The Solidarity movement of the early 1980s not only triggered a transformation in Polish society. It forced a fundamental reconsideration of the nature of socialism throughout the Soviet Union and Eastern Europe. Solidarity will be seen as one of the most important social movements of the century.

Michael Kennedy develops a theoretical conception of Soviet-type societies by analyzing Solidarity's significance on three levels. First, he explains the background to and nature of the conflict between Solidarity and the authorities by examining the relation between the distribution of power and movement strategies. Second, he considers the implications of Solidarity's struggle for the theory of the Soviet-type system's reproduction and transformation by offering a critique and synthesis of relevant theories of class and civil society. Third, he examines the internal constitution of Solidarity in terms of gender and, in particular, cross-class alliances. He argues that because engineers and physicians were dependent on the self-organized working class in this conflict between civil society and state, professional projects had to be recast in visions suitable to the alliance. In a concluding chapter, he explores the implications of his analysis both for understanding *perestroika* in the Soviet Union and more generally for reformulating a critical sociology of Soviet-type societies.

Professionals, power and Solidarity in Poland is the most informed and the best-documented study of Solidarity to date. As Soviet-type societies are in transition, there is a pressing need for theoretical reconceptualization. Kennedy's pathbreaking study will become essential reading for specialists and students of Soviet and East European Studies, and of modern Poland in particular; specialists in political sociology and the sociology of social movements and for activists in radical politics.

PROFESSIONALS, POWER AND SOLIDARITY IN POLAND

Soviet and East European Studies: 79

Editorial Board

Soviet and East European Studies, under the auspices of Cambridge University Press and the British Association for Soviet, Slavonic and East European Studies (BASSEES), promotes the publication of works presenting substantial and original research on the economics, politics, sociology and modern history of the Soviet Union and Eastern Europe.

Soviet and East European Studies

PROFESSIONALS, POWER
AND SOLIDARITY
IN POLAND

A critical sociology of Soviet-type society

MICHAEL D. KENNEDY

Assistant Professor of Sociology, The University of Michigan

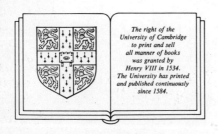

The right of the
University of Cambridge
to print and sell
all manner of books
was granted by
Henry VIII in 1534.
The University has printed
and published continuously
since 1584.

CAMBRIDGE UNIVERSITY PRESS

Cambridge
New York   Port Chester
Melbourne   Sydney

Published by the Press Syndicate of the University of Cambridge
The Pitt Building, Trumpington Street, Cambridge CB2 1RP
40 West 20th Street, New York, NY 10011, USA
10 Stamford Road, Oakleigh, Melbourne 3166, Australia

First published 1991

Printed in Great Britain at the University Press, Cambridge

British Library cataloguing in publication data
Kennedy, Michael D.
Professionals, power and Solidarity in Poland: a critical
sociology of Soviet-type society.
1. Poland. Social movements, history
I. Title
303.4'84

Library of Congress cataloging in publication data
Kennedy, Michael D.
Professionals, power, and Solidarity in Poland: a critical
sociology of Soviet-type society / Michael D. Kennedy.
    p.   cm. – (Soviet and East European studies: 79)
Includes bibliographical references.
ISBN 0–521–39083–4
1. NSZZ "Solidarność" (Labor organization) – History. 2. Poland –
Social conditions – 1945– 3. Poland – Politics and
government – 1945–1980. 4. Poland – Politics and government – 1980–
5. Power (Social sciences) 6. Elite (Social sciences) – Poland.
I. Title. II. Series.
HD8537.N783K46 1990
306'.09438 – dc20   89–77368CIP

ISBN 0 521 39083 4 hardback

CE

Contents

Tables

Acknowledgments

Many have contributed to this work over the years. IREX provided a fellowship for the ten months of my stay in Poland in 1983–84. Dissertation advisors Gerhard Lenski, T. Anthony Jones, Craig Calhoun, Maurice Simon and Richard Simpson also contributed a great deal in their advice in preparation for the project and in their criticism and support later. Many people in Poland also have offered considerable support. To risk naming any means leaving out some who were very helpful, but Jolanta Babiuch, Bogdan Cichomski, Danuta Duch, Anna Firkowska, Jan Hoser, Krzysztof Jasiewicz, Aleksandra Jasińska-Kania, Jadwiga Koralewicz, Andrzej Krajewski, Marek Latoszek, Bogdan Mach, Irena Reszke, Piotr Sielewończyk, Renata Siemińska, Magdalena Sokołowska, Jadwiga Staniszkis, Anna Titkow, Edmund Wnuk-Lipiński and especially Ireneusz Białecki, Grzegorz Lindenberg, Witold Morawski and Włodzimierz Wesołowski offered so much good advice and guidance that I have not been able to take advantage of it all. Therefore, I alone bear responsibility for what arguments follow, but I owe many insights to their willingness to explain Polish life to an American sociologist.

I have revised and expanded the dissertation considerably, so that much of what appears in this text is different from that which I wrote in 1985. I am indebted to the Joint Commission on East European Studies of the American Council of Learned Societies and the Social Science Research Council for the 1987–88 post-doctoral fellowship that allowed me to go beyond what I had written before. Grants from the Center for Russian and East European Studies and from the Rackham Graduate School of the University of Michigan in 1987 provided research assistance by Konrad Sadkowski to help me incorporate more original documents from 1980–81 in this study. A faculty grant and fellowship from the same Rackham Graduate School in 1989 also helped refine the theoretical critique found in chapters 4 and 5. Part of chapter 6 is a revised and expanded version of an article with Ireneusz Białecki that appeared in *Eastern European Politics and Societies* volume 3, number 2 (1989). Chapter 8 is also revised and expanded based on an article published in *Social Forces* volume 65, number 3 (1987).

My colleagues at the University of Michigan have also contributed a great deal to this new and improved argument. My students in social theory have helped me understand the difficulty of translating critical sociology across unfamiliar cultures. Marty Whyte and our students in comparative communism have helped me understand better the limits and possibilities of generalization across actually existing socialisms. Geoff Eley, Ron Suny, Roman Szporluk and Mayfair Yang have helped me understand the relationship between civil society and socialism in a discussion group sponsored by the Comparative Studies in Social Transformation program of the University of Michigan. Pat Preston has offered fine and timely typing and computer assistance deadline after deadline. Howard Kimeldorf, Roman Szporluk, David McQuaid and Akos Rona-Tas have read portions of the manuscript, and Geoff Eley, Marty Whyte and Barbara Anderson the entire manuscript. I am indebted to their careful readings and helpful comments, as well as to those of the Cambridge University Press reviewers, although I cannot claim to have satisfied all of their concerns.

Elizabeth Bourquin Kennedy has helped me the most in this long project. She has mediated the ups and downs discovery and frustration yield. She has been subjected to repeated readings of various "key" passages. She clarifies my thinking, criticizes my inconsistencies and assures me that I will work it through. A better partner I could not imagine. Liz managed this even while carrying our daughter, Emma Louise, whose birth on May 1, 1989, enriched our lives even more. To Liz and Emma this work is dedicated.

Abbreviations

AK	*Armia Krajowa* (Home Army)
CPSU	Communist Party of the Soviet Union
DiP	*Doświadczenie i Przyszłość* (Experience and the Future)
KOR	*Komitet Obrony Robotników* (Committee for the Defense of Workers)
KPN	*Konfederacja Polski Niedpodległej* (Confederation for an Independent Poland)
KPP	*Komunistyczna Partia Polski* (Communist Party of Poland)
KPRP	*Komunistyczna Partia Robotnicza Polski* (Communist Workers' Party of Poland)
KRN	*Krajowa Rada Narodowa* (National Council of Poland)
KSC	*Komitet Samoobrony Chłopów* (Farmers' Self-Defense Committee)
KSS-KOR	*Komitet Samoobrony Społecznej-KOR* (Committee of Social Self-Defense – KOR)
KZ-KFS	*Komitet Założycielski – Krajowa Federacja Samorządowców* (Founding Committee of the National Federation of Self-Management Bodies)
MKS	*Międzyzakładowy Komitet Strajkowy* (Inter-Enterprise Strike Committee)
NOT	*Naczelna Organizacja Techniczna* (Supreme Technical Organization)

NSZZ	*Niezależny Samorządony Związek Zawodowy* (Independent Self-Governing Trade Union)
NSZZPNTiO	*NSZZ Pracowników Nauki, Techniki i Oświaty* (NSZZ of Science, Technics and Education Employees)
OBS	*Ośrodek Badanii Społecznej* (Center for Social Research)
PKWN	*Polski Komitet Wyzwolenia Narodowej* (Polish Committee of National Liberation)
PPR	*Polska Partia Robotnicza* (Polish Workers' Party)
PPS	*Polska Partia Socjalistyczna* (Polish Socialist Party)
PRL	*Polska Rzeczpospolita Ludowa* (Polish People's Republic)
PSL	*Polskie Stronnictwo Ludowe* (Polish Peasant Party)
PZL	*Polski Związek Lekarski* (Polish Physicians' Union)
PZPR	*Polska Zjednoczona Partia Robotnicza* (Polish United Workers' Party)
ROPCiO	*Ruch Obrony Praw Człowieka i Obywatela* (Movement for the Defense of Human and Civil Rights)
SDKPiL	*Socjaldemokracja Królestwa Polskiego i Litwy* (Social Democracy of the Kingdom of Poland and Lithuania)
SMO	social-movement organization
ZLP	*Związek Literatów Polskich* (Union of Polish Writers)
ZNP	*Związek Nauczyczelstwa Polskiego* (Union of Polish Teaching)
ZOMO	*Zmotoryzowane Odwody Milicji Obywatelskiej*
ZOZy	*Zezpoły Opieki Zdrowotnej* (Teams of Health Care)
ZPP	*Związek Patrioty Polskich* (Union of Polish Patriots)
ZSL	*Związane Stronnictwo Ludowe* (United Peasants' Party)
ZZLP	*Związek Zawodowy Lekarzy Polskich* (Trade Union of Polish Physicians)
ZZPSZ	*Związek Zawodowy Pracowników Służby Zdrowia* (Trade Union of Health-Care Employees)

Introduction

The Solidarity movement of 1980–81 transformed Polish society and the nature of socialism in Eastern Europe. In its five hundred days, this trade union and social movement put to rest any lingering hope that Poland's Communist Party could represent the interests of the working class or of the Polish nation. The vast majority of Poles came to identify with Solidarity and the alternative future it advanced. In 1981, Adam Michnik, one of Solidarity's leading intellectuals, wrote that it was "too soon to give a sociological profile of this movement" (1985: 129). As Solidarity enters the Polish parliament in 1989, the time has come for sustained sociological analysis of this movement and the principles for which it struggled.

Solidarity's alternative rested upon the principles of social self-organization. This principle recognizes the right of all social groups to form their own organizations in order to articulate their own demands and to defend their own interests. In this, Solidarity sought to construct a civil society, where pluralism and an open public sphere would reign over the state instead of the state reigning over them.

The principles of a civil society challenge fundamentally the organizing principles of Soviet-type society.[1] Where the Soviet-type system is based on the unity of state and society, civil society depends on their separation. Where the Soviet-type system acknowledges no antagonistic interests, civil society assumes them to exist and prepares rules to adjudicate among antagonists. Where the Soviet-type system is founded on the belief that a single party can rule in the interests of the whole of society, civil society assigns no group or organization that right without recurrent contest.

Solidarity's social construction of civil society in the Soviet-type system did not reproduce the antagonistic principles listed above, however. Civil society depends on a state regulating social contracts through law; Solidarity constructed a society in opposition to the

1

authorities and the state. Civil society encourages the formation of different social groups with different interests; Solidarity organized different occupations and different political tendencies into a single trade union and social movement. Civil society has been based historically on a system of private property; Solidarity's base lay among skilled workers organized in large factories with little, if any, interest in private ownership of their places of employment.

Although Solidarity opposed the Soviet-type system, in many ways Solidarity resembled the proletarian movement upon which the Marxian vision of socialism was to be built. Socialism was to be based on the organized movement of skilled workers, as Solidarity was. At this moment in socialism's construction, the proletariat was to be the majority of society, as Solidarity was. Socialism was to increase workers' control over the means of production, as Solidarity aimed. Socialism was to bring a new kind of freedom to humankind, where bourgeois freedoms would be made meaningful by rights in the economic sphere. Solidarity sought to establish these bourgeois freedoms in a system claiming to have realized already these social and economic rights. Despite these affinities, Solidarity claimed no Marxian legacy, and many of its most outspoken members declared their opposition to the socialist tradition.

Solidarity's rejection of Marxism was not because it lacked consciousness. Indeed, considerable self-consciousness was essential to participation in a "self-limiting revolution." There was a common understanding in Solidarity that an unbridled revolution would bring failure by inviting Soviet and Warsaw Pact invasion. This movement of over 9 million men and women exercised considerable self-restraint in order to avoid providing provocations for a violent repression of their challenge.

Solidarity thus merits study for its distinction as one of the most important social movements in world history. Not only did it mobilize considerable resources in a relatively sparse environment, but it was also unprecedented among social movements in its self-limitation and progress toward constructing a civil society in a Soviet-type system.

Solidarity is also important given its contribution to the political transformation of Poland. Its organization in 1980–81 was obviously a precondition for the 1989 round-table negotiations that led to the first parliament with an organized opposition in Soviet-type society. Without the fundamental transformation of Polish society in the first two years of the 1980s, Solidarity could never have survived its life underground and thus been able to return to open public leadership in

1989. For those who search the social roots of the systemic transformation of Soviet-type society, the development of Solidarity in
1980–81 is central.

The distinction between totalitarianism and authoritarianism once
rested on their different potentials for returns to democracy. Poland's
democratic transition thus demands our own return to prevailing
conceptions of the Soviet-type system. Although the totalitarian
framework went out of favor in most Western circles in the 1960s, the
preferred modernization and Marxist perspectives also failed to anticipate the kinds of changes the decade of the 1980s produced. It also
seems unlikely that existing models will help us with the kinds of
change likely in the 1990s. The social and systemic transformations of
Eastern Europe in this past decade demand our own theoretical
transformations in reformulating the theory of Soviet-type society.
Central to that reformulation is a reconsideration of its power
relations.

If we understand power relations as "relations of autonomy and
dependence in social interaction" (Giddens, 1979:93), we are led to
consider how sets of rules and resources enable actors to expand their
opportunities for action. We are also moved to consider how those
same rules and resources might limit actors. Two general paradigms in
Soviet studies[2] deal with such "asymmetrical conceptions of power,"
as Lukes (1978) terms it. The political paradigm, in which we can
include both totalitarian and interest-group approaches, emphasizes
state power. It deemphasizes the power relations which constitute
social relations, assuming them to be derivative of party and state
initiatives. Another approach derived from this political school does
emphasize, however, the significance of the social. The return of civil
society as both an actor and a normative goal has made the political
approach more attuned to the non-state and non-party spheres in
Soviet-type society. This focus on civil society also invites consideration of social movements. Such a redirection of inquiry thus moves
Soviet studies toward a more relational perspective on power, one
which searches for sources of autonomy even in the most apparently
powerless.

The political economic or Marxist perspective has always worked
with a relational and asymmetric sense of power. The very logic of
class exploitation and struggle indicates this notion of inequality and
conflict within relations of autonomy and dependency. But the
Marxist perspective has had the most intellectual power in capitalist
systems. Its focus on class has presented certain dilemmas in its

treatment of Soviet-type societies and has led to a variety of conceptual revisions of class and emancipatory praxis. It has even led several schools of Marxism to embrace the concept of civil society as one means to resolve the dilemmas of a workers' movement struggling against actual socialism.

As Soviet-type societies are in a period of transition, so are the theories which purport to explain them. No doubt we shall see in the near future many revisions that normalize the anomalies real-world practice creates for these theories. But unless these revisions are based on historical sociological argument, the new theories will be most appropriate for the latest news headline, not for sustained scholarly inquiry. This volume aims to contribute to this general theoretical revision, but on the foundation of a historical sociological analysis of the social phenomenon that inspired much of the theoretical revision: the Solidarity movement of 1980–81.

What was Solidarity, why did it form and how did it develop? How, in particular, is Solidarity connected to Poland's history? In chapter 1, "The historical genealogy of Solidarity," I explain how nationalism and communism came to be perceived as antagonistic; why there is so little trust in Poland for the Communist Party; and why religious consciousness seemed so important to the Solidarity movement's identification.

In chapter 2, "The nature and causes of Solidarity," I analyze alternative accounts of the 1980–81 movement. I consider on the one hand various analyses which explain Solidarity as the "outcome" of structural factors, and on the other, Solidarity as the "meaningful" product of actors' intentions. I also consider those approaches which try to integrate structure and action through Marxist and resource-mobilization theories. In chapter 3, "Solidarity movement as emancipatory praxis," I offer a synthetic interpretation of the 1980–81 movement that draws on the critical analysis of existing theories. I explain Solidarity as a product of a peculiar set of power relations, and as an attempt to restructure those power relations. Its transformative strategy was above all "pragmatic," but because its class base was among workers, Solidarity's theory of change might best be called one of "socialist pragmatism."

Such an inquiry into the causes and aims of Solidarity presupposes an understanding of the *nature* of Solidarity. What was Solidarity? Certainly it was a social movement and trade union, but what was its distinction? Who and what did it represent? One of the principal conclusions of chapter 3 is that this movement was an *alliance* between different social groups with different conditions of existence. One of the most important questions that could be asked, therefore, is how such an alliance was created. To understand the meaning of Solidarity one must not only explain the nature of the conflict between it and the authorities, but also the internal constitution of the movement itself. Although one might consider the rural–urban alliance (Halamska, 1988; Hann, 1985), I focus on the alliance central to Solidarity's core: that between professionals and workers.

In chapters 8 and 9, I explain why engineers and physicians belonged to this trade union and social movement whose base was skilled workers in large factories. One of the social conditions which has enabled East European communist parties to retain their position is the reproduction of divisions between professionals and workers. Explaining this cross-class alliance is therefore fundamental to understanding Solidarity's internal constitution and why it posed such a challenge to the reproduction of the Soviet-type system.

Such a question of cross-class alliance does not emerge from a study of the period, however. The discourse of Solidarity and the discourse of many texts on the movement emphasize its fundamental unity. This was important, because the authorities wished to undermine Solidarity by stressing its class divisions. Although I argue in chapter 3 that Solidarity is best conceived as an emancipatory movement, this does not assume that its internal constitution represented a voluntary unity based in equality and mutual recognition. Women, for instance, were excluded from most of the politically significant spheres of the movement, even when they were the majority of the occupation represented. I shall discuss this problem in chapter 9, when I analyze the relationship between Solidarity and physicians.

Although professionals and workers were both in the movement, their copresence reflected not the elimination of class but the accomplishment of class alliance. Even here, however, this was not entirely a "voluntary" alliance, as professionals were dependent on the self-organized working class. This dependency is not surprising, as professionals were also dependent on the political authorities before (chapter 7). But these questions of dependency do not derive from the period so much as they derive from the metatheoretical tools we bring to its analysis. It is necessary to consider a more general level of analysis to find reasons why these differences within the movement are important for understanding Solidarity.

In chapters 4 and 5, I consider modernization, Marxist and political models of Soviet-type society in order to clarify the nature of the debate around Solidarity, and to explain how my analysis of Solidarity might illuminate these more general approaches. In chapter 4, "Solidarity, modernization and class," I argue that modernization perspectives fail to make asymmetric power relations problematic, and therefore do not serve us well in understanding *how* recent transformations, as that inspired by Solidarity, have occurred. Instead, modernization perspectives translate the conflict over systemic change into a conflict between the old and the new.

Marxist models also are problematic in so far as they continue to emphasize class as the central feature guiding social change and structuring power relations. Because the state–society tension is the fundamental axis of conflict in Soviet-type society, class analyses typically are revised to take this into account. But when this state–society conflict is subordinated to a class conflict, the potential contribution of class analysis is lost. This is exemplified in studies which base their work on "self-management." Alternatively, those class analyses which search for class identities analytically distinct from political power have great promise.

Many of these Marxist perspectives are drawn to theories of civil society. Indeed, when civil society is added to the totalitarian framework, Marxist models and political models prove to be quite complementary. In chapter 5, "Solidarity, culture and civil society," I discuss this affinity and note that civil society and the proletariat are, in each system, both the actor and the definition of universality. But where class interest theoretically unites the proletariat, civil society's universality rests on contradictory foundations: romantic cultural nationalism and a utilitarian moral actor. Such a contradiction leads its theorists to overlook questions of political economy and class alliance to focus on cultural or legal theory. This blind spot undermines the great potential of civil society as an analytical and political concept. This is most clear with the case of Solidarity in 1980–81, but also threatens the prospects for emancipatory transformation in the 1990s.

Social transformation is occasioned not only when those powerless restructure their situation, but when authorities restructure theirs. The analysis of power relations in Soviet-type society thus requires not only an analysis of the constitution of resistance, but also the formation of domination. In chapter 6, "A theory of power relations in Soviet-type society," I offer a structural account of the patterns of autonomy and dependency that shape social relations between authorities and society and within the authorities. I argue that the authorities are more constrained in their use of power than we normally assume, and workers through collective organization are potentially more independent. In chapter 7, "Professionals, power and prestige," I extend this model to professionals to explain how they normally are dependent on the authorities for their own power. This structural foundation for the analysis of domination and professional dependency provides a point of departure for the analysis of class alliances of 1980–81 presented in the following chapters.

This volume analyzes Solidarity at three levels, therefore: at the level of the movement in its conflict with the system and the authorities; at the level of systemic theory in order to see more clearly against what, for what and with what Solidarity struggled; and at the level of the movement's internal constitution, in terms of gender, but especially in its class alliances. I have titled this work "A critical sociology of Soviet-type society" because I intend with this analysis of Solidarity and Poland to contribute to the construction of a more adequate approach for explaining the reproduction and transformation of Soviet-type society. I believe that the kind of sociological theory most useful at this time is one that adopts a critical epistemology. A critical perspective puts at its center those matters central to defining the distinction and prospects of Soviet-type society: power, praxis and socialism.

Socialism has been the principal "counter-culture" and utopia of capitalism (Bauman, 1976). Developments in Communist Party-led societies have always affected the popularity of socialism in capitalist societies, but the democratic transformations we are witnessing in these societies have a potentially different impact than previous developments. These changes may lead to the final abandonment of socialism as a progressive alternative to capitalism, or lead to a new vision of socialism which can provide capitalist subjects with an emancipatory alternative. Critical sociology has a normative commitment to discovering such alternatives embedded within the present. Clearly, the transformations of Soviet-type societies are essential data for reformulating that commitment.

If the normative commitment to emancipation is the "interest" of critical sociology (Habermas, 1971), the typical substantive focus of critical sociologists is power. Other perspectives address power, but critical perspectives generally find in the unequal distribution of opportunities for action the basis for recurrent patterns of social life and the reasons for change. Critical sociologists often focus on how the strong dominate or exploit the weak. By exposing the mechanisms of this injustice, these sociologists hope to facilitate the making of an emancipatory alternative. The making of this alternative is emancipatory praxis, the third leg of critical sociology.

Beyond the demystification of domination, critical sociologists generally search for what James Scott (1985) has called "the weapons of the weak," or those power resources which enable resistance to domination and perhaps its progressive transformation. One of the principal power resources of the weak is their collective mobilization into social movements. Alain Touraine (1984) even argues that social movements should be the new central problem of sociology, because by clarifying the vision of movements, the sociologist facilitates their independent action and capacity for self-regulation, and thus contributes to an "affirmation of the rights of the subject" (pp. 125, 135). But how movements translate their resources into institutional transformation is a central problem too. The assumption that some clearly defined list of what makes socialism should be supplanted by a socialist pragmatism that makes both movement strategy and institutional transformation subject to experience-based reformation.

This study thus works within the critical sociological project by making power, praxis and socialism its underlying motif. Although I hope it contributes to the growth of the critical sociology of Soviet-type society, and helps to reconstruct the more general critical sociological project, it is not designed to be read only by those who share my general orientation.

This volume is organized in four parts. For those readers less interested in theories of Soviet-type society and primarily interested in Poland and Solidarity, part 1, "Solidarity and social transformation," and part 3, "Professionals and Solidarity," can be read on their own. Likewise, for those who are primarily interested in general theories, part 2, "Solidarity and the theory of Soviet-type society," can be read without parts 1 and 3. Although this selective reading is possible, I discourage it. I have made every effort to integrate these sections in order to show why simultaneous work at both specific historical and general theoretical levels of analysis facilitates the proper elaboration of each. In the final part of the book, "Critical sociology and Soviet-type society," I summarize the book's main arguments and tie them to an agenda for future theory and research.

Part I

Solidarity and social transformation

1 The historical genealogy of Solidarity

The Polish Solidarity movement can be said to have begun on August 31, 1980, when an inter-enterprise strike committee in Gdańsk signed an agreement with the authorities granting the right to form independent trade unions in Poland. It is misleading to begin an analysis of Solidarity with that day, however. Strikes raged throughout Poland in the preceding weeks of that summer. A Pole became Pope of the Roman Catholic Church less than two years earlier, reinforcing the identity of nation and church. The previous decade was an economic roller coaster, with a boom in the first half of the 1970s and bust in the second. The technocratic spirit of that decade was a response to a death of ideology in the previous years, after the hopes of an anti-Stalinist communist reformation in 1956 yielded anti-Semitic and anti-intellectual maneuvers instead. And all of these Polish historical developments have taken place within a context of Russian/Soviet–Polish tension and global cold war.

It is impossible to consider adequately any social movement *ex nihilo*. This is the common historical critique of timeless sociology, but this charge has special power in the case of Solidarity. The movement was historically self-conscious, with its participants grounding their present struggles in those of the past. One particularly powerful example of this historical self-consciousness can be found in a document written by leading Solidarity activists that called for the formation of a self-governing republic. Part of that document was a discussion of the movement's genealogy:

> The idea of the self-governing republic has deep roots in our national culture which is part of the European civilization shaped by Christianity as well as in the tradition of workers' movements and traditions of democracy and tolerance. This is not tantamount to an idolatrous reverence for the past. It means, however, that we have the duty to continue the work of those who preceded us and to avoid

11

their mistakes and weaknesses. This we must remember when we define our present positions with reference to our genealogy. We consider ourselves to be the continuation of the traditions of the Polish left; in the first place, of those of the left who were fighting for the independence of Poland. However, we wish to overcome the blunders and weaknesses of that tradition. We state emphatically that our basic principle is the supremacy of man, of the human individual over other values and goals of any collective ... We are aware of particularly strong links with the traditions of the Polish Socialist Party and the Polish peasants' movement ... We have our forebears in the Polish underground state at the time of the German occupation and in its Parliament which in unspeakably difficult conditions maintained unity in the multiplicity of programmes and ideas. We revere the programme of the Polish Peasants' Party, then conceived, and the programme of the socialist Freedom, Equality and Independence movement. The traditions of struggle against any form of totalitarianism, whether communist or fascist, formed in the interwar period, were continued after the war in the struggle against communist power. We mean both the efforts of the legally acting leaders of the Polish Peasants' Party and the consistent refusal to accept the Soviet dictate, voiced by the socialists under Kazimierz Pużak and the leaders of the underground Freedom and Independence Movement. The totalitarian dictatorship was never fully victorious in our country. It had to contend with the people, gathered round the church, the peasants, fighting against collectivization, the workers of Poznań in June 1956, with the October movement of workers, student and intellectuals. It had to contend with the coastal workers in 1970, with the workers of Radom, Ursus and other centres in 1976, with the students and intellectuals in 1968. Part of our tradition is the Workers' Defence Committee KOR which, in the pre-August days, launched both the idea of creating self-governing independent institutions and the idea of friendly co-operation with other nations. We are continuing the tradition of the unofficial paper *The Worker* and of the founding committees of the free trade unions. We see the realization of the basic unity of different social trends in the ISTU Solidarity. We wish to stress that we claim no exclusive right to these traditions. (Onyszkiewicz and Wujec 1981, quoted in Raina, 1985:449–50)

This document does not represent all of the Solidarity movement. Other parts of that movement drew on different traditions and even on the same traditions reconstructed in different ways. Nevertheless, different tendencies within the movement were based in large part on various historical identifications. Historical genealogy is thus critical to analyzing the character of the Solidarity movement.

At the same time, these different traditions and disputes over their meaning already illustrate the foolhardiness of considering *the* historical genealogy of Solidarity, given that there was no single logic within history which produced it. Space does not allow us to consider the debates over the appropriate reconstruction of this legacy either. Not only are we unable to address the typical historiographical disputes, but many of the archival materials essential to a well-informed discussion of these matters are not available. Under Gorbachev's *glasnost'*, a Polish–Soviet commission to investigate the "blank spots" of their post-October Revolution history has been established and access to the data could be improved. But even with such access, that aspiration requires another book with a different, historiographical, intention.

It would be equally misleading, however, to ignore this history just because of its complexity. We should set the stage for Solidarity with a review of the movement's significant historical antecedents, for it is through these historical specifics that the peculiarly Polish variation on the Soviet-type theme has been established by Poles and can be understood by us.

There are common political–economic systems across Soviet-type societies, but no society is "essentially" the same as any other. Nor is any concrete society the pure type representing this system of power relations. The Soviet Union is the historical prototype of this system, but we would be misled if we were to think its totality was transmitted to other societies. An abstraction of that totality was transplanted to Eastern European societies, but comes to life only in interaction with the particular historical and cultural components of the life world it encounters. Thus, the abstracted Soviet-type political economy underlies Soviet-type societies, but its interaction with distinctive cultures and histories produces different forms of social reproduction and social transformation. To consider Solidarity, we must consider how Polish history and culture themselves transformed the Soviet-type system.

There have been several major social transformations which any critical study of Soviet-type society must consider. They include (1) the origins of the nation's communist movement; (2) the conditions under which revolution was made; (3) the formation of Stalinism; (4) Stalinism's subsequent transformations; and (5) the success of the system's transition from an economy based on extensive accumulation to one relying on a more intensive form of accumulation. The particular variation on a theme established in each of these stages sets the range of possibilities for subsequent patterns of reproduction and trans formation. These transformations are themselves, however, shaped by the relationship between the dominant forms of identification guiding liberation movements in the twentieth century: communism and nationalism.[1] In some countries, communism or socialism and nationalism can reinforce one another, or at least not prove contradictory. In Poland, however, communism and nationalism have become antagonistic principles in the inter-subjective life world of most Poles.

Poland, socialism and the communist movement

Polish workers and intellectuals were prominent in the rise of European socialism. Utopian socialist programs were advanced by the 1831 emigré group, the Polish People (*Lud Polski*). Prominent individual emigrés also considered themselves socialist, including Romantic poet Adam Mickiewicz. Utopian socialist programs were mainly agrarian, as industrialization came late to most of Poland. Utopian socialism appeared finally in Poland in the 1840s, but never gained much support, given the hostility of both gentry and peasants to collective ownership. After the failed 1863 uprising, a new generation of Polish emigrés participated in the founding of the first Working Men's International Association. These activists provided the link between utopian socialism and modern socialism for Poles (Cottam, 1978:8–19). Marx and Engels themselves paid close attention to the struggles of Polish revolutionaries. Marx initiated a First International document of support for the Polish independence struggle. The Polish independence struggle also informed discussions of foreign proletarian policy for the Second International (Lichtheim, 1961:85, 103; Walicki, 1983:30, 54–55).

Polish printers in Lwów organized the first Polish trade union in 1870 and the first socialist-led strikes among Poles occurred in Poznań in 1871–72 (Davies, 1984:539). In 1882, Ludwik Waryński and others formed the first Marxist group in Poland, the Proletariat. Leading Polish Marxist intellectuals also came on the European scene in this period, including Kazimierz Kelles-Krauz and Stanisław Brzozowski. In 1892, the Polish Socialist Party was formed in Russian Poland, although there were also smaller socialist or social democratic parties organized in Galicia and Prussian Poland. The Polish–Jewish Bund was organized in Vilnius in 1897. The socialist movement was also represented in a number of other smaller parties. The central point is not this diversity, but that socialism was one of the major themes in Polish social and political life in the last quarter of the nineteenth century and beginning of the twentieth. National independence for Poland was equally important, however, if not more so.

Poland was partitioned among the great empires of Central and Eastern Europe at the end of the eighteenth century, and was not to regain political independence again until the end of World War I. Several uprisings were launched in this period to regain national sovereignty, but all were crushed. These uprisings have left a legacy that glorifies resistance to external occupation and places national independence as a central value in Polish political culture. The socialist movement in Poland faced, therefore, dilemmas that did not preoccupy activists in the centers of the empires. How should national independence figure in the socialist agenda? Given the internationalist sentiment of the socialist movement, should a separate state for Poland be part of the movement's goals at all? This tension in Polish socialism has been a recurrent theme in the political struggles defining Poland through the present. It was especially apparent, however, in the different programs of various tendencies in the pre-war Polish Socialist Party, as well as in its difference with the forerunner to the Polish Communist Party, Social Democracy of the Kingdom of Poland and Lithuania (*Socjaldemokracja Królestwa Polskiego i Litwy* or SDKPiL).

The Polish Socialist Party (*Polska Partia Socjalistyczna* or PPS) initially gave equal place to national independence and social reform. This synthesis ultimately proved unstable. In 1906, the PPS-*Frakcja Rewolucjna* (Revolutionary Faction) broke to promote a military strategy while the PPS *Opozycja* resisted this turn. In 1913 the PPS-*Lewica* broke with the PPS in order to establish a more militant working class based movement. By August 1914 the prospect of national independence reunited the first two factions, while in 1918 the PPS-*Lewica* joined with the SDKPiL (Tomicki, 1983).

The SDKPiL did not promote independence. Rosa Luxemburg, its most prominent theorist, in fact argued in her thesis on economic development that Russian Poland is so integrated into Russia that it should not seek independence from it (Luxemburg, 1899 [1977]). This theme recurred even after Polish independence was regained in 1918. On December 16–17, 1918, the SDKPiL and PPS-Left united to form the Communist Workers' Party of Poland (*Komunistyczna Partia Robotnicza Polski*, KPRP). As the Russian and German revolutions took place on each side of them, the leaders of this new party reasoned that capitalism itself was about to fall and that therefore bourgeois politics and partial social democratic reforms were inadequate in the face of the revolutionary opportunity surrounding them (Tomicki, 1983:202–3).

Although the German revolution failed, the 1919–20 war between the Bolshevik and Polish governments justified communist hopes for revolution, especially when the Soviet military reached Warsaw's Vistula River. As the Soviet army advanced, provisional governments of communist councils were set up and a Provisional Revolutionary Committee for Poland was established. The Soviet forces ultimately were turned back and revolution defeated. Polish communists later lamented that they relied on hopes for military victory too much, as they were isolated from workers and the left in their support for the Soviets (Dziewanowski, 1976:91–94). Polish-born Marxist Isaac Deutscher (1984:97) called the Soviet march on Warsaw "a real tragedy for the Polish CP, because it pushed the Polish proletarian masses towards anti-Sovietism and anti-communism." Ignacy Daszyński, the socialist premier of the short-lived (from November 7–14, 1918) "Provisional People's Government of the Polish Republic," defended the war to Western socialists by referring to the historical union of the Ukraine and Belorussia with Poland, Poland's right of state and the "threat of Bolshevism" (Tomicki, 1983:238). By the end of 1921, the KPRP lost a significant proportion of membership, even in Dąbrowa, Warsaw and Łódź, its strongest areas (de Weydenthal, 1978:14).

The communist movement regained some of its strength over the next decade as economic difficulties increased and as it began explicitly to support Polish national independence, although it never attained the following of several other left groups and the left itself claimed the electoral allegiance of only about one-fourth of the population.[2] An even greater problem for the communist movement than division on the left was its own internal strife. Control over the KPRP alternated between its left and right wings, as each leadership made "errors" that inspired its removal. Some of these errors involved domestic strategy, as in the right's failure to take the initiative in the strike waves of 1923 (Tomicki, 1983:271), but they also occurred as a consequence of foreign policies. The Polish communist right-wing leadership protested the attacks on Trotsky by Stalin, Zinoviev and Kamenev. After their victory, Stalin and Zinoviev dismissed this leadership as well as the leaderships of the German and French communist parties for interfering in Soviet internal affairs. That was made official in the third national congress in 1925, at which time also the name of the Polish party was changed to the Communist Party of Poland (*Komunistyczna Partia Polski*, KPP). The left came to power only briefly, for when Stalin allied with Bukharin to form the "rightist line" against Zinoviev and Kamenev, Polish left-wing leaders who sided with Zinoviev were dismissed (Deutscher, 1984:99–102; Dziewanowski, 1976:107–16). Fearing a right-wing coup d'etat, this communist leadership initially supported Piłsudski's coup in 1926, but during the coup Piłsudski arrested and interned leading communist activists. This error coincided with the COMINTERN decisions to repudiate united-front tactics and to expel Bukharin as head of the COMINTERN. The left wing of the party once again regained power, and purged the right wing of the KPP. By the early 1930s, struggles within the Polish Communist Party intensified even further, as the COMINTERN sought to eradicate all Trotskyite and other dissenting influences in its member parties. Stalin was especially interested in eliminating the Luxemburgist influence on the Polish party, which he considered to be the Polish variety of Trotskyism. The Polish party expelled those who dissented from the new line of struggle against social fascism (i.e. social democracy), including Deutscher, and in the process lost a significant portion of its membership (Dziewanowski, 1976:137; Deutscher, 1984:110–22).

When COMINTERN reverted to united-front tactics in 1935, the KPP followed suit and sought a united front with the PPS and Jewish Bund. Its activists worked with the rank-and-file members of the left parties in Warsaw, Łódź, Kraków, Lwów and other regions. Leading left-wing socialists in the PPS also pushed for united-front tactics (Tomicki, 1983:350–53), but most of the national leaders of both parties continued to distrust the KPP, since they had a reputation first as Soviet agents and only second as ideological comrades (Dziewanowski, 1976:141–45). This lasted only until 1937–38, when nearly all Polish communists on Soviet territory were executed, sent to concentration camps, or in some other way disappeared. At least 5,000 communists were killed. Those prominent Polish communists who survived did so by virtue of being recruited into the Soviet security service or of being interned in Polish prisons (Davies, 1984:545). And sometime in 1938, the Polish Communist Party was officially dissolved by the Soviets.[3]

More than in any other European country, communism and nationalism were at odds in Poland before World War II. Other communist parties were heavily influenced, if not manipulated, by the Communist Party of the Soviet Union (CPSU), but this relationship was far more problematic for Poland. Poles and Russians have competing claims to being the great historical Slav nation, for reasons of demography and imperial legacy. This rivalry was compounded by tsarist domination of Poland. Such a cultural antagonism need not have been reproduced after the October Revolution, but the Polish–Soviet war of 1919–20 managed to translate tsarism into communism for many Poles. The manipulation of the Polish Communist Party by the Soviets and its ultimate destruction by Stalin provided a final justification for why communism and Polish national interests were antagonistic, at least in a multipolar world. That world ended in 1939, as the bipolar world came into existence.

From World War to Cold War

On September 1, 1939, Hitler launched against Polish forces the world's first *Blitzkrieg*. Seventeen days later, in accord with the Ribbentrop–Molotov pact of August 23, 1939, Soviet forces invaded Poland from the east. With this invasion from east and west, a new bipolar world came into being, Germans and Russians temporarily allied. Poland's alliances with Britain and France mattered little, as Poland was within one month erased from the political map.

Between 1939 and 1945 over 6 million Poles were killed by Germans, of whom nearly half were Jews. Many died in war operations, but the systematic extermination of both Jews and other Poles in death camps accounted for nearly 90 percent of all human losses. Poland's Jewry and intelligentsia were the special object of Nazi attention. In May–August 1940, during the *Ausserordentliche Befriedungaktion* (Extraordinary Pacification Campaign) 10,000 Polish intellectuals were sent to Dachau, Buchenwald and Sachenhausen, while 3,500 municipal and political leaders were executed near Warsaw (Davies, 1984:447). Richard Lukas (1985) estimates that approximately 45 percent of Poland's physicians and dentists, 15 percent of its teachers, 30 percent of its clinicians, 18 percent of its clergy, 40 percent of its professors and 57 percent of its lawyers died during the war. Jan Hoser (1970) figures that between 35 and 50 percent of Poland's engineers died between 1938 and 1945.

Soviet occupation of eastern Poland between 1939 and 1941 reinforced preexisting antagonisms. Various categories of people, ranging from former members of Russian prerevolutionary parties to aristocrats to members of the Red Cross were immediately rounded up when the Soviets crossed Polish borders. Between 1 and 1½ million of these Poles were then deported to Siberia. Almost half of these victims died by the time amnesty was declared in 1941 (Davies, 1984:447–49;

Kostecki and Mreła 1986:20; Gross, 1988). The event which symbolizes this period of Soviet occupation for many Poles is the murder by Soviets of over 4,000 Polish officers in the Katyn forest.[4]

The relationship between Polish and Soviet authorities changed over the course of the war. When the Nazis invaded the USSR in June 1941, imprisoned Poles were granted amnesty and a Polish army responsible to the Polish government in exile was allowed to form on Soviet soil. At the same time, the Soviets were also organizing pro-Soviet Polish groups: the Union of Polish Patriots (*Związek Patriotów Polskich* or ZPP) and the Polish Workers' Party (*Polska Partia Robotnicza* or PPR). In 1942–43, Polish–Soviet relations deteriorated significantly. The independent Polish army left the USSR and Polish units were formed under Soviet command. Diplomatic relations between the London-based Polish government and the Soviet Union were cut off after the 1943 discovery of the Katyn massacre's graves.

In November and December of 1943, the PPR organized the National Council of Poland (*Krajowa Rada Narodowa* or KRN), an underground parliament to rival the London government. As the Soviet Army crossed the old Polish border on January 4, 1944, smaller leftist groups joined the council, but the PPR remained the dominant force within it (Dziewanowski, 1976:171–72). This body was superseded by the Polish Committee of National Liberation (*Polski Komitet Wyzwolenia Narodowego* or PKWN), established July 21, 1944, in Chełm. It claimed sole executive authority over the struggle for Polish liberation, although only the Soviets recognized its proclamation. Recognizing that the Soviet-backed PKWN sought political domination, the London government ordered its Home Army (*Armia Krajowa* = AK) to revolt against the Germans and take Warsaw before the Soviets could liberate it for them. While Polish communists inside the capital fought alongside the Home Army, Soviet forces across the Vistula remained inactive, ignoring the appeals of the Home Army commander for help. After nearly two months of fighting, Soviet planes dropped food and supplies, but that turned out to be too little too late. The Polish resistance surrendered on October 3, 1944, after losing at least 225,000 people. This decimated the military strength of the London government, and opened the door to pro-Soviet Polish forces. The Soviet domination of Polish politics was formally recognized by the allies in conferences in Teheran in 1943 and at Potsdam and Yalta in 1945. These meetings ultimately produced the new global order (Fehér, 1988) and the cold war that followed.[5]

For Poland, this new global order meant that the London government and the Home Army were to be effectively excluded from governance. Consequently, civil war raged during and after Soviet liberation (de Weydenthal, 1978:50). Home Army leaders were imprisoned, charged in a Moscow court with illegal activity as the American and British ambassadors watched (Dziewanowski, 1976:185–86; Davies, 1988). The only London-based party to partici-pate in the formation of the government was the Polish Peasant Party (*Polskie Stronnictwo Ludowe* or PSL) of Stanisław Mikołajczyk. This party claimed the largest membership of any of the parties, but its influence was effectively undermined in a variety of ways, from intimidation to politically inspired murders. The 1947 elections were rigged to give the communist-led Democratic Bloc 80 percent of the votes. Mikołajczyk then was accused of being a spy and subsequently fled to London (Kostecki and Mrela, 1986:49–52).

Although London-based groups were effectively excluded, there were other alternatives to the communist PPR. A reconstructed Polish Socialist Party had been formed. It was about the same size as the PPR and included some elements from the pre-war PPS *Lewica*. Between 1945 and 1948, this PPS maintained a separate identity and indeed held out a different vision of socialism from that which the PPR offered (Reynolds, 1978:517–18). It was a short-lived opposition, as the inten-sification of cold war and Stalin's pressures forced the collapse of an independent PPS. The final blow came when its leadership submitted to communist pressure and purged 100,000 members in 1948 for ideological insubordination (de Weydenthal, 1978:56). Later that year, the parties were merged into the Polish United Workers' Party (*Polska Zjednoczona Partia Robotnicza* or PZPR) (Davies, 1984:571–72). Two other parties remained officially independent of the PZPR, the Demo-cratic Party and the United Peasants' Party, the latter formed out of the communist-organized peasant party and the remnants of Mikołaj-czyk's party.

An alternative to PPR hegemony in these formative years could also be found in the independent action and organizing of workers themselves. Strikes and other protests raged in several centers, especially in 1946–47, when the PPR attempted to introduce work speed-ups, similar to the Russian Stakhanovite work programs. Police units and firearms were used to break these strikes (Reynolds, 1978:529–34). This independent worker activism anticipated the importance of worker self-organization in subsequent decades.

The most important conflict in this period was within the Commun-ist Party itself. The two principal factions were divided over the Polish party's autonomy from the Soviets. One group sought to imitate the Soviet method of socialist construction, while the other, emphasizing Poland's peculiarities, advocated a more distinctive national road. The latter faction's leader, Władysław Gomułka, was dismissed from leadership for his "nationalist deviationist" tendencies in 1948, expelled from the party in 1949 and later imprisoned. Bolesław Bierut became the party's leader, and with that, the Stalinist road began in Poland.

World War II and its aftermath reinforced the tension between the Communist Party and Polish nationalism. The main resistance to Nazi aggression was not the communist movement, as in Yugoslavia, but the resistance forces associated with the old government. The Soviets in fact imprisoned the leaders of the main Polish resistance in the last days of the war. Unlike Hungary, Czechoslovakia and Romania, the pre-war Polish government was not tainted with collaboration with Nazi forces. Instead, it was the communists who were compromised by their association with the Soviet invasion of eastern Poland in 1939–41. Effective exclusion of the London government and its supporters from authority in post-war Poland further undermined the chance that the communist movement and Polish nationalism could be reconciled. That possibility was ultimately buried when the PPS and the Gomułka wing of the newly created PZPR were eliminated. Communism and Polish nationalism had been perceived as potentially antagonistic before World War II. By 1948, the principal recurrent theme of protest for subsequent decades had been established: the identification of communism with foreign occupation and repression.

This identification is not, however, adequate to explaining the Solidarity movement. The communist authorities had several alternative possibilities in over thirty years for overcoming that identification in Poland and building legitimacy.[6] (1) Postwar political and economic reconstruction enabled the creation of a new cadre of loyal activists and new expanded intelligentsia and working class. But agricultural collectivization, conflict with the Roman Catholic Church and persecution of non-communist resistance fighters undermined this post-revolutionary Stalinist base for legitimacy. (2) The "Polish October" of 1956 created another potential base for regime legitimacy when new PZPR leader, Gomułka, threw out many Soviet advisors, ended collectivization, facilitated workers' self-management and encouraged a new wave of liberal discourse. This potential was also lost as the authorities pulled back from economic and cultural reforms, repressed their own students in March 1968 and participated in the invasion of Czechoslovakia a few months later. (3) The replacement of Gomułka with Edward Gierek after the murder of scores of workers on the streets in 1970 also opened up new opportunities for overcoming the association of communism with foreign occupation and repression. Gierek's practice of "consultations" with workers, the increasing standard of living and growing opportunities for travel abroad were potential foundations for another kind of regime legitimacy. But regime corruption and incompetence turned this technocratic–consumerist vision into an economic crisis, which in turn provided one set of conditions essential for Solidarity's formation.

Another set of conditions for Solidarity's formation usually centers on the significance of the Catholic Church and its identification with the nation. This association is not intrinsic. The religious foundation for Solidarity rests instead on the "political economy of truth" in Soviet-type societies, and the ability of Pope John Paul II to generate in his visit to Poland in 1979 an alternative emancipatory language and cultural identity for workers. But this alternative identity was not so obviously important at the close of World War II.

Polish Stalinism

The government formed after World War II was primarily a product of Soviet military might. Poland was consigned to the Soviet sphere of influence and her domestic politics were dictated in large part by Stalin, or those executing policy sought to fulfill his wishes (Brzezinski, 1967; Torańska, 1987). Polish Stalinism was thus a product of Stalin's personal influence, but the extremes of Stalinism in collectivization, mass terror and personality cult were more limited in Poland than in other countries. Indeed, it was not self-evident from the start that communist rule in Poland would be so disastrous. For some groups, communist rule promised improvement.

Although comparatively few Jews remained in Poland after their extermination during the war and their emigration afterwards, Jews, perhaps more than any other ethnic group in Poland, welcomed the Soviet liberation. Checiński (1982:8) explains, "not only did they owe their life to the Soviet victory over the Nazi murderers, but, before the war, it had been the Left, including the Communist faction, that fought anti-Semitism in Poland and proclaimed the abolition of all forms of national, racial, or religious discrimination as a principal aim."

Given the measure of anti-Semitic sentiment in parts of the gentile Polish population, the link of Jews to Russian communist liberation intensified Polish–communist antagonisms. Jews had been more closely tied to the communist underground armies than to the London government's Home Army during the Nazi occupation of Poland too (Lukas, 1985), and continued to be prominent in the post-war communist government until 1968 when anti-Semitic ideology was used by some Polish communists to attack student activists and communists with Jewish origins. Polish–Jewish relations color the nationalist–communist relationship.

Despite this national factor, Polish communists had several opportunities for building legitimacy through economic and social reconstruction. The whole population was exhausted from the terror of Nazi domination and some groups already were suffering terribly in the Second Republic before the war. There was hyperinflation through 1926, high unemployment among urban and especially rural workers and ethnic conflict between Poles and the sizeable minority groups including Ukrainians, Jews, Ruthenians, Belorussians and Germans (Davies, 1984:404–15; Hann, 1985:28–35; Pearson, 1983:160–69). Most Poles were ready for a new order that promised to be more equal and just. In fact, Poland's economy recovered much more quickly after World War II than it did after World War I (Taylor, 1952). If historical comparison is one basis for acquiring legitimacy, Polish communists were advantaged by the tragedies of human experience overseen by their predecessors.

The communists also needed to fill positions of a whole new state and economic apparatus. This gave the new ruling party an opportunity to create a cadre more directly indebted to them. State administration increased its number of jobs from 172,000 before the war to 344,000 in 1949 (de Weydenthal, 1978:62). The party's drive to industrialize also created structural conditions that enabled massive rates of upward social mobility for peasants, workers and their children. Intra-generational social mobility was especially great, producing a favorable attitude toward the new regime and creating a relatively quiescent and inexperienced industrial labor force (Kolankiewicz, 1973).

The PZPR faced greater challenges with other groups. The peasantry was the largest part of the Polish population at the end of World War II. Land reform was part of the 1944 PPR plan for reconstruction, and in the period immediately after the war the communists increased their support in the countryside through it.

Under Soviet pressure, however, on July 6, 1948, the party announced plans to collectivize agriculture. Between 1949 and 1951, peasants resisted collectivization by drastically reducing agricultural production. By 1953, the party announced its agricultural policy to be a failure and through 1956 reduced its rate of collectivization, recognizing the "balance of power in the countryside" (Korboński, 1965; Torańska, 1987:296). In this attempt to collectivize, the party lost much of the rural support it had won through its agricultural reform.

Through 1948, the party followed a policy of coexistence with the Roman Catholic Church. The communists interfered relatively little with Church activities and the Church also held its hand, avoiding open confrontation with the government. A war of words nevertheless escalated through the 1940s into more severe confrontation. The government charged the Vatican, the Polish Church hierarchy and numbers of Polish priests with anti-Polish and anti-state activities. On June 30, 1949, the Vatican decreed that all Communist Party members and sympathizers would be excommunicated, announced through the Voice of America (Markiewicz, 1981:80). By 1950, over 500 religious persons had been arrested (Dziewanowski, 1976:245). In the same year, all Church property, except for church buildings and churchyards, was confiscated (Davies, 1984:580). A brief truce was signalled between the Church and state on June 14, 1950, but could not last as the Cold War intensified. On February 9, 1953, the government issued a decree in which appointments to Church administrative positions had first to receive government approval (Markiewicz, 1981:110). From the Church's viewpoint, this was one of the most severe violations of the 1950 agreement (Wyszyński, 1983:36). Tensions grew after this confrontation, resulting in the arrest of Cardinal Wyszyński on September 25, 1953, and his imprisonment for over three years. By 1954, nine bishops and hundreds of priests were imprisoned (Dziewanowski, 1976:251).

The party could not build legitimacy by attacking an overwhelmingly popular Church. Whether the party could have pursued any other path is difficult to say, however. This was not just a domestic conflict, and rather reflected a larger one between the Vatican and Moscow. Within Poland, both sides seemed to want the 1950 agreement to succeed (Wyszyński, 1983:20–23). It seems that such wishes could not be realized in the cold world atmosphere facing both communists and clergy in Poland.

The government's imprisonment of Home Army veterans also hurt the chances for the development of legitimacy. The AK was widely and accurately perceived as the largest Polish force against the Nazi occupation. The AK, together with the Peasant Battalions, had about 400,000 men in its forces, in comparison to the communist army which never had more than 10,000 (Davies, 1984:466). Between 1950 and 1955, thirty-seven pre-war Polish officers were sentenced to death and dozens more were imprisoned (Checiński, 1982:56).

Although the PZPR created a loyal group of Communist Party members, and a potentially sympathetic working class, it only exacerbated prior tensions that non-communist Poles felt towards a Soviet-sponsored Communist Party because of its persecutions of the Church, peasantry and Home Army veterans. Poland's Stalinism was nevertheless mild in comparison to the terror in Hungary and Czechoslovakia. Indeed, this relatively mild version gave Polish communists a second chance for winning legitimacy.

Revisionism's promise and failure

Josef Stalin died in 1953. Władysław Gomułka, purged from the party in 1949 for his "nationalist deviationist" tendencies, and imprisoned in 1950, was released from prison in 1954. In 1955, some of the most hated members of the security apparatus were dismissed, and purged from the party. At the twentieth Communist Party congress of the Soviet Union, Nikita Khrushchev attacked Stalin's personality cult. Shortly before, the Communist Party of Poland, dissolved in 1938, was rehabilitated by the Soviets. Less than one month after the twentieth CPSU congress began, Poland's party leader, Bolesław Bierut, died under mysterious circumstances in Moscow, and Edward Ochab became first party secretary. On April 20, 1956, 28,000 people were granted amnesty and 1,000 political prisoners were freed. Various front groups asserted greater independence from the party. Workers elected trade union officials by secret ballot and independent workers councils were formed. The Sejm (the parliament) began to act more independently, and universities sought the restoration of old academic freedoms. Three years after Stalin's death, his legacy in Poland was being dismantled.

In this same period, intellectuals intensified their attacks on the suppressions of various freedoms (Raina, 1977:21–36). Economic conditions also deteriorated significantly by 1956. Peasant resistance to collectivization reduced the food supply in the cities. The tremendous bias toward capital goods in the first six-year plan also led to severe shortages of consumer goods on the market. The dissatisfaction grew as the six-year plan of 1949 reached its end, and culminated in the "Poznań Uprising" led by a workforce with a pre-war militant union tradition from the H. Cegielski or ZISPO complex.

On June 28, 1956, more than 20,000 and perhaps as many as 100,000 demonstrators took to the streets to demand better wages, more apartments and fairer taxes. Although initially peaceful, rumors that the workers' negotiators in Warsaw were arrested turned parts of the crowd violent. One group freed prisoners and obtained weapons from the local prison. Soldiers, tanks and airplanes were used by the authorities to restore order. Official estimates put 53 dead and 300 wounded, but at least 74 people had been killed and over 400 required hospital attention (Dziewanowski, 1976:265; Maciejewski and Trojanowiczowa, 1981).

This uprising, the scores of strikers killed by communist authorities and the other smaller strikes and demonstrations of the time dominated the discussion at the Seventh Plenum of the PZPR Central Committee. They initially tried to attribute the tragedy to "imperialist agents" and "provocateurs," but under public pressure, the party finally acknowledged the justification of the protests. The internal party struggle grew more intense in that plenum, as some called for a halt to cultural liberalization, while the majority of the party recognized the need for changes. Gomułka regained his party rights in this meeting, and several new faces were added to the politburo. Over the following summer, more changes in economy and society were initiated and by mid-October, at the Eighth Party Plenum, Gomułka returned to power as first party secretary (Dziewanowski, 1976:266–72; Brzezinski, 1967:247; Checiński, 1982:111).

The drama of Gomułka's return contributed once more to the possibility of legitimacy for the party. For the first time, a communist was to become leader of Poland *despite* the wishes of the Soviets. In fact, Khrushchev and other Soviet leaders flew to Warsaw, and it was widely believed at the time that they threatened invasion by Soviet troops if various pro-Moscow figures were removed from power. Word of the visit leaked out, and street demonstrations in favor of Gomułka took place. An armed Internal Security Corps under a Gomułka ally manned key buildings and Warsaw arteries. The Soviet leaders for various reasons (Brzezinski, 1967:250–60) backed down and returned to Moscow. Soviet-sponsored Minister of National Defense Konstantin Rokossowski was replaced by a Gomułka supporter. Rokossowski returned to Moscow with about thirty highly ranked Soviet generals and thousands of lower-ranked officers (de Weydenthal, 1978:92; Dziewanowski, 1976:283–84).

Not only did it seem that Gomułka stood up to the Soviets, but within one month he secured various concessions from them (de Weydenthal, 1978:93). Gomułka's apparent resistance to the Soviets gave him an opportunity that no other communist has ever had, or perhaps will ever have again in Poland: the chance to achieve legitimate leadership. His criticism of Stalinist practices, imprisonment by Stalinists, defiance of Soviet might and the creation of greater equality in Poland–USSR relations led people to believe that something different was about to happen. He was a *symbol* of something new and appealing to virtually everyone (Brzezinski, 1967:333–34).

Gomułka's first months in power represented a genuine social transformation of Stalinism. The security service virtually disappeared from public life and censorship was almost completely inactive (Checiński, 1982:123–24). The peasants spontaneously decollectivized agriculture. The new five-year plan was to be gradually recast so as to provide better consumer goods and services. Over the summer, workers spontaneously organized councils in factories, and under Gomułka's tenure they were legalized. Other new and relatively autonomous associations were formed. Cardinal Wyszyński was released from house arrest one week after the October plenum, and shortly thereafter a Church–state commission seeking better dialogue was established.

The transformation of 1956 was one in which all sectors of society were actively engaged. Workers (especially those in large factories) took the initiative to form councils; peasants decollectivized agriculture; intellectuals formed discussion clubs and filled the media with new and exciting criticism; the party had an internal revolt in which someone initially opposed by the Soviets gained power. These groups were, however, acting autonomously. They were, of course, aware of other events, which bolstered their own aggressiveness in seeking change. But there was not cooperation across strata; the party did not even help workers organize the councils. While autonomous, all sectors saw the party's transformation as the means through which their own aspirations could be fulfilled. What was desired by all of the groups was security and stability, and Gomułka seemed to be able to provide it.

In Gomułka's search for stability, new conciliatory relations with workers, peasants and the religious were made, but he also sought to establish more rigid control over the party. By May 1957, Gomułka asserted the need for a reinvigorated democratic centralism, and criticized "dogmatists" and "revisionists" alike. Over the next few years, the ranks of the liberal revisionists were devastated (de Weydenthal, 1978:97). The intellectual thaw represented by that Polish October also grew cold. The periodical that symbolized the transformation, *Po Prostu*, was closed down in 1957. By 1963, the liberal atmosphere had clearly ended. Even the allocation of privilege to travel abroad became the province of public security officers (Raina, 1977:73). The University of Warsaw was the only place that retained most of its intellectual freedom through this period (Karpiński, 1982:106). In fact, it was only because the university remained so free that the next confrontation in 1968 could even occur (Kuroń, 1973). While most of the political–cultural promises of October were being broken, the economic reforms promised in 1956 were also being dismantled.

Already in 1953, the economic and social crisis prompted the party to criticize its application of the Soviet model to the Polish economy. At the Seventh Central Committee Plenum in 1956, a scheme for the decentralization of the economy was approved, but in implementation, its decentralizing character disappeared (Zieliński, 1973:15). In mid-1957, central planning still determined at least 80 percent of output and by 1959 "hardly a vestige of freedom survived in determining employment, technological change and the purchase of raw materials and supplies" (Woodall, 1982:35–36). Hopes for expanded economic democracy also went unfulfilled as the independent workers' councils, spontaneously formed over the summer of 1956 and legislated into legal existence by Gomułka shortly after the October Plenum, were eviscerated. On November 19, 1956, the very progressive Workers' Council Law was passed. According to this bill, two-thirds of the members of the council had to be from the manual working class and "it would have a right to scrutinise and to comment on the annual plan, profits and performance, to agree to any changes in the internal organisational structure and production process of the enterprise, to approve of the distribution of profits between wages and bonuses and the newly created Factory Fund, and to approve the appointment of the Factory director" (Woodall, 1982:171). This bill affected those places (mostly large factories) that had already formed councils spontaneously, since it appeared that the party tried to hinder the development of new councils after "October" (Kolankiewicz, 1973:109–10). The councils and factory managers were interested in decentralizing the economy, but decentralization would loosen the grip of the central administration on individual factories and thus reduce its power (Kolankiewicz, 1973:109).

The autonomy of the councils was almost completely eliminated in 1958 by a new law on the establishment of the "Conference of Workers' Self Management." The independent councils were subordinated to this organ, which was formally composed of the councils, the enterprise party committee, the official trade-union factory council and the enterprise director himself. In practice, this body was dominated by management and functionaries of bodies controlled by the party (Woodall, 1982:172). There were no modifications in this law until 1978, when the role of workers' councils was further reduced officially (Woodall, 1982:182). In just two years, what appeared as a new stage in economic democracy became a repetition of centralized domination.

October 1956 had promised great things, and seemed to confirm the viability of revisionist strategy: that it was possible to reform the system from within by working through the Communist Party. Between 1956 and 1968, hopes for system transformation lay in the success of this strategy. In fact, Brzezinski (1967:343) believes that intellectuals intentionally avoided working with the workers' councils so as to ensure the greatest possible chance for a successful revisionist strategy. But revisionist hopes were crushed in the 1960s.

In order for revisionism to be successful, two conditions must be met: there must be a faction of the party both sufficiently powerful and sufficiently interested in reform, upon which those outside the party can rely; and there must be opportunities for independent public expression which the liberal faction in the party can use in their struggles for power within the party. Both conditions were destroyed, as liberal members of the party like Władysław Bieńkowski were removed from leadership and the organs for independent expression were crushed (Rupnik, 1979:64). Until Gorbachev, the military suppression of the Prague Spring appeared to represent the end to revisionist strategy. In Poland, the end came a little earlier.

New struggles

It is difficult to say *why* Gomułka backed off from the reforms promised in October, but it seems important to bear in mind that Gomułka himself was not the generator of reform. The councils were not the result of party initiative, despite the 1956 law. They were formed by workers themselves. Intellectuals formed their own discussion clubs and journals. The party did not initiate cultural liberalization. The social turbulence surrounding the Polish October was, however, used by Gomułka and his supporters to gain power within the apparatus. Once he had power, further disruptions only endangered his influence. Hence, the more important question may not be why Gomułka backed away from the Polish October, but rather what happened in society to undermine faith in him and his party. What changed the language of the opposition from a vocabulary based on revisionism to one based on conflict between society and the authorities?

Intellectual dissent continued through the 1960s, and party reactions became more severe. In 1964, thirty-four leading intellectuals wrote to the prime minister and decried censorship and "paper shortages" as deleterious to national culture. There was no official reaction until the letter was reprinted in the foreign press and broadcast over Radio Free Europe. Fourteen of the letter's signatories then found it impossible to publish their work in official publications. In that same year, two future Solidarity advisors prepared an "Open letter to the party." Jacek Kuroń and Karol Modzelewski presented an extended empirically based Marxist–Trotskyite critique of the Polish condition, based on the existence of a struggle between the working class and what they called the "central political bureaucracy." Ultimately, they argued, the working class would rise up and overthrow this new ruling group: "Revolution is inevitable." In 1965, after the letter was smuggled out of Poland and published without the consent of either of the authors (Checiński, 1982:180), Kuroń was sentenced to prison for three years and Modzelewski for three and a half. On the tenth anniversary of the Polish October, philosophers Leszek Kołakowski and Krzysztof Pomian offered critiques of the party's fulfillment of the October legacy. In turn, the party denounced them and expelled them from the party.

Most of these controversies centered around Warsaw University, since it was among its frequenters that the ideals of the Polish October were best preserved. One of those ideals was freedom of speech. In 1964, there was a demonstration in support of the signatories of the "Letter of the thirty-four" on the campus. In university discussion clubs, the Ribbentrop–Molotov pact, reasons for recurrent recessions in Soviet-type economies, the lack of society-wide freedom of speech and the need for political pluralism were all discussed. Given these discussions, different currents of political thought were developing, but whatever the perspectives, all groups, even the campus Maoists, were in favor of pluralism and against totalitarianism (Kuroń, 1973:96).

Another reason that the new struggles centered around Warsaw University was that most of the university activists in the PZPR itself were advocates of system liberalization, freedom of speech, significant autonomy for trade unions and so on (Kuroń, 1973:97). They argued that it was occasionally necessary to act *against* party dictate, especially when promised reforms were never realized. These overt conflicts between intelligentsia and party were not the only new struggles to emerge in this time. Struggles within the party achieved a new level of intensity.

Party factions are rarely well characterized by the labels they adopt or are given (Staniszkis, 1984a:293–98; Białecki, 1985). Liberals and conservatives often support the same programs, but have different visions about who should be in charge. The labels are more useful to identify allies and enemies than describe real positions. In 1956, faction labels helped exonerate, in the eyes of society and especially the party rank and file, certain members of the ruling elite from responsibility for the Stalinist tragedies. Certainly, all members of the leadership had a collective responsibility for the tragedies of Stalinism, but by creating faction labels, transforming equally complicit individuals into the "good" and the "bad," the liberal and the neo-Stalinist, the anti-democratic and anti-Semitic, certain leaders from the period of Stalinism managed to escape responsibility for their collective actions. But it was these same people who survived the transition from Stalinism who found themselves under attack at the end of the 1960s.

Mieczysław Moczar, minister of the interior from 1964 and a leader of the faction called "the Partisans," used nationalist and anti-Semitic rhetoric in an attempt to dislodge from power the disproportionately Jewish group who remained at the top of party hierarchies since the days of Stalin. Moczar's anti-Semitic machinations set political struggles for the next several years (Checiński, 1982:156–71; Dziewanowski, 1976:291–92; Raina 1977:45–47, 65–69, 104–8). It was his bid for power, in conjunction with the resistance of Polish students and intellectuals to the suppression of free intellectual activities at Warsaw University, that provoked the next major clash between authorities and part of society.

During the 1967/68 school year, a production of Adam Mickiewicz's *Forefather's Eve* (*Dziady*) was run at the National Theater in Warsaw. The play was very popular for its literary content, but also for its political message, as relevant in 1968 as it was when Mickiewicz wrote the play after the 1831 uprising against the tsar. When lines expressing anti-Russian sentiment were recited (like "We Poles have sold our souls to Moscow for silver rubles" and "Everyone sent here from Moscow is either a jackass, a fool, or a spy") the audience applauded vigorously. The play ran for a long time, and some believe that Moczar protected it so that it would become an embarrassment to Gomułka. Gomułka finally shut it down on January 30, 1968. After that last performance, the student audience marched toward Mickiewicz's monument on Krakowskie Przedmiejście Street, where they were met by police. Thirty-five people were beaten, taken to police headquarters or fined (Checiński, 1982:228).

In the following month, students at the university circulated a petition protesting the play's cancellation. Over 3,000 signatures were collected and the petition was sent to the Sejm on February 16 (Karpiński, 1982:110; Raina, 1977:115). Later that month, a meeting of the Warsaw chapter of the Union of Polish Writers (*Związek Literatów Polskich* or ZLP) defied the authorities' demand to endorse the play's cancellation, and instead called it a "glaring example" of the authorities' interference in Polish culture (Karpiński, 1982:112). Conflict intensified when two students, Adam Michnik and Henryk Szlajfer, were expelled from Warsaw University.

Four days later, a student demonstration was organized to protest against the spring's events. In the course of the demonstration, "outsiders," later learned to be "worker activists" from factories and volunteers in the citizens' militia, shoved demonstrators. These activists eventually left in their buses when the rector issued a vague statement thanking them for their help. As students left the campus two hours later, however, the ZOMO (*Zmotoryzowane Odwody Milicji Obywatelskiej*), a paramilitary riot squad, beat students with their truncheons (Karpiński, 1982:113–15; Raina, 1977:125–28).

These events escalated into a major confrontation, because they were tied into the largest anti-Semitic campaign Europe had suffered since Hitler's terror. Gomułka used the occasion of the Arab–Israeli war to initiate an "anti-Zionist" campaign against several leading Jewish communist leaders. Gomułka's use of anti-Zionist propaganda gave Moczar's group free reign to use that vocabulary in their own struggle for power. They went very far to establish that a "fifth column" existed in Poland, one that included all Jews, including communist Jews. Checiński (1982:215) recalls that when he was still a member of the Polish military counter-intelligence, he was shown a document reportedly stolen from the Ministry of Internal Affairs based on the tsarist "Elders of Zion." The anti-Semitic campaign was also waged against students.

In the press, "ringleaders of the disorder" were called "Zionists in league with West Germans." Extra names with a decidedly non-Slavic ring were added to the list of demonstration leaders (Karpiński, 1982:117). Three days after the demonstration, Warsaw University students and faculty protested the beatings and anti-Semitic press accounts, and demanded reinstatements of rights for students and faculty arrested or expelled from the university, and guarantees of academic freedom and university autonomy (Karpiński, 1982:118). Other institutions of higher education in Warsaw supported the university's demands. Confrontations between the police and from 5,000 to 20,000 demonstrators in Warsaw's streets continued that same afternoon (Raina, 1977:129). The next day and for several days thereafter, demonstrations by university people took place in Gdańsk, Lublin, Poznań, Wrocław, and Kraków.

In response to the urban intellectual support, the party initiated rallies in factories, wherein students were told to go back to their studies and calls for a purge in the "Party of Zionists" were made (Karpiński, 1982:120, 126; Raina, 1977:133). Moczar was using his influence to deepen divisions between workers and students, but also to create an opportunity for him to take power from Gomułka. Warsaw University students in turn occupied one of the halls on campus. High-level state functionaries and Warsaw University faculty were then dismissed (Karpiński, 1982:132). After another protest rally, whole departments were eliminated, 1,600 students expelled and student leaders imprisoned (Karpiński, 1982:135; Raina, 1977:145–46).[7]

These events not only have meaning for the formation of party factional struggles, but also for the formation of the opposition. Starski (1982:25–56) argues that there has been a process of oppositional formation in Poland, and that the March events of 1968 were key in teaching intellectuals that they could not hope for change coming from within the party, nor could they force the party to change from outside by themselves. In 1968, the students chanted "Poland is waiting for her Dubček" (Rupnik, 1979:68). Because no faction existed which was motivated or strong enough to play the revisionist role, and because the students' plea was met with violent repression, the March events can justifiably be called a "generation-making experience" (Starski, 1982:35). The violence launched against students and the crudity of the anti-Semitic propaganda destroyed any lingering hopes for revisionism among the intelligentsia as the means toward the humanization of communism. The Warsaw Pact's annihilation of the Prague

Spring was probably the final proof. The memory of 1968 is a principal factor in Poles' skeptical reception of Gorbachev's *glasnost'* and *perestroika*.

Many intellectual advisors to Solidarity were weaned on the March events. Through their participation in the trade union, March 1968 has taken its place beside workers' revolts as part of the opposition's historical self-consciousness. In 1981, a memorial to the March 8 protest was erected at the gates of Warsaw University. The inscription begins with a quotation from the Polish writer Cyprian Norwid, and follows with a memorial to the March events:

> We must not bow to circumstances and let truth stand behind closed doors.

> On this place on March 8, 1968, students demanding freedom of speech were dispersed. The events of March have become a symbol of the suppression of free thought, the destruction of national culture, and the unity of Polish society. Today in sympathy returning justice to the wronged, we place this plaque as a warning to future generations.

> Students, Employees of UW, Workers of Warsaw

Workers, Gomułka and Gierek

With Soviet aid, Gomułka managed to weather the intellectuals' protests and Moczar's first challenge. Moczar appeared unreliable to the Soviets, especially when it became known that one of his editorial allies planned to reconsider the Katyn Massacre in the Polish press. Rather than threaten Polish–Soviet relations, Gomułka reinforced them by ordering Polish troops to participate in the Warsaw Pact invasion of Czechoslovakia in 1968. At the Fifth Congress of the PZPR in November of that year, the Soviets put all their support behind Gomułka, and helped him retain his leadership. Moczar advanced to candidate member of the Politburo and secretary of the Central Committee for Security Matters, but no further (Ascherson, 1982:93; Raina, 1977:161).

The March events, and indeed the entire post-October history of opposition seems to be dominated by the protests of intellectuals rather than working-class opposition. That appearance is partially a result of the bias among Polish historians. The social history of the working and peasant classes fares poorly in comparison to the histories of notables and literati. Nevertheless, it was true that workers were relatively quiet during Gomułka's tenure, although not all were completely passive or antagonistic to protests from the intelligentsia (Raina, 1977:139–40). During the 1960s, workers occasionally protested working conditions and compensation, but their actions remained localized and quickly resolved. This changed in 1970.

On December 12, 1970, the Council of Ministers announced a change in the industrial wage scale and the pricing system for consumer goods. Some goods were lowered in price, but the prices of the most essential items went up (Ascherson, 1982:100; Singer, 1981:157). In economic terms, the price hikes may have been long overdue, as there were no mechanisms that changed prices automatically with changes in the costs of production. Whatever the macroeconomic "necessity," the move ignited popular protest on the Baltic coast.[8]

On Monday, December 14, workers began to stage demonstrations. A major protest occurred in Gdańsk, outside the shipyards.[9] Several thousand workers assembled and marched on to the center of town, where, in front of the district party headquarters, they shouted "we want bread" and "the press is lying." Later in the day someone attempted to burn the party headquarters. The next day, over 10,000 people demonstrated. This time they succeeded in burning the regional party building and main railway station. According to the authorities, 6 people were killed, 300 people were wounded, and 128 people were arrested in the conflict.

In both Gdańsk and nearby Gdynia, a curfew was introduced that evening. Tanks and armored vehicles were brought in overnight. The following morning, four men were killed as a throng of workers left the Gdańsk shipyard and marched toward the surrounding tanks. An occupation strike was declared in the shipyard and strike committees were established across the coast. Conflicts between workers and authorities intensified. Thirteen workers were murdered at the gates of the Gdynia shipyard. In Szczecin, the District Party Committee headquarters was set on fire, and at least sixteen workers were killed by the military. By the weekend, workers on the coast were occupying a range of enterprises. In Szczecin, a parallel city government based on an inter-enterprise strike committee was established. Most of the factories in Warsaw were on strike too, and a nationwide general strike was called for the following Monday. Violent conflict was widespread and revolution seemed possible. Official figures put the number of dead at 45 and 1,165 wounded; unofficial estimates of the figures of those killed are closer to 200–300 (Ascherson, 1982:100–102; Green, 1977; Karpiński, 1982:158–60; Singer, 1981:166–71; Starski, 1982:41).

Gomułka sought from the Soviet leadership support for his confrontational strategy. Brezhnev refused and advised a political solution, eroding Gomułka's power within the Polish party. On December 19, Gomułka fell ill and an emergency meeting of the politburo was called. On December 20, at a Central Committee meeting, Edward Gierek, the Silesian political boss known for his successful technocratic leadership, became first party secretary. Apparently, this was a more-or-less Polish choice, since the USSR did not seem to intervene (Dziewanowski, 1976:328). Among Gierek's first acts were a promise not to raise prices any more for the next two years, the introduction of a new bonus scheme and a new housing program.

After bringing down Gomułka through protest, workers felt confident to continue pressing for the elimination of any price hike and wage-system restructuring. The Warski shipyard workers in Szczecin staged an occupation strike in the middle of January in response to a false newspaper report that they were ready, willing and anxious to meet new production quotas. Among their demands were a return to the pre-December 12 food prices, democratic elections to party, trade-union and workers' council positions and guarantees of safety for present and past strikers (Karpiński, 1982:164–65; Singer, 1981:172–78). In response, the new first secretary, Gierek, and the new prime minister, Piotr Jaroszewicz, came to negotiate with them. Gierek conceded to some of their demands, including an elimination of the wage reform. After nine straight hours of negotiations, the occupation strike was called off, but without resolving the matter of food prices (New Left Review, 1972). The workers maintained their independent strike committees, continued to hold mass meetings and supervised new trade-union elections in the shipyards.

Strikes nevertheless continued in other parts of the country, with the next major confrontation in the textile city of Łódź. As early as February 13, over 10,000 women workers in seven mills were on strike, with workers occupying the Marchlewski plant. The prime minister went to consult the strikers, but he could not repeat his Szczecin "success." The strikers insisted on a return to pre-December 12 prices before returning to work. As strikes continued there and elsewhere, Gierek and his team had no alternative: the December price hike was withdrawn completely on February 15 and gradually relations in production were "normalized" (Green, 1977). By summer, the party felt its position firmly enough consolidated to fire the most militant workers from the Szczecin shipyards. But the price freeze, having become a symbol of the *modus vivendi* between party and workers, had to remain intact (Singer, 1981:181). When the party planned to raise prices again late in 1972, workers in Gdańsk, Szczecin, Łódź, Warsaw and Katowice mines struck. The price hike was put off again, but now with thirty Katowice miners arrested (Green, 1977).

The strength of a mature working class became evident to all in this conflict. Where intellectuals could be beaten into submission in 1968, the authorities had to bargain with the workers in 1970–71. Their occupation of plants, halting production and aggressiveness on the streets made them far more formidable than students occupying university buildings. Ultimately, the workers' simplest demands (concerning the food prices) were conceded by the party. The demands for democratic elections to workers' bodies were never, however, fulfilled outside of Szczecin, and those accomplishments gradually disappeared even there. It might be said that where intellectuals had lost faith in revisionism in 1968, the workers had no reason yet to doubt that revisionism could work for them. They could rely on refinements in the existing institutional structure of Poland's Soviet-type system and the promises of the party leadership.

Gierek's economic and social transformation

While Gomułka's economic reforms never amounted to anything, economic reform was Gierek's first priority. Gierek's political success rested on the reform's success. Gierek did not have Gomułka's personal popularity. Gierek had to keep the prices of basic goods down, and turn around the economic decline Poland had suffered in recent years. By 1983, the dream of making Poland the second Japan of the world economy was a popular joke, but in the first half of the 1970s a glorious economic revival seemed quite possible.

For the last four years of Gomułka's tenure, real wages for Polish workers had risen very slowly, and for some groups had even declined (Green, 1977). In order to fulfill his promise, Gierek had to increase rates of investment substantially to modernize Polish industry as well as improve levels of consumption to pacify an already rebellious population. Unlike Gomułka, who sought a more autarkic economic development in the last years of his rule, Gierek turned westward for help. He borrowed extensively: long- and medium-term debt to advanced capitalist countries expanded from $1.2 billion in 1971 to $7.6 billion in 1975 to $23.0 billion by 1980 (Nuti, 1981[1982]:22). In addition to incurring debt, Gierek's reform also involved yet another attempt to decentralize the economy (Farrell, 1981).

From 1972 to 1974, the average yearly increase in investment was 24 percent (Farrell, 1981:299). Much of the technological development came from foreign licensing and expanded trade with the West. In 1971, Poland had $2.3 billion in export receipts from advanced capitalist countries, $5.7 billion in 1975 and $9.9 billion in 1980. Import outlays for goods and services from the West increased from $2.0 billion in 1971 to $8.7 billion in 1975 to $10.3 billion in 1980 (Nuti, 1981[1982]:22).

Living conditions improved dramatically in the first years of the seventies. The average growth rate of consumer-goods production as a percentage of producer-goods production increased, from 67.3 percent in 1961–65, to 70.2 percent in 1966–70, to 95.3 percent in 1971–74. Real wages increased by 40 percent for the first five years of the seventies; in the 1960s they increased only 20 percent (Green, 1977). The consumption of meat increased between 4.7 and 7.2 percent in each year of Gierek's first half-decade (Farrell, 1981:302). Poles recognized the improvement; by 1975, three out of four Poles believed that their own material conditions had improved (Pravda, 1982:170). Restrictions on travel to the West were also reduced; 114,000 Poles visited capitalist countries in 1970, while in 1975 approximately 316,000 people took such a vacation (Kostecki and Mreła, 1986:666). This combination of improved consumption at home and the opportunity to travel abroad suggested to many Poles and Westerners alike that Poland was indeed on a course of liberalization and economic development.

Although consumption had improved, all was not quiet. Power struggles continued within the party and in society at large. Moczar launched an attack against Gierek in May of 1971, though Gierek managed to survive and consolidate his power (Dziewanowski, 1976:319–20). Gierek also moved against dissenters. Thirteen members of the *Ruch* (The Movement) were sent to prison for their "anti-state" activities (Raina, 1977:205–9).

The first years of the decade were quiet in comparison to what followed the presentation of a new constitution to the public in December 1975, however. In the 1952 constitution, power belonged to the working people in towns and countryside, as in the new version; but the new version also proposed that (1) the PZPR would be recognized as the leading force of the country, (2) a citizen's rights would depend on the performance of a citizen's duties, and (3) there would be unshakeable fraternal bonds with the Soviet Union. Poland's intellectuals and the Catholic hierarchy strongly protested against these additions, and managed to convince the party to back down; the phrase about rights was eliminated and the other two were watered down (Raina, 1977:190–221). This event foreshadowed one alliance between intellectual opposition and the Church. The foundations of an alliance with workers were laid one year later.

Gierek tried to build support for his leadership through technocratic reform and consumer revolution. He also tried to build legitimacy by tying the party to more peculiarly Polish historical traditions. He linked the PZPR to the "native radical tradition" and restored the ancient royal castle in Warsaw. One of his advisors even drew an analogy between the role of the party and the role played by Poland's elected kings of the sixteenth century (Dziewanowski, 1976:319). Gierek also tried to resecure the party's working-class roots through "consultations." Green (1977) calls these consultations "ideologically inconsistent," since Poland was already supposed to have been a socialist or popular democracy; how could it only now consult the population? Gierek frequently met with workers, as he did in Szczecin, ostensibly to understand better what they wanted. In 1971 alone he had 171 "grass-roots meetings" (Dziewanowski, 1976:318). Between 1971 and 1975, he held about thirteen meetings with Baltic shipyard workers. These meetings gradually lost the electricity and confrontational quality characteristic of the first Szczecin meeting, and evolved into stage-managed media presentations (Green, 1977).

Although ceremonial ties with the working class increased under Gierek, his leading cadre lost commitments to communist morality. The fever attached to the loan-generated consumerism seemed to eliminate any egalitarianism from the consciences of the economic and political elites. This was a departure from Gomułka's era and especially Gomułka himself.[10] Although Szczecin workers complained in their 1971 meeting with Gierek about managerial privileges (New Left Review, 1972), by 1976 there was far more about which workers could complain.

Alex Pravda (1982) calls Gierek's attempts at economic bribery a "premature consumerism." Gierek may have successfully convinced the population that consumerism was a worthwhile trade-off for greater democracy, but he failed at providing the means for the continued consumerist revolution. By the mid-seventies, economic difficulties provoked more labor unrest. Although there were several slowdown strikes on the Baltic coast in 1974, and strikes and demonstrations took place in Warsaw and Radom in 1975 protesting against economic conditions, the next major challenge to the authorities took place in 1976. On June 24, price increases averaging around 60 percent were announced abruptly, without the consultation on which Gierek prided himself. Wage supplements were also administered, but in an extremely inegalitarian way, increasing in size as the wages themselves rose (de Weydenthal, 1978:164–65; Raina, 1977:231).

The party showed some evidence of having learned something from 1970, however. They tried to introduce the change when many people were already on summer vacations, and not when they were planning a major holiday. This greater wisdom could also be seen as an indication that this was not a provocation to strengthen the hand of some party faction, since it was introduced in such a way as to minimize society's antagonism. In fact, thirty minutes were set aside for consultations in the factories on the following day (Green, 1977). The consultations were inadequate, however, as workers throughout the country rebelled. After the regional party secretary refused to meet with demonstrating workers in Radom, the strikers stormed the party headquarters, and then set fire to it and to the secretary's official residence. The police used water cannons and tear gas to stop the workers, killing as many as seventeen workers in the conflict (Green, 1977; Raina, 1977:232–35; Singer, 1981:183–84). The price hike was withdrawn that evening.

As in workers' rebellions in 1956 and 1970, the party initially decried the participants in the Radom confrontation as hooligans and criminal elements. Be they hooligan or not, the conflict forced the party to back down again, and Gierek a week later was seeking new consultations with the masses, trying to explain the necessity of the changes. Sugar was rationed eventually, but with the help of a low-interest Soviet loan, meat went unrationed and without a change in price.

Though it appeared that Gierek did not understand how workers would react, he had learned something from Gomułka's failures. Rather than confront the workers initially and then give in, as Gomułka, he chose to back down immediately and engage in a more selective repression. That strategy helped create the alliance which ultimately led to his fall.

The authorities dismissed from employment at least 2,000 and perhaps tens of thousands of workers for political reasons (Green, 1977). Over 2,000 people were arrested, and at least twenty-five people finally were imprisoned. Activists from both working and intelligentsia classes were beaten by the militia. Indeed, less than a year later one activist was killed by the authorities (Karpiński, 1982:196; Raina, 1977:274–78; Starski, 1982:50).

Immediately after the 1976 rebellion, dissident intellectuals wrote letters to Polish officials for an improved dialogue between authorities and society and a more genuine democracy, and to foreign leaders to intercede on behalf of workers who were being punished for their militance. A group of fourteen Polish intellectuals also organized themselves into the Committee for the Defense of Workers (*Komitet Obrony Robotników*, KOR) on September 23, 1976. Through both national and international appeals, the committee raised a good deal of money to support victimized workers and their families. By mid-October 1976, ninety-eight families were already being supported on a regular basis by KOR's activities (Raina, 1977:255). Perhaps the most useful of activities was their composition and dissemination of bulletins on the trials and other related events. Conflict continued to intensify. Letters of protest from dissidents at home and critics abroad were sent to the authorities. Hunger strikes were staged in Warsaw. Finally on July 22, 1977, a general amnesty was announced.

Grzegorz Bakuniak and Krzysztof Nowak (1987) argue that the sociological vacuum between the social network of family and friends and identification with the nation which Stefan Nowak (1981) describes was partially filled in this period. S. Nowak (1981) describes an atomized society, devoid of identification with organizations or other secondary groups. Bakuniak and K. Nowak contend, however, that the workers' successes in forestalling price hikes gave them a new sense of their own power and means for identification with their class. In addition, the government's subsequent attempts to indict the protesting sectors of society as irresponsible also gave these sectors a new common identification, even though they previously had no contact. This was mainly a "negative" identification, prefiguring the creation of sides to be found later in Solidarity, between us (*my*) and them (*oni*).

An explosion of new organizations and their publications also helped to fill this sociological vacuum during this period. KOR continued to be active and extended its membership to include twelve others. It also changed its name to KSS-KOR, the Committee of Social Self-Defense-KOR (*Komitet Samoobrony Społecznej*), reflecting its broader scope. Its informational bulletin and bimonthly bulletin, *Robotnik* (*The Worker*, named after the pre-war Polish socialist newspaper), inspired the proliferation of other *samizdat* publications. Other independent and critical associations also emerged, including independent students' associations, the Farmers' Self-Defense Committee (*Komitet Samoobrony Chłopów* or KSC), the Movement for the

Defense of Human and Civil Rights (*Ruch Obrony Praw Człowieka i Obywatela* or ROPCiO) and various founding committees for free trade unions. Other than the nationalist Confederation for an Independent Poland (*Konfederacja Polski Niepodległej* or KPN), most of these groups were non-ideological, seeking for the time being only a wider and more dynamic civil society and more autonomy from the Soviet Union (Curry, 1983; Rupnik, 1979). Other bodies also emerged that were not necessarily oppositional, but were also critical of the party's policies or the prerogative it aggregated to itself. The "Flying University" developed, an apartment-to-apartment discussion group of forbidden ideas, similar to that which existed in World War II. *Zapis*, an independent writers' journal under the editorship of KOR activist Kazimierz Brandys, published uncensored articles. "Establishment" critics in the *Doświadczenie i Przyszłość* (DiP) (Experience and the Future) group also presented stinging attacks on government policies (DiP, 1981).

Why could these groups proliferate? Some have argued that Western contacts obliged Gierek to become more liberal at home, to ensure continued cooperation abroad. This account is more misleading than it is explanatory, however. Multinational corporations are not intrinsically devoted to civil liberties and human rights; indeed, in some cases, most notably Chile in the transition from Allende to Pinochet, they are directly responsible for governmental brutality. Even today in Poland, Western finance institutions are not committed to strengthening Solidarity at the expense of sound business investments.

Nevertheless, Western governmental support for loans was predicated on a kind of convergence theory, where greater economic aid and modernization would lead to greater liberalization in domestic policy. Gierek understood this linkage in Western policy circles, and sought to confirm their understandings so as to continue to receive Western aid. In this sense, then, the diminution of cold war and the generation of multipolarity in international relations enabled liberalization at home, even if not so directly as crude convergence theories would suggest.

There was also no strong party faction ready to provoke a major incident in society, and challenge Gierek's rule. Gierek was too ruthless in his reconstruction of the party, and eliminated many of the pockets where factional formation had previously taken place. Under these conditions, Gierek's version of "repressive tolerance" seemed to be a good strategy for continued domination. Writers would have their outlets and be less resentful of official censorship. Further, because Gierek did not change the official rules, he could assure the Soviets that he was not tearing down any of the central pillars of Soviet-type society.[11]

These independent groupings foreshadowed the two alliances crucial for the formation of Solidarity. On the one side, because intellectual dissidents involved themselves directly in the affairs of workers, rather than remaining preoccupied with their own affairs, they overcame one of the traditional barriers separating strata. On the other side, left dissident intellectuals began to cooperate with Catholic intellectuals. Catholics were very active in setting up these groups and left intellectuals recognized the importance of their support (Michnik, 1977b). Intellectuals from the religious and the left cooperated in the defense of workers and human rights. In fact, it was Poland's Catholicism which ultimately cemented the alliance.

The religious prelude to Solidarity

After Pope John Paul I died in October 1978 after a very brief tenure, the College of Cardinals elected the first non-Italian pope in 455 years: Kraków Archbishop Karol Wojtyła. The election of Wojtyła, who assumed the papal name John Paul II, provided a new angle on Polish poet Adam Mickiewicz's description of Poland in the 1830s as "The Christ of Nations." The institutional and cultural power of the Roman Catholic Church was now tied in Wojtyła's person to the Polish nation. Wojtyła's election and subsequent visit to Poland from June 2–10, 1979, might even be regarded as the midwife of the Polish Solidarity movement, as it provided a new cultural foundation for national self-identification, and the organizational experience for mobilizing it. Two of Poland's leading writers convey the symbolic significance of the Pope's visit to Poland.

> In this dismal country of hypocrisy, cant and disregard for human dignity, the Pope's words harmonised with the thoughts of every Pole. He called for dignity, respect for man, truth, justice, law and tolerance. He clearly indicated those responsible for Poland's decline. He personified the potential greatness, the hopes and aspirations of the whole nation. (Szczypiórski, 1982:112–13)

> The Pope expressed the thoughts of those great crowds of Poles, the thoughts and memories that had been falsified; he spoke to them out of his own experience and expressed their own much-abused truth. Their best truth, I would say. These are dark years; this is an age of

evil prophets. Using the words of a good prophet, the Pope gave access to what is brightest in them and of which they had been aware from time immemorial. He cleansed them of everything that had been rendered opaque and stony by years of adversity and falsehood, preaching ideas that the church in Poland had not always expressed with such ardent conviction. (Brandys, 1983:86)

These authors are not Catholic intellectual activists, and thus their portrait of the Pope's visit makes his presence in Poland appear all the more extraordinary. But how could those who are not believing or practicing Catholics find in a pope's words their own identity?

Branko Horvat's political economy of socialism (1982) emphasizes that the pervasiveness of the lie in Soviet-type society resurrects truth as a central feature of class struggles in this system. There is no social force in Poland which can claim "truth" better than that which considers itself eternal. It can achieve no better force than when it is embodied in a charismatic figure. Pope John Paul II became the personified Church and Nation. Church and Nation seemed everlasting in comparison to the decades of communism. But before the Pope, they seemed truthful only as a historical memory in opposition to communism. They became a living truth when they were resurrected in the Pope's person. Communism therefore was pushed further from meaningfulness in the Polish life-world, becoming even more an alien power system that seeks only to destroy what is good in the Polish experience. Communism, if legitimate for pragmatic reasons before, now became antagonistic to a new truth that was eternal. This new truth was less in the meaning of the words the Pope offered than in their mutuality and their public novelty.

As S. Nowak (1981) documents in surveys, before Solidarity and especially before 1976, Poland was a private society. Poles identified with the abstracted concept of the nation and with their families. Intermediate associations of professions or trade unions were meaningless for the construction of self. With the absence of regular public-opinion reporting, whether one's opinions were common to a larger public or not was hard to know (Jones, Bealmear and Kennedy, 1984). But when 15 million people participated in meetings with the Pope (Szczypiórski, 1982:112), the population recognized that they had something in common. They were a community.

The Pope's simple religious vocabulary, a vocabulary neither of theologians nor of dogmatists, also had a liberating effect. Marxism provides the vocabulary of utopia in capitalism, but when its words are appropriated by a communist party in the East to justify its rule, their emancipatory potential is emasculated. When "exploitation," "class struggle" and "socialism" itself are words associated with an order which few respect, these words will not inspire the imagination of an alternative future necessary to the struggle for it. Staniszkis (1979:168) calls this the "semantic problems of workers' protest." The words of Marxism often describe what workers want, like self-government and democracy, but since these are the same words the regime uses to describe its own activities, workers are shamed by using the vocabulary of their oppressors. But the Pope's words presented them with a vocabulary in which concern for human rights and for human dignity would become the verbal arsenal with which intellectual and worker could in common criticize the regime without shame. Michael Szkolny (1981:9–10 [but see also Bakuniak and K. Nowak, 1987; Bauman, 1981; Michnik, 1981]) put it this way: "the symbolism of religion has become the unique language capable of expressing ideas of social emancipation; it is a language symbolizing at once the continuity of Polish cultural heritage, the ancient struggle for national independence, and the self-identity of the individual in a world of social relations dominated by the state."

Finally, the Pope's entire trip was organized outside of the state and its organizations. Gierek, although allowing the visit, did not facilitate it. He did not provide organizational or communications support. "Society" did it on its own, without the help of the regime, and it was in this sense that the Pope's visit was a dress rehearsal for the formation of the self-organized and self-governed trade union. People learned that they could organize themselves to pursue goals they themselves established (Starski, 1982:55).

Thus, there was indeed a religious prelude to Solidarity's formation that became a leitmotif in the movement's symbolism. But the Catholic symbolism should not be understood as a "natural" identification between Poles and Catholicism. The Pope's message became central not because it is intrinsically valid, but for several sociological reasons: (1) the pervasiveness of lies and distortions in Soviet-type society makes claims to "truth" more sensible to the system's subjects; (2) claims to truth are enhanced when they can be associated with everlasting identities, which in this case were nation and Church; (3) these identities become living only when a population can assign them to a charismatic individual. The religious message was translated into the Solidarity movement because it provided (1) the movement with a cultural self-identification; (2) an emancipatory vocabulary; (3) the model for self-organization.

Conclusions

Solidarity's historical genealogy is controversial for several reasons. First, different parts of the movement will reclaim different aspects of Polish history to establish different tactics in the present. Second, these events reclaimed are inherently controversial, given the limited data available and the divergent meanings these events have for participants in the events and their descendants.

There is another aspect to this genealogy, which is perhaps the most controversial. It is tempting to portray any historical development as the inevitable outcome of a prior development, especially when considering Marxism. Ironically, dogmatic Marxism's views on the iron laws of history are replicated in their ideological opponents' views on the inevitabilities of communism's degeneration from bolshevism into Stalinism and of the impossibility of Stalinism's reform. The historical genealogy of Solidarity that I prefer relies on a mode of historical reasoning whose thought experiments might be considered analogous to probabilistic accounts where likelihood increases with proximity to the final outcome. As such, the summer of strikes which preceded the signing of Solidarity is so closely tied to the character of Solidarity itself that I leave them to consideration in the next chapter, on Solidarity. The election of Wojtyła as Pope and his visit to Poland is, however, analytically distinguishable from the formation of Solidarity. It did not have an explicit working-class identification as Solidarity did, but it bequeathed to the movement a living identity that united the nation and made communism even more an alien system encroaching on the Poles' life world.

Communism has, of course, always born a tentative relationship to Polish nationhood, but it would be a mistake to argue that this antagonism derives from an incompatibility between socialism and Polishness. Poles, like other European nations, were engaged in socialist politics from the First International through the beginnings of World War II and even immediately after it. And indeed, many see in Solidarity a true socialist movement in all but name. It would also be a mistake to establish the conflict between communism and Polish nationalism on the basis of national tensions between Russians and Poles. There have been many opportunities since the Partitions for these cultural differences to have been overcome, or at least reduced. But at each moment of historical alternativity, these national tensions have been augmented rather than reduced.

Instead of communism breaking down the Polish–Russian tension

through internationalism, the Polish–Soviet war of 1919–20 reidenti-
fied it. Instead of Polish communist politics becoming part of a left
national tradition, it became a puppet and ultimately a victim of Stalinist policy. Instead of the Soviet Union becoming an ally of Polish
struggles against Hitler's Germany, it became another enemy in 1939
and again in 1943–44. Instead of a Polish road to socialism being established, in 1948 Stalinist practice destroyed gains made in the countryside, and pushed the Church and nation away from communist politics through persecutions of Catholicism and Home Army veterans.

Gomułka had a chance of restoring a Polish road to socialism in
1956, but after a two-year honeymoon, the gains of October were
being lost. The hopes for revisionism among the intelligentsia were
destroyed by the anti-Semitic and anti-intellectual politics of 1968, and
crushed with the invasion of Czechoslovakia. Gierek promised a new
road for Polish politics, one that relied less on Marxism–Leninism and
more on a successful economic transformation and consumer revolution. For a time, it appeared that Gierek might succeed, as he consolidated his own position within the party, crushed the minimal dissent
that existed in the beginning of his decade, and initiated a period of
economic prosperity. But even this rejection of ideology and embrace
of consumerism failed in 1976 and especially in the end of the decade.

By emphasizing these moments of historical alternativity, I do not
mean to suggest that those responsible for building the communist
movement simply made "errors" that the perfect theoretical apparatus or insight of retrospective thinking could have avoided. There certainly were structural forces moving each actor to do as he did. The
Polish–Soviet war was based partly on the fears of socialism failing in
one country, but also the aggressiveness of Piłsudski and the Entente
powers. The fall of the Polish road to socialism in 1948 was not just
based on Gomułka's own failure to perceive the balance of power. But
we also have instances where agency created a greater range of historical alternativity. The resistance of "Stalin's puppets" to collectivization suggested this possibility, as did the imprisonment of Gomułka
rather than his execution. Private agriculture has facilitated the emergence of the generalized market, and the existence of a living victim of
Stalinist repression created greater chances for revisionist success. We
can, of course, only engage these thought experiments to consider the
implications of actions taken other than those realized. But the alternativity of the past is critical to recall for it to be retained in the present.

Many in the Solidarity movement would prefer to see a straight line
drawn from the 1919–20 war, or at least Yalta, to Solidarity. This

picture of historical inevitability led some activists to overemphasize the movement's power and internal unity, as well as to limit the movement's strategic range. They were neither prepared for the historical alternative of their own demise on December 13, 1981, nor were they prepared for an alliance with the Party opposition. In a sense, their own "dogmatic" thinking about the past led them to an inflexible analysis of the present. In chapter 2, I should like to take that lesson to heart by considering different models of the Solidarity movement and learn from them what structural limitations and what alternative strategies faced this exemplar of emancipatory praxis.

2   The nature and causes of Solidarity

The Solidarity movement of 1980–81 was an organized attempt by over 9 million people to transform the structures that organize Polish life. In chapter 3, I argue that Solidarity is best understood as a form of "emancipatory praxis." In this chapter, I consider how other authors have conceptualized this movement, and how they have explained its emergence. I begin with a discussion of the immediate conditions which led to Solidarity's formation. What characterized the strikes of 1980 and how did they lead to the formation of an independent trade union? In the next section, I turn to the more abstract structural features which called those immediate conditions into play. In particular, I consider the economic, social and cultural features structuring Polish life at the end of the 1970s. Then I turn to a more agent-centered account of the 500 days of Solidarity in order to derive its "meaning." Here, the understandings activists had of their movement are considered. Finally, I consider those approaches which try to link structure and action more directly. In particular, I examine Marxist and resource mobilization accounts of Solidarity.

The immediate conditions of Solidarity

Most observers agree that without drastic economic decline, Solidarity would never have formed. This assumption of course implies that "compensatory" needs (Bahro, 1978) can live up to their name. Had the Polish economy been able to continue its boom of the first half of the 1970s, Solidarity would never have formed. Poland's consumerism would not have been "premature" (Pravda, 1982). But Soviet-type economies, apparently as much as capitalist ones, if not more, are subject to periodic crises. Investment cycles lead to somewhat consistent patterns of growth and recession in these economies, although the intensity of the swings varies from one country to another, with Poland facing among the most extreme alternations. (Drewnowski, 1982; Mihalyi, 1988; Staniszkis, 1984a: 248–77). Poland's economy approached crisis at the end of the 1970s. Gierek's economic strategy had hinged on successful exports to repay the huge debts Poland incurred in Western loans. A combination of internal and external problems made debt repayment impossible and contributed to a disastrous economic situation, manifested in an overall negative rate of growth (Nuti, 1981 [1982]).

The economic decline forced Gierek to look for ways to save the country from collapse. What had been a long time overdue in economic terms, but was politically infeasible, was finally undertaken. On July 1, 1980, a new price scheme was announced for meat. With this response to crisis, Gierek translated an economic crisis into a socially meaningful event sparking workers' self-organization. In contrast to 1970 and 1976, the change in the price of meat was neither dramatic nor universal. Gierek obviously learned something from past attempts. Since 1977, there had been special "commercial shops" where more meat was available for higher prices. The new price scheme, its implementation left to local officials, was to shift greater supplies of meat from the state-run shops to the more expensive ones. A minor official appeared on television and announced the change, leaving intentionally ambiguous the scope of change.

Workers and society also had learned. Although many analysts suggest activist intellectuals were the ones to promote the notion of independent trade unions to workers in the 1970s (Kolakowski, 1983; Lipski, 1985; Pravda, 1983), Roman Laba (1986, forthcoming) argues convincingly that some of the most militant workers on the coast were already demanding their own independent trade unions in 1970. Whatever the source, by 1978 a few activist workers, future leaders of Solidarity, were forming small groups advocating the creation of independent trade unions. In Katowice, Kazimierz Świtoń organized the "Workers' Committee," later called the Free Trade Union of Silesia. In Radom, another free trade-union group was founded. Inspired by the 1979 publication of a Charter of Workers' Rights in *Robotnik*, workers in Szczecin established the founding committee of the Free Trade Unions of Western Pomerania. Probably the most significant free trade-union group was the Committee for Independent Trade Unions for the Baltic Coast. It included in its ranks some of the most prominent future Solidarity activists: Lech Wałęsa, Andrzej Gwiazda, Alina Pieńkowska, and Anna Walentynowicz (MacShane, 1981:44–46; Wałęsa, 1987). Despite a wave of strikes in July, demands for an independent union would not take root until the second part of August.

In July 1980, approximately 81,000 people in 177 enterprises, especially in industry, construction and transportation, engaged in strikes (Błasiak, 1987:139). Strike committees were organized in these enterprises. They pressed managers for compensatory wage increases and other improvements in working conditions. On orders from above, managers complied. Portable meat wagons even took extra supplies to the strike centers. Confrontation generally was avoided by giving in to the demands of the well-organized and militant sectors of the workforce. Humor summed it up: "Lenin, they argued, got it wrong when he said 'those who do not work do not eat'; Poland has reached a higher stage: here, 'those who do not strike do not eat meat'" (Singer, 1981:212). The workers in Lublin achieved the most in this period. Their eight-day city-wide strike won pay increases and a more egalitarian distribution of privilege. But few enterprises asserted the need for independent unions (Laba, 1986:63). That innovation was to wait until the coastal region took center stage. This first period, between July 1 and August 16, nevertheless was important, as it revealed the basic structure upon which Solidarity would be built, in its class base, principal power resource and identity.

The class base for this movement was above all workers, as engineers and other professionals generally did not participate in the strikes (Żukowski, 1987:181). Workers avoided street demonstrations and arson, and instead concentrated on far more effective occupation strikes. When Stefan Olszowski pressed for a forceful suppression of the strikes, the current chief of the army, Wojciech Jaruzelski, advised that the army would have to storm "500 fortified castles" and no Polish officer would dare issue a command to fire under such circumstances (Starski, 1982:62). These strikes were also beginning to give workers more of a regional identity. The largest factories in a region sometimes engaged in solidarity strikes with those in smaller enterprises (Drążkiewicz and Rychard, 1981). Although there were few demands for an independent union at this time, this wave of strikes clearly established the common interests, common resources and common fate of Polish workers. This linkage was improved when the strike committees in individual factories established formal ties through *inter-enterprise* strike committees. On August 18, Szczecin and Elbląg formed such committees. On August 26, Wrocław formed one, and then on August 29, Jastrzębie. Gdańsk was the first, however, on August 16.

Gdańsk was officially a "free city" before World War II, but was under German hegemony. After the war, it was awarded to Poland. The town was repopulated by Poles, overwhelmingly of peasant or small-town background, of which 20 percent came from the eastern lands lost to the Soviets. In 1950, only 11.4 percent of its population was native, although nearby Gdynia was relatively stable. The whole area industrialized and urbanized very quickly, however, and created a disproportionately large and skilled labor force. The labor force was inadequate to the demand for people to undertake the dangerous and difficult work of the shipyards. Consequently, there was a very high turnaround in employment there. Even during the prosperous years of the decade, Gdańsk shipyard workers indicated in a 1972 survey considerable dissatisfaction with their wages and their work. According to surveys in 1975 and 1977, these already poor conditions were perceived to have declined. Official trade unions were perceived less and less as workers' allies: in 1977, 36 percent of the shipyard workers thought the unions represented the interests of the authorities, while in 1979 50.5 percent did. Only 8.3 percent of the workers thought the unions represented workers' interests (Latoszek, 1987:32–44).

General economic and working conditions prepared workers to strike, therefore, but the immediate incident which moved the Lenin shipyard workers was the dismissal of a crane operator, Anna Walentynowicz. She was a member of the 1970 strike committee and of the committee for the Free Trade Unions of the coastal region. Management had similarly fired future Solidarity leader Lech Wałęsa years earlier. On August 14, the founding committee of the Free Trade Union distributed leaflets in the shipyard demanding her reinstatement as well as higher wages and cost of living allowances. The shipyard workers began their strike.

Wałęsa and Walentynowicz were elected to the Lenin shipyard strike committee. The committee formulated several demands: the reemployment of victims of politically motivated dismissals; the erection of a monument to workers killed in 1970; guarantees against future reprisals for this strike; and a 2,000 złoty per month wage increase in addition to family allowances comparable in size to those already received by the security police. Just two days after the Gdańsk strike began, management compromised on the wage increase: the Lenin shipyard workers were to receive a 1,500 złoty increase in their monthly package. The strike committee then voted to suspend the strike. Wałęsa even declared "We've won." Various activists, including those from other plants, challenged Wałęsa and the committee on how they could abandon other plants still striking. These smaller plants would never realize their demands without the support of the largest concentration of workers in the area. In what proved to be a historical turning point, Wałęsa and others overturned the committee decision, and with the remaining workers in the shipyards, initiated another occupation strike in solidarity (Orchowski, 1980; Wałęsa, 1987).

Solidarity strikes had already become common in other parts of the country. In their analysis of the evolution of strikes in the Warsaw area, Drążkiewicz and Rychard (1981) found that the larger factories, after having won their demands, would strike on behalf of smaller factories. Economic crisis thus was not the only precondition for the formation of the movement. Also critical were the primary social relations that provided the foundation for the class solidarity within enterprises as well as across them.

Gdańsk sociologist Marek Latoszek (1987) interviewed 500 families of shipyard workers, refinery workers and engineers in the Gdańsk area in 1978–79. According to these respondents, public associations did not have much influence on what happened, and therefore people retreated to private life. But this did not mean they were isolated and atomized. Extensive primary relations, from the extended family to neighbor and friendship networks, reinforced a new class identity for both shipyard and refinery workers. Most of the family's close friends originated in the man's place of work, in contrast to engineers, whose friendships from school days predominated (pp.178–82). These primary relations enabled workers to generate a sense of class unity, and on that basis, led workers to establish the solidarity, discipline and low incidence of non-conformism that eventually allowed them to win their demands from the authorities in that August. Strong primary social relations that coincided with relations of production enabled solidarity to reach across sectors which might have been cut off from one another by a more corporatist representation of interest.

Although some values crossed class lines, workers had few informal contacts with those outside their class (Latoszek, 1987). There was a virtual caste system in the shipyard, where engineers and professionals formed the highest caste, technicians the next, with different categories of workers, more and less skilled, more and less permanent, following (Wałęsa, 1987:42). Nevertheless, as the strikes intensified and demands grew, the lines of struggle defining allies were redrawn higher and higher. Initially, foremen would try to negotiate, but finding that they could not satisfy workers' demands, the authorities' representatives would have to be found from higher and higher up (Drążkiewicz and Rychard, 1981). The pattern was given its pure form in Gdańsk. When the solidarity strike in Gdańsk was called, an Inter-enterprise Strike Committee (*Międzyzakładowy Komitet Strajkowy*, or MKS) was formed out of the enterprises in the area. By 9.30 on August 18, about 40 striking enterprises were represented in the Gdańsk shipyards; by 2.00, over 100 enterprises were included, and so it grew (Orchowski, 1980:13).

Over several days representatives of the government and of the workers met and talked, their conversations broadcast over a loud-speaker system so that the mass of striking workers could keep track of the bargaining. In the first set of negotiations, the authorities had been represented by the factory manager and Union of Socialist Youth leader, who conferred by telephone with the district party leader, Tadeusz Fiszbach. In the second round, when the MKS was formed, the workers demanded that a highly ranked government representative should talk with them. Deputy Premier Tadeusz Pyka came to Gdańsk, but tried to avoid negotiating with the MKS, and preferred to deal with individual enterprises. He realized agreements with most groups, except the transport workers, who demanded he negotiate with the MKS. The government Council of Ministers also refused to accept the demands Pyka negotiated with the other enterprises. Solidarity was thus born in part out of choices: the transport workers' solidarity, and the reticence of the Council of Ministers. After this break with Pyka, striking workers decided that the only negotiations to take place would be between the MKS and the government's representative (Kemp-Welch, 1983:21).

The authorities next sent a higher-ranking deputy minister, Mieczy-sław Jagielski, for negotiations with the MKS on August 23. Jagielski initially sought to drive a hard bargain. The workers had presented him with twenty-one demands, including traditional ones for higher wages and better consumption conditions. But there were also new demands, including better health conditions, freedom of the press, radio and television time for Church services and, most significantly, the establishment of free trade unions. Jagielski ignored some of the demands, and adopted a "wait and see" approach on others. All Jagielski offered on unions was a reform of the existing ones.

While the negotiations and strikes were taking place, a reshuffle of leading party leaders occurred. At the Fourth Party Plenum on August 24, Gierek's group in the politburo was decimated, although Gierek himself managed to survive. Without supporters, however, party leaders are powerless. After a leadership fight between two leading party figures, Stefan Olszowski and Stanisław Kania, Gierek was removed from his position as party first secretary and Kania took his place. Kania's victory was important for charting the future of the Solidarity movement. Olszowski had become convinced that the movement was a dangerous anti-socialist force and favored "harsh decisive action" (Ascherson, 1982:155). Kania, on the other hand, was not given to rash action, despite his background in the security services. By his election, Kania and his supporter Wojciech Jaruzelski managed to avoid a violent confrontation with the workers and give the August agreement a chance (Wałęsa, 1987:179). Their hand was strengthened when Admiral Janczyszyn, commander of naval forces, refused to commit the forces under his command to fight workers (Ascherson, 1982:162).

Strikes and inter-enterprise committees were not limited to the tri-city area. By the end of August, inter-enterprise strike committees had been established in Gdańsk, Szczecin, Elbląg, Wrocław and Jastrzębie and strikes were taking place in every Polish province, especially where these inter-enterprise committees had been established, plus Kraków, Warsaw and Torun. Approximately 750,000 workers in about 750 enterprises struck in this period (Błasiak, 1987:145). Although the Szczecin inter-enterprise committee negotiated with the authorities mostly on their own (they had only two intellectual advisors) the Gdańsk MKS had seven principal advisors.[1] The advisors and the authorities had traveled in the same circles, and some even knew one another personally. They shared the same semantic capabilities, and the same expectations as to what was and was not possible. The workers did not. The intellectuals never dreamed that the authorities would agree to the independent trade unions (Kowalik, 1983; Staniszkis, 1984a:38–72; Touraine, et al., 1983:38). The authorities probably did not foresee that outcome either. As solidarity strikes on behalf of the twenty-one points spread throughout the country, the MKS won verbal concessions on all of their demands, including the right to establish independent trade unions. On August 31, under a crucifix and using a souvenir pen of the Pope's 1979 visit, Lech Wałęsa signed the agreement that was to allow the formation of the *Niezależny Samorządny Związek Zawodowy* (Independent Self-Governing Trade Union) *Solidarność*.

Wojciech Błasiak (1987) finds two periods in these two months. In the first, between July and August 16, the mass movement begins to assert its identity as a syndicalist workers' movement. In the second, between August 14 and September 3, the *center* of the movement crystallizes. Gdańsk becomes the territorial center of the entire Solidarity movement, and the shipyard workers its occupational center. The formation of this center facilitated the emergence of a third stage, from September 3 to October, in which the movement crystallizes on the periphery.

In September, over 1 million workers and 800 enterprises engaged in strikes largely in support of the Gdańsk accords. Much of the strike action took place in Poland's "periphery," in the provinces of Białystok, Piotrków, Trybunalski, Bielska-Biało, Suwałki, Jelenia Góra, Bydgoszcz, Opole, Olsztyń and Legnica. Strikes in these regions were often more general and sharper than those which preceded them, due in part to the "quasi-feudal" character of the local authorities. These authorities struggled desperately against the formation of independent unions in their districts. With the formation of a nationwide Solidarity movement on September 17, and the consequent establishment of strong center-periphery ties, peripheral activists were able to defeat local authorities and establish independent trade unions (Błasiak, 1987:145–50).

The immediate conditions of Solidarity's formation thus involve structural elements: macroeconomic crisis, strong intra-class primary social relations and authorities who were simultaneously centralized and ineffective (see chapter 6). But these structural factors were turned into the conditions of Solidarity by a new generation of worker–activists who promoted new forms of struggle. It was the "innovations" of occupation strikes, solidarity strikes, inter-enterprise strike committees, independent trade unions and national solidarity that enabled the movement Solidarity to be born and cause a major, if temporary, transformation of Soviet-type society.

All accounts of the Solidarity movement incorporate these "immediate conditions" in one fashion or another. But there are considerable differences among approaches in the way in which they explain Solidarity. Some agent-centered approaches, as Touraine *et al.* (1983), focus on the meanings the movement had for its participants. For him, the movement was formed *because* of participants' desires to challenge the class which ruled, and to establish greater democracy and national independence. Other approaches look to the "structural" or "objective" conditions that caused these meanings to develop. One also can distinguish a variety of structural levels. There are those most macroscopic structures considered in chapter 1, including Cold War relations, the imperial domination of nations, rapid industrialization and the cultural constructions of history. These set the most general frameworks within which social action takes place. There are also the smaller-scale, shorter-term structures we considered in this section: economic crisis, strong intra-class primary social relations and the contemporary structure of the authorities. But there are also "deep structures" which exist but can be observed only indirectly in their manifestations. There are fleeting structures which endure only in the moment of encounter. We shall consider these other kinds of structures in chapter 3. The important point to keep in mind at this point is that these different structures bear different relationships to one another and to agency. The main problem is to understand their distinctions and clarify their relationships.

These various structural and agent-centered approaches are not so much competing as they focus on different aspects and thus might offer compatible accounts of Solidarity. But there are also competing accounts of Solidarity's formation which remain at the structural level. As Skocpol (1979) sought to find the "causes" for social revolutions, these accounts seek to explain the macrostructural conditions which produced Solidarity as an outcome in 1980–81.

The structural peculiarities of Poland in 1980–81: Solidarity as outcome

Area specialists often explain developments in their regions as rooted in some cultural soul. Some claim that Poland defies generalizations from or to its experience. But every society is to some extent "exceptional" and the task for the sociologist is to extricate that in a society which explains its exceptionalism. One also must establish the nature of the exception. Certainly, the most exceptional characteristic of Soviet-type Poland is Solidarity's formation. But how does one explain such a development? Macrocausal analysis[2] is difficult to use in this case because only one consequential independent trade union has emerged in Soviet-type society. Does that then mean we cannot establish what is significant and what is not in explaining the emergence of Solidarity? Must we accept the common explanation that the movement is unique and the fruit of Poland's entire history and culture? A similar problem emerged when political scientists and area specialists tried to explain why the "Prague Spring" developed in Czechoslovakia. From the voluminous literature, Susan Bridge (1975) distilled no fewer than twenty-five hypotheses on the origins of "socialism with a human face." While she tries to develop a theory by creating predictive hypotheses from postdictive explanations, her approach is limited ultimately by her focus on a single event. Because all prior events are logically linked to the Czechoslovak reform, it is impossible for her to isolate spurious factors from critical antecedents, or to separate the necessary from the sufficient condition (Kennedy, 1982).

Another method to explain exceptionalism is to "contrast contexts" (Skocpol and Somers, 1980). Paul and Simon (1981) employ this in their comparison of the 1980 Polish revolution and 1968 Czechoslovak reform. Both events had two broad features in common: "a movement toward fundamental change in the political system . . . and the active involvement of a popular movement in the creation of new political structures" (Paul and Simon, 1981:25). The authors acknowledge similarities between events, but emphasize differences. They conclude that the Czechoslovak and Polish movements represent instances of competitive and consolidated pluralism, respectively. Poland's unified opposition was made possible because of (1) intense Polish nationalism; (2) focused nationalistic hatred for the Russians; and (3) a common religion. Czechoslovakia's pluralism was competitive (in which separate interest groups pressed individually for their own ends and not together, as in Solidarity) because the movement lacked these Polish conditions (Paul and Simon, 1981:38). A second level of explaining differences between societies rests in their contrasting political cultures: the Czechoslovak impulse toward pluralism and the Polish impulse toward unity (1981:39). Paul and Simon explain how the Czechoslovak and Polish challenges differ from one another, in how social and cultural factors influenced the character of socio-political challenge, but they don't explain why challenge emerges in the first place. The implication is that these various challenges are culturally specific responses to the problems of modernization. Cultural antagonisms often take precedence in explaining the origins of transformation in Soviet-type society.

Although he recognizes the importance of the food shortage and economic crisis, Alexander Matejko (1982) considers the structural roots of the Polish opposition to lie in the conflict between models of socialization. The authorities wish to shape an "immature" society according to their own version of the truth, while society aspires to have "freedom to choose" one's own pattern of values. Matejko specifically opposes Marxist class analysis for explaining the system's antagonisms. He finds the "ruling managerial class" to have too few privileges, either in consumption or in continuity, to be a real ruling class. Matejko instead emphasizes antagonistic cultural traditions in Polish life. The Soviet pattern (itself inherited from tsarist Russia) of artificially suppressing private interests in favor of putatively public ones was imposed on Poland. This pattern destroys any traditionally Polish sense of the public good and leads to an individualistic ethos incapable of collective sentiment. Any accurate sense of that beyond one's immediate sphere becomes impossible given censorship and the relative lack of resources held by opposition forces.

There had always been resistance to this Soviet pattern in Poland, from the anti-communist underground after World War II through the various episodes discussed in chapter 1. But it was the working class, with its religious foundations, that ultimately was responsible for the emergence of an effective political opposition that culminated in Solidarity, Matejko argues. It sought to organize itself against the exploitation and irrationality of a ruling group whose power is based on Soviet support and an alliance with the extreme right wing of Polish politics. A new opportunity for a Polish cultural pattern was restored in Poland by Solidarity, as individuals established their own self-governing associations independent of the authorities and their culturally retrograde pattern. For Matejko, therefore, socio-economic changes are the "sufficient" conditions which translate the more fundamental cultural antagonism into a social conflict. Jean Woodall (1981) offers an account designed to supplement those that emphasize cultural factors. In this, she considers the social factors which led to unrest in Poland, in particular the policies of the authorities and class relations. In so doing, she raises issues which bring her closer to Marxist analysis.

Although the food prices were the ostensible cause of protest, Woodall writes that there were more systematic deprivations of consumption at issue, where real wages declined significantly in the last years of the decade. But additionally important is the changing nature of social relations within and across classes. Management is poorly trained, if at all, in business administration. Lower management "passes the buck" to senior management, even while the size of management as well as its perquisites grow. When combined with the decline in workers' income, this managerial privilege contributed to greater class antagonisms. As the postwar baby boom entered the labor force with its higher educational qualifications, a common generational resentment to blocked opportunities for upward mobility inspired their antagonism toward the authorities and more solidarity with those workers with few managerial aspirations. Simultaneously, factory authorities developed a more insulated and technocratic style of management that failed to take into account the interests of the workforce. Thus, the new technical intelligentsia developed an allegiance with workers at the same time that ties between the cultural intelligentsia and workers were being established through KOR.

This model resembles a Marxist account in so far as both consider class relations, but Woodall departs self-consciously from Marxism by emphasizing that this is a conflict over social control of the means of consumption rather than production. Woodall also departs from Marxist accounts epistemologically. Marxists usually adopt a "realist" epistemology, emphasizing not only empirically accessible conflicts, but also the structurally hidden causal mechanisms that generate systemic contradictions.[3] Woodall remains more at the "contingent" and "empirical" level of social analysis. Norgaard and Sampson (1984) offer a more "realist" account which seeks not only contingent explanation but also systemic analysis. They also use a variation on the macrocausal approach, in so far as they explain Poland's exceptionalism with reference to developments in other Soviet-type societies.

They propose three kinds of factors explaining the Polish developments: structural (those relevant to all Soviet-type societies); nation-specific (which includes the cultural); and conjunctural (having to do neither with Soviet-type nor national features intrinsically, but with external features like world politics, economy or climate). They argue that Solidarity was a "symptom of structural contradictions latent in East European socialism ... These contradictions attained concrete form in Poland because of nation-specific Polish conditions, and they were sharpened by conjunctural developments of an economic and political nature" (1984:774).

Norgaard and Sampson emphasize economic difficulties in the transition from extensive to intensive capital accumulation and the need for democratization as the principal structural factors underlying the Polish crisis. The structural factors also have a subjective side; as economic growth and social mobility decline, group consciousness grows and tends to challenge the system. The conjunctural factors include the world economic crisis and its effect on Eastern Europe; the link between Western economic dependence and regime legitimacy; the "coming of age" of Poland's postwar baby boom, which generated unresolvable strains; and climatically induced crises in agricultural production. They claim that on structural and conjunctural grounds, Poland and Romania are particularly vulnerable to major social challenge. Hungary, the German Democratic Republic and Bulgaria had made some strides toward necessary economic reforms, thus lessening the severity of structural contradictions. Romania, on the other hand, failed to develop a "Solidarity" because of national features. There are six significant nation-specific conditions underlying the Polish crisis: (1) a poor perception of regime competence; (2) low regime legitimacy; (3) weak regime unity; (4) high societal homogeneity; (5) the availability (in the Church) of alternative centers of power; and (6) a prior experience of struggle. Romania, while similar to Poland in the first and second factors, had strong regime unity, low societal homogeneity, no alternative center of power and no prior experience of struggle. Certainly, Poland is characterized by the exceptionally low legitimacy of the Communist Party, and minimal regime competence, given repeated failure to institute economic reforms. But I believe that Norgaard and Sampson overrate regime unity and the other three factors are better consolidated into the more comprehensive rubric of the historical constitution of the opposition.

While there is little doubt that the Romanian Communist Party is more unified than the Polish party has ever been, Gierek's Communist Party was a more unified party than the Poles had seen for years. Gierek had centralized his power by eliminating many of the niches that formerly bred internal party opposition. He eliminated the possibility for strong factional development and consequently eliminated the likelihood of a revisionist solution. Norgaard and Sampson (1984:787) correctly note, however, that in the latter half of the decade Gierek's leadership "succumbed to the demands of regional and sectional interest groups." But how important is this kind of leadership failure for explaining the development of Solidarity?

A strong and decisive party probably could not have prevented the development of Solidarity through the use of force as the Romanian leader, Nicolae Ceausescu, broke the Romanian miners' strike in 1977. Jaruzelski himself believed that the use of force against workers occupying factories in 1980 would be the equivalent of storming fortresses. Jaruzelski's implementation of martial law was successful in 1981 only because society itself was exhausted and unsure about whether the promise of a restoration of economic rationality was better than the glory of self-organization. The use of force, in Gdańsk and Gdynia in 1970 and in Poznań in 1956, only pushed Poland close to the brink of civil war. A unified leadership against an antagonistic and active society is of comparatively small value. For a unified leadership to be effective, it must also have a greater measure of legitimacy.

Societal homogeneity, alternative centers of power and prior experience of struggles are part of the historical constitution of the opposition. It is less useful to conceive of them separately. The experience of prior struggles is certainly the most critical of the nation-specific factors, because they provided lessons for activists and provided symbolic capital upon which the masses of workers and intelligentsia could draw in their struggle against the authorities, as the genealogy beginning chapter 1 illustrates. The Church as an alternative center of power has existed since the communists took power, but it was only in the process of struggle that it began to side with the opposition actively. That alliance began in 1975 with the dispute over the new Polish constitution, and support grew with the struggle to establish an independent peasants' trade union. Other significant alternative centers of influence were formed as hopes for revisionism lost favor in the opposition. Although Polish society is comparatively homogeneous, especially in its ethnic and religious composition, the barriers between intelligentsia and working class have existed historically in Poland as in other East European societies. In fact, the social and cultural distance between the intelligentsia and other classes might be said to be greater in Poland and Hungary than in Romania, Bulgaria or Yugoslavia (Connor, 1979:29–105). Those barriers were only partially dismantled as each stratum learned of the other's indispensability to opposition. The Polish intelligentsia was alone in 1968 and the workers alone in 1970. The combination of economic crisis and the lesson of the likely failure of isolated protests is what brought the strata together.

We are left with a complex explanation of Solidarity as outcome. Single case studies cannot find which factors are necessary and which are sufficient, or which are spurious and which are essential. Comparative historical studies can tell us what about Poland in 1980–81 makes it different from its own past and from other societies with common systems. But we are left with a variety of apparently necessary factors whose relative importance cannot be assessed. One alternative to this is to move toward public-opinion studies. Ireneusz Białecki (1987), for instance, tests various theories of Solidarity. He compares the theories of "failed expectations," of the "revolt of the powerless" and of a "conflict of values" using public-opinion data from 1980 and 1981. He finds in the distribution of opinions little support for the economistic or "failed expectations" theory. Those who were most deprived and those belonging to the new middle class were not distinguished in their opinions from other groups and one another in the survey. On the other hand, those who were least critical of the system tended to be those most powerful: those who simultaneously belonged to the government's unions had higher managerial status and were party members. There was also support for the cultural theory: the majority of respondents rejected the official values upon which the system is based. Thus, if we can use public-opinion data on opposition to the authorities as representative of the meaning of Solidarity, we can say that Solidarity was a revolt of the powerless whose roots lay in a cultural antagonism between society and the system. It was not a revolt of the new middle class of professionals and skilled working class.

One need not tell these analysts of public opinion that the distribution of attitudes is not the same as the movement itself. They recognize this and suggest only that by using public-opinion surveys to test alternative hypotheses we can come closer to explaining the reasons for the Solidarity movement's formation. But like the comparative historical studies which explain Solidarity as an outcome, they treat the movement as a single coherent phenomenon, whose explananda are more important than the nature of the movement.

This presents two problems. First, by treating Solidarity only as an "outcome" of social and cultural factors, the *mechanism* connecting structural phenomena (cultural antagonisms or class exploitation and impoverishment with the movement) remains unexplicated. These macrostructural accounts are not wrong, and, indeed, such non-reductionist macrosocial accounts are necessary to provide a meaningful context for the mechanism explaining the formation of Solidarity. But they are not adequate without that mechanism (Levine, Sober and Wright, 1987). The causal mechanism linking macrostructural phenomena only can be provided through the explication of the meaningful activity of individuals. In these accounts of Solidarity as outcome, the movement's *construction* by living actors is assumed, more and less acknowledged, but beyond identifying the attributes of the actors, treated as sociologically unimportant. Without this causal mechanism, structural accounts are of limited utility to a critical sociology which seeks from the past lessons for the future. Praxis cannot be treated only as an outcome, and must be understood also as a means to realize an outcome, where different choices and strategies have alternative consequences. Fortunately there are several major accounts which emphasize how living actors made the social movement.

Secondly, these alternative accounts also show the difficulty in explaining Solidarity as a *single* outcome. One of the most important factors explaining attitudes toward the regime, for example, was locale. On the basis of nationwide surveys, Krzysztof Jasiewicz (1988) advocates the "hot spots" theory, where region of residence is the most important factor explaining support for the government: Warsaw, Wrocław, Gdańsk and Łódź were significantly more likely to oppose the regime than were those cities in the rural northeastern sector of the country, for example. This suggests potential interactions between region and other "causes" for Solidarity. It also shows the dangers of offering a single account for the rise of Solidarity in *Poland*, since it rose in some areas before others. One challenge for future researchers is to explain *how* the movement for self-organization, initiated on the coast (Laba, forthcoming), was translated from one region to another, thereby showing the actual construction of the movement in various conditions.[4] Another challenge is, of course, to consider the alternative meanings of the movement itself.

A sociology of historicity: the meanings of Solidarity

French sociologists Alain Touraine, François Dubet, Michel Wieviorka and Polish sociologist Jan Strzelecki (1983), along with a team of Polish sociologists,[5] have produced an invaluable analysis of the inner life of Solidarity, using the principles of sociological interventionism.[6] Their book clarifies the internal meanings of the movement. Solidarity, they argue, had three basic identities revolving around its function as a trade union, as a force for democratization and as a movement for national independence.

Some of their research sites had one kind of identity more than others. Those from Katowice and Gdańsk, for instance, identified their movement more as a union than anything else: "the activity of the trade union was constantly defined in terms of class struggle, even when these were not the words used by the militants" (Touraine *et al.*, 1983:41). In this, Touraine *et al.* find similar interests as those held by workers in the West. Polish workers' solidarity across workplaces is generated not only by their common class, however, but by their common difficulties as consumers with the state-run system of distribution too. Thus, they are not only concerned with the workplace in their class struggles, but also with the entire political–economic organization of social life, and the unjust distribution of privilege that it represents.

Nationalism is a common theme for Polish history and the experience of Solidarity. It has three primary manifestations: (1) pride in "authentic" cultural and historical expression; (2) an association of Polishness with Catholicism; and (3) hostility toward Russia as an imperial occupant of Polish territory. The first is exemplified by Solidarity's invitation to exile Czesław Miłosz to read his poetry in Poland and by the drive to reconsider the Katyn massacre and other blank spots of Polish history in public and school life. The second manifestation is more complicated, as the Church was characterized variously in different research sites: as identical to the nation, as an ally in the defense of civil society, and as an institutional body with its own conservative interests. In general, Solidarity sought to remain institutionally distinct from the Church, even if it drew heavily on religious symbolism. "True Poles" characterized the last manifestation of nationalism, where national independence was considered the principal goal of Solidarity (Touraine *et al.*, 1983:44–49). Of the regions Touraine studied, Wrocław best characterized this nationalist theme. Demographically speaking, highly educated males seemed most extreme in this regard (Touraine *et al.*, 1983:167). Organizationally, national independence was more important to delegates of Solidarity's congress, while the union rank and file found its union identity basic ("Czym Jest Solidarność,"1981).

Democracy is the third leg of Solidarity's identity. This leg is also multifaceted, composed both of "the sovereignty of the people" and "individual freedoms," although this latter civil libertarian notion predominated in discussions of democracy. This is particularly obvious in the call for a "separation of powers," where judges and enterprise managers should become separate from the authorities and their *nomenklatura* (Touraine *et al.*, 1983:49–51). This emphasis on individual rights and civil society could directly promote professional-class interests, but this does not automatically mean that it is antagonistic to workers' class interests. For the democracy which was promoted was also one which increased the responsibility of professionals and those in authority to those whose interests they should serve (Kennedy and Sadkowski, 1990). Those in the Warsaw–Mazowsze region especially emphasized this democratic aspect.

Despite different emphases among social groups and various regions of the country, these three aspects were united within Solidarity. "In the spring of 1981, the trade-union, national and democratic dimensions of Solidarity's action were not only linked: they were fused to such an extent that no one would risk putting himself on the fringe of the movement by adopting one dimension, or even a combination of two of them, to the exclusion of the others" (Touraine *et al.*, 1983:55).

Touraine *et al.* (1983) theorize this unity on the basis of the team's sociological intervention research. They demonstrate the unity with references from these group interviews. With these examples, they provide an extraordinarily useful picture of the impression activists wish to convey about their movement. Much as their general theoretical approach, Touraine *et al.*'s book on Solidarity is an attempt to help clarify the vision Solidarity invoked in its attempt at social transformation:

> The constantly reaffirmed aim of Solidarity was to free society from the totalitarian domination of the Party. In the factories, rank-and-file militants were just as clear about this as their national leaders. They did not speak of a workers' state, rarely of "true socialism," and even less of the total independence of Poland. They wanted to drive the Party from their lives, and to limit it to its proper functions within the state, so that a free society might once more exist. (Touraine *et al.*, 1983:56)

This vision could be approached in a variety of ways: (1) as a revolutionary unionism, typified by Silesian workers; (2) in the spirit of the Gdańsk agreement, referring to the Baltic coast's emphasis on legal conditions for independent unions; (3) as a defensive populism where the "little guy" was defended from the powerful, as "true Poles" wished to defend Poland from the USSR; and (4) as a movement to create political democracy, characterized by the Warsaw intellectual movements. The more a position embraced all of these tendencies, the more likely it could influence the whole of the movement (Touraine *et al.*, 1983:174). As the fall of 1981 approached, the movement's unity was threatened by these various tendencies splitting off from the compromise position realized in the spring. Nevertheless, the movement retained a synthesis of its working-class, democratic and national elements throughout its life, even if the relationship among these elements changed over time. The movement developed by way of "its own internal dynamics, the evolution of its opposition, and the changing situation" (Touraine *et al.*, 1983:86).

This says relatively little about how or why the movement itself could influence society. What allowed the movement to form in the first place? Why did the movement for working-class rights, democracy and national renewal not take other paths? These questions are not emphasized because Touraine *et al.*'s major interest is to clarify the movement's self-understanding, not to challenge it with a series of alternative routes or counter-factual questions. The aim of Touraine *et al.*'s research was to help researchers and activists alike in understanding the movement, to engage "in a joint enterprise in which the actual and potential meanings of the movement were gradually brought to the surface" (Touraine *et al.*, 1983:104). Presumably these meanings were already existing under the given conditions; Touraine did not ask how these meanings could change under new conditions, or how dependent these meanings were on the conditions in which they were formed. To place too much emphasis on alternative conditions, I presume, would lead to too great an emphasis on the structure Touraine (1984) seeks to minimize in sociology.

Touraine *et al.*'s method creates a portrait of Solidarity as a cultural construct by its members. They intentionally avoid examining the systemic limits of transformation (Touraine *et al.*, 1983:64). They approach them only in so far as they are discursively formulated by Solidarity activists in group sessions, the contents of which were in turn shaped by relying on various unnamed written sources and the "comments of Polish intellectuals" (Touraine *et al.*, 1983:103).

Touraine's portrait of Solidarity is thus from the point of view of its members, in a dual sense: the data come, by and large, from discussions involving Solidarity activists and the aim of this research is to facilitate the goals of these activists. But this can lead to difficulties.

The only constraints on Solidarity's character that Touraine's analysis emphasizes are those which movement participants themselves initially recognize, or acknowledge after lengthy discussion. Structure intervenes only through the real or potentially discursive acknowledgment of movement participants. This captures many important aspects, but leaves some in the dark.

Most obvious of the constraints which Touraine's method could capture is the "geo-political" reality in which the movement struggled. The threat of Soviet invasion is a constraint everyone recognized, and the principal reason for the movement's "self-limiting" character. This was also extended to caution about attacking the Polish United Workers' Party directly. Although the party represented Soviet domination, its destruction would mean Soviet invasion (Touraine *et al.*, 1983:66–68). The episcopate of the Church also reminded Solidarity frequently of the borders it should not cross (ibid., pp.68–70).

This geo-political reality generated an internal conflict within the movement: between moderates and radicals, and later pragmatists and fundamentalists (Touraine *et al.*, 1983:75–79). These tendencies were not clearly defined, but could sometimes be identified with certain individuals or regions. These distinctions tended to be based on the attitude toward compromise and negotiation with the regime: radicals wanted little if any of either, even if they too recognized the need to preserve the party at least as a figurehead. This generated another tension within the movement, as the rank and file became increasingly frustrated with their leadership and its apparent weakness in self-limitation. But Touraine *et al.* (1983:77) write that it is certainly not the case that "the base is radical or fundamentalist and the advisers moderate or pragmatist, and to conclude [therefore] that the principal rift is between the base and the top, the workers and the intellectuals?" But why not?

Touraine *et al.* offer few reasons other than the fact that discussions among their rank and file militants' groups were little different than the debates at the national level (Touraine *et al.*, 1983:91). While this may be true, it does not mean that there were no such gaps between rank and file and leadership. If pragmatism is derived from the "internalization of limits," would we not suspect those responsible for negotiations with the authorities to be those most likely to recognize the necessity of these limits? Touraine *et al.* (1983:142) say as much when they discuss the Solidarity congress in September, and how Wałęsa and his "barons" wanted more centralization and reliance on "expert" (pragmatist) advice which diverged from the likely rank-and-file interest in greater democracy and decentralization. Touraine *et al.* identify this as a break between gradualists and those inclined toward rupture with the regime. But why would this not be associated with rank in the union, which is itself correlated with discussions of the difficulties of a self-limiting revolution?

Would a discussion in group sessions among rank-and-file militants of the same problems which led the union barons to become more pragmatic not also encourage workers to develop the same internalized limits? Can we assume that these militants would come to these conclusions without sociological interventionism? Only if we assume that the research groups "pull out" only what is already there. It seems equally likely, however, that the research groups' discussions create the very attitudes the researchers seek to generalize to the rest of the movement. Thus, there may indeed have been a potential rupture between leadership and rank and file in the making, given the tightrope that self-limitation forced the union leadership to walk.

Another constraint on Solidarity's action was the economic crisis everyone recognized. And this crisis grew larger every month of

Solidarity's legal existence. The fault for the crisis was laid typically at the incompetence of the regime or Soviet pillaging of the Polish economy. Beyond this blame, Solidarity discussants also acknowledged that workers would have to lose some of the protections and security they enjoyed. Trade unionists were actually calling for the creation of unemployment in the name of "economic laws" (Touraine *et al.*, 1983:70–71).

This last issue suggests further difficulties in Touraine *et al*'s. analysis. They come to this conclusion on the basis of one discussion in Warsaw that Solidarity was willing to rebuild the economy along lines that would introduce unemployment and other capitalist artifacts. We are to be convinced of this on the basis of one quotation from a rank-and-file member of the union. We know nothing of this group nor of this particular individual. We know nothing of how representative these views were, even though there are several public-opinion surveys and public documents which suggest that even if the intelligentsia was in favor of radical market reforms, workers were not. Of course, "sociological interventionism" cannot achieve the representativeness of a public-opinion survey; but in the process of clarifying the vision Solidarity held of itself, it need not perpetuate the myths which helped tie it together. In particular, one cannot assume that Solidarity as a movement, or the "rank and file" as a group, supported market reform. What is more, how does one distinguish between support in a discussion group, and the kind of support which would eliminate one's job? This is something we cannot discover in such focus-group discussions. Touraine's own discussion of the Solidarity congress suggests this.

At this congress in the fall of 1981, the trade-union element of the movement was hardly represented. It might be argued, they write, that Solidarity was ready to accept "price increases and unemployment, and to take responsibility for these in exchange for political guarantees" (Touraine *et al.*, 1983:144). In the very same paragraph, however, Touraine *et al.* note the "deterioration" of the working-class component of the movement. But what does this mean? Apparently, it means that it failed to move with the rest of the movement toward political discourse, illustrated by their attacks on everyone in the leadership but Wałęsa. Does the working-class component cease to be part of Solidarity with this rejection? Even though this book is a lengthy discussion of the differences in the movement, Touraine *et al.* exclude this element without providing justification.

Touraine *et al.* subsume the potential conflicts between the leadership and rank and file, as well as the conflict between professionals and workers, into a conflict between democrats and nationalists. Why? This is especially confusing when the "true Pole," Jan Rulewski, received only 9 percent of the vote for union president, and the working-class populist, Marian Jurczyk, 25 percent. Touraine *et al.* dismiss the significance of the working class "defensive populism" because it does not evolve in the same way as the rest of the movement? Do they minimize the split between leadership and rank and file because it does not have the same cultural resonance with the union's multiple identities as the tension between democrats and nationalists?

The problems I have listed above (the identification of movement and market reform; the denial of embryonic internal conflicts between leadership and rank and file; and the subsumption of working-class identity into nationalist politics) derive from a common problem: Touraine *et al.* have few means, other than the interaction produced by the interlocuter, to penetrate beneath discursive "appearances." Indeed, Touraine *et al.* are quite ambiguous on this question of whether there are "real" mechanisms beneath what actors recognize or acknowledge. Although "hidden" mechanisms can produce mythological forces, uncritically accepting myths that Solidarity created for itself, of itself, does not help the movement uncover the best form of struggle.

One of the first identities that Touraine makes of this movement is that its base was in the working class. Although there are firm grounds for identifying it as such, it begs an important question: what was the significance of the extensive participation in leadership of those with higher educations? Although only 8 percent of the labor force in 1980 had higher educations (Rocznik Statystyczny, 1983:59), over one-third (12 of 33) of the top activist officials of the union were highly educated (Pakulski, 1986:72). The highly educated were also likely to be leaders of the regional bodies of Solidarity: about one-third (21 of 62) of the members of the Upper Silesian regional commission, the most "working-class" region among Touraine *et al.*'s research sites, were highly educated ("Wybory", 1981). There is considerable controversy over the proportion of delegates to Solidarity's September congress who were from other than the working class; the *Wall Street Journal* (September 10, 1981:29) reports about 70 percent came from the intelligentsia, while Polish sociologist Stanisław Starski (1982:154) suggests that informal polls put the working class at about 60 percent (except for the Warsaw delegation, where the intelligentsia carried about 60 percent of the delegates). Touraine *et al.* accept the image Solidarity presented of itself as a "unified" movement of the nation when they accept its working-class character. Although I, too, find that interpretation appealing, it is too readily accepted when the aim of analysis is the "self-clarification" of Solidarity's vision. For, in that amplification, the myths of the movement are reproduced.

Indeed, the possibility of difference, if not antagonism, between professionals and workers (as professionals seek reconstruction and workers seek defense, as in the fall of 1981) or farmers and urban consumers (especially as food shortages grew and hunger strikes were initiated in July 1981), or men and women (never acknowledged, but potentially ever present) is not discussed by Touraine *et al.* Likely, too, is that discussion groups would suppress these differences, as they emphasized the conflict with the Soviet Union or the party, not with one another. Systematic silences, like explicit acknowledgments and arguments, are data which deserve interpretation.

There are certainly constraints on Solidarity's activity that participants in the movement declined to recognize. Certain "myths" were critical to maintaining the very unity Touraine *et al.* praise, and thus they avoid challenging them, much less exploding them. The notion that there were no significant divergent class interests among Solidarity activists is exemplary in this regard, as a discussion of self-management and economic reform will illustrate. Likewise, the question of whether Solidarity's refusal to ally with party reform movements was an asset or liability in the movement's aspirations was mentioned only in passing (Touraine *et al.* 1983:72), even though most outside observers and even a few insiders, like Warsaw's Wojciech Lamentowicz, argued this to be a key problem which Solidarity refused to resolve.

Should critical sociologists not ask whether Solidarity's own cultural constructs limited its possibilities for action? Could we not ask whether the suppression of both differences of interest in the union and their articulation was more alienating than empowering, as Staniszkis (1984a:113) suggests? If we ask the Solidarity activists these questions, and they dismiss them as products of Western sociology and irrelevant to Solidarity, are we truly irrelevant?

Touraine *et al.*'s methodology relies in large part on a variation of the Schutzian postulate of adequacy, where verification depends on the subjects of analysis validating the interpreter's analysis. It thus fails to link action to the system, except in so far as action is directed toward the "cultural stakes" of the struggle, which in this case was the form of life the Polish nation was to take. But in so doing, the analysis of action can only be grounded in the meaning various actors give it. The role of the analyst is to clarify the meanings held by different actors. There is no immediate way to question whether there are suppressed differences of interest, because we cannot derive from the system any potential interests. Unrecognized and unacknowledged systemic constraints on social action cannot be found in this culturalist account of Solidarity's meaning. For example, nowhere is it asked explicitly whether the struggle Solidarity constructed was a feasible means of social transformation, a question I shall address in chapter 3.

Touraine *et al.*'s book is extraordinarily useful for conveying the meanings held by different participants in the Solidarity movement. It is also very good for conveying the evolution of the movement, but Touraine *et al.*'s analysis does not explain the evolution of this movement in terms of the systemic constraints on action that are not acknowledged by movement participants. Nor can they convey the meaning of this movement for world history, unless we come to accept structure as defined by cultural stakes, and these cultural stakes merely as products of social learning. What of the constraints that are not known? What of the determinations of action that are not acknowledged? What of the accomplishments that are not recognized? Marxism has, of course, been characterized by its concern for the "hidden" laws of history and the "real" contradictions of modes of production and their social formations. If we are interested in the link between structure and action in 1980–81, the best place to begin is with a Marxist analysis of Solidarity.

Structure and action: class analysis and resource mobilization

One of the reasons Marxism is one of the most appealing forms of critical sociology is that it incorporates both structure and action in its analysis. Class, or relations of production, is simultaneously a structure and form of action, as it is embedded in a deep structure called a mode of production that depends on the strategic action of systemically formed actors for its reproduction and possible transformation. Because Solidarity was in large part, if not predominantly, a workers' movement, it would seem that Marxism offers an extremely useful approach. The principal barrier to this Marxism is, however, the uncertainty about how to analyze the context in which the struggle takes place. In what follows, I shall consider Stalinist,

Trotskyist and Polish Marxist accounts of Solidarity. In the first two cases, their global analysis of Soviet-type society structures their interpretation more than their analysis of Solidarity informs their global analysis, thus rendering systematic shadows in their analysis of Solidarity. In the last case, however, Solidarity's "meaning" overwhelms the theoretical apparatus so as to undermine Marxism's analytical contribution.

Albert Szymanski was an exceptional American Marxist sociologist. Although one might disagree with his Stalinist type of Marxism (e.g. Singer, 1984), it is undeniable that he confronted some of Marxism's greatest problems. Rebellion by workers against a workers' state is certainly one of the most serious. Szymanski (1984) argues that the 1980–81 Solidarity movement was the consequence of four features of Polish socialism (which exists within an international contradiction between US militarism and Soviet support for national liberation and socialism): (1) a tension between a centralized and decentralized model of socialism; (2) a class struggle between intelligentsia and workers; (3) unreasonably high consumer expectations for a newly industrializing country; and (4) specifically Polish conditions. These particular conditions center on (1) the weakness of the Communist Party in Poland between 1938 and 1944; (2) the intensity of the Cold War between 1948 and 1955; (3) the strength of the Catholic Church; and (4) the chauvinist traditions of the Polish intelligentsia. For Szymanski, the crisis was ultimately the consequence of the impurity of socialist construction in Poland. The party, given its weakness, was forced to "compromise" with the Church, peasantry and intelligentsia. It had to buy off the population with unreasonably high rates of development and increases in living standards. The mass membership of Solidarity never really challenged socialism or the Communist Party's leadership of Poland, he claims, but rather sought an increase in living standards and a decentralized model of socialism. What anti-communist sentiment there was came from anti-communist intellectuals (KOR social democrats), who influenced the workers from the start, but finally assumed leadership in the fall of 1981. Szymanski argues that they planned to overthrow the government and eliminate socialism in Poland. As a consequence of these conditions, the Solidarity movement was internally contradictory, he argues. It embraced incompatible demands of antagonistic classes (peasants, workers and "middlemen"). Even the workers' demands were contradictory, seeking free markets as well as egalitarian demands for full employment, and increased levels of consumption but reduced work-weeks (1984:120). Szymanski excuses the party's loss of support and the workers' rebellion by explaining how the conditions of Polish socialism's construction differed from "ideal" conditions for the construction of a better socialism. In the process, he maintains unreasonable assumptions.

Szymanski assumes that the Communist Party *must be* the representative of socialism. Socialism, he argues, was produced spontaneously in Poland after World War II. But he does not, and cannot, demonstrate that Communist Party rule is the same as this period's popular movement to socialize industry and redistribute land (chapter 1). He also explains the party's unpopularity with its being forced by Cold War conditions to impose a rapid industrialization plan on the country rather than pursue a more gradualist, decentralized model. The party could have survived this imposition, however, if it had not been so weak between 1938 and 1944 (which prevented it from restricting or "rooting out reactionary influences" (1984:127)). Its "weakness" was mostly a consequence of its destruction by Stalin, of course. Szymanski reproduces in analysis the principle of party infallibility that the Solidarity movement, and the entire post-revisionist opposition in actual socialism, has struggled against. Under what conditions does the party cease to be an embodiment of socialism? Nowhere does Szymanski even pose the question, and thus fails to raise a basic issue for critical sociology, and an essential question for Solidarity.

Szymanski argues that challenges to the Communist Party and socialism were not made by the majority of the union. Those workers who did so were only influenced by anti-communist forces like the Church, Western right-wing trade unions, professional economists, intellectuals from KOR or the KPN and the intelligentsia which became the leadership in most places. Even working-class Wałęsa was associated with KOR, and thus became anti-communist. But this interpretation flies in the face of the data Touraine *et al.* (1983) and others present. More revolutionary action against the party was *resisted* by segments of the intelligentsia, because they recognized that an unlimited revolution would only reintroduce Soviet military occupation. Only if one assumes the party equals emancipation and anti-regime activities equal counter-emancipatory activity is there reason for indicting the working class for having false consciousness in the Solidarity movement. If class interest is going to retain any analytical power, it must avoid preposterous extensions into identification with parties. Class interest begins to lose its utility once the point of production is left and questions of politics are asserted.

Oliver MacDonald (1983) provides an alternative, and much better informed, Trotskyist account of Solidarity and the general crisis which gave rise to it. MacDonald (1983:14–16) considers Solidarity a workers' movement *sui generis*, with a socialist program generated out of its working conditions. It was

> the collective effort by the elite industrial and transport workers of the country – party and non-party workers – to lead the society out of its crisis ... Formulated democratically with great care, they [their social demands] bound together the more politically conscious section of workers with the broad majority and they indicated principles which were by no means the commonsense of some undifferentiated society: workers should be compensated for striking; there should be a flat-rate increase for all employees [helping the lowerpaid]; the commercial shops and hard currency shops should be closed; the privileges of the police and party apparatus should be abolished, as should special stores; family subsidies should be equalized; there should be rationing rather than free-floating prices, and a massive shift in spending towards social welfare. This programme was classic in the socialist egalitarian assumptions underlying it. So too were the radical democratic freedoms called for in the twenty-one demands: freedom of speech, the press and publication.

MacDonald nevertheless acknowledges that this workers' movement never identified itself as socialist, and in fact took pains to distance itself from the symbols of socialism. But this is because the workers identified socialism with the PZPR, and had no alternative socialist tradition with which to identify (1983:21). In the absence of socialist alternatives, the workers' movement was dominated by an anarcho-syndicalism married to currents of Polish nationalism.

This movement faced its main opponent in the state bureaucracy and its allied regimes abroad. Although the nationalization of the means of production moves these systems toward socialism, according to MacDonald, the internal mechanisms of the Communist Party prevent the workers from participating in governing their society. Hence, the crisis is derived from the system's "transitional" status between capitalism and socialism, with workers obliged to engage a political revolution against the party. Solidarity ultimately lost because it lacked the proper program, argues MacDonald. Solidarity adopted a marketization and self-managing economic policy that violated the workers' egalitarian spirit. It also failed to link up with reformist elements with the PZPR, which might have enabled it to promote an anti-Stalinist Marxist program that would culminate in the political revolution MacDonald finds essential. The roots of this programmatic failure lie partially in the Church hierarchy's attempts to "weaken working class resolve," and the intelligentsia's attempt to "assume influence over its [Solidarity's] direction." But mostly it lies in the inadequate vision of Solidarity's own "anarcho-syndicalism." Essentially, Solidarity failed to understand its own internally contradictory identity as trade union, political party and quasi-state institution, which a proper socialist program would resolve.

MacDonald's approach exemplifies Marxism's ability to integrate structure and action. The undemocratic structure of Poland's political system leads to crises which only the industrial working class has the strength to face. But this class does not automatically have, by virtue of its social weight, the power to transform society. It requires intelligent analysis and a proper program. With appropriate humility, MacDonald acknowledges that no such program exists, and thus calls on the Western left to take the analytical field from the "Kołakowski's and Brzezinski's." But how is this program to be derived? Who is to make it? And what are the criteria that enable us to evaluate its socialist content?

Although Szymanski and MacDonald are quite distant in their estimation of ruling communist parties, their evaluation of socialism remains similar. They find certain essential ingredients of a socialist system in central economic planning, full employment and other social rights. They find these social rights to be really existing in Soviet-type societies. They have similar estimations of the workers' movement: that it "failed" because it did not have the proper vision. Both find the advice of the intelligentsia and the indigenous ideology of the workers inadequate: skilled industrial workers must be the foundation of socialism, but they are not able to generate the appropriate transformative program on their own, and can be taken over by anti-socialist ideologues. For socialism to be successful, according to these accounts, another socialist vision must take root in the working class. But the contents of that vision lead them to deny many of the programmatic elements Solidarity found essential, including movement away from the centrally planned economy. This dogmatic resistance to Solidarity's pragmatism leads these Marxist perspectives to fail to appreciate the contribution Solidarity might make to rethinking emancipatory praxis.

Solidarity's vision of a market economy is a major challenge to many currents of Marxist thinking. But might that challenge not suggest a transformation of Marxism, rather than demand a change in Solidarity? The Marxist tradition, after all, has been sufficiently flexible to incorporate other major changes. Marxist class analysis does not always identify skilled workers as the foundation of transformation in these systems, nor does it always find outside agencies the appropriate source for ideology. In this spirit, Solidarity might be understood best as a kind of pragmatic critique of Marxist praxis and utopia. But some of these Polish pragmatic revisions of Marxism go so far as to abandon not only articles of Marxist faith about socialism's essence, but also some of Marxism's most important analytical insights into social relations. One set of Marxist revisions has gone especially far in making Marxism serve Solidarity by removing class based on relations *in* production[7] from the picture.

Kostecki and Mreła (1984:134) argue that raising the question of worker–peasant–intelligentsia relations feeds into the party's attempt to continue "pulverizing" society. "Class analysis" thus undermines a natural alliance among all the incapacitated in Poland. It is not surprising that Kostecki and Mreła would be critical of accepting, even as a point of departure, the party's distinction of social groups, given their own engagement in struggle. Instead, they prefer to follow Kurczewski (1982) in seeing Solidarity as primarily an alliance between the professionals and skilled working class. Indeed, this struggle is less an alliance than it is the emergence of a new agent of transformation, the "new middle class," or that group which is paid better than the unskilled manual class, but without the decision-making power of the elite.

Stanisław Starski (1982) extends this approach into a more Marxist account by reconstructing class and class struggle. For him, class struggle in Soviet-type society is a conflict between a class which "owns the state" and a differentiated labor force united by its common employment by that state. The systemic contradiction lies between state ownership of the means of production and the socialized character of production which calls for greater decentralization of decision making. In fact, discussing favorably some Polish literature, Starski (1982:187) argues that it is the dispossession of a share in policy making, not the dispossession of the means of production, which makes the new, ruled class. Solidarity

> is a trade union in that it recognizes that the basic common denominator of the members of the class of state employees is the fact that they sell their labor to the state. However, it is also clear that by doing so Solidarity is recognizing and revealing the basic structure of state socialist society which is political domination by the ruling class from which all other kinds of domination follow. (1982:209)

In this, Starski provides the extension most Marxist revisions have sought to make: to identify new ruling and ruled classes, so the class struggle which defines much of critical sociology can continue unabated. Socialization of the means of production and socialism can remain its utopia. Utopia is characterized by

a dismantling the state's repressive machinery and subjecting it to regular democratic control to prevent a gradual renewal of the ruling class's ability to manipulate all social strata with threats of terror;

b reconstructing democracy and especially democratic forms of control and coordination of all spheres of social life, to prevent a ruling class gaining a monopoly on decision making power;

c working out a democratic means of running the state (understood to be the sole political framework of all political processes) which cannot be discarded at present for both internal and external reasons. (1982:240)

Although this is a very attractive development over Szymanski's Marxism in that it is more critical of the regime itself, Starski's Marxism generates problems that are not present in MacDonald. Starski allows the search for new antagonistic classes to override what are perhaps equally significant bases for identity that structure action. Starski's (1982:16,48) class of state owners is in constant search for those who could be coopted into an alliance. This strategy of cooptation is, in fact, the principal "tie" which holds together the ruling group and its vassals and which makes the authorities such an ineffective "ruling class" (chapter 6). But this characteristic also makes an identification of a *ruled* class of "state employees" problematic, for such a class includes everyone, as nobody has exclusive decision-making power. The ruled class therefore becomes conscious not only as a consequence of learning through anti-statist struggle, but also when these politically disenfranchised state employees believe that they have no career trajectory that might escalate them into the ranks of the decision makers. When professionals are much more likely to enter these decision-making ranks, we have the basis for an old-style class conflict based on relations in production. When they are denied entry, we have the basis for a real class alliance. Although MacDonald (1983) does not note this distinction between professionals and workers, his identification of the skilled working class as the "truly" emancipatory class opens up the question for discussion.

Starski's (1982) book is among the most useful works on the Polish self-limiting revolution, but it ultimately suffers by refusing to allow its insights to break it free from an unrewarding search for the new class struggle that defines the totality of the conflict. Class analysis of social movements allows a link between structure and action to be found, but it also can blind us to other possible connections between structure and social transformation. "Resource-mobilization" studies promise much the same without granting priority to the relations of production in shaping struggle. This perspective therefore offers a more "flexible" account, that might better capture the resources that structure action in Soviet-type society.

Elizabeth Crighton (1985) employs a resource-mobilization perspective to explain Solidarity's developments. Although distributional, ethnic/national and post-materialist concerns are separated into distinct movements in the West, the Solidarity movement in Poland embodied all of them being a "total social movement." It is therefore unique among movements in industrial societies for the broad scope of its demands, its size and the speed with which it grew, and its capacity to build alliances among different groups. This much we know from Touraine, but what does the resource-mobilization approach suggest for why this occurred as it did? Crighton argues that Solidarity's access to resources and its organizational structure in large part decided how it mobilized and built alliances.

The resources which Solidarity had available to it were primarily "intangible" – organizational ability and legal expertise as well as strong social bonds resting on loyalty and obligation – in part compensating for its limited (although not non-existent) tangible resources (money, means of communication, etc.) (Crighton, 1985:119–21). Thus, "natural groups" with preexisting normative bonds and loyalties were essential to Solidarity's formation (see also Latoszek, 1987). These "natural" groups were also cross-class alliances, whose formation was relatively unproblematic. The relatively small class and cultural differentiation in Poland minimized class antagonism, while the nature of resource competition in Poland demanded their cooperation (Crighton, 1985). Crighton finds the various groups allied with Solidarity to be more cooperative than competitive, despite the fact that they belong to the same social-movement "industry." They competed less with one another for several reasons: (1) they "specialized" in various tasks – specializing in concerns that focused on their own niche in the occupational structure;[8] (2) overlapping memberships in various social-movement organizations (SMOs) also smoothed the conditions of alliance making; (3) repression demanded cooperation among SMOs in self-defense; (4) political centralization also restricted the opportunity for incompatible, even different, strategies in pursuing aims;[9] and (5) the goals Solidarity pursued, given its alliance character, had to be broad and general. The "total social movement" therefore has its roots in the distribution of resources in the state socialist system and the organizational structure of the movement itself.

This perspective also hints at the conditions of success for social transformation by Solidarity, something that Touraine avoids by and large. In particular, decentralized organizations will be likely to generate broad support and new ideas and even transform the values of its members more effectively than centralized movements; but the latter tend to be better coordinated and more likely to begin institutional transformations (Crighton, 1985:128). Indeed, the combination of these features in Solidarity might help explain the tension of the rank and file with the leadership Touraine's approach sought to minimize. Touraine also avoided the question of coalition between sections of the authorities and Solidarity, much as Solidarity avoided it. Resource mobilization suggests this to be a key factor in translating movement goals into institutional transformation (Crighton, 1985). Clearly, this was a controversial issue which the moralistic anti-political politics of Solidarity did not allow it to address (Staniszkis, 1984a).

The resource-mobilization perspective raises issues and questions no other perspective has, and therefore illustrates its considerable utility. But because it has no "global" theory of Soviet-type society, it is presented with major problems. First, it fails to identify what kind of institutional reforms are associated with the struggles of which kinds of groups. This is a critical question in so far as the character of the movement is influenced by both the groups which compose the movement and the goals that it sets for itself. Indeed, it might be argued that Solidarity could survive as a "total social movement" only by avoiding questions of institutional reform. On the other hand, certain kinds of institutional reform might be compatible with maintaining the alliance of divergent interests the movement represented. This we shall consider in chapter 3. Second, this approach fails to anticipate which groups should become mobilized. In this sense, it shares much with Touraine when it takes the mobilization of the group as a point of departure and does not ask which groups are most likely to be at the base of a social movement and under what conditions other groups are likely to participate. Finally, without any explicit normative foundation, resource-mobilization accounts are agnostic in their movement commitments. This is not a necessary element of the perspective, as Morris's (1984) "indigenous" transformation of the theory suggests. But it does raise the question as to whether emancipatory commitments might not lead the analyst to search more diligently for resources among the movement participants and for self-reliant strategies than to conclude that alliances with portions of an elite are necessary for institutional transformation.

Points of departure

This chapter's analysis of various accounts of Solidarity and its formation suggests the difficulty of evaluating the relative strength of approaches. Depending on one's concern, whether it is in the search for Solidarity's meaning or its structural origins, one is led to embrace different kinds of theories and methods which may be unsuitable for other interests. My analysis of Solidarity is motivated by the foundational concern of critical sociology: a search for the conditions which make possible emancipatory social transformation.

The various structural approaches we have considered in this chapter have identified a number of features which have made Poland in 1980–81 distinctive. Poland's rapid industrialization, the authorities' alternating relations with the West, and society's cultural and political antagonisms with the East provided the general macrosociological conditions which enabled Solidarity's rise. Particularly in Gdańsk and other Baltic areas, strong primary social relations within the working class and overextended and ineffective authorities made Poland a likely place for workers' opposition. This likelihood was increased by an economic and agricultural crisis combined with the coming of age of Poland's postwar baby boom. Poland's major distinction from other East European societies lies in the historical constitution of its opposition, however.

This historical constitution, as I emphasized in chapter 1, is filled with "alternativity," with other options that might have been taken. This notion demands, therefore, that we pay attention to the choices and strategies pursued by various groups and individuals. Without choice there can be no alternatives. And without understanding the meanings attributed by individuals to their world, we cannot evaluate their choices.

Touraine helps us understand the meanings of Solidarity, and how it came to be constituted as a social movement with three legs of identity: as a trade union, a democratic movement and a force for greater national independence. But because Touraine remains at the level of actors, and refuses to go beyond what they are willing to recognize, we are left without a way to discover unacknowledged conditions of action and the unintended consequences of that action. In particular, we are unable to answer the questions which Solidarity activists hesitated to consider. In order to do that, one needs a theory of the structure which conditions social action.

Marxism is based on just such a relational approach, based as it is on a construct, the relations of production, which is both a manifestation of a deep structure, the mode of production, and enabled by strategic action by primary actors, social classes. But Marxism serves analysis well only when its global theory of structure clarifies the principal foundations of social action. Marxism faces considerable difficulties in this regard when it comes to Soviet-type societies.

Marxists like Szymanski are loathe to recognize that the Communist Party may not represent the emancipation of the working class, and therefore interpret Solidarity as a misguided force. Although Mac-Donald does not hesitate to join Solidarity in the condemnation of the PZPR, he too finds Solidarity basically misguided, because its plan for action did not conform to his global theory of socialism, and of the source of crisis in Soviet-type society. In effect, these Marxists could not integrate Solidarity's pragmatic approach to social transformation, because they have no account of how and when to transform their own global theory of socialism.

One solution is to allow the conflict engendered by Solidarity to define new classes and new struggles, as Starski does. But in this, we lose one of Marxism's distinctions: the search for hidden structures that, under other conditions and different choices, might lead to alternative outcomes. In Starski's revision, Solidarity defines the essential structure of Soviet-type society. But to conflate class with the social movement represented by Solidarity violates the Marxist notion that relations *in* production structure action. Starski's Marxism makes Solidarity an expected consequence of the Soviet-type system, not one that is problematic. To find class relations the only fundamental condition structuring action in the case of Solidarity undermines the analytical potential of Marxism in the analysis of Soviet-type society.

The resource-mobilization perspective is therefore quite useful for understanding Solidarity, given its flexibility in the analysis of structure and action. Class relations become one of several important structures shaping the opportunities of social movements. But this approach, unlike Marxism, does not have a global theory of Soviet-type society and thus cannot tell us *why* a movement like Solidarity emerges. It also cannot help us understand the relationship between the various possible institutional transformations offered in those 500 days and the social groups constituting Solidarity. In addition, without a general theory of the deep structure which shapes the conditions of Solidarity, we cannot anticipate how structures influence one another, and whether a change in one will produce changes in others.

Ultimately, I find the attempt to integrate different levels of structural analysis and agent-centered approaches essential to understanding Solidarity better, and developing critical sociology further. This means that we should ask how the autonomous and mutual transformations of different levels of structure and agency reshape the conditions for social change. How do actors use the knowledge of the structural constraints and possibilities of their context to expand the limits of the possible and approach the conditions of the desirable? In other words, what are the conditions of emancipatory praxis in Soviet-type society? In chapter 3, I shall offer one answer with regard to Solidarity in 1980–81.

3 The Solidarity movement as emancipatory praxis

To argue that the Solidarity movement of 1980–81 is a case of emancipatory praxis is deliberately provocative. Praxis is normally associated with Marxist discourse, and is understood in that context as conscious human activity that enables life and reproduces structures. It is also conscious activity that transforms structures, thus creating new forms of life (Petrovic, 1983). Emancipatory praxis refers to such transformative activity that produces greater opportunities for freedom and human self-realization.

Few associated with Solidarity would dispute an account which describes their movement's goal as greater freedom. But emancipatory praxis is normally associated, given its Marxist roots, with the struggle for socialism. Few in Solidarity would argue that they struggled for socialism. Nevertheless, in many of its aspects, from its working-class base to the struggle by workers to realize greater control over their enterprises, Solidarity resembled a socialist movement in all but name.[1] But the differences which Solidarity raised with really existing socialism are as important as the similarities the movement had with socialist principles. As such, to label Solidarity a form of emancipatory praxis invites socialists to reconsider their own critical perspectives and find within Solidarity material for the reconstruction of their theoretical and political frameworks. Solidarity provides a case that can illuminate the pragmatist critique of Marxism in which the link between class struggle and emancipation must be inductively determined, not deduced from laws of history (Dewey, 1938 [1973]).

Emancipatory praxis is also important for the analytical link the concept establishes between strategies, structures and normative standards. There is a normative commitment embedded within emancipation, of course. The success of a movement does not depend on its organizational survival or conquest of state power, but whether it contributes to the realization of the ethical principles for which it stands. To use the term "emancipatory praxis" therefore holds up a movement to some normative standard, and invites a critical appraisal of its choices and accomplishments in that regard. And as pragmatists argue, it also suggests that normative standards themselves could change as conditions diverge from those under which the original standards were formulated.

Emancipatory praxis also emphasizes the significance of choice. Choice is involved in the selection of values, both by activist and by theorist, but strategy is even more obviously a matter of decision. One strategy will be more effective than another for realizing normative goals. This often depends on the strategist's ability to find in the dominant structures weak links, and points of strength in that which enables resistance. At the very least, therefore, emancipatory praxis directs attention to the structures which movements seek to overturn and the structures which enable them to struggle. But often it moves beyond that too. Emancipatory praxis normally asks us to recognize different kinds of structures, and to establish their linkage. Which structure is most important to change in order to assure the stability of transformation? Which structure is the most feasible to change given the resources of a movement? What enables the movement to expand its resources? Upon what structural conditions does the form of the movement depend?

There are thus several moments to an analysis which makes "emancipatory praxis" its central concept. One is to explain the interaction of different structures, and how those structures combine within a given conjuncture. Another emphasizes the alternative choices within existing settings, and how those choices shape the different possibilities within a conjuncture. These can be combined when one identifies how decisions, made and unmade, reproduce or reshape the structural possibilities of the future. One also considers how those possibilities relate to the normative claims the movement makes. In sum, one of the greatest challenges facing critical sociology is to identify the "degrees of freedom" each setting has available to it, and how, in turn, the actions in these settings reshape future settings so as to move toward the desirable.

In the following analysis of Solidarity, I argue that workers' self-organization laid the foundation for the successive evolution of Solidarity, but was not enough, by itself, to ensure the realization of the movement's aims. Some kind of strategy was necessary to transfer control over the economy from the authorities. Self-management was a brilliant move in this regard, in as much as it enabled an alliance

all those in the world of work. But self-management came too
imately, the authorities' resistance to this and other changes
1 Solidarity down a no-win avenue, where cooptation or revo-
were its only alternatives. Neither could enable the realization
lidarity's aims. It does suggest, however, that progress toward
the reconstruction of a new emancipatory praxis could have been
realized by Solidarity had the authorities been less resistant to compromise with the movement.

The evolutionary logic and choices of Solidarity

Włodzimierz Pańków (1987), who was part of the Touraine
research team, argues that there are three stages to the evolution of
Solidarity:[2] the first stage, between August 1980 and March 1981, was
characterized by its unionist or syndicalist identity. In this stage,
self-organization was its principal concern. The authorities responded
to demands in a piecemeal fashion just as they had in the 1970s. This
culminated in a fight over "free Saturdays" and the Bydgoszcz attack.
Both events showed Solidarity that the authorities would not tolerate a
workers' opposition in the long term, and that therefore the movement had to change its focus to an economic or institutional transformation of Polish society. Between March and late September 1981,
Solidarity moved into its *economic* stage, where self-management and
economic reform became central. It sought to limit and divide the
power of the authorities in this. Although self-management was
initiated by people outside of the union, the union nurtured self-
management efforts. Some movement leaders found that this concern
for the autonomy of workers and the world of work could unite
various classes in the movement. Workers and their representatives
were not sufficiently interested in this option, while the authorities
proposed their own economic reform package. This led to terrible
compromise legislation in September. The final stage, between September and the imposition of martial law on December 13, 1981, was
characterized by *political* concerns above all, where the establishment
of political clubs characterized positive efforts, and refusals to consider
a coalition government with the Party negative energies. These
political concerns were provoked by the appearance of intransigence
on the part of the authorities, given their failure to concede on matters
of the media and the failure by the horizontalists and others to
generate real internal party reform. Self-limitation made sense as a
strategy only when it promised progress. By the fall of 1981, economic

crisis and political stalemate provided few options for Solidarity other than to become more expressly political. But the threat of Soviet invasion made overt political opposition only a defensive strategy, not a transcendent one.

Each stage of Solidarity's evolution set new conditions for what could be accomplished in the subsequent stage. This breakdown of the movement's evolution is an extremely useful organizing principle for discussing the opportunities and constraints facing the emancipatory praxis of the movement and groups within it. Solidarity's formation illustrates these opportunities and constraints of action very well.

Self-organization as self-defense

In December 1980, Adam Michnik observed that the government's behavior toward Solidarity was "odd." The authorities had failed to see the union as an opportunity, and instead saw it only as a threat to its omnipotence (Michnik, 1985: 112). Michnik could use the term "odd" without irony only if public responsiveness was the structural predisposition of the authorities. The Gdańsk accords were not, however, an indication of a new governmental predisposition. The authorities continued to be structured by their old pattern of rules and resources, whose deep structure remained the same even while its manifestation was being reshaped in struggle.

One of the structures shaping Soviet-type society is the "organizational hegemony" of the Communist Party, in which rival organizations with essentially alternative programmes are forbidden (Fehér, Heller and Markus, 1983: 157; chapter 6). When the authorities agreed to allow Solidarity's formation, they violated that principle and apparently transformed the system into something different. But the deep meaning of the system had not been changed. The system meaning of Polish power relations continued to depend on a perverted substantive rationality.

According to the constitutions of Soviet-type societies, the goal of social organization is the construction of socialism. But the definition of socialism and means by which it is obtained are defined by the party itself. The Communist Party therefore embodies substantive rationality, and no external standard can be used to evaluate its ability to realize this rationality (Bauman, 1972: 137; Fehér, Heller and Markus 1983: 143–467). Although the Communist Party of the Soviet Union could claim this virtually sacred status with its position as the incarnation of the hierophantic October Revolution (Jowitt, 1987), East

European parties were too far removed, especially by the 1970s, to claim that status in good faith. They could, nevertheless, claim a special privilege. In Poland, the Polish United Workers' Party is the group which can appeal most effectively to the Communist Party of the Soviet Union for national privileges. It thus can claim a kind of "perverted" substantive rationality (see chapter 6). While its organizational hegemony was eliminated with the August agreement, its claim to perverted substantive rationality was not. This "deep structure" motivated the authorities to try to restore the organizational hegemony that would improve the image of the party in the eyes of the Soviets. Likewise, Solidarity activists restrained themselves from overthrowing the party, acknowledging that it must remain at least the titular head of People's Poland to prevent Soviet invasion. In this way, the movement became self-limiting even while the authorities continually used their resources to undermine an already cautious movement. One of the first moves of the authorities was to reintroduce into the document ending organizational hegemony an acknowledgment of the party's "substantive rationality."

During the Gdańsk negotiations, the authorities' representatives asked the workers to accept a political formula acknowledging the "leading role of the Communist Party." This would minimize the shock to systemic identity that the end of organizational hegemony represented. The experts (without Staniszkis, who believed this an unnecessary and potentially dangerous compromise) encouraged the MKS presidium to accept this clause. The compromise was accentuated by Jagielski in his closing speech. Later, various groups of people, including members of the Movement of Young Poland, protested to the workers' representatives. Dispute raged within the MKS, and was only partially settled by Wałęsa's fervent appeal to the crowd emphasizing that they would be given their *own* unions, which would in practice offset the submission of society to the leading role of the party (Staniszkis, 1984a: 57–62). Already the deep structure of systematic identity led the authorities to maneuver in a way that made the self-defense of self-organization paramount in union strategy. The self-defense of self-organization also gave Solidarity its particular cross-class identity and national scope.

One of the first groups to self-organize in Warsaw was the Independent Self-Governing Trade Union of Science, Technics and Education Employees (*Niezależny Samorządowy Związek Zawodowy Pracowników Nauki, Techniki i Oświaty* or NSZZPNTiO) (Krzemiński, 1983: 328–44). On September 4, 1980, in a Warsaw apartment, approximately sixty people from some thirty employment sites, especially the Polish Academy of Sciences and the University of Warsaw, assembled to declare the foundation of their own independent union. This would replace the old and non-representative *Związek Nauczycielswta Polskiego* (ZNP = Union of Polish Teaching). The new Union formed relatively quickly, as the organization was based on the dense network of personal ties within Warsaw's intelligentsia. Those who were involved in the March 1968 protests were especially important in the union's foundation. This separate union of Warsaw's intelligentsia lasted only through October 30, at which time it dissolved into Solidarity. On the coast, the Gdańsk intelligentsia immediately joined with the Inter-Factory Strike Committee and did not assume any separate identity. In Warsaw, however, the social environments of the intelligentsia and working class were more isolated from one another. Organizing efforts in the factories and among the intelligentsia took place relatively separately.

At the first meeting of NSZZPNTiO on September 4, Zbigniew Bujak, the leading worker activist from the Ursus plant just outside of Warsaw, and several other worker activists from the Ursus, Huta Warszawa and TEWA plants, appeared to invite the intelligentsia to join in the regional Mazowsze union they were trying to organize. At this time, the intellectuals preferred to establish their own union that would represent their own special interests and social identity (Krzemiński, 1983: 347–48). Krzemiński (1983: 395–96) argues that they resisted this association for fear of the "tyranny of the majority": that if their union was merged into the workers' union, their special interests could not be represented and would be subordinated to the workers' demands. They were nevertheless supportive of the workers' union, recognizing that their own self-organization was the fruit of the workers' self-organization in Gdańsk. This position was retained through the first NSZZPNTiO congress on September 11. At its second congress on October 15, however, this question of the NSZZPNTiO's relationship to Solidarity became the central issue for debate. By this time, the government had begun to organize its new branch unions, which it called "autonomous." This put NSZZPNTiO in a difficult position. Because of the array of different organizations, it was difficult to establish which union was on whose side. If the intellectuals' union was to remain separate, this would lend legitimacy to the government's "autonomous unions." For strategic reasons, the members of NSZZPNTiO decided to dissolve their union into national Solidarity (Krzemiński, 1983: 412–31).

As this example of the Warsaw intelligentsia suggests, divergent occupational interests led some parts of the intelligentsia to form their own unions. But the nature of the conflict moved them to merge into the larger workers' organization. The conflict also worked against the formation of a very decentralized independent union movement.

While the agreement provided for the formation of independent trade unions on the coast, other regions had to fight their own local authorities for the right to form their own unions. Within a couple of weeks, most of the regions had formed their own committees with local demands and a demand to be included in the twenty-one point Gdańsk agreement. The relationship between these various regions was not clear from the outset, however. Most of those on the periphery wanted to be part of a national organization, thereby strengthening their position in the face of the local authorities. The Gdańsk presidium, with Wałęsa at its helm, preferred a more decentralized structure. Wałęsa was skeptical that another centralized union could resist being coopted and moved away from local interests. Indeed, he argued, if they wanted a centralized union, he could have accepted the offer to become head of the old centralized union apparatus (Wałęsa, 1987: 154).

Despite this initial controversy, Wałęsa and other Gdańsk leaders drafted a document for registering a nationwide union. By September 17, a single union based on one set of statutes was founded, although its executive body remained relatively weak (Holzer, 1984: 112–14; Laba, forthcoming; Wałęsa, 1987: 152–58).[3] This move toward centralization was especially important for those struggling to form independent unions on the periphery (Błasiak, 1987), although relatively unimportant for core regions, at least in the short term.

This move to make a more centralized national union was thus motivated by the interpretation by activists of the structure of the conflict. Because the authorities were themselves nationally organized, self-defense mandated national self-organization. Unlike the authorities, however, Solidarity did not form a firm executive branch given the dangers of cooption that represented. Solidarity did not, therefore, "mirror" the structure of their opponents. Instead, they analyzed that structure and formed an opposition which they believed could provide for the greatest defense of an independent union. This is especially clear in the case of the *form* of self-organization. In particular, should it be territorially or functionally organized?

The structure of negotiations encouraged opposition activists to adopt an organization that would be based, as the old official unions, on economic sector. Demands over resources and working conditions were formally decided by various ministries, as the Ministry of Light Industry, Construction and so on. The authorities preferred such an organization. A corporatist breakdown is more effective for the reproduction of power relations than a class or territorial identity for the independent union movement. The greater the fragmentation, and the more this fragmentation is inconsistent with spatial proximity, the greater the ability for the authorities to coopt the movement with its own people or lure self-organized movements into cooperation with the authorities for the privilege the authorities could delegate. The authorities could have reproduced the model of "semi-feudalism" Gierek employed in the 1970s with self-organized smaller groups, achieving a kind of "Mexican" corporatism (Duran-Arenas and Kennedy, forthcoming).

In the first weeks of self-organization, workers in different regions often negotiated by branch over wages. The authorities tried to break the self-organization movement by acceding to the old unions and refusing to deal in good faith with independent union activists (see chapter 9 for health-care workers in this regard). This recalcitrance by the authorities finally led the nationwide Solidarity group to declare a one-hour warning strike on October 3 to protest at the authorities' failure to live up to the Gdańsk accords. The strike was a considerable success, demonstrating the potential power, through solidarity, of a new nationwide union (Holzer, 1984: 117–20; Staniszkis, 1984a: 64–68). It also demonstrated the need for self-organization which transcended enterprise, branch or occupational identification.

In its recalcitrance, the authorities contributed to the national organization of Solidarity. Had the authorities been able to cooperate with new independent unions and encourage a narrower form of self-organization based on occupational, functional and regional differentiation, an organization like Solidarity would have become far less likely. But the authorities were either unwilling, or unable to adopt a new systemic identity. Had there been a different, more innovative regime in the USSR, another alternative road to self-organization might have been taken in Poland. Instead, the authorities insisted on the formulaic "leading role of the party" and the sanctity of Poland's "international alliances." This was so significant that the authorities, without authorization, inserted these into the text of Solidarity's registration agreement on October 24. This act ignited new calls among the union rank and file for a nationwide general strike.

Finally, after negotiations between the authorities and the union's National Coordinating Committee, and after Party Leader Kania and Prime Minister Pińkowski visited Moscow, the authorities compromised. The Supreme Court invalidated the judge's modifications and settled for a statement on party leadership in an annex to the union statutes. From the start, therefore, the authorities sought to reduce the significance of these new independent organizations. Ironically, the very deep structure of "substantive rationality" which made self-organization so threatening also moved the authorities to adopt a strategy that unintentionally generated a self-organized movement more independent and more solidary than it might have been otherwise.

With Solidarity firmly organized and its old unions a failure, the authorities had to adopt new strategies to counter Solidarity. The authorities tried to "ignore" the union by making important decisions without consulting it on relevant matters (as in the case of cutting back "free Saturdays" in January 1981). It also introduced new "autonomous" unions as an alternative to the old discredited unions and Solidarity. This strategy can be illustrated best in the case of health care (chapter 9). The most significant resource on the side of the authorities in this struggle was the threat of coercion, however. But it had to be applied in a new way, given the new structure of power relations.

There are two principal forms of coercion in postwar Poland that are the basis for systemic reproduction: direct personal coercion and the threat of invasion. Personal coercion was not useful for reproducing the power of the authorities during the 500 days of Solidarity's legal tenure. Even between 1976 and 1980, when there were no large independent organizations to defend the harassed, KOR and other groups made the politically motivated prosecution of worker activists difficult. The authorities consequently knew that direct unjustified attacks by the militia would provoke strong protests by the movement. Solidarity, too, gave the authorities few justifications for any attack. Hence, the authorities, or parts thereof, were forced to find or create reasons that would justify repression of the union's leaders or the entire union itself. The "Naroźniak affair" is one example of this.[4]

On November 20, Warsaw regional police conducted a raid on the union's Mazowsze branch office and found a confidential government document called "On the Present Methods of Prosecution of Illegal Anti-Socialist Activity." The police arrested a young union activist, Jan Naroźniak, and a clerk in the prosecutor's office, Piotr Sapielo, who supposedly passed the document to Naroźniak. The prosecutor charged Naroźniak with disseminating state secrets, which, if he was convicted, would earn him a five-year sentence.

The Mazowsze union was incensed, and demanded the release of the two. Leaflets were distributed on which was written "Today Naroźniak, tomorrow Wałęsa, the day after tomorrow – you" (Ash, 1983: 91). The union saw this as the first direct attack by the secret police against its membership. If Naroźniak and Sapielo were not released, the union threatened a regionwide strike. They were not released and several workplaces, including the Ursus tractor plant, went on strike on November 24, resolving not to return until Naroźniak was freed. The regional leader, Zbigniew Bujak, held a news conference the same day, and presented the authorities with five more demands, including a demand for an investigation into the methods of the Polish secret police. On November 26, the region's union delegates voted to call a general strike alert. By this time, Huta Warszawa also went on strike.

Raina (1985: 20–21) argues that Bujak was overstepping the bounds of his leadership of a *trade union*, by becoming expressly political. He accounts for this move by noting that the confidential document indicted several of Bujak's advisors, and this was his way of repaying them also showing his capacity for leadership. Whatever personal motivations, this political escalation would become increasingly likely over time, given the authorities' strategies to undermine the union, and the association of the secret police with the structure of domination that Solidarity sought to overturn.

The fundamental power resource enabling the reproduction of Soviet-type society in Poland is coercion and violence. Although the Soviet Army was the initial symbol of this domination, the riot police (zomo) and secret police have come to replace them. Their obvious privilege reinforces the resentment Poles have for this reminder of the basis of their order. Thus, in addition to calling for legal restraints against police attempts at intimidation, Solidarity activists sought to force the militia to relinquish many of the privileges they previously enjoyed.

Not surprisingly, the police were eager for revenge. Starski (1982: 96) believes that the party leadership sought to restrain the secret police from taking matters into their own hands. Certainly, the "moderates" in the party, those who allowed the formation of the union in the first place, were restraining them in order to avoid violent confrontation. They were only partially successful. A few things could have been attributed to the police:

a tear gas canister had been hurled into a Warsaw shop where the assistants wore Solidarity armbands; delegates to the "Rural Solidarity" National Congress which was due to begin in Poznan the next day (March 8) had been "warned off" by plainclothes men; in Nowy Sacz a local Solidarity chairman had been found dead – hanged – in mysterious circumstances; . . . an "unknown assailant" attacked one of the senior members of KOR. (Ash, 1983: 148–49)

But in contrast to what the militia would have liked to do, these were probably relatively minor. Moderates probably recognized that selective repression would not intimidate the union, but provoke confrontation. While the moderates in the party recognized the danger of police attacks against union members, the secret police themselves were hard to control. In Bydgoszcz in March, they finally let loose.

On March 19, supporters of Rural Solidarity were to have a chance to present their arguments at a session of the Provincial Council, at the end of the session during "questions and opinions." The chairman of the council presidium broke off the meeting abruptly, without hearing the protesters. The union supporters, along with about forty-five of the local councillors, refused to leave the hall and both groups stayed on to work out a joint communiqué. Then provincial officials reappeared five hours later, requesting that the remaining councillors join them in another room for private discussions. About forty of the councillors left, and an official then appeared requesting that the remaining people leave. After the peasant delegation refused, about 200 police forced out the approximately thirty-five union supporters, making them run a "gauntlet" as they exited. The demonstrators were forced to run between two lines of police, who beat them as they ran. Twenty-seven people were injured, and three had to go to hospital, including Jan Rulewski, an outspoken member of Solidarity's national commission. Rulewski seemed to have been a special target, since one of the police cried out in the scuffle, "Get Rulewski" (Ash, 1983: 152; Persky, 1982: 200–3). These events were replayed on the Polish television news.

Solidarity and the authorities seemed to be on the verge of war. Posters were put up throughout Poland, depicting the three injured men and *Provokacja* (provocation) written below. The population responded with demonstrations and strikes. The union's position was that this was a deliberate provocation by those hardliners who sought to unseat Jaruzelski, then prime minister. Whoever instigated this attack, it was certainly not the action of a united leadership, much less a united apparatus. The uniformed police filmed the beating, but were not participants. In fact, one of them "wept publicly because of his impotence to prevent it" (Starski, 1982: 119).

There is also good reason to believe that these actions were instigated against Kania and other moderates by Stefan Olszowski and his supporters in a bid to usurp the moderates' power (Staniszkis, 1984a: 82–83, 203). Kania was away in Budapest, Jaruzelski was busy with Warsaw Pact maneuvers on Polish soil, and Rakowski was receiving the West German foreign minister when the beatings took place. The incident also took place in Stefan Olszowski's parliamentary constituency (Ash, 1983: 152). Subsequently, Olszowski and his allies sought to declare a state of emergency, which certainly would have led to Kania being ousted. The remarks of the liberal journalist and party member, Stefan Bratkowski, in reference to this incident are perhaps the most convincing: "Our hardliners stand for no programme except the concept of confrontation and disinformation . . . Today they are trying to involve the whole Party leadership in a clash with the entire society. With incalculable consequences, they are trying to provoke society to behavior justifying the use of force " (Ash, 1983: 154–55).

Solidarity's national commission deliberated when, not if, to call a nationwide general strike in response to the attack. After debate, a four-hour warning strike was to be called on March 27, and if no resolution was reached by the end of March 31, a full-fledged general strike. In addition to the demands of punishing those responsible for the attack, other demands, including the registration of Rural Solidarity, were made. The warning strike went as planned, and the union was well prepared, and even intent on carrying out the second strike.

Party members even on the Central Committee protested the attack. Kania used this to his advantage, and, employing a labelling process similar to that which took place in the 1956 transformation, blamed the attack on party "hardliners," like Olszowski. His labelling was so successful that Olszowski and his allies were convinced to resign the Politburo, even though their motion to declare martial law had earlier carried that same body. Finally, on March 30 negotiations between Wałęsa and Rakowski produced an agreement and the general strike was averted (Ascherson, 1982: 265; Ash, 1983: 155–57; Raina, 1985: 81–104; Staniszkis, 1984a: 203–4).

During this period, police attacks on union members had a different meaning. Before Solidarity, the attacks were meant as intimidation. Now, they were only a provocation to the movement to confront the authorities. Hence, it seems unlikely that anything less than a *complete* repression of the union, such as occurred on December 13, 1981, would not be designed to limit the union's significance. Rather, these occasional attacks were probably prompted by some faction within the authorities who would try to use the confrontation between society and authorities to spark a change in leadership. This change could have been accomplished in an internal coup d'etat, or perhaps with a little help from their military allies.

The secret police and hardliners within the party might have welcomed an invasion. It seems that several times an invitation was extended. If a general strike had taken place in Bydgoszcz, it would have broken the rail connection between East Germany and the USSR, at a time when Warsaw Pact forces were conducting maneuvers in Poland. In June, Starski (1982: 124) notes that secret police were defacing monuments to Soviet aid in World War II, in order to make it seem that the union was losing control over its "anti-socialist" elements, and thereby to necessitate Soviet invasion.

Although the Soviets never invaded, these "invitations" to the Soviet Union had a latent effect of making the population more cautious, and more worried about the real thing (Starski, 1982: 124). As time went on, hints about neighborly aid in the preservation of socialism intensified, and people grew more aware of the possibility of foreign invasion. Data from surveys conducted in 1980 and 1981 suggest this. In 1980, 47.6 percent of the population felt that the current socio-political and economic situation of the country endangered Poland's independence, and in 1981, 52.2 percent (11.3 percent in 1980 and 17.4 percent in 1981 said it was difficult to say) (Jasiewicz, 1982: 129). These responses did not reflect a fear of the West, but rather of the USSR or Warsaw Pact.[5] Of course, the intimidation of potential Soviet invasion is what kept Solidarity from going further than it did; as Jacek Kuroń (1981) said, they did not want to lure the wolves from the woods.

Coercion and its threat thus had mixed results. Random police beatings no longer served this function, and were rather used to strengthen the hand of one faction within the authorities against another. But references to the possibility of Soviet invasion limited the significance of the union's independence. Poland's geo-political realities prevented the independent union from becoming a full-fledged revolutionary movement. This "self-limitation" was a consequence of strategic decisions made by movement participants themselves. They were obliged to figure out the maximum transformation that could be made given the structural constraints of the geo-political situation. If they could not overturn the existing order, they might transform it from within by encouraging self-organization in other spheres. The existence of an independent industrial union that could protect other less powerful groups was essential. Other organizations were formed and existing ones acquired a new independence from the authorities.

Independent professional advice on matters of social policy was not common in Poland before Solidarity. The boldest initiative, *Doświadczenie i Przyszłość* (DiP or Experience and the Future), was prevented by the authorities from even holding public forums on social policy in 1979. By 1981, under Solidarity's protection, not only were open debates held on such matters, but official professional bodies openly dissented from government policy. The Polish Economic Association, for instance, supported an alternative economic reform package from what the authorities offered (Staniszkis, 1984a: 213). The United Peasants' Party, the Democratic Party and the pro-regime Catholic group, Pax, undertook internal democratic reforms and took more and more independent stands from the PZPR. Even the Sejm began to act increasingly like a Western parliament. It debated the proposals sent to it by the party and split votes on proposals. Members of the party rank and file also tried to organize themselves into horizontal structures to try to reform the PZPR itself.

Various groups also founded new autonomous organizations outside of Solidarity. In January and February 1981, there was a national student strike centered mainly in Łódź seeking (1) the creation of an independent student union (*Niezalezńe Zrzeszenie Studentów*), which held its first national congress in Kraków in April; (2) the elimination of the obligatory courses in Russian, Marxist–Leninist ideology and military training; and (3) a more autonomous and internally democratic university structure (see Lutyński, 1982; Persky, 1982: 177–80; Wejnert, 1988).

Peasants had previously been "represented" by the *Związane Stronnictwo Ludowe* (ZSL = United Peasants' Party) and by small agricultural circles. But neither the ZSL nor the circles were truly autonomous. As early as September 1980, peasants began to press for the legal registration of their own unions including *Solidarność Rolników Indiwidualnych* (Solidarity of Individual Farmers), *Solidarność Wiejska* (Rural Solidarity) and *Solidarność Chłopska* (Peasant Solidarity) (Ash, 1983: 111; Halamska, 1988; Starski, 1982: 112). By October they had about 1.2 million members out of 3.2 million private farms (Staniszkis, 1984a: 97). The authorities argued that most of the peasants did not need unions, since they were self-employed and did not have to defend themselves against any boss. Eventually, after the Bydgoszcz crisis and support by the Church and Solidarity, peasants registered their united union in May (Ash, 1983: 110–34).

The opportunity for self-organization occasioned by the independent trade union, Solidarity, was taken by virtually all social groups. This kind of transformation was in the interest of all groups in civil society, given that it allowed them (1) to establish a more autonomous identity, (2) to articulate group needs and (3) to negotiate on that basis. There was a differentiated response to this opportunity, however.

The authorities resisted the establishment of truly autonomous organizations, as we have seen above (pages 87–97). To the degree that social groups remained dependent on the authorities in this embryonic civil society, they were reluctant to join the new union. Instead, they would join the "new" branch unions which officially broke with the Central Council of Trade Unions, under whose control they previously existed. These old unions turned new were supposed to be "independent" of both Solidarity and the government, but their independence from the government is suspect, since they faced no difficulty in securing legal registration (Starski, 1982: 113).

The majority of virtually all eligible socio-occupational groups joined Solidarity (table 3.1). The differentiation we see is derived from the degree of dependence various occupational groups have on the authorities (chapter 6). Those whose careers are more dependent on the authorities were more likely to join branch unions and less likely to join Solidarity. Although this thesis of dependency will frame my argument on engineers and doctors in chapters 8 and 9, it is applicable to other groups as well. I have not carried out extensive research on teachers, but they seem to be a particularly good example in this regard.

Teachers joined Solidarity in lower proportions than any other widely eligible group. They were not very likely to join the branch unions, but they did join their old "autonomous" union, *Związek Nauczyczelstwa Polskiego* (ZNP) as often as they joined Solidarity. There are several possible reasons. Distance of Solidarity from the concerns of teachers clearly is not an explanation, given that a restoration of authentic Polish literature and history was a major theme in the movement's self-identification. Teachers' socio-economic standing, too, is not a good account. Although they are not so well situated on the second economy as physicians and others (Fiszman, 1972:95), neither are nurses or other highly feminized occupations who also joined in considerable numbers. The characteristics of the old union

Table 3.1. *Selected occupations and union membership (in percentages)*

Occupation	Solidarity	Branch Union	Other	None	Number
Skilled worker, heavy industry	86.7	3.3	–	10.0	60
Skilled worker, light industry	74.1	10.2	1.9	13.9	108
Foremen	73.5	14.2	2.0	10.2	49
Technicians	71.1	15.5	–	13.3	45
Skilled and semi-skilled workers	69.0	15.0	1.0	15.0	100
Doctors and others with higher education (other than engineers and economists)	68.2	4.5	4.5	22.7	22
Middle-level personnel	66.7	16.7	7.1	9.5	42
Physical–mental workers	62.3	12.3	6.6	18.9	106
Nurses, nursery-school teachers, etc.	62.3	18.9	7.5	11.3	53
Unskilled and agricultural workers	55.4	14.9	5.9	23.8	101
Peasant-workers and the like	53.3	11.1	3.3	32.2	90
Bureaucrats and administrators	51.7	22.4	6.7	19.1	89
Higher cadre, specialists and engineers	51.7	31.0	1.7	15.5	58
Teachers	47.5	2.5	45.0	5.0	40

Source: adapted from W. Adamski (1982: 183–84).

might be relevant, however, given that the ZNP is a direct descendant of a pre-war association with reasonable prestige. But probably the most significant factor is the rather isolated and highly politicized nature of work facing schoolteachers. Appointments and work performance are more closely scrutinized with political criteria than in other kinds of jobs. Not surprisingly, therefore, party membership is relatively higher among teachers than among other non-managerial intelligentsia occupations. Teachers are more "dependent" on the authorities than are workers and more than other occupations like engineers and physicians.

Independence from the authorities depends on the possession of power resources that are not "delegated" by the authorities. Teachers have power in the classroom because they are appointed by political authorities, but they remain dependent on these authorities because they can be replaced with others. Managers in enterprises have power in factories because they are similarly appointed, but they are relatively more independent than teachers, given the greater demands of their work and the greater difficulty in replacing them. Physicians are relatively more independent than either of the previous two groups because, while their license to practice is granted by the authorities, physicians are much more difficult to replace. They nevertheless remain obliged to the authorities for their facilities, and thus remain, collectively, dependent on the authorities. Although I elaborate this theory of dependency in chapter 6, I introduce it at this point in order to emphasize workers' self-organization as the principal autonomous power resource which enabled Solidarity.

Workers' self-organization is more significant than any other group's independence because workers, especially skilled workers in large factories, are scarce relative to the demand for their services. There are not many workers waiting to replace them. Workers' occupational strikes also can halt production and reduce the material resources at the disposal of the authorities, thereby undermining, fairly quickly, the power of the authorities. The threat of a strike can do much the same thing. But in a crisis-ridden economy, as Solidarity's was, the strike became less and less useful for Solidarity. The strike was perceived as not only a source for pressuring the authorities, but by some as contributing to the overall economic crisis that was undermining Solidarity. By October 1981, a significant proportion of Poles believed that strikes should end. At the same time, a hard core of rank-and-file activists pressed for more strike pressure (Ash, 1983:251). Thus, by October, the strike became a less useful weapon in so far as it began to undermine national solidarity.

One innovative strategy for coping with this problem was to transform the nature of the strike. On October 23, 1981, Solidarity adopted an innovation produced earlier by Łódź workers: the "active strike" (*strajk czynny*). This strike form could have enabled Solidarity to retain its principal power resource against the authorities, while refraining from magnifying the economic crisis and undermining national solidarity. In this strike, workers continue to produce but then distribute the fruits of their labors independently of the state. Hence, an alternative economy would be formed. Its promoters, most notably Zbigniew Kowalewski of Łódź, believed that this form of struggle was the most radical kind of self-organization, because it would also be a form of self-management. It would also be the basis for a genuine revolution, where workers, under the protection of workers' guards, would take control of production and distribution away from the bureaucracy and replace it with a form of local self-government based on workers' councils. If this localization of

control proved insufficient, the promoters of the active strike anticipated the formation of a self-management chamber within the Sejm
(Kowalewski, 1982).

The active strike was an important extension of workers' self-
organization, but promised neither strategic nor systemic solutions.
On a practical level, the active strike was not pursued in many
circumstances (Ash, 1983: 255), nor did the national leadership of
Solidarity enthusiastically support the strategy. A general active strike
was planned for Łódź on December 21, however, and Kowalewski
(1982: 236) believes that his region's success in the effort could have
brought other provinces into the revolutionary struggle. I believe that
Kowalewski is right to argue that a regionwide active strike in Łódź
would have brought other provinces into the struggle. The authorities
would have used force to break the Łódź strike, and national sympa-
thy as it was, other regions would have moved in solidarity. The active
strike was, as Kowalewski acknowledges, a *revolutionary* strategy. It
effectively abandoned Solidarity's self-limitation, and with the
promise of Soviet invasion, would have ended the prospects of
peaceful transition.

It also offered no clear alternative for organizing production and
distribution. Kowalewski (1982: 234) cites the reaction of experts to his
strategy: "Seizure of economic power during the active strike, and
hence the establishment of rule by workers' councils, may lead to the
replacement of the central bureaucracy by another bureaucracy, and of
one authoritarian system of allocation and decision making by
another." Kowalewski defends his strategy with reference to the
capacity of workers to organize an alternative economy on its basis.
But I know of no scheme worked out by workers or anyone else that
takes these objections seriously. There is no question that direct
workers' control was popular among many workers. It is another
question as to whether it offered a genuine institutional transformation of Poland's first economy. I believe that the active strike can
be seen only as an extension of workers' self-organization which, I
argue in the next section, is inadequate to the task of *systemic*
transformation.

In effect, a *social* transformation of Soviet-type society was achieved
in Poland between August 1980 and May 1981. Although the deep
structure of "substantive rationality" continued to organize every
group's actions, its former manifestation, organizational hegemony,
had been eliminated. It was eliminated on the basis of the self-
organization of skilled workers in large factories, for they provided the

"threat" – the occupational general strike and later the active strike – which forced the authorities to tolerate this explosion of pluralism. Not all actors were equally able to organize themselves, given variations in dependency on the authorities. Nevertheless a civil society, in which pluralism, publicity and legality reigned over the state rather than the state over them, seemed to be on the verge of restoration.

Pluralism had been established and, with the resources these independent groups had at their disposal, "publicity" was also being realized. Each organization had its own publications, and this put more pressure on the official press to be more responsible in its own public statements. "Legality" was not, however, a condition that could be established on the basis of initiative from below alone. It required a negotiated compromise with the authorities, whose state apparatus had to be the vehicle of legislation. All actors in this uncertain birth of civil society knew that pluralism and limited publicity were no guarantees that legality could be established, given that the problems which generated the movement, the economic crisis and substantive rationality, were still the fundamental features shaping action.

Self-organization to self-management

Independent trade unions and other autonomous organizations can be significant in a purely defensive capacity. Like Western trade unions, they could remain concerned with defending the rights of their constituency against the authorities. Lenin ultimately argued that workers need their own organizations in order to protect themselves from the state and that "strike struggles" could be legitimate weapons (Bettelheim, 1976: 391–92). But Polish autonomous organizations in these 500 days were forced by the structure of conflict to consider more active measures.

Corrupt elites have always earned the ire of workers and peasants, and their dismissal has been at the center of protests and strikes in 1970–71, 1976 and 1980–81 (Ascherson, 1982: 177; Ash, 1983: 125, 141). Society thus attacked government corruption, just as it had in times past. But these movements also had to seek control of their own affairs, given the principles of civil society and the structure of the authorities.

Self-management is one form of "legality" upon which a socialist civil society might depend. Self-management ideally limits the intrusive rights of the party's substantive rationality. Internal democratization of various institutions could provide the self-regulating control and procedural justice that offset the arbitrariness and irrationality associated with past party practices.

Students not only sought to create an independent students' union, but from the start they struck for self-management for the university.[6] University autonomy has been at the center of student demands at least since the 1968 protests. This drive for self-management is a logical step, because student demands center on the determination of their curricula. Since most of their demands in some way oppose political interference in education, by getting the party out of university affairs, the need for constant conflict with the party is eliminated. Because the students are not as powerful as workers in large factories (occupation strikes of universities are much less threatening than similar strikes in productive factories), a single victory at a time of support from the workers would be all the more valuable. Repeated confrontations with the party would probably mean losses for the students. The "legalization" of self-management is therefore essential for the preservation of the normative foundations of civil society. This also extends to workers and the self-management of the productive enterprise.

In Western societies, the existence of independent trade unions *per se* is not antagonistic to the principle of private ownership of the means of production. Unions can be coopted into the status quo by bargaining away their potential radicalism for higher wages and benefits. But the independent unions in Soviet-type societies are radical by their very existence, since they subvert the party's claim to substantive rationality. They have nothing to trade off with the authorities but their very independence. And in a crisis economy, as Poland faces, the party has nothing to offer workers in exchange for cooptation. Hence, authorities and independent organizations are forced into a struggle over the management of the organization's milieu. The milieu of Solidarity was the economy itself.

The union's strength depended on the active support of its members, either in strikes or in the threat to strike. As the economy deteriorated, people became more tired, wanted a restoration of order, and placed more blame on Solidarity. Some union activists even believed that the government was intentionally "starving" the people (Michnik, 1985: 125). An indication of this dissatisfaction and its danger for the union can be seen in a comparison of two surveys conducted in 1980 and 1981: in 1980, a random sample of the Polish population was asked about who was responsible for delays in the realization of the Gdańsk agreement; in 1981, another sample was asked about who was responsible for the deepening of the economic and political crisis.

Although the questions from each year are different, the data suggest the population began to feel more negatively toward Solidarity. In 1980, the government was held responsible by itself by 61.5 percent of the respondents; in 1981, only 39.7 percent thought so (Mokrzyszewski, 1982: 111). Data from these same surveys also show that the proportion of people who strongly supported the union declined from 57.9 percent of the population in 1980, to 33.2 percent in 1981, the proportion of those who did not support the union rose from 4.5 percent in 1980 to 13.9 percent in 1981, and the proportion of undecided rose from 5.6 percent in 1980 to 15.2 percent in 1981 (Mokrzyszewski, 1982: 117).

The union had two choices to offset this decline: it could try to divorce itself from responsibility for the economic crisis, which would have been almost impossible, given government propaganda; or it could try to turn the crisis around, which may have been unlikely, but was the only way out. This was a major change from the initial strategy of avoiding responsibility for matters over which workers could have little control. Even at the time, "self-management" was perceived by some workers as something that would divert the workers from their primary task of organizing independent trade unions (Norr, 1985). This move toward institutional transformation among sectors of Solidarity demonstrated the range of choices facing Solidarity, and potential differences in interest.

Among some skilled workers but especially young engineers and technicians, self-management was attractive as it offered a means to introduce a more "rational," and less "political," form of economic production (Kennedy and Sadkowski, 1990). In April 1981, activists from seventeen enterprises formed the Network of Enterprise Organizations of the Independent Self-Governing Trade Union Solidarity (*Sięć Organizacji Zakładowych NSZZ "Solidarność"* = *Sięć*). By the time their proposal for "social enterprises" was put forward, more than fifty enterprises belonged to the "network." In this plan, they sought a way to reconstruct the failing economy's functioning that was combined with the organization of workers' councils. Activists recognized that if the workers' movement was to remain energized at the rank-and-file level, and if it was not to be defeated by the ruined economy, independent organizations would have to take a more active role in production and the administration of the economy. This movement was to some degree independent of the activists in the union, and occasionally they were even at odds (Norr, 1985; Staniszkis, 1984a: 26). The network nevertheless produced a plan in June 1981 that Solidarity later endorsed.

In this "social enterprise" scheme, the enterprise was to be run by democratically elected workers' councils, which would be responsible for appointing the factory manager and negotiating with trade unions. The state would exert control over the enterprise through various economic instruments like taxes, custom duties and credits, but not through direct political control. This was aimed at reducing the influence of central administrative planning on the economy, since the network activists believed that planning was "the main source of this country's economic crisis." This self-management scheme was intended to be "an instrument of economic rebirth" and was to use workers' initiative to "overcome the economic depression" (Persky and Flam, 1982: 179). This diverged from arguments advanced by Marxists like MacDonald (1983), for Sięć argued that central planning was the instrument by which authorities ultimately dominate society.

The authorities in turn attacked the network. They opposed its ideas, likening them to Yugoslav and Czech (Ota Sik) "revisionism," the Soviet "workers' opposition from the 1920s," "anarchy" and "contemporary bourgeois theories of reinvigorating socialism" (Norr, 1985: 105). They denounced this plan, replacing it with one of their own. The government's plan used similar slogans as the social enterprise scheme. Both supported the "three Ss," samorządność (self-management), samodzielność (independence or self-resourcefulness) and samofinansowanie (self-financing).[7] While they used the same words, the two plans differed dramatically. The government plan not only limited the significance of workers' councils, but it also narrowed enterprise autonomy. The authorities' plan rejected the network's radicalism on central planning; the former retained some vaguely defined administrative measures, including the right for the authorities to make managerial appointments. The network's plan, on the contrary, made the manager subject to enterprise-council election alone. They also envisioned different types of property ownership: the authorities sought to retain state ownership, while the network advocated a form of limited employee ownership, where workers are entrusted by society to use its property. Finally, the network envisioned self-management to incorporate enterprise autonomy and workers' democracy, while the authorities wanted to legislate different aspects of the reform in separate acts (Morawski, 1987: 89–94).

These divergent plans reflected the struggle over the context of action. The authorities' power resources were based in part on their control over the economy through central planning and *nomenklatura* (chapter 6). The network plan attacked both. According to one Solidarity document (see also Touraine *et al.*, 1983: 94): "The system which ties political to economic power, based on continual party interference in the functioning of enterprises, is the main reason for the present crisis of the Polish economy. The so-called *nomenklatura* principle rules out any rational cadre promotion policy, rendering millions of workers who do not belong to any party second class citizens" (Persky and Flam, 1982: 214).

The final legislation to which the Solidarity presidium and the authorities agreed was a compromise between these strategies. It particularly disappointed and discouraged network activists for its effective abandonment of control over managerial appointments with the authorities (Norr, 1985: 99). The manager is appointed by the authorities if it is an enterprise of "central importance to the national economy" and if it is a public utility (Morawski, 1987: 95). This meant that 1,500 of the largest enterprises would have their directors appointed by the authorities, in places where self-management was strongest (Kowalewski, 1982: 232).

Although this was less than what the activists sought, it did represent the institutionalization of some change. The very compromise was achieved in part because non-communist members of the Sejm demanded this compromise legislation (Ash, 1983: 213–14). Before martial law, about 50 percent of enterprises had introduced some of these self-management elements. But this was temporary, since it depended on the tactical alliance of workers and management. With martial law and the transformation of power relations, few enterprises remained interested in self-management (Morawski, 1987: 108). But even without martial law and the compromised legislation, Norr (1985: 98) doubts that the radical introduction of self-management could have turned around the economic crisis which proved Solidarity's undoing. This self-management compromise also turned out to be unsatisfactory to the first national congress of Solidarity. In the first stage of this congress (September 5–10), Solidarity resolved that it would conduct a referendum on the appropriate scope of self-management if the Sejm refused to do so before it initiated legislation. After the legislation was issued on September 25, the second meeting of Solidarity's congress (held between September 26 and October 7) denounced the two bills and made plans to hold a referendum on them. They also criticized the Solidarity presidium for consenting to the legislation, charging that experts had "excessive influence" (Raina, 1985: 392–419). This debate began to reveal the internal contradictions of "self-management."

Self-management was argued by its proponents to be in the interests of "society." Solidarity too accepted this argument by and large. The party also argued self-management to be in its interests, but clearly there was considerable disagreement over what "self-management" means among these sides in the conflict. The party would not relinquish control over the economy, even in self-management, while the network used self-management to eliminate that power base of the authorities. But there was disagreement over self-management in Solidarity, too (Norr, 1985). Although subsidiary to the larger conflict between authorities and society, the potential conflicts between self-management as economic rationality and as workers' democracy cannot be overlooked. Only after pressure by the Touraine research team did the Gdańsk discussion group recognize the potential for conflict between workers in unions and workers in management (Touraine *et al.*, 1983: 110); those in Silesia resisted the idea that workers would ever strike against self-management *workers'* councils, although they would distrust engineers and experts if they were in charge (Touraine *et al.*, 1983: 120–22). In the end, self-management and opposition to *nomenklatura* in the enterprise was not so important to these groups as it was in Warsaw (Touraine *et al.*, 1983: 110). In Warsaw, the professional aim of self-management became most apparent: as a vehicle for restoring "rational economic criteria" to enterprise decisions (Touraine *et al.*, 1983: 131). In addition, they saw this self-managing transformation of the enterprise as a means for limiting the power of the party and liberating society from autocratic rule (Touraine *et al.*, 1983: 132). But what would *negotiations* between union representatives and self-management representatives look like, when these representatives are elected by the same workers (Norr, 1985: 101)? Here one of the principal difficulties facing a "socialist civil society" appears.

These fragmentary data suggest that professionals were more likely than workers to discuss self-management, and even more likely to be interested in it. They were more likely to advocate an "expert" type of self-management, while workers, if they were interested, were more likely to see it as a means of democratizing their workplace. Self-management was in one sense a "logical" extension of the self-organizing effort given that it sought to create another institution in civil society. It contributed in particular to the pluralism and legality that distinguish civil society from the dominant structure of Soviet-type society. But beyond this "freeing" of production from the state, it is difficult to decide what self-management entails. In particular, until "pluralism" is reintroduced as divergent and potentially antagonistic interests *within* civil society, negotiation fails to acquire much meaning, or at least necessitates the generation of a new meaning. It requires that economic interests of differently situated actors be acknowledged, and institutional means for negotiated compromise be provided. This is a major step away from the societal solidarism represented by Solidarity. Indeed, the different visions of self-management suggested some of the changes that might be essential.

Although the network was the leading group promoting self-management, on October 17 another self-management alliance established the founding committee of the National Federation of Self-Management Bodies (*Komitet Założycielski – Krajowa Federacja Samorządowców* = KZ–KFS). Kowalewski (1982: 231) finds the network oriented toward parliamentary democracy and self-management within a "technical" framework. The federation based its efforts more on workers' councils and the active strike. The class base of the network was professionals and technicians, while the federation was based more on workers. But this break in the vision of self-management is as one would expect in the constitution of a socialist civil society. Self-management offers a viable strategy for systemic transformation only so long as these alternative tendencies within it recognize their mutual necessity and construct a means to negotiate their differences. This, of course, is no small feat, but is the next step in the evolution of emancipatory praxis in Soviet-type society.

Self-management, therefore, was an important step in the evolutionary logic of Solidarity, and an important part in the constitution of civil society. But it also represents dilemmas and contradictions which the movement was not well prepared to address. In particular, self-management, much like democracy, raises problems of conflict and its resolution that the solidaristic ideology of the movement was ill prepared to anticipate. The movement was more inclined to address "cultural conflicts" (between pragmatists and nationalists, for example) than it was to examine systemically derived conflicts, such as those based on classes. This is a major problem with all strategies of emancipatory praxis that base their struggle on a culturally constructed, or class-based, unity, as we shall see in the next section of the book. For now, however, I retain focus on the conflict between authorities and society.

Compromise legislation on self-management was enacted by the Sejm at the end of September. But this legislation did not signal the start of a new stage for self-management; instead, the growing crisis in the economy and the apparent failure of the party to cooperate sincerely with Solidarity led to a new, political, stage. Demands centered on new elections and referenda, new parliamentary bodies and new organizations of experts. As politics became more critical, the unity of Solidarity also began to break down, even more as "true Poles" and revolutionary unionists sought confrontation and moderates wanted to back off; as reconstructionists continued dialogue with the authorities, and populists resisted compromise. Ultimately, the push for political activity proved unstoppable. If the movement did not "evolve" with its most extreme elements, and therefore limit them, invasion would have seemed inevitable. Thus, although calls at Solidarity's national congress for free elections to parliament and for other "nations" of the Soviet Union and Eastern Europe to embark upon "the difficult road of struggle for a free trade-union movement" (Persky and Flam, 1982: 189) seem "radical," they were also the result of a strategy of self-limitation: including "radical" elements in the larger organization to control them. Although the nationalists were therefore limited, they set the tone of this period.

This political escalation of Solidarity's struggle is where my analysis of Solidarity ends, for it is here where the self-limiting movement began to lose its identity. The severity of the economic crisis and the intransigence of the authorities throughout the term made the coup d'etat of December 13, 1981, virtually unavoidable. The only alternative the party faced was to put an end to its claim to substantive rationality by accepting a genuine partnership with society. Although they took such a step in the spring of 1989, in the winter of 1981 this would have led to the Soviet invasion of Poland. Jaruzelski took the obvious road with the coup. Strangely enough, this option was not so obvious to Solidarity. Their leadership was confident that there could be no military repression of the movement.

Solidarity's strategy and praxis

The failure to prepare for a military coup is often cited as one of the major strategic failures of the Solidarity movement. I disagree. Once the military is engaged in repression, the possibilities for emancipatory social transformation fade, and "resistance," not transformation, becomes the keyword. Groups seek to preserve their identity, not move toward a restructuring of the institutions which oppress them. Also, although some hoped Jaruzelski would take the opportunity of martial law to introduce reform, he could not succeed. Social transformation relies on initiative from above and below. In martial law, Jaruzelski destroyed, temporarily, the energy of the nascent civil society. Thus, the key questions on strategy and emancipatory praxis center on how institutional transformation could have been realized in the 500 days. Timothy Garton Ash (1983: 285–304) reviews the familiar litany of "strategies" available to Solidarity. I agree with his general argument, but I reformulate and add to it so that it takes account of the various dimensions I have proposed as central to a critical sociology of Soviet-type society.

Those who argue that Solidarity was impossible from the start or that it went too far employ the same logic: that it could never survive by virtue of the union's incompatibility with the system in which it lived. Ash is right to argue this logic is entirely inadequate, for it fails to incorporate the data that Solidarity did in fact form and develop for 500 days in 1980–81. It effected a social transformation of Soviet-type society, even if it was temporary. Solidarity could not effect a lasting change, however, because the "deep structure" of the system could not be challenged. But this need not mean that Poland was doomed to martial law or invasion, for (1) the conditions reproducing the deep structure (military alliances or the character of the imperial center) could change or (2) the relationship between the "deep structure" of substantive rationality and its manifestations in organization could change. This relational change is similar to what Ash (1983: 287) means when he argues that the Polish authorities might find a negotiated compromise with Solidarity more in their self-interest than an invasion or revolution. Such a compromise depended on several things: (1) the ability of the "hardliners" in the authorities to force the "moderates" to bargain with Solidarity in order for the latter to maintain their own status; (2) the ability of Solidarity to negotiate in good faith with the authorities (here I assume party moderates negotiate only out of fear of alternatives); (3) the possibility of rendering a substantive and formal agreement; (4) the ability of the authorities to maintain agreements that they sign with the union; and (5) the tolerance of the USSR for compromise.

Available materials suggest that the USSR was willing to examine "compromises," although how much compromise it would tolerate before it would invade was unclear. Solidarity was able to negotiate "in good faith" with the authorities, although this ability declined over time. When party moderates were unable or unwilling to maintain agreements or even reach agreements with the union, the rank and file became increasingly frustrated with "pragmatism" and enamored with a fundamentalism found in nationalist populism or revolutionary unionism.

It is often assumed, however, that this break between leadership and rank and file in the union was inevitable, that the rank and file could never adopt the pragmatism of the leadership. But, as Touraine's research groups suggested, discussion of the dilemmas facing Solidarity led its discussants to ever more pragmatic positions. Thus, an even more decentralized, less bureaucratic movement than Solidarity, one with even greater "communicative rationality," might have allowed greater integration between levels, and less difficulty for the movement to retain self-limitation (for a similar argument, see Pańków, 1987: 129). As pragmatic theory would suggest, therefore, role-taking and negotiation facilitate the choice of the optimal means to realize desired ends.

The authorities, while struggling with Solidarity, also had their own internal conflicts; but these conflicts were not structured in such a way as to force one faction against another, one clear group of hardliners against another group of moderates. Instead, the very power relations constituting the authorities made alliances and consistent strategies impossible, and therefore made unlikely the ability of the authorities to fulfill agreements reliably. An alternative to this internal party ambivalence would have been a successful "horizontalist" transformation of the party in the summer of 1981. This movement sought to eliminate democratic centralism from party relations and institutionalize a radically decentralized model of party–state–society relations. Had the horizontalists succeeded, a new actor in the authorities might have appeared, rendering many assumptions about the constitution of the authorities (as in chapter 6) irrelevant. Solidarity might have been able to prevent the horizontalist defeat had it been more actively interested in party affairs. At the very least, they should have sought allies in the adversary and not treated it as such a homogeneous entity (Pańków, 1987: 129). But the virtues of this strategy are unclear too, as the CPSU pressured Polish authorities directly to assure the defeat of the horizontalists (Ash, 1983: 292). Any faction that would have allied with Solidarity might receive the same.

Finally, the contents of agreements were increasingly difficult to draw over time. No institutional framework or even "spirit" of agreement could satisfy the increasingly antagonistic interests of authorities and society by the fall of 1981. The compromise on self-management reform came too late. Society sought revolution within a framework the authorities could endorse.

These comments suggest that other conditions might have produced other outcomes. Had the USSR been more encouraging of innovation and compromise (as we see with Gorbachev) or had the economy not been in such crisis (as at the beginning of the 1970s with considerable Western aid), the possibilities for negotiation on the part of the authorities in the former case, and of both sides in the latter, would have been greater. But without economic crisis and imperial homogenization it is doubtful that such a popular movement would have emerged in the first place.

More relevant to Solidarity-style praxis is a consideration of alternative strategies, for they might have reshaped political and social conditions to allow a more lasting transformation. Had Solidarity been able to move directly for compromise legislation on self-management from the start, or had the authorities been more willing to compromise on self-organization from the start, the conditions for a negotiated settlement for this conflict between state and society might have been realized. One Solidarity analyst suggests that the "strike weapon was relied upon too frequently as the form of pressure" and that it was ineffective against those who do not own property. Simultaneously, however, worker self-management was often too inconsistent in its aims (Pańków, 1987: 129). Thus, had Solidarity been able to establish a coherent positive plan for *institutional* transformation from the start, the chances for a lasting compromise and systemic transformation may have been greater.

Clearly, however, these alternative strategies were unlikely, given that (1) the authorities had not considered altering the deep structure of their identity, (2) they had no plan for cooperating with society to override the resistance in their own planning apparatus and (3) society itself had not sufficient interest or experience to initiate an institutional reform from the start. Self-organization seemed more than enough. The immediate outcome of Poland 1980–81 suggests that it is not. For future emancipatory movements in Soviet-type society some strategy must be made for negotiated compromise with the state in order to effect an institutional transformation that makes self-organization an element of the system's functioning, not an antagonistic principle to it. This is one reason why the changes of 1989 in Poland offer so much hope.

Another argument altogether on Solidarity's choices is to argue that

Solidarity never went far enough; that it should not have reformed or transformed the system, but rather that it should have tried to eliminate it. Many "true Poles" and revolutionary Marxists agree in this common support for a cataclysmic end to the system. Most Solidarity activists would disagree, arguing that violence and blood-shed have rarely produced the claims which motivate destruction. It was this violence, after all, that initiated the system in Poland; to use violence to tear it down is likely to replace the system with something worse. Even more, to assume this option from the start is to make any peaceful negotiation impossible (Ash, 1983: 297). The outcome of a violent struggle is too difficult to predict, and too risky to begin.

Whatever the risk, revolutionary Marxist theorists and "true Poles" demanded that partial efforts could never solve the problems that moved Solidarity to action. The only basis upon which such claims could be made is to grant sacred status to the global theories informing their analysis of the Soviet-type system. But these theories deserve no such sanctity, given Solidarity's own unexpected accomplishments. The movement's pragmatic strategy, based on what were effectively socialist movement foundations, suggests that Solidarity was creating a kind of emancipatory praxis based on a socialist pragmatism.

Conclusions

To conclude this chapter on Solidarity with a discussion of strategy implies that praxis is about historical choice. Given the sociological penchant for the analysis of "structures," speculating on alternative possibilities derived from other decisions is an important contribution, even if it only provokes debate. But to imply that choice is all that matters, and that the "right strategy" is somehow out there, waiting to be discovered by a new Lenin, is sociologically irresponsi-ble. Strategy is only one part of the praxis which might transform structures.

In order to identify the praxis of which one writes, however, the understanding of strategy and choice is essential. What is Solidarity, after all? Can we understand the praxis we wish to explain by referring to its official policies, size, formal organization and demographic make-up? Certainly these are important ingredients to its identity, but they are but the shell of what defines its character. The "meaning" of Solidarity must be found in the self-understanding of its participants. Touraine *et al.* (1983) provide good reason to believe that Solidarity was a movement based on a multiple identity: a trade-union movement that also struggled to realize democracy and national self-determination. The mix of these three ingredients varied by region, occupation, gender, organizational level and local culture, but the discourse around these three points helped construct the movement's aims and form. The self-understanding of Solidarity activists should also contribute to the historical meaning of the movement. This historical meaning has been understood in ways almost divorced from this hermeneutic perspective, however. Most common is that Solidarity represents the failure of socialism and the confirmation of capitalism's systemic superiority. Capitalism's ideologues are not the only theorists to freeze Solidarity into ideological lenses, of course. Syzmanski's theoretical acrobatics to preserve the identification of the Communist Party with socialism show the dangers of treating the self-understanding of a movement's participants with disdain. Variations in dependent variables rely as much on the data one chooses to describe them as they do by their proposed explananda.

For those engaged in critical sociology, the self-understanding of a movement's participants is even more essential. The implications of the Solidarity movement for future praxis can only be grasped by a simultaneous hermeneutic and critical analysis of this self-understanding. The transformative goal of critical sociology works through the self-consciousness of potentially emancipatory actors; to deny the relevance of the self-understanding of Solidarity's actors denies a normative foundation essential to the critical project. Touraine's project is outstanding in that regard, as it not only elucidates the premises of the movement's participants, but challenges them to discuss and defend these ideas so that both participants and researchers develop better understandings of the praxis in which the movement engages. One of the most important ingredients of self-understanding is the analysis of structures which constrain and enable action. A movement's participants are the best situated to recognize some patterns, although they do not necessarily see, or will not acknowledge, all of them. Critical explanation must incorporate both recognized and hidden structures.

Praxis is in part an outcome of the intersection of a variety of structured settings. Solidarity too was an outcome of an intersection of structured settings varying in breadth, depth and time. As the cultural theorists emphasize, Solidarity was the outcome of the antagonism between a Russian/Soviet sponsored political economy and a Polish culture, an antagonism rooted in a historic rivalry to become the dominant Slavic nation, but reproduced through Comunist Party rule.

The contemporary manifestation of this historical tension is found in the contradiction between systemic and social legitimacy that shaped regime activities. This contradiction moved the authorities to allow "society" to preserve an independent identity through primary social relations and the Church. It also allowed society to construct a genealogy of struggle against the Communist system, a memory essential for Solidarity's construction. These structural features rooted in culture and foreign oppression were acknowledged by Solidarity participants, reflected in their yearning for national self-determination, demands for the democratization of the Soviet-style polity and the self-limitation of the revolution.

Solidarity was also, however, a consequence of the particular political economy organized in postwar Poland. It was in part a class struggle of workers and young intelligentsia against an incompetent, self-serving set of vassalized authorities who helped to generate a nationwide economic crisis at the end of the 1970s. This same political economy, however, created a new workforce that, especially in places like Gdańsk, developed strong primary social relations essential for the foundation of solidarity upon which the union was built. Indeed, it was this overwhelmingly working-class component which enabled the summer 1980 occupation strikes to demand independent trade unions. Those better aware of the regime's identity knew such a demand impossible; the workers' "ignorance" enabled them to succeed where the "well-informed" would fail. Ultimately, however, the different understandings of the structures in which praxis was engaged led to internal difficulties for the movement. Participants in the movement recognized the problems imposed by a self-limiting revolution, and why some would be moved to fundamentalism and others to pragmatism. Most, though not as many, participants recognized the need to institutionalize with self-management the nascent civil society that self-organization generated. Few analysts, however, discovered nascent class differences in this promised civil society.

Phrases like "civil society against the state" (Arato, 1981) capture this image of a united society against the authorities and their imperial backers. Many analysts who preferred the use of class instead argued that Solidarity created a new "class for itself": the class of state employees whose nucleus was a "new middle class" of skilled workers and professionals (Kostecki and Mreła, 1984; Kuczyński, 1983; Kurczewski, 1982; Starski, 1982). Indeed, other than the "strategic" or cultural differences implied in the conflict between pragmatists and fundamentalists, many movement participants were reluctant to acknowledge any other internal tensions shaping social action. Analysts were even more unlikely to raise any question of divergent class interests *within* the opposition, given that such a suggestion was also a strategy of those whom Solidarity combated. Szymanski (1984) was one of the few Western analysts who emphasized it.

Those who analyze Solidarity as a "class for itself" homogenize the differences within the movement. If Solidarity represented a single class, there is no need to examine the contradictory interests or alternative aims within the movement. But for those who emphasize civil society against the state, one should imagine these divisions critical. It is particularly interesting that Touraine did not pursue this question, as he identified with the civil-society model, and his own data pointed time and again to difference. Although he dismissed it, his discussions suggested rank-and-file divergence from the leadership. They also noted disproportionate influence by professionals over the movement. Touraine also recognized the divergent interest in self-management between classes, yet smoothed over that difference by emphasizing its strategic necessity. He did not discuss the gendered quality of Solidarity, but his activists did not recognize it either. Touraine thus clarified the self-understanding of Solidarity, but may not have improved its vision. The vision of social movements is improved not only when that which they see is made clearer, but when new aspects of their existence are brought into view.

The vision of social movements depends, in part, on the constructs with which activists understand their world. Solidarity's vision was derived from the social experience of its activists, but also from elaborated accounts of the "nature" of communism and of the Soviet Union. These accounts go beyond immediate experience to define what is and envision what could otherwise be. A critical sociology of Solidarity should thus not only clarify the meaning of the movement in terms of its participants' self-understanding. It should also reconsider those accounts which inform the meaning of Solidarity and of other forms of praxis in Soviet-type society.

In part II of this volume, I consider those elaborated accounts, those general theories, of Soviet-type society. In particular, I examine modernization, Marxist and political/civil-society models in light of the preceding analysis of Solidarity. I show why it is difficult to construct an analysis of Solidarity's struggle within a modernization framework. I argue that problems with analyses of Solidarity by MacDonald and Kowalewski derive from an internal contradiction within Trotskyist thought. The ambivalence of self-management as praxis also derives from more general problems with its "classless" quality. And the dominant model underlying Solidarity, that of civil society against totalitarianism, undermined Solidarity's own struggle in its failure to go beyond culture and history to identify conflicts and alternative futures. I follow those two chapters of critique with a third chapter elaborating a structural theory of power in Soviet-type society based on relations of autonomy and dependency. This theory, I argue, not only provides a conceptual apparatus to understanding the reproduction of Communist Party rule, but also a vehicle to understanding its transformation. I use this general approach to explain in chapter 7 the position of Polish professionals before 1980.

This move toward general theory is important for two basic reasons. First, and most obviously, Solidarity moves us to reconstruct the general theories which underlie our vision of Soviet-type society. Few theories anticipated that a social movement would emerge out of the working class and that it could unite the entire society in struggle against the state. Those theories which did anticipate such an action generally did not expect workers to articulate the demands that Solidarity did. This section should appeal, therefore, to those whose interests lie in theories of socialism, but not only to them. These three chapters are also important for those who wish to understand Solidarity and Poland better. Without considering more general accounts of Soviet-type society, there is no way to enter the discourse of Solidarity and of Polish life critically. This is demonstrated very nicely with regard to the question of the class alliances forming Solidarity and the relationship of those alliances to the construction of civil society.

What conditions allowed professionals and workers to ally in Solidarity, and what conditions endanger that alliance? If counterfactual conditions are not anticipated, the ability of an emancipatory movement to deal with that which threatens its identity is undermined. This question of alliance between professionals and workers is not only an important question for the praxis of critical sociology, but it is also basic to theorizing the alternative for which Solidarity struggled. If the post-Marxist theorists are right (which I believe they are), Solidarity's telos, or utopia, was the creation of a civil society. Solidarity's struggle against the authorities was unquestionably a step toward the creation of that society, in that it generated some of the pluralism and publicity essential to its makeup. Simultaneously, however, Solidarity's struggle suppressed some of the questions that the institutionalization of civil society raises. There are two basic problems in this regard: (1) what is the relationship of the state to the creation of civil society in Soviet-type society; and (2) what kinds of classes and class differences does this socialist civil society represent?

These questions rely on different sets of materials for their answer. The question of the role of the state in the creation of civil society requires a comparative analysis of different periods of transformation in Soviet-type societies. Ideally, the Solidarity movement's grass-roots transformation is compared with instances of transformation initiated from above. In the final chapter to this volume, I compare briefly Polish Solidarity with Gorbachev's *perestroika*, and the possibilities and barriers each strategy represents in the struggle for a socialist civil society.

The other question cannot be addressed adequately without the creation of this civil society. But some of the answers to it can be anticipated by considering material from the Solidarity movement itself. By explaining the *structural conditions* underlying the alliance, we can anticipate what changes might endanger the alliance between professionals and workers in the process of transformation. With this concern in mind, I consider in chapter 8 the structural conditions underlying the alliance between Polish engineers and workers in Solidarity.

As this chapter has illustrated, however, structural analysis is only part of a good critical sociology of social transformation. With this in mind, in chapter 9 I shall consider the process by which Polish physicians and workers came to be active allies in Solidarity. Here, the *meanings* surrounding the transformation of society and of health care will be addressed.

Those interested only in Solidarity can turn to part III of this volume, but to do so runs the risk of failing to understand entirely why questions of class alliance are important not only for the theory of Soviet-type society, but for the future of Poland and Eastern Europe.

Part II

Solidarity and the theory of Soviet-type society

4   Solidarity, modernization and class

T. Anthony Jones (1984) identifies three basic approaches to the study of Soviet-type society: the political–economic, the political and the industrial. Jones advocates the industrial model within a general modernization approach and evaluates models on the degree to which they facilitate the comparison of societies. His analysis overstates the unity in political and political–economic models, but this classification of approaches nevertheless serves as a useful point of departure for this overview. In what follows, I consider the relevance of modernization theory for understanding Solidarity and developing a critical sociology of Soviet-type society. I then turn to a more extended analysis and critique of various political–economic approaches. I conclude this chapter with a review of the strengths and weaknesses of these approaches. In the following chapter I consider whether the "political" models of totalitarianism and civil society overcome the limitations of the political–economic models.

Industrialism, functionalism and normative commitments

Jones (1984) finds the industrial-society model superior to the political and political–economic models he considers because it opens the way for a dynamic analysis of these societies and their comparison with other societies with similarly developed technological bases. The common tendency for all industrial societies to become increasingly complex with technological development serves, for him, as a useful point of departure for sociological analysis (Jones, 1976). It provides a dynamic approach and directs analysts to problems of social structure, unlike the political and political–economic models which focus on politics and class respectively. Jones points to the use of this model by Eastern European and Soviet sociologists and the results of their studies as evidence of the model's potential fruitfulness.

This modernization perspective helped undermine the old totalitarian approach and direct attention to the important changes undertaken in Communist Party-led societies after Stalin. R. V. Burks (1970) exemplifies this modernization challenge when he uses technological change to explain political reforms in Eastern Europe. The basic problem with Stalinism, he argues, was its inefficiency and unpredictability. National leaders recognized the economic problems associated with coercion and feared the instability that terror delivers. They also became obliged to find new bases for legitimacy as the Soviet leadership granted them greater autonomy. One of the methods they typically used was to try and improve their nation's living standards. But centralization of the economy presented certain inefficiencies which are incompatible with "industrial maturity." The basic problem was "the inability of Stalinist central planning to provide automatic institutional responses to new situations" (Burks, 1970:288). Thus, leaders were moved to an economic reform based on some measure of pluralization, which in turn undermined the Communist Party's leading role. Although Burks wrote at the end of the 1960s, the general modernization perspective has become the dominant view in most studies of Communist Party-led societies. Western writers emphasize the fundamental problems of Soviet-type systems in modern, more complex societies. The old commitments to equality, social security and centralization must give way to a more decentralized system with greater efficiency and innovation if these societies are to compete with the capitalist West. The more comprehensive the reform, the greater the chance of success (e.g. Hewitt, 1988).

The industrial model was promoted by those in the West who wished to move away from the totalitarian model's normative foundations to a less controversial emphasis on technology and social structure. The modernization perspective succeeded partly because it offered a naturalistic and scientific rhetoric for studying the problems of Soviet-type societies. The starting point of the industrial model is that modern societies have certain *needs* which each industrial society must meet. There is a hypothetically optimum form of social organization toward which advanced societies converge as they evolve toward increasing complexity. Given these needs and the tendency for societies to adapt forms of social organization to meet them, the research agenda of the modernization perspective usually involves the identification of (1) the institutional forms which satisfy these needs and (2) an analysis of their compatibility with one another. Problems emerge when certain needs are not being met, or when needs of one subsystem are subverting the satisfactory functioning of needs in another subsystem. The most common example of this strategy is to point out how the politically motivated emphasis on equality in Soviet-type society has led to inefficiency in the economic sector. As societies become more technologically developed, the system, or its leading sector, attempts to introduce mechanisms which would restore a dynamic equilibrium to the system functioning, which in the example above usually means a diminution of equality as the price of greater economic efficiency. Both problems and their solutions therefore "emerge" from the social system itself.

The assumptions of the industrial model embody a holistic functionalist orientation, characteristic of an early Durkheimian sociology, in which the analytical priority of the whole and its needs takes precedence over the needs of individuals and groups in researching human societies. The power and priorities of different groups in systems are not the motor of change in such functionalist modernization approaches. System needs and relationships among subsystems are their main problem. Modernization theories nevertheless need some kind of actor to translate the problems of these systems into solutions. There are generally two actors that translate: the political leadership and the highly educated.

At the end of the 1960s, modernization theory found its most suitable object of analysis in the Prague Spring. At the end of the 1980s, it is finding it in the *perestroika* of the Soviet Union (cf. Lewin, 1988). In both cases, professionals are the most important in reform, given the "modern scientific, technological, administrative and intellectual tasks of the reform" (Lewin, 1988:124). We also find a political leadership open to social scientists and other experts (Zaslavskaja, 1988). In both cases, political leaders make calls for reform on the grounds that an advanced economy requires sound scientific foundations. Mikhail Gorbachev says that *perestroika* "means a decisive turn toward science, a business-like partnership between it and practice with a view to achieving the highest end results, the ability to place any initiative on a firm scientific footing and the willingness and ardent desire on the part of scientists actively to support the party's course of renewing society" (cited in Zaslavskaja, 1988:267). Modernization theory thus "works" in the sense that the authorities and their advisors adopt it as a guide to social change.

The modernization perspective thus is not only attractive to Western social scientists: Eastern European and Soviet sociologists also have used this perspective to provide us with a far better understanding of these societies' characteristics and tendencies. Even before large-scale reform, academics adopted these industrial models in research as a reaction to the crude or vulgar Marxism that predominated in party ideology, and that attempted to dominate sociology. Indeed, the perspective proved quite compatible with the prerogatives of the Communist Party.

During the Stalinist era in Poland and other Soviet-type societies, sociology was disbanded in the universities (Kolankiewicz, 1979; Walaszek, 1977). The discipline was considered subversive, as it offered a perspective on society that could challenge orthodox Marxism–Leninism. Its independent research also could serve as a means to translate private problems into public issues (Jones, Bealmear and Kennedy, 1984; Mills, 1964). In order to overcome the suspicions of the authorities, sociology had to appear non-threatening. The best means to assure security and continued funding for research was to help the dominant party in the construction of its vision of socialism. Ideally, the concepts and approaches of Marxism–Leninism would have been used, but the theory had been effectively turned into a state ideology by the end of Stalinism, and the potential for its creative application all but destroyed.

Polish culture and intellectual life have historically been linked to the West. It is not surprising that Polish sociology should have been so anxious to reestablish its contact, after the isolation of the Stalin years, with international, especially US, sociology. The renaissance of Polish sociology began in the late 1950s and early 1960s, during the heyday of North American functionalist sociology. Although Poland's own sociological traditions have continued through the present day, the functionalist industrial model found fertile soil in People's Poland. Polish (and other Eastern European and Soviet) sociology developed what some have called "socialistic functionalism" (Gouldner, 1970; Strasser, 1976).

Functionalism is said to be rooted in conservative political traditions (Lenski, 1966:15). Its arguments on stratification can provide scientific justification for the persistence of the status quo. The aspects of functionalism that the industrial-society model incorporates into its perspective also imply a kind of inevitability about the continuation of inegalitarian systems of power and privilege (Giddens, 1987). Polish sociological research took up the questions of the functionalist industrial models, with the appropriate political results. Some of this research could basically replicate the work found in the capitalist West. The examination of industrialization's effects on the lifestyles of people or on patterns of social mobility could direct attention away from the political–economic organization of social life, and toward a seemingly inevitable and autonomous process of technological development. Research focusing on the effects of the scientific–industrial revolution could serve to direct attention to the anticipated economic successes of socialist development. The socialist functional model encountered more problems in the study of inequality, given the egalitarian claims of the authorities. Research indicating inequality's multidimensionality (as in the "decomposition of class attributes") could nevertheless justify the party's claims of growing egalitarianism in spite of inequality's functional necessity. In short, the functionalist industrial model proved to be the safest sociological perspective in a society where social criticism, inherent in some other perspectives, could be dangerous. This is even the case for understanding Solidarity.

Kazimierz Doktór (1982), although claiming a Marxist perspective, explains Solidarity as representative of a more general phenomenon of industrial conflict. First of all, there is the inevitable conflict between those with power and those without, as Dahrendorf (1959) argued. In Poland, he continues, industrial conflicts acquire political consequences because the economic subsystem has insufficient autonomy from the political subsystem. This lack of autonomy becomes all the more problematic as the industrial system becomes more complex. Conflict also intensifies as living standards fail to improve adequately and the gap between the rhetorical celebration of workers and their actual satisfaction grows. Ultimately, real socialism becomes incoherent, but nevertheless remains stable. Reforms fail because individuals do not break their old political routines: "Inertia, conservatism, orientation toward equilibrium and stability thus gain an upper hand over dynamism, radicalism, and striving for innovations" (Doktór, 1982:80).

There are relatively few accounts of Solidarity that are rooted in such an industrial model. Doktór's account suggests why. Discourse on Solidarity virtually demands some kind of affirmation of the movement, even if critically rendered. Doktór, then director of the Institute of Philosophy and Sociology of the Polish Academy of Sciences, could not do so. He affirmed the importance of renewal and the dangers of "inertia," but tried to "normalize" Solidarity as just another industrial conflict.

Doktór also did not identify real actors in his analysis. The main conflict is not between authorities and society, but between those who wish to retain the old ways and those who wish to introduce greater rationality, he argued. He identified only a general tendency toward conservatism and stability among "old political routinists, frozen groups within central administration, and big socio-occupational groups (civil servants and clerical workers, and even engineers and economists)" (p. 79). The challenge represented by Solidarity is transformed into a normal feature of industrial systems. The alternative suggested by the conflict is a new "equilibrium" which the authorities themselves could introduce were it not for the inertia of others (p. 80).

This approach, although acknowledging the "ultrastability" of the system, fails to credit Solidarity with anything more than being a revolt by the powerless. Solidarity is a consequence of the system working poorly, not a consequence of the system itself nor of the emancipatory yearnings of knowledgeable actors. Thus, we are unable to understand what makes Solidarity different from other conflicts, why Solidarity formed in Poland in 1980–81 and not elsewhere, and what a greater empowerment of Solidarity might contribute to an alternative Polish society. Few in the West would use this industrial model to explain Solidarity, therefore.

In sum, although modernization and functionalist theories are often used, in the East and West, to explain systemic problems and to justify top-down reforms, they are generally less suitable to analyzing movements from below like Solidarity. Neither are oriented toward explaining socially constructed actors transforming society. The only actors they typically incorporate are political leaders or the highly educated, whose role is to translate the problems of archaic systems into modern solutions. Modernization theories are also not generally interested in linking the demands of social movements to alternative systems that are not existing elsewhere. Indeed, modernization theories are drawn to a defense of the rich and powerful because it is their systems which typically exhibit the greatest adaptive success in the world system.

Modernization theory nevertheless can contribute in another way to the theory of systemic change advocated by those in Solidarity and those engaged in transformative struggles elsewhere. Hungarian, Polish and Soviet social scientists have resurrected the notion of system "needs," which political domination and economic planning have ignored, but with a price. "Spontaneous" processes emerge from a malfunctioning controlled system in order to compensate for the dereliction of the system, thus confirming the "naturalness" of these needs. The inevitability of certain basic social features of industrial societies becomes, instead of a tool to justify the status quo, a tool in the transformation of society (e.g. Misztal and Misztal, 1986–87). Much as Merton (1967) and Gans (1972) argued, therefore, functionalism is not inherently conservative, and work done within the modernization perspective need not be considered unimportant for the critical sociological agenda. But functionalism and modernization theory are easily drawn toward a defense of the powerful and a portrait of the inevitable, even when engaged in critical analysis. This is nowhere more apparent than in the analysis of inequality.

Walter Connor (1979) establishes "equality" as the goal of socialist politics and evaluates its desirability on the grounds of its realization in Soviet-type society and its compatibility with the preservation of liberty. He accepts the conservative premise that the establishment of equality necessitates state intervention, which in turn restricts individual liberty (1979:25, 332). Since he places a greater value on liberty, he rejects socialist goals *a priori*. But the body of his book documents that these societies have not even been successful in creating an egalitarian society, and therefore the socialist project neither preserves the liberty that democratic capitalism protects, nor even achieves socialism's goal of equality. "Inequality, of whatever magnitude, seems likely to remain a problem; socialism surely shows no signs of outgrowing it" (Connor, 1979:306). Even without the same conservative commitment, Gerhard Lenski (1978) concludes on the basis of his review of "Marxist experiments" that inequality is inherent in society, and that any attempt to introduce economic equality probably leads to an expansion of political inequality.

The Solidarity movement not only struggled to realize civil society, but also a fundamentally more egalitarian society. Those who accept functionalist arguments on the inevitability of some form of inequality, or equality's incompatibility with liberty, will find in Solidarity's aims a basic contradiction. Their systemic analysis would recommend to Solidarity that it abandon these mutually incompatible aims, and strive instead to restore civil society, and with that, an economy based on private property and market relations. In this sense, the emancipatory quality of their sociology stops once a modern or capitalist society is founded.

Critical sociology faces considerable difficulty in the study of Soviet-type society. Instead of challenging the myth of value-free sociology, it enters a field which is already loaded normatively. The first challenge to this conservative hegemony in Soviet studies was launched by the very kinds of sociology which critical sociology has criticized in studies of capitalist societies. The "value-neutral" modernization approaches enabled considerable progress in researching the various subsystems of Soviet-type society, both by Western and Eastern social scientists. But as the opportunity for systemic and social transformation comes to Soviet-type society, a new kind of critical sociology in Soviet-type society has become necessary.

Social science can serve several functions in the study of social transformation. It can help, as Tat'yana Zaslavskaja (1988) urges, to formulate plans for reform, provide reliable feedback on these changes and understand better the "human factor" so as to channel it into the direction "society" needs. But that presupposes that the powerful can recognize the direction society wants to move and are predisposed to move in that direction. It also assumes that the system itself has its own needs, which social scientists merely recognize. Solidarity's experience suggests that society, once self-organized, can also indicate "directions" for change and must be self-organized in order to assure that those directions are followed. What is more, its "needs" may be different from those which modernization theorists find feasible or possible.

Human societies have heretofore been organized on the basis of directions from authorities, be they in ruling classes or ruling parties. One of the obligations of a critical sociology is to help realize visions from below, and not just help implement plans from above and without. Solidarity's alternative vision embraced both equality and liberty. How might that alternative be realized in Soviet-type society? One place to turn to look for an answer is Marxism.

Marxism, class and democracy

In capitalist society, Marxism is certainly the most important tradition in critical sociology. It is also an important critical tradition in Soviet-type society. But what is Marxism?[1] Given that there are no longer any institutional foundations for establishing what is and what is not Marxism (as Marxism has moved from disciplined parties to the naturally contentious academy), it becomes an open-ended mode of inquiry which could be identified with critical sociology in general. It seems that beyond a commitment to praxis toward socialism, there is little that is distinctive to the Marxist perspective now, except perhaps for the conceptual centrality of class.

There are many reasons to consider class and class struggle as the central concepts of Marxism. Although the *Communist Manifesto* served primarily as a political pamphlet, for many the idea that "the history of all hitherto existing society is the history of class struggle" is the core of Marxism. Trotsky's debate with John Dewey affirmed the importance of class analysis for distinguishing Marxism from bourgeois and petty-bourgeois moralism (Trotsky, Dewey and Nowack, 1973). More recent debates over the proper way for considering the anti-systemic force that will transform capitalism into socialism suggests that the centrality of "class" is at the root of a distinction between Marxism and "a new true socialism" (Wood, 1986). The proper way of framing "class" in Soviet-type society also seems to distinguish "Marxist science" from "utopian socialism" (Mandel, 1982; Silver and Tarpinian, 1981; Tarpinian and Silver, 1982). In general, many Marxists would identify their work as "scientific" on the basis that Marxism has discovered the priority of the relations of production in organizing social life, structuring praxis and identifying an emancipatory alternative.

Critical sociology is based on the analysis of domination, praxis and utopia, but there is considerable disagreement among critical sociologists as to the centrality of class in these moments and their analysis. Should domination be identified mainly on the basis of class? Ought praxis be based primarily on class struggle? Can utopia be considered in terms of classlessness? These debates over class are particularly important for Soviet-type society. Before we consider class in the critique of actual socialism, we should note how it can be used to legitimate it.

The number of accounts establishing the relationship between Marxism, Leninism and Stalinism is daunting and need not be considered here.[2] I believe Gouldner's (1980) argument resolves the problem adequately: that because the writings of Marx and Lenin are sufficiently broad and internally contradictory, some of their arguments can be used to legitimate Stalinism. Of course Marx and Lenin are not responsible for this. Marx died decades before the revolutions of 1917. Lenin vehemently defended one-party rule after the revolution, but in his last years he began a struggle against "bureaucratic distortions," advocating party and governmental reconstruction, bureaucratic reduction and removing Stalin from power (Bellis, 1979:30–55; Bettelheim, 1976:437–530; Lewin, 1968). Lenin even argued for independent organizations that could protect workers from potentially antagonistic authorities (Bettelheim, 1976:391). Beyond Marx and Lenin, the Bolshevik tradition itself contains alternative critical currents with, among others, Bukharin and the Workers'

Opposition. Of the Bolsheviks, Trotsky provided the most systematic and consequential critique. To a considerable degree, the success of reform from above as an emancipatory strategy depends on the capacity of reformers to draw upon, or reconstruct, alternative currents within the Bolshevik tradition as models for transformation.

Stalin's transformation of Marxism and Leninism completely removed its emancipatory critical edge. Class analysis instead became a means of ideological obfuscation, where domination is disguised as a form of unity (Marcuse, 1958). According to the official 1939 *History of the Communist Party of the Soviet Union (Bolsheviks)* (Commission of the Central Committee of the CPSUC(B): 342–44), all exploiting elements are eliminated in this new Soviet Union, and workers, peasants and intelligentsia cooperate with one another in the construction of socialism. Stalinist analysis of Soviet-type society therefore is a kind of class analysis without exploitation and conflict. Classes are merely groups with different roles in a harmonious order. This is class analysis without the critical edge.

Beyond official Stalinist ideology and its reproduction in some Western communist parties, there are also independent Western Marxist interpretations which work within the Stalinist framework. These interpretations first of all assume that socialism can be constructed in a single society[3] and secondly affirm the authentically socialist character of the Soviet Union. Mandel (1982) charges Silver and Tarpinian (1981) with a Stalinist perspective in their work, but Szymanski's (1979) book about the Soviet Union might be the best example of Stalinist assumptions in Western Marxist sociology. Szymanski (1979) argues that there is a basic unity to Soviet society, even if it is a "technocratic state socialism" where professionals are more influential than manual workers. There is no class exploitation, he argues, for while these influential groups do have greater decision-making power, they do not make decisions to benefit themselves, but to guide Soviet society according to a technocratic ideology of efficiency. While this portrait of Soviet society is relatively unproblematic when transformation is not on the agenda, as it was not under Brezhnev, it clearly becomes inadequate in a period of conflict and struggle, as under *perestroika*. It is especially inadequate when transformation is moved from below, as with Solidarity, because this perspective fails to raise the question of whether the structural position of a communist party in Soviet-type society is associated with exploitation and domination (chapter 2). In that sense, it shares with modernization theory a view of Soviet-type society as basically non-antagonistic.

Such Western Marxists as Szymanski are few, as most offer a critique of Soviet-type society. The variety of Marxist critiques is daunting, however, and they all cannot be reviewed here (see Bellis, 1979; Fehér, Heller and Markus, 1983; Kelly, 1985; Lane, 1984; Park, 1987). I consider only a few major theorists, so that we can focus on the major themes in the critique of Soviet-type society rather than the more subtle differences among them. These themes revolve around the role of class in characterizing the nature of domination, praxis and utopia in Soviet-type society.

Trotsky, bureaucracy and democracy

The central Marxist critique of Soviet society comes from its "outcast prophet," Leon Trotsky. Trotsky's critique is so important that Perry Anderson (1983:55) finds his argument unsurpassed in the analysis of Stalinism. Subsequent sovietologists have only developed its empirical side and failed to offer an alternative, integrated theory, he argues. Among Marxist analyses of Solidarity, Trotskyist accounts, as that of MacDonald (1983), are also among the most sophisticated. Trotskyist accounts are, however, restricted by three fundamental problems in the paradigm: an ambivalent class analysis; a contradictory assessment of democracy in socialism; and overreliance on strategy to explain the outcomes of praxis. In what follows, I illustrate how each of these problems are apparent already in Trotsky's analysis.

The severity of Trotsky's critique grew over time and his mature argument can be found in *The Revolution Betrayed* (1937 [1972]) (Anderson, 1983; Beilharz, 1979; Bellis, 1979:56–92). This book was written as a response to Stalin's claim that socialism had been constructed in the Soviet Union, an interpretation which itself originated as a challenge to Trotsky's theory of permanent revolution (Knei-Paz, 1978:339–48). The basic outlines of Trotsky's critique continue to influence many Marxists, most prominent of whom is Ernest Mandel (1978, 1981, 1982).

Given Trotsky's central role in the initial years of the Soviet Union, it is not surprising to see his point of departure based on the degeneration of the original revolution. The October Revolution itself was a genuine proletarian revolution, he argued. The main problem facing the Soviet Union was that it had to apply socialist methods to solve pre-socialist problems (Trotsky, 1937 [1972]:57). In so doing, the bureaucracy managed to separate itself from the political control of the masses (p. 35), which led to the leadership becoming a "preparatory regime transitional from capitalism to socialism" (p. 47). This does not mean, however, that continued economic development would inevitably lead to the construction of socialism, as Stalin claimed; the future of socialism in Soviet society depended on the "struggle of social forces" on an international scale (pp. 48–49). Socialist dictatorship was to prepare for its own demise (Trotsky, 1937 [1972]:52). But in order to do so, it had to raise the productivity of the economy under conditions of state ownership. This led to the creation of the transitional regime, based on the state's dual character. It was socialist in that it defended "social property," yet also bourgeois because it distributed privilege on the basis of capitalistic measures (p. 54). By 1936, the Communist Party ceased to be representative of the workers' real interests. The Leninist Communist Party died when the tactical suppression of factions turned into a permanent policy (p. 100). The bureaucracy had become ascendant, outgrowing its social function of promoting economic development, becoming an independent social force (p. 113). The Soviet Thermidor was thus the "triumph of the bureaucracy over the masses" (p. 105).

For Trotsky, planning and the nationalization of the means of production were progressive steps, but this did not ensure that property was really in the hands of the masses. "State property becomes the property of the whole people only to the degree that social privilege and differentiation disappear, and therewith the necessity of the state" (p. 237). For socialism to triumph in the transitional regime, the working class has to rise up and overthrow the bureaucracy, which has become the parasite of the working class. But workers must be cautious, because the bureaucracy, whatever its shortcomings, protects the existing "socialist" relations of production. Hence, he believes, the working class will only cast out the most corrupt bureaucrats until world socialist revolution returns to the agenda (pp. 285–86). When world revolution appears, a renewed Leninist vanguard would lead the struggle.

Class, in terms of relations of production, remains at the foundation of Trotsky's analysis. The nature of a revolution depends on the class of its revolutionary personnel (Beilharz, 1979:139). Definitions of Soviet society as transitional depend on its relations of production being socialist and its distribution of privilege being bourgeois. The agent of transformation remains the working class, even if led necessarily by a regenerated Leninist Party.[4] The bureaucracy is not a class (Trotsky, 1937 [1972]:248–52), as class is based on relations of production, and those relations are socialist. The bureaucracy is only a "commanding stratum," and the working class remains the dominant class. The bureaucracy exists by virtue of the proletariat's weakness. Much as Marx (1852 [1977]) explained the growth of French bureaucracy in terms of class, Trotsky also accounts for the rise of Soviet bureaucracy through an analysis of proletarian weakness as a ruling class.

If class is to retain conceptual consistency with previous usages, Trotsky is right not to call the bureaucracy a class. It is constituted differently, not on the basis of the relations of production but on the basis of positions in an administrative hierarchy (see also Bauman, 1980). Thus, his image of domination in Soviet-type society is not based on a new ruling class but on the domination of a bureaucracy with its roots in the working class.[5] But what does this emphasis on a *political bureaucratic* domination, rather than a new form of *class* domination, do to Trotsky's class analysis? If class relations are fundamentally socialist, then what of our understanding of praxis and utopia? Can they be defined adequately in class terms? If bureaucracy becomes the central form of domination, why then would praxis and utopia not change to one that more directly attacks the dangers of bureaucracy? Why would the principal praxis and utopia of struggle in Soviet-type society not come to be based on political struggle instead of class struggle? Indeed, might not the struggle for democracy come to be identified with proletarian class struggle, and thus the peculiarity of class analysis (as the analysis of forms of struggle over the appropriation of surplus value) disappear? Trotsky's analysis of praxis, in fact, ultimately emphasizes *political revolution* rather than social revolution for just these reasons.

Alternatively, why could we not reformulate the concept of class so that domination could also be class-based, and class struggle and classless society remain secure in the center of critique? In fact, a large group of Trotsky's American followers challenged their leader's notion of non-class domination with their own emphasis on "bureaucratic collectivism," in which they argued a new type of ruling class had emerged (Bellis, 1979:93–128; Knei-Paz, 1978:418–27). We shall consider this thesis of a new class in a subsequent section of this chapter. Suffice to say here, Trotsky argued until his assassination against the new-class thesis with all of its implications.

Trotsky defended the authoritarian state in the first years after the revolution. In *Terrorism and Communism* (1920 [1961]), he justified the proletarian state's domination of the citizen with a legitimizing reference to similar structures of domination in military authority. Trotsky began a more critical line as early as 1923. In *The New Course*, he began to argue that a political revolution was necessary to restore a Communist Party that was truly Leninist, in which there would be "debate, criticism, the free airing of opinions, and a collective form of decision-making," although discipline in action and submission to the party would continue to be essential (Knei-Paz, 1978:369–80). Intra-party democratization thus would be the key to restoring the emancipatory project. He believed this could be achieved through internal party reform until as late as 1932 (Knei-Paz, 1978:414). Later, he believed an entirely new Leninist Party would have to challenge Stalinism. Through his life, however, Trotsky continued to emphasize praxis in Soviet society as the *transformation of the organizational structure of politics*. In addition to organizational change, *cultural transformation* was essential, necessitated by organizational inertia and the conservative institutionalization of the party itself (Knei-Paz, 1978:369–80). Not only were opportunists joining the party, but even the older idealists began to lose their revolutionary commitment.

Trotsky's position eventually evolved beyond an emancipatory praxis that focused on the party alone. In 1933, he called for the transformation of the organizational structure of Soviet society itself. He revised the position he took in 1920 on trade unions, and now considered independent occupational associations essential to workers' defense, so long as the state is coercive and classes remain (Bellis, 1979:81). He even called for the restoration of civil liberties and independent political parties.[6]

> It is not a question of substituting one ruling clique for another, but of changing the very methods of administering the economy and guiding the culture of the country. Bureaucratic autocracy must give place to Soviet democracy. A restoration of the right of criticism, and a genuine freedom of elections, are necessary conditions for the further development of the country. This assumes a revival of freedom of Soviet parties, beginning with the party of Bolsheviks, and a resurrection of the trade unions. (Trotsky, 1937 [1972]:289)

With this move to the democratization of society, Trotsky begins to acknowledge what Rosa Luxemburg and Karl Kautsky also emphasize in their critiques: the mutual necessity of formal democracy and socialism.

Kautsky (1919 [1964]) based his critique of bolshevism on the belief that democracy was central to the socialist project and that the forces of production had to be built higher than the Russia of 1917 enjoyed. Without the latter, large-scale industry would not be sufficiently developed and the proletariat would not be of sufficient size and or have sufficient interest in socialism. The democratic side of his concern included a commitment to a strong parliament. He argued for the importance of universal equal suffrage and civil liberties, even for the political opposition. This text is the principal foundation for what has been called the "social democratic" critique, which Lenin (1918 [1975]) so vehemently denounced in "The Proletarian Revolution and the Renegade Kautsky." But this critique of bolshevism was not restricted to those who were "reformists."

Like Lenin, Rosa Luxemburg identified herself as a "revolutionary" socialist, opposed to the reformist strain predominating in the Second Socialist International dominated by the German Social Democratic Party. But while revolutionary, she was not a bolshevik, and took great pains to separate herself from the bolshevik vision (see Mattick, 1978:19–48). Luxemburg anticipated the danger that a vanguard party, claiming to act in the historical interests of the working class, would not remain committed to general class interests. The only protection against the degeneration of a probably necessary initial dictatorship lay in the use of dictatorship to extend democracy and freedom to the masses, not to suppress it (Luxemburg, 1918 [1961]:78). While she praised the "courage and farsightedness" of the bolsheviks, she also criticized them on democratic grounds. She praised parliaments (p. 62) and argued that freedom of press and assembly were essential to a democratic socialism (p. 67).

> Socialism in life demands a complete spiritual transformation in the masses degraded by centuries of bourgeois class rule ... Without general elections, without unrestricted freedom of the press and assembly, without a free struggle of opinion, life dies out in every public institution, becomes a mere semblance of life, in which only the bureaucracy remains as the active element. Public life gradually falls asleep, a few dozen party leaders of inexhaustible energy and boundless experience direct and rule. (pp. 71–72)

Luxemburg is known for her commitment to class analysis, as in her (1899 [1977]) argument that Poland should not seek independence from Russia but become part of a larger socialist revolution. But her class analysis was supplemented by a vision of an alternative clearly grounded in mass initiative and freedom, of which democracy was a central ingredient. It is not, therefore, surprising to find that the basis for her critique of the Bolshevik experiment is in its disregard for "democracy."

The Trotskyist, Luxemburgist and Kautskyist critiques of Soviet type society note how the centralization of political power crushes socialist victory and how important "democracy" is in the struggle for socialism. Luxemburg and Kautsky agreed that civil rights and vital parliamentary institutions were essential to socialist construction. The Trotskyist position was different initially, arguing above all for the restoration of debate within the party, even if democratic centralism would prevail in the execution of policy. Over the years of his exile, Trotsky gradually abandoned his hope that transformation could be driven from within the party, and advocated a praxis and program of socialist construction that looked more like what Luxemburg and Kautsky supported decades earlier. Trotsky began to support the "self-organization of society" through independent trade unions and political parties.

This emphasis on democracy in the Marxist analysis of praxis in Soviet-type society nevertheless continues to rest on class foundations. It continues to assume that the most significant divisions within society are based on class. The denial of rights to workers is what indicates the denial of the socialist project. It is workers who must organize themselves, and express themselves. And it is the distribution of society's surplus in ways antagonistic to workers' interests (reflected in their poverty or in their limited say over how it is distributed) which indicates the distance of actual socialism from genuine socialism. This democracy thus rests on a future image of classlessness and the absence of antagonistic interests. This suggests a basic tension between class analysis and democracy. Democracy is essential only when there are differences of interest. Without such differences, one need not debate, one need not compromise, one need not have alternatives. Is this democracy of which Trotsky writes, therefore, only a transitional project itself?

For Trotsky, trade unions are themselves transitional, necessary only until the disappearance of classes. As such, trade unions, and perhaps democracy itself, are ancillary to the struggle for socialism and classlessness. The continuation of democratic institutional features indicates the distance of the real from the ideal. While they are themselves necessary in praxis, for Trotsky, pluralist structures are antagonistic to a utopia of classlessness. This is their fundamental ambivalence in the class analysis of actual socialism: while struggle for "democracy" denotes praxis against a form of non-class political domination, democracy becomes incompatible and redundant in a utopia where there is no domination and no antagonistic interests.

Trotsky's critical theory of Soviet-type society illustrates better than other Marxist approaches the instability of a Marxist analysis which identifies a non-class basis for domination. When domination is identified with bureaucracy, politics or something else, praxis tends to be identified on some basis other than class. The appeal of a utopia defined exclusively in terms of classlessness then declines. To the extent that this other foundation legitimates other bases for struggle, the utopia must take into account the transcendence of difference on these terms. This might be realizable in terms of race and gender, where a non-racist and non-sexist society can be imagined alongside of classlessness. Most Marxists today would argue in just such terms.

If the organization of society itself produces differences of interest, the viability of the assumption of a future unity and homogeneity which underlies a non-racist, non-sexist and classless society is called into question. No Marxist would argue that the need for administration will disappear in human society. Indeed, the only way to assure that administration would not separate itself from the masses is to make it subject to politics. And the only way to assure that these politics are consistent with the wishes and needs of the masses is to assure a democracy of equal participation and civil rights. But this very assurance implies differences of interests, for without that assumption, democracy is superfluous. Democracy, then, must assume an equal, not subsidiary role, in the identification of utopia. But with that, the adequacy of class recedes as the central concept organizing critical sociology. Indeed, the very homogeneity associated with a class or with classlessness becomes antagonistic to the emancipatory project. This is most apparent in the question of the relationship between state and economy.

Although Trotsky notes that uncontrolled bureaucratic power leads to inequalities in the sphere of distribution, he finds no relationship between bureaucratic power and one of the principal instruments of its domination: central planning (Fehér, Heller and Markus, 1983:11–14). On the contrary, for Trotsky a planned economy is essential to the building of socialism (Trotsky, 1937 [1972]:285). He assumes central planning to be a neutral tool in the construction of a classless society, much as Lenin believed Taylor's capitalist techniques in the organization of work compatible with workers' rule (Corrigan, Ramsay and Sayer, 1978). Planning can organize economy in the general interest and becomes a central part of his socialist utopia because in a classless society planning is the instrument of a unified society.[7] But how does this planning represent a unified interest? Clearly, the bureaucracy cannot be expected to realize this interest on its own, as it can sever its subservience to the working class and society. The ruling party which is supposed to oversee the bureaucracy can itself degenerate and fail to serve the universal interest too. A renewed Leninist Party might serve such a function, but how would that party realize universal interest under conditions of political pluralism, where one would expect it to compromise with political parties that represent interests of other classes, class fractions or other groups differently constituted? Would compromise with these parties not limit the capacity of the renewed Bolshevik Party to construct socialism in the general interest? Or might the general interest be redefined as the compromise of competing interests? And, if so, might this appeal to the general interest be camouflage for some particular interest? And, especially problematic for those socialist societies that are underdeveloped, how does one reconcile the construction of a society on the basis of proletarian power when the working class is a minority? Trotsky's support for political pluralism bears important tensions with his continued commitment to central planning and an image of a future society that is without conflicting interests.

This ambiguity of pluralism in his image of the classless society's construction and his continued commitment to central planning undermine the radicalism of Trotsky's "democratic" critique. He ultimately fails to challenge the central features organizing domination in Soviet-type society. A privileged leading party and central planning are considered entirely compatible with the realization of classlessness. Democracy is subordinated to the twin assumptions of class analysis: the homogeneity of class interest and the unity of classlessness. In general, we might hypothesize that *to the degree that class remains central to the critique of Soviet-type societies, these twin assumptions legitimating democratic centralism and bureaucratic domination remain unassailed*, and thus one of the most significant problems for a critical sociology of Soviet-type society is left untouched.

As the central problems of domination in Soviet-type society remain untouched, the analysis of praxis remains inadequate in Trotsky's work. Trotsky ultimately relies on the objective interest of the working class to guarantee that their revolutionary action will yield socialist fruits. Revolution is successful when the objective interests of the working class are translated into the needs of the moment by a leadership which understands both the conjuncture and the alternative that will emancipate that class. Because the objective needs of the working class are based on the establishment of an economy organized by the plan, success or failure depends on the quality of

leadership in establishing that formation. Leadership becomes syno-
nymous with strategy and conjunctural analysis, and the success of
revolution becomes dependent on that leadership (Beilharz, 1979:141–
43). But leadership does not incorporate a redefinition of the goals of
socialism themselves. While strategy and choice are certainly important factors in shaping a movement's success, it is hard to recognize in
Trotskyist analysis when strategic failure is the decisive element, and
when it is not, as Beilharz (1979) argues. But perhaps even more
problematic, it is hard to assess when elements of the socialist
program itself should change. Trotsky eventually recognized that
societal democracy or civil society constituted an important ingredient
for the alternative to the Communist Party's mono-organizational
system. Trotsky came to this conclusion by analyzing the struggles
against Stalinism within the Soviet Union. But can we not also come to
the conclusion that Stalinist centralized planning is itself antagonistic
to socialism, and socialist markets are complementary, as Harrington
(1989) argues? The struggles within Poland by Solidarity would
suggest so, and yet MacDonald (1983) finds Solidarity's program of
marketization and plant autonomy the decisive feature which held
back the victory of the working class in Poland in 1981. But he can
make this claim only if he can deduce, from Marxist theory, the
necessary socialist ideology. As Dewey (1938 [1973]) suggested of
Trotsky, this conflates means and ends in the analysis, and practice, of
social change. It assumes, and does not demonstrate, that socialist
ideology would have enabled the emancipation of Polish workers.

Trotsky's critique of Soviet-type society is valuable for its identification of principal conflicts and emancipatory actors. Its emphasis on
leadership and strategy is perhaps overdone, but helpful in overcoming the structuralist bias against analyzing the role of choice in social
change. But ironically, the Trotskyist approach denies agency in
redefining the emancipatory alternative. And the capacity for redefining this alternative is essential for moving beyond the vanguardist
politics embryonic in Trotsky's analysis, and helping to define a new
critical sociology of Soviet-type society.

Trotsky's theory of the transitional society is itself transitional, as it
rests on a class problematic but denies that class adequately characterizes praxis and domination. The consequent reformulation of
critique then suggests the antinomies of classlessness as utopia.
Conflicting interests can be constructed on bases other than class, and
their resolution cannot be accomplished without the compromises
accompanying the pluralism of independent trade unions and political

parties. But this pluralism bears an unstable relationship to central planning, inasmuch as this economic control is supposed to be the instrument which transforms antagonisms into unity, even while pluralism implies the legitimacy of difference. These antinomies are ultimately resolved by relying on the fetishization of the socialist program, which can resolve fundamental antagonisms through a leadership that considers strategy, but not the normative foundations of its project.

To the extent that the Marxist project introduces bureaucracy and democracy, its critical project becomes unstable. When domination is not based on class, and as it comes to be identified as bureaucratic in form, it tends to lead to a revision of the emancipatory project along the lines of democracy discussed above. Thus, it is not surprising that much of the Marxist debate has instead turned to the question of whether a new ruling class has emerged in Soviet-type society. This question could be put into the framework of whether capitalism has been restored, but that is another issue (see Bellis 1979:114–21, 129–222; Park, 1987).

A new ruling class

The thesis of a new ruling class as bureaucracy has a long lineage. Bakunin warned that Marx's dictatorship of the proletariat would lead to the class rule of state engineers; in 1899, Polish anarcho-syndicalist Waclaw Machajski was also skeptical of the emancipatory commitments of the intelligentsia (Knei-Paz, 1978:419–20). Bruno Rizzi, Max Schachtman and several other Western analysts have suggested the ruling-class thesis (Bellis, 1979:93–236), but the book, *The New Class* (1957), by Yugoslav Milovan Djilas is the central text in this tradition. Although Djilas (1969) later breaks with "historical materialism," the argument of his earlier work is consistent with Marxist analysis. He argues in contrast to Trotsky that socialist relations of production have not been created. Instead, another ruling class with control over the means of production has replaced the bourgeoisie.

> Ownership is nothing other than the right of profit and control. If one defines class benefits by this right, the Communist states have seen, in the final analysis, the origin of a new form of ownership or of a new ruling and exploiting class. (p. 35)

> The new class may be said to be made up of those who have special privileges and economic preference because of the administrative monopoly they hold. (p. 39)

> The new class obtains its power, privileges, ideology, and its customs from one specific form of ownership – collective ownership – which the class administers and distributes in the name of the nation and society. (p. 45)

> The emergence of the new class has been concealed under socialist phraseology and, more important, under the new collective forms of property ownership. (p. 47)

Although Djilas holds a different view on the character of the leadership and the underlying relations of production, both he and Trotsky hold similar views on the basic contradiction: between the ideal of social ownership of the means of production and the reality of a single group directing production in its own interests (Djilas, 1957:65). Djilas resolves the ambiguity of non-class domination by defining the bureaucracy as a new ruling class.

Polish critical theorists Jacek Kuroń and Karol Modzelewski (1966) also identify a new ruling class in the "central political bureaucracy." They differ from Djilas and Trotsky, however, in that their identification of this group's dominance is not related to its personal consumption. Instead, its class interest is to increase its power and influence within the country and across the globe by developing the means of production under its control.[8] But they remain more within the Marxist problematic than does Trotsky by arguing that praxis is defined by a class struggle to realize a *true* socialization of the means of production. But like Trotsky, the form of class struggle is to be found in the political, cultural and organizational democratization of society, through workers' councils, independent trade unions, a workers' militia and a pluralism of political parties.

There are differences among the many perspectives which suggest the emergence of a ruling class. There are, nevertheless, common points: (1) control over the means of production defines the ruling class; (2) the ruling class includes the bureaucracy, or certain levels of it, and/or enterprise managers; (3) class struggle to effect true socialization of the means of production is the central praxis; (4) class society is counterposed to the utopia of a classless one.

Although class now becomes the central concept in explicating domination, praxis and utopia, the central difficulties of the Marxist critique of actual socialism still are reproduced. The identification of a new class domination fits better with the classless utopia, but praxis is rarely identified with change in political economy. When the struggle against the ruling class is explained, the argument depends on the democratization of political and social organization. This reinforces

Trotsky's position that praxis in Soviet-type society calls for political revolution, not social. It also calls into question the centrality of class for a critical sociology of Soviet-type society.

The revision of the Trotskyist position to identify bureaucracy as a ruling class cannot overcome the dilemma of Marxian critique. Inasmuch as the means of production are controlled by a group which has its roots in the formal organization of the political power of the society, the praxis against this "ruling class" must ultimately be a praxis which reorganizes political power. Because this praxis therefore relies on a "political" revolution, the identification of the ruling group as a class becomes virtually superfluous and inconsistent with the main thrust of the critique, as is the case for Kuroń and Modzelewski (Bellis, 1979:204). The only way in which class analysis could regain its conceptual centrality would be to challenge the political economy of the bureaucracy's power. And that involves a challenge to central planning itself, which in turn calls into question the Marxist critique of property relations and the market. But, in so doing, Marxist analysis becomes more relevant to the emancipatory praxis of Solidarity.

Self-management as praxis and utopia

The principal Marxist innovation in response to this challenge is the idea of "self-governing socialism" (Horvat, Marković and Supek, 1975; Horvat, 1982). In many ways, this approach is quite compatible with the "post-Marxist" critique I consider in chapter 5: both retain an Enlightenment commitment to the utopia of the free association of producers rationally deciding their own lives; both identify with the modern extensions of the French Revolution in the ethical trichotomy of freedom, social equality and human solidarity (Horvat, 1982:224–32). But the self-management approach remains closer to Marxism in terms of self-identification and areas of concern. In particular, it seeks to redefine the *political economy* of socialism. Yugoslav Branko Horvat's book (1982) acknowledges the essential connection between political economy and Marxism in its very title.

Self-managing socialism begins with a critique of actually existing socialism, which it labels "etatism." An etatist society is one whose ruling strata claim allegiance to socialist tenets, especially in its elimination of private ownership of the means of production and an end to class exploitation; but it also revises the socialist heritage in an important sense: it makes a virtue out of the strong authoritarian state, despite the socialist expectation that it would wither away.

This ruling class is caught between its new status and its own legacy which denies that it should exist as a ruling class. The ruling class is therefore more obliged to lie than rulers in any other system: to proclaim its virtues and hide its failures. It is obliged to hold itself up to higher standards than other systems, and more ruthlessly to suppress any criticisms of itself. It is obliged to live up to some parts of its legacy (as in providing basic welfare) in order to hide those other elements (most notably the absence of a ruling class) which deny its historical link to socialism (Horvat, 1982:462–71). This lie can be perpetuated by discouraging individual emancipation and modern rationality, and instead creating new forms of "traditional" authority. It is not surprising that in such a system, therefore, actors are drawn to genuinely traditional forms of authority with longer lasting claims to truth, as the Church (chapter 1).

Generally, the guiding principles of etatism developed as a negation (*Verneinung*), not a supersession (*Aufhebung*), of those guiding capitalism. Because leading forms of capitalism are characterized by private property, the market, money, interest, individualism, spontaneity and democracy, etatist socialism *must* be characterized by state ownership of the means of production, planning, moral incentives and commands, collectivism and dictatorial state control over all spheres of social life (Horvat, 1982:23–25). The one exception to this negation is the centrality of science, for in both societies it is central, ideologically. In practice, in etatist society pre-bourgeois values of authority, not reason, and beliefs, not facts, are preeminent. This is apparent in the suppression of individual responsibility and reason in favor of organizational will. Consensus is not established by reasoned discussion, but through faith (Horvat, 1982:28–43).

The 1917 October Revolution began as a socialist revolution with self-management in various work units and territories organizing social life, but within months socialism was crushed as the state centralized power into its own bureaucratically sponsored organizations. The other Central European revolutions after World War I also moved spontaneously toward self-management, but foreign and domestic state power crushed self-governance there too (Horvat, 1982:135–56). These political and military tactics destroyed the spontaneous and natural drive toward classlessness.

Classlessness is not specially dependent on economic categories for Horvat, and rather is opposed to any form of domination based on property or authority. Social classes exist whenever groups of persons occupy systematically different positions in regard to some kind of power, standard of living or measure of prestige. Thus, economic power has no special ontological priority in this Marxism. Nevertheless, class is constructed within the social organization of work, broadly defined to include economic and political activities. Exploitation becomes "any socially conditioned form of asymmetrical production of life chances," and class struggle is the "fundamental social conflict between order givers and order takers." Compliance can be achieved through physical or symbolic coercion, typically identified with state power. Or it can be achieved through incentives, be they status-generating, material or normative. The incentives distributed by authorities differ in each system – material in capitalism and "moral" in etatism – but the fact that they are distributed by some to others means that the former rules and the latter is ruled. In general, therefore, those who rule are those who are in the position to control most coercive resources and distribute most incentives. They continue to rule, as the ruled cannot imagine viable alternatives (Horvat, 1982:57–65).

Given this flexible account of power resources, one does not find any priority given to a "class analysis" of etatism, if we understand this analysis as one which goes beneath political appearance to discover real control over the allocation of surplus product. It is enough to argue that the state controls the surplus. Horvat identifies the etatist structure of inequality in terms of politics, and the ruling class in terms of its political monopoly (Horvat, 1982:81). As such, even in this "marxist political economy of socialism," politics is central in its definition of the ruling class, and politics is "the problem of socialist society" (Horvat, 1982:232); "not the expropriation of private property but the expropriation of political authority is the necessary and sufficient condition of socialism" (Horvat, 1982:321). States and politics must therefore be transformed and decentralized.

Horvat does not advocate multiparty pluralism, however. He finds political parties to be cartels which restrict individual influence. Social movements are far more attractive forms of political organization, because they rise and fall with the significance of the problems motivating them (Horvat, 1982:308–27). The state must be decentralized too. This can be accomplished by the separation of powers into distinct administrative branches which deal with rule making, rule application, rule adjudication, institutional control, recruitment and administration (Horvat, 1982:283–306). This decentralization of political power and the acknowledgment of the importance of social control over government reflects a major departure from the harmonious unity suggested by some visions of the classless utopia: "Socialism eliminates class conflicts but not all conflicts; class interests, but not diversity of interests. Conflicts have to be resolved and diverse interests brought into harmony" (Horvat, 1982:301).

This decentralization of politics and state does not pose major problems for the traditional utopia of Marxism, inasmuch as Marx's own praise for the 1871 Paris Commune relied heavily on democratic control of societal administration. Trotsky also comes round to identify pluralism and political compromises as essential to the construction of socialism (if not in its realization). But how does this acknowledgment of the diversity of interests translate into the economic sphere? Horvat is quite different from Trotsky in the Yugoslav's commitment to analyzing the economic foundations of this political class's power.

Against state ownership of the means of production and an etatist organization of production which emphasizes the unity of political and economic leadership, administrative appointment from above, and one-man management in economic organization, Horvat counterposes a socialist organization (Horvat, 1982:188–90) and social property in production. Truly social ownership of production is implied when every member of society "(1) has the right to work; (2) has the right to compete for any job, according to his personal capability (consistent with the specifications of the job); (3) has the right to participate in management in equal terms and (4) derives economic benefits exclusively from his work and none from property" (Horvat, 1982:237).

Social property relations depend, however, on the supersession of central state planning as the sole instrument organizing economic activity. Instead, this planning must be part of some optimal combination that also includes markets, economic regulation, information and non-market inter-organizational coordination. The state does not, however, control the market or planning; regulation is accomplished through a federation of various associations in the economy and at the various territorial and functional levels of the state (Horvat, 1982:328–67).

Most of Horvat's discussion focuses on what socialism should look like. This is an important part of the critical project inasmuch as it provides the alternative vision with which to evaluate the existing order. It also suggests that the "core" of this revised Marxism has little to do with substantive propositions about the preeminence of class and more with the centrality of a vision of the non-alienated individual (e.g. Marković, 1977). Not surprisingly, this emphasis on utopia in defining Marxism leads to a major reformulation of praxis.

One homogeneous class with its own interests struggling against another is superseded by a vision of various social movements, none ontologically fundamental, struggling to organize themselves and achieve self-governance. In fact, in etatist societies, the intelligentsia plays the central role in this struggle by restoring meaning to the hijacked slogans of the original revolution. Workers ultimately are likely to engage in collective action and struggle for their own trade unions to protect their interests in work. Both struggles lead to self-management, although workers' self-management will probably appear first (Horvat, 1982: 468–71). Class is replaced by self-organization and self-management as the central concepts organizing the analysis of praxis, even while classlessness remains the foundation of utopia.

By this revision, Horvat overcomes the basic dilemma of the Marxist critique of actual socialism. The opposition between the homogeneity implied in class and the diversity implied in democracy is resolved in favor of the latter. Equality, pluralism and negotiated consensus become mutually important partners for socialism. Their compatibility is established through their linkage in the decentralized organizational structure of self-management.

This alternative is probably the most developed foundation for a critical sociology of Soviet-type society. It is especially useful for a more general understanding of Solidarity's struggle, inasmuch as the Polish movement becomes an example of a more general praxis of self-organization and self-management in Soviet-type society. There are, nevertheless, important problems associated with this revision of Marxism.

In general, this revised Marxism treats cultural factors as secondary to the natural impetus of humans to struggle for a genuine socialism based on self-management. This is reasonable in light of the comparatively great legitimacy socialism enjoys in Yugoslavia, but it is more questionable when we turn to Poland. Workers struggle there too for self-management, but whether they associate this struggle with Marxism and socialism is doubtful. When they fail to associate the struggle with Marxism, they fail to find foreign capitalist investment and ownership of their means of production problematic. And thus, self-management, if still a part of the transformative struggle in

Poland, can become an ally to capitalist rationalization, rather than to the socialization of the means of production.

It is even more doubtful whether the majority of the Polish intelligentsia still wishes to identify its aspirations with that of the unfulfilled socialist vision. It is unlikely, therefore, that the intelligentsia will play its strategic role in the transformation of etatism into socialism. If the intelligentsia plays a significant role in the transition to socialism, culture becomes even more obviously important to explaining the alternative futures of actual socialist societies than if we are to rely on workers' class interest in socialism alone.

Culture becomes even more significant when the struggle over "truth," and not just control over the means of production, is a central ingredient to praxis. Indeed, one likely reaction to the association between lies and the identification of truth through praxis or pragmatism is to return to the eternal standards of truth offered by tradition or religious authority. In this sense, any critical sociology which downplays cultural factors loses its ability to explain the problem of "truth" in praxis. We especially cannot assume that all etatist societies have the same cultural commitment to a "true" socialism. "Truth" might come to be defined in ways which are antagonistic to equality and self-government by the associated producers. Cultural affinities for authoritarianism and religious hierarchy might make claims to truth and egalitarian self-governance especially difficult to realize.

Self-management was, nevertheless, a central problem in the struggles of Solidarity, and in this Horvat provides a valuable structure for explaining praxis in Soviet-type society. But there are radically different strategies for a self-managing transformation. These differences need not be linked to culture, and might be explained through a more traditional class analysis. The self-managed revision of Marxism effectively eliminates class as an important analytic category, however. It redefines ruling class in terms of political authority, and redefines praxis and utopia in terms of self-governance. While this formulation of critique captures an important dimension of the basic struggle, it tends to overlook the subsidiary struggles that make alliances between different classes accomplishments rather than automatic. If all citizens have an equal interest in self-management, their coordinated activity is merely a problem of adequate consciousness and sufficient power against the state. But does that not answer *a priori* a question that should be asked? Do all groups have an equal stake in self-managing socialism? Do some groups benefit by an alliance with an etatist order? No matter the utopia, the problem of class alliances should be made central.

A new foundation for class relations

One revision of class analysis that challenges the problems faced by Trotsky and illuminates issues avoided by self-management theorists can be found in the perspective promoted by Konrád and Szelényi (1979) and Szelényi's more recent work (1982, 1986–87, 1989). Although they share important elements of Djilas's (1957) thesis for the Stalinist period, Konrád and Szelényi are sensitive to the emergence of a new kind of class structure in Soviet-type societies which enables the intelligentsia to be potentially on the road to class power.

Their analysis follows Machajski's work, in that they believe the intelligentsia uses its vanguard role as the fulfiller of the historical interests of the working class only to establish its own class domination (Konrád and Szelényi, 1979:3, 139–42). Thus, the Communist Party is the vanguard of the intelligentsia's class domination (Szelényi, 1982:312). In these systems, superior teleological knowledge, rather than property ownership *per se*, guarantees the right to dispose of society's surplus. Hence, to gain the right the bourgeoisie enjoys by virtue of its property ownership, one must have "specialized knowledge," and hence, be some kind of intellectual to become part of the ruling class in rational redistributive systems (p. 46).[9]

The class structure of these societies is potentially dichotomous, with the intelligentsia at one end and workers at the other (p. 145). There are, of course, middle strata, who neither possess redistributive power nor engage in directly productive labor, like lower-level supervisory personnel. But these strata wind up becoming the "vassals" of the dominant and a buffer between them and workers (p. 146). The dominating class thus not only extends to those who directly redistribute the surplus, but to all those who "create and maintain the rational–redistributive ethos, and make out of it an ideology which pervades the society's entire culture" (p. 76).

The party continues to be dominant, but it rules in the interest of the intelligentsia. Contrary to its ideology, it does not rule in the general or workers' interest. Workers, for example, do not enjoy higher wages, better living conditions or greater privilege than the intelligentsia. Neither do they enjoy any greater say in managing their own or society's affairs than workers in capitalism (pp. 171–78). In one sense, Soviet-type societies are even worse than capitalist societies, since workers are never permitted to organize their own independent organizations. Programs of the most liberal party reformers have consistently failed to advocate the establishment of independent workers' organizations, although independent intellectuals' organizations are advocated (p. 174). The final proof for the non-working class character of the party is that worker dissidents systematically suffer greater penalties than intellectual opponents of the regime (p. 175).

The Communist Party is not entirely a party of the intelligentsia, however. The party is both the mass party of the intelligentsia and the cadre party of the workers (Konrád and Szelényi, 1979:179). Intellectuals make up the bulk of the party's membership, but party membership also provides a vehicle by which children of workers can escape their parents' class position. The party's ruling elite also remains somewhat separate from the intelligentsia *en masse*. It reserves to itself the right to make all decisions, and to locate its superior vision of the general interest over the perhaps superior technical knowledge of the intellectual (p. 182). Hence, the technocrat's bridle at the yoke of the irrational political domination of his technical expertise is a sign of his exclusion from direct political rule (p. 179).

Although excluded from direct rule, the intellectual's involvement in active domination of the society has increased. Stalin's purges of intellectuals, of course, showed that they were by no means direct rulers. But these purges yielded too much power to the secret police for the safety of the ruling elite themselves, and hence, the ruling elite sought a new solution where they created a "rationally controlled system of conflicts between the intellectual class and ruling elite" (p. 187).

Szelényi (1982:312) later argues that in the early stages, the party was the vanguard of the intelligentsia as a new dominant class. Under Stalin, it becomes the intelligentsia's potential enemy, but with economic reforms, and as the economy gains more autonomy from politics, the intelligentsia begins to assert its dominant class position. Thus, although the ruling elite continues to rule, it includes the intelligentsia, and especially its technical component, into the ranks of ruling class. There is thus a "joint exercise of power" between elite and intelligentsia, with the elite retaining hegemony (p. 201).

The most basic struggle since Stalin is between this alliance and workers. Konrád and Szelényi's case for the antagonistic class relations between classes rests on two bases: (1) the existence of a structural conflict of interest between classes; and (2) the relatively privileged position of the intelligentsia in comparison to the working class.

The intelligentsia is united in its belief that superior knowledge should determine the distribution of surplus; workers have an alternative principle, being that those who actually produce the society's wealth should decide how it should be distributed. This conflict, in fact, reproduces the alternative ideas of socialism present in classical socialist theories (Szelényi, 1982:313). But this class antagonism will only develop when the political becomes relatively separated from the economy and society; until then, intellectuals and workers will be united against the ruling elite in their common wish to create basic civil liberties (Szelényi, 1982:323).

Proof of the preferred class position of the intelligentsia *vis-à-vis* workers can be seen in the increasingly superior position of intellectuals since Stalinism's demise. Its standard of living has improved more than workers' and their security from the ruling elite's repression has increased. Technocrats, more than humanist intellectuals, are especially secure. When the ruling elite crushes revisionist challenge, and prevents the emergence of a more liberal political order, the technocrat becomes an obedient servant, "exacting compensation for its subordinate status in the form of a higher level of material rewards" (p. 212). This is an unstable compromise, however.

Technocrats do not enjoy their subordination to the ruling elite, and may have to decide, at critical historical junctures, whose side they are on (p. 215). When Konrád and Szelényi were writing, they observed that the ruling elite had launched a "counter-offensive," reining in the economic reforms and liberal cultural policies won in the heyday of compromise. The elite has tried to position the technical intelligentsia against humanist intellectuals, and especially prevent any alliance of technocrats with the working class. It has tried to buy off sectors of the intelligentsia and working class with greater privilege (p. 219).

What of the chances for a historic alliance of technocrats, humanist intellectuals and workers against the ruling elite? Konrád and Szelényi (1979:220–21) recognize that for the technocracy to throw off the elite's domination, it may have to allow other social groups to articulate their own interests, much like the French bourgeoisie had to allow the masses their own say and organizations in the eighteenth-century democratic revolution. Marginal, drop-out intellectuals may also appear to articulate the workers' interests, but to do so, such an organic intelligentsia of the working class will have to challenge their own class's right to dispose of surplus, and replace it with a principle of workers' legitimacy to such disposition, based on the workers' creation of the surplus, or its possession of labor power (p. 224).

While there is the chance that marginal intellectuals will become an organic intelligentsia for the working class, there is an even greater possibility for a tactical alliance of workers and the entire intelligentsia against the ruling elite in their common wish for creating "transactive socio-economic relations."

> The workers have a stake in the technocracy's reform proposals insofar as they aim to link productivity and wage scales more closely and assure that capital and labor will flow without administrative hindrance to more economically efficient branches of the economy. Such reforms would ... give a powerful impetus to the development of the consumer goods industries and agriculture, and they would make room in a more rational and less overextended state budget for larger and more rapid wage increases. (p. 230)

While this makes possible a tactical alliance, the workers' interests in their own associations in self-management and independent unions could later challenge the intelligentsia's privilege to decide the allocation of surplus on the basis of its superior knowledge. But if the workers are not given their own power centers, technocracy itself has no protection from the ruling elite (p. 232). Hence, the intelligentsia finds itself between two power centers, ruling elite and workers, and its choice of ally becomes subject to the patterns of future struggles.

Thus, should the intelligentsia overthrow the ruling elite, and assume the sole dominant class position, it will do so only in alliance with the working class. But in so doing, it will have allowed the workers their own organizations, which will limit the intelligentsia's own power. The intelligentsia might then become the sole dominant class, but its own hegemony will be more limited than that which the ruling elite enjoyed. The workers' ideology will therefore become something of an opposition ideology, not replacing rational redistribution as such but limiting its redistributive power in "articulated conflict systems" (Szelényi, 1982:314–15). That could mean, then, that the relatively privileged position of the intelligentsia will actually deteriorate.[10]

Given the surprises these societies have offered in the last three decades, it seems too bold to rule out any particular direction of transformation. Ivan Szelényi's (1986–87) autocritique of his work with Konrád finds that the future domination of the intelligentsia should be considered only as one possible alternative future, and by 1985 less likely than it appeared in 1975 because of the short-sighted stubbornness of bureaucracy and the growth of small private business. Given these developments, Szelényi finds several alternative alliances possible.

One such alliance is between industrial workers in heavy industry and cadre intellectuals, or party bureaucratic elite, against any market-based technocratic reform. Alternatively, we could find an alliance of the technocracy and the emergent petty bourgeoisie. The final possibility is an alliance of the "popular forces" (workers, petty bourgeoisie and intelligentsia) against the authorities. This future Szelényi finds least likely, even though it was characteristic of Poland in 1980–81. He believes Solidarity to be an accident deriving from the intransigence of Polish bureaucracy. He doubts that such an alliance as was Solidarity's could survive, as this alliance is most threatening to the authorities, and one most readily repressed.[11]

This revision of the class analysis of Soviet-type societies overcomes several of the difficulties in Marxist critique discussed so far. First, it does not fall into the trap other Marxist analyses have by identifying a ruling class with a set of politically or administratively defined positions. This revision is, however, a major departure from identifying class on the basis of relationship to the means of production, though it nevertheless does continue to make the disposal of surplus value key to the identification of classes. Second, the praxis implied by his analysis is not just a political revolution, but also a transformation of political economy from centralized planning into "transactive socio-economic relations." This market transformation thus challenges the traditional Marxian identification of socialism with planning. But it does identify praxis with the struggle over surplus value, and thus brings class back in. In this, Szelényi is entirely compatible with self-management theorists.

Third, while this perspective carries forward the assumption from class analysis that one's interests are determined structurally, it avoids identifying class interest with a logic of history. It therefore moves beyond *evolutionary* Marxisms by positing several alternative futures for class alliances. In Szelényi's autocritique, class interests do not determine class alliances. Instead, various historical and sociological conditions lead to different alliances of classes with divergent interests. *A critical question in the analysis of reproduction and transformation of Soviet-type societies, then, is under what conditions different class alliances are made.* Where the private sector is underdeveloped and the entrepreneurial class is insignificant, as in most Soviet-type societies outside of Hungary, the question centers on which way the intelligentsia will turn. What factors might lead to the fulfillment of the new class project, where the intelligentsia allies with the ruling elite against the working class? What factors might push it to risk its already privileged position to ally with the working class in opposition? These questions are not posed when self-management is assumed to be the common interest of society against the state.

Fourth, like the self-management theorists, this argument also moves away from an undefined utopia of classless society. Szelényi (1986–87) finds that this utopia is too dangerous in its use by the new class itself, as a means of justifying their own domination. Instead, he prefers an alternative based on "the diversification of class power" (p. 140), where workers play the bourgeoisie and "new class" off against one another. This is an important theoretical departure, inasmuch as it tries to reconsider the utopia of critical sociology.

In another text, Szelényi (1979:204) regards the question of whether civil society is or is not identical with capitalist economy the central problem for both Eastern European and Western socialist theory. These alternative statements are not too far from one another, inasmuch as they both make central the idea that some kind of pluralism of power resources is essential to the emancipation of society, and that the only way in which such a pluralism can be guaranteed is by reconsidering the place of capitalist relations of production in the emancipated society.

Trotsky's failure to establish the economic foundations of political domination led to an unresolved tension between the centrality of class in his critique and his commitment to democratic pluralism. This tension is not resolved by labelling the politically dominant a ruling class, for this approach still fails to challenge the political–economic foundations of their rule. The self-management theorists do manage to resolve the tension, however, by establishing these very political–economic conditions. But in the process they identify the ruling class as political and praxis as self-management, retaining only classlessness as a normative foundation. Indeed classlessness is made deliberately compatible with difference as other sources of identity, from ethnicity to region to function, are acknowledged as reasons for institutionalizing procedures for compromise in socialism. Szelényi also reconciles pluralism and class analysis, but while class is the centerpoint of his analysis of domination and praxis, he rejects classlessness as utopia.

Szelényi's pluralism is certainly less utopian, indeed consciously so. Does this pose any disadvantages? Should we argue that Szelényi's trade-in of classlessness for class pluralism weakens the normative power of his critique of Soviet-type society? Does this set of alternatives mean that the only way in which class can be compatible with a commitment to pluralism is if its analytical priority disappears in the analysis of praxis and domination or as a normative foundation? The disappearance of class in the analysis of domination and praxis in actual socialism is by no means a guarantee that democratic pluralism will gain equal footing with classlessness in utopia. Rudolph Bahro's *The Alternative in Eastern Europe* (1978) is the last Marxist critique of actual socialism we shall consider in this chapter. It too claims to jettison class from its analysis of domination and praxis while retaining an unrevised vision of classless socialism as its utopia.

The new praxis

Rudolph Bahro (1978:183–202) rejects the value of class analysis for developing an emancipatory project in advanced industrial societies, since "the subject of the emancipatory movement is to be found in the energetic and creative elements of all strata and spheres of society" (p. 326). This rejection is mostly based on a pessimistic view of the universality of the interests of any class. Hence, "the whole problem of general emancipation must be placed on a new basis, as far as its practical political form is concerned" (p. 202). But while no class possesses universal interests, as Marx thought the proletariat to have, Bahro thinks that the intelligentsia is the most likely opponent of the Soviet-style system of domination. In this, the intelligentsia assumes a fundamentally different role than that offered by Szelényi: from oppressor to savior.

Bahro's faith in the intelligentsia is based on his analysis of the structure of domination in what he calls "actually existing socialism" or "proto-socialist" society. The idea of domination depends, of course, on the notion of emancipation. Emancipation, for Bahro, is the "overcoming of subalternity on a mass scale" (p. 271) or the "liberation of individuals from all socially determined limitations on their development."[12] Bahro (1978:255) argues that it occurs when

> men are positively placed in a position to appropriate creatively the social totality – or to put it another way, to make subjectively their own the quintessence of the overall cultural achievement that mankind has so far produced or reproduced ... that everyone can acquire all the individual abilities that correspond to the general level of the existing productive forces and system of regulation.

The intelligentsia is in the forefront of struggle because their social location most dramatically confronts the reality of oppression and the potential of emancipation in Soviet-type societies. The scientific revolution that the advanced Soviet-type societies have undergone has created a mass of intellectually developed laborers who have a capacity for abstraction and hence greater ability to realize the emancipatory project (p. 175). Being involved in mundane tasks throughout the day, the common laborer fails to have the psychic energy or social consciousness to demand the fulfillment of "emancipatory needs," and is satisfied more easily with other "compensatory needs" that stultify rather than encourage the emancipatory project. Bahro considers consumerist satisfaction as a typical compensatory need, and an emancipatory need as the self-realization of the personality in a wide sphere of activities (p. 272). Given the growing recruitment of society's members to the intelligentsia, the prospects for a real revolutionary emancipatory project are enhanced.

The basis for revolt in Soviet-type societies is the "surplus of human expertise" (p. 176). Although all individuals, given the "universal natural endowment of the human brain," are capable of more than their social situations allow, those who have learned the dialectical structures of philosophy, mathematics and art "are capable in principle of understanding any problem, no matter how complex, and moreover, understanding it more profoundly than would be necessary for egalitarian social communication" (p. 177). While the highly educated thus have the potential to engage in the planning of their society, the bureaucratic domination of the society impedes their creative contribution. Like Hirszowicz (1980) and Szelényi, Bahro recognizes that the professional is well integrated into the system, but he goes one step further to recognize how that integration is incomplete. While the bureaucratization of the specialists' social consciousness integrates them into the status quo, it also forces them to engage in a *reservatio mentalis*, in which each individual distances himself from the role he is forced to perform (p. 317). The more the system produces members of the intelligentsia, the greater the inability for the bureaucracy to absorb, through providing compensatory needs, the emancipatory interests the intelligentsia's greater consciousness inspires (p. 319). This happens in two ways: first, there are more professionals outside the apparatus itself; and second, those within the apparatus also become potential opponents of the status quo, because of their failure to identify with the role their job demands of them. In a sense, the lines of struggle cannot be drawn between occupations or levels in a hierarchy, but go right through the heads of the intelligentsia employed in the apparatus (p. 320).[13]

This "surplus consciousness" (having the ability to manage affairs without having the power to do it) exists on a continuum that extends down through the social structure to the immediate producers. It is especially strong, however, among specialists in social policy, since, although their work is both detailed and linked to ideal representations of society, they are devoid of any real power (Bahro, 1978:326). Thus, the emancipatory potential of any group comes from the distance between its ability and desire to manage society and its actual power to do so.

To this point, I find Bahro's argument compelling. As I shall argue in part III, professionals are indeed frustrated by the political domination of their expertise and, given the opportunity, are eager to throw off the yoke of political domination. This observation is not inconsistent with Szelényi's views either, since in his analysis too the intelligentsia would only become the sole rulers when they could oust the political rulers from their hegemonic position within the ruling alliance of political elites and intelligentsia. While Szelényi sees the triumph of the intelligentsia as the final step toward their class rule, Bahro, however, does not believe that the intelligentsia would institute a system that would systematically favor its own status.

His faith in the future's progress does not rest on the virtue of the intelligentsia themselves, but rather the role of a new League of Communists. He acknowledges that members of the intelligentsia are, by their education, better equipped to put forward self-interested programs, but it is the obligation of a new genuinely emancipatory party to block unjust claims by socially powerful groups (p. 352). His party is to be organized as the "collective intellectual, which mediates the reflection of the whole society and its consciousness of all problems of social development" (p. 362). This new party would not represent the intelligentsia's interest, however, but rather universal interests in the emancipatory project. What constitutes the emancipatory project? The dismantling of the traditional division of labor, since this social characteristic is the main impediment to the equal appropriation of culture (p. 364).

Bahro takes great pains to show how his new revolutionary party would differ from the degenerated parties that rule. He claims they must be organized differently from the existing communist parties: they must be open to all social forces; they must have unimpeded communication; state institutions must be responsible to society and not to the party; and changes would be made by the party by its convincing the society as to the correctness of the party's position (pp. 363–70). In this, there is little difference from Trotsky's reliance on a vanguard.

There are several serious problems with Bahro's interpretation, however. First, the party is in a weak position to effect changes, or even to block the domination of the intelligentsia, since its power relies only on the persuasiveness and intellectual quality of its arguments (p. 362). Second, since the party is open to all social elements, it seems doubtful that the division of labor will be attacked, given the potential capacity for intellectuals to assume prominent positions in such a party and as much as any other group they would probably promote their own interests. Thus, although I am suspicious of Bahro's faith in a revolutionary party for continuing to push for an end to the social division of labor, it seems reasonable to think that the organization of the Soviet-type society moves professionals to opposition.

Bahro is forced to rely on the vanguard party in his view of transformation because he remains tied to class analysis, despite his disavowal of its usefulness. While he has discarded classes from his critique, he nevertheless continues to put imputed interests to the center of his analysis. Workers, although no longer a coherent class in proto-socialist society, cannot recognize their own "real" interests. Their comparatively limited education also limits their capacity to articulate their own emancipatory needs. Thus, in public discussion, the intelligentsia will be able to put forward its own agenda better than workers and, without the revolutionary party, workers would become the disadvantaged class once again. In order to realize truly universal interests, and not just return to a situation where various groups conflict over their own immediate interests, Bahro needs an organization to lead that possesses the vision of a Platonic philosopher king or Hobbesian sovereign to recognize society's interests. Thus, while Bahro explicitly rejects class analysis, his utopia remains that of class analysis: a unified, classless society.

The faith in the possibility of a group representing truly universal interests is what separates Bahro from both Szelényi and Horvat, and what makes the former opt for a Leninist solution, and the latter move toward models of socialist pluralism. Szelényi is suspicious of any claim that one group can represent the universal interests of the whole. Bahro, despite his skepticism of the possibility, ultimately is forced to take up that faith, since his utopia, the elimination of the division of labor, is a goal likely to be resisted by the only group whose "superior consciousness" would enable them to push for such an emancipatory need.

Alvin Gouldner presents a compromise between these positions. Gouldner (1979:83–85) recognizes that the intelligentsia would articulate its own selfish interests, but since it "subverts all establishments, social limits, and privileges, including its own . . . [and] bears a culture of critical and careful discourse which is an historically emancipatory rationality," it can thus be considered as a universal class, albeit flawed. Relying on the possibilities of open and free discourse to guarantee emancipation seems to put the cart before the horse, however. Intellectuals can, as the experience of Soviet-type society suggests, succumb to the attractions of power resources that go beyond superior argumentation. Indeed, it seems that the universalism guaranteed by open debate requires some kind of institutional foundation to guarantee its preservation. A "diversification of class power," following Szelényi, is one such base. Another requires more sustained attention to the political realm, as the Solidarity movement suggested.

Reflections on Marxist critiques of Soviet-type society

Trotsky's analysis of Soviet-type society is the intellectual ancestor of most Marxist critiques of Soviet-type society. Except for a few contemporary theorists like Mandel, most have moved away from Trotsky's thesis because it is, like the regime it described, transitional. By denying a class basis to domination, Trotsky implicitly calls into question whether a praxis and a utopia based on class is adequate to critical sociology. This theoretical instability has led in several directions. Most common for Marxists has been the attempt to reinstate the centrality of class. One can define domination in Soviet-type society as a kind of class domination similar to that in capitalism, requiring the same kind of class struggle and relying on the same image of a classless utopia. This state-capitalist thesis is, for reasons that I have not pursued here but that have been documented adequately elsewhere, hardly a satisfactory solution (Lane, 1984). Another option is to consider that a new kind of class domination has emerged, as Djilas and those in the bureaucratic collectivist school argue. This solution is also inadequate, because this form of "class rule" is based on an administrative hierarchy, not on production relations. In this, I find much of what Trotsky argued persuasive. But, more problematic, this position also replicates Trotsky's problem when it promotes a praxis that focuses more on the democratic reorganization of social life, and fails to challenge the political economy which grants the ruling group its power: central economic planning.

The third strategy is to challenge statist economic planning directly by calling for an alternative of self-managing socialism. This makes explicit the political–economic foundations of class rule, even if that class is politically constituted. It changes praxis, however, by de-emphasizing any particular group or class as the transformative agent, and instead argues that all groups must engage in their own self-organization and self-management. Class returns as a significant concept only when classlessness identifies the organizational revolution self-management represents. But because this strategy minimizes the significance of class in praxis, it fails to raise the problem of class alliances and antagonisms in the construction of classlessness. Nevertheless, this is probably the most systematic and best developed of all Marxist critiques.

The fourth option reformulates the nature of class relations in actual socialism, as Szelényi has done. As the former, this approach makes explicit the political–economic foundations of class rule. But because it focuses on class rather than self-management in praxis, it invites a reconsideration of class alliances. In particular, it raises the question of the possibilities for domination by the intelligentsia along with the political elite, or for opposition by the intelligentsia in alliance with the working class. In addition, this asks whether the reemergence of a petty bourgeoisie might be a progressive development for the working class, in which the working class might play off one master against the other. This is one of the most promising directions for class analysis in so far as it recognizes the distinctiveness of domination in this system and is most sensitive to the importance of recognizing divergent interests and thus pluralism. It is also the most uncertain in its consistency with the Marxist tradition, as it finds much of the classical liberal argument on democracy sound.

The last option which treats class centrally is to deny one is engaging any kind of class analysis, but carry forward some image of a unified society and common imputed societal interest in struggle, as Bahro. This leads one into a cul-de-sac: the only way to achieve the classless society enabling unity is to reproduce the same kind of elitist political organization which helped structure the domination of actual socialism from the start.

Another option altogether for critical sociology is to take Trotsky's theoretical dilemma in the other direction and consider whether, in fact, domination, praxis and utopia in Soviet-type society should not be discussed in terms of class, but rather in terms of politics and culture. The Marxist critiques we have considered here treat cultural differences among Soviet-type societies as barely relevant, if at all, and, except for Bahro, the cultural constitution of classes as minimally important. Questions of political organization are treated more seriously by Szelényi, and especially by Horvat, but typically with reference to class. Need politics and class be tied so? Should culture not be brought in more directly? Could a critical sociology of Soviet-type society do without class? The answer to that question depends on the theoretical possibility of substituting some kind of state-domination model for one based on class, and on replacing the classless utopia of emancipatory politics with a civil society.

5 Solidarity, culture and civil society

Jones's (1984) critique of the political model of Soviet-type society, especially in its totalitarian version, rests on its overemphasis of the political and relative ignorance of social structural features. He also argues that the political model is limited by its static character. Subsequent approaches within the political genre, like the interest-group approach, have allowed for these societies' greater pluralism, but they are still constrained by their political focus.

But is the totalitarian model not the ultimate critical approach? The most vociferous opponents of Communist Party-led regimes frequently call these societies "totalitarian." Ronald Reagan, for instance, won widespread popularity in Poland when he called the Soviet Union "an evil empire." Much of the Eastern Central European opposition itself uses the term "totalitarian" (Rupnik, 1988). Certainly, in the common use of the term "critical," "totalitarian regimes" and "evil empires" are severe denunciations. They are less useful for an *immanent* critique, however, inasmuch as the totalitarian approach assumes that no change can come from within. The totalitarian model tends to lead its proponent to the view that totalitarian systems are invincible in the face of domestic challenge. The Hungarian revolution supposedly destroyed that belief in totalitarianism's immutability (Fehér and Heller, 1983).

Although this revolution may have changed the beliefs of totalitarian theorists on the theoretical *possibility* of internally driven transformation, neither the policies of its political adherents nor the problematics of its theoretical proponents give much credence to that eventuality. For example, Reagan's policy on the Sandinistas in Nicaragua, whom he called totalitarian, was based on their American-funded military defeat. Theorists of totalitarianism who study the Prague Spring tend to discount the possibility that internally driven change could have yielded real transformation (Krystufek, 1982). The choice by many in the Polish opposition to use the term "totalitarian" is sometimes motivated more by political than analytical interests.[1] But there is also an analytical moment in this choice of terms, as it suits their mode of transformative praxis.

The conceptual transformation of totalitarianism

One of the major distinctions among forms of transformative praxis in actual socialism is drawn on the basis of how much significance is granted to change within the Communist Party. Initial struggles against Stalinism generally relied on revisionist strategy (Michnik, 1976 [1985]). To the degree that transformation rests on change initiated within the Communist Party, one can say the transformative praxis is guided by a strategy of "revisionism" (Rupnik, 1979). Revisionism characterizes the Polish October of 1956, the Prague Spring of 1968 and Soviet *perestroika*.

Another strategy of transformation rejects any reliance on changes in the Communist Party itself, and relies exclusively on external pressure on the party. Here the main impetus for change comes from below. It is a form of struggle associated with Adam Michnik's "new evolutionism" (Michnik, 1976 [1985]) and later Polish Solidarity itself. It can be called a transformative praxis of "self-organization" or "civil society." The model of totalitarianism has been adopted and transformed by this strategy with peculiar consequences.

The model of totalitarianism implies stagnation. Transformation depends on external gestures. But since the failed 1956 Hungarian revolution, few in the Eastern European opposition have believed that the West would intervene on behalf of any transformation. The failure of the West to intervene in 1956 demonstrated the significance of the Yalta Agreement and of the superpowers' "spheres of influence" (Fehér, 1988). Thus, to adopt the totalitarian model without modification would lead to a fatalist politics, an absence of political imagination, a smooth extension of the present with no possibility for real change.

The totalitarian model was transformed by the Polish opposition by limiting the system of totalitarianism to the political sphere. Society was no longer conceptually part of totalitarianism, and thus could act independently. The totalitarian authorities remain stagnant, but transformation becomes possible due to a new external force: the independent society. Thus, when Solidarity activists use the totalitarian model, they continue its tradition of rejecting the possibility of immanent transformation, but only because they emasculate totalitarianism by redrawing the borders of its system. Their system is drawn on political terms alone, with "society" resting outside its boundaries. Hence, there is even skepticism about whether Poland deserves the term "Soviet-type society." Poles have argued with me that yes, the *system* is of the Soviet-type, but the *society* is separate. Can one imagine a Marxist saying a system is capitalist, while its society is not?[2]

This is a peculiar use of the notion "totalitarian", and is a considerable departure from its original usage. The original term was developed to illustrate the penetration by a government of all spheres of society, not just those spheres characteristic of government penetration in capitalism. William Kornhauser (1959:123), for instance, defined it so: "Totalitarian dictatorship involves total domination, limited neither by received laws or codes (as in traditional authoritarianism) nor even the boundaries of governmental functions (as in classical tyranny), since *they obliterate the distinction between state and society*." This Polish conceptual transformation is nevertheless consistent with the original model because the alternatives underlying critique remain political. Classical totalitarian approaches employ the liberal/dictatorial *polity* difference in their critique. Transformation is typically based on an escape from single-party dictatorship and a return to public freedom through multiple-party parliamentary politics. This political pluralism is to be one of the fundamental points upon which the "good society" can be constructed, with the good society being one in which civil liberties and "freedom" reign. The "social question," i.e. poverty and economic inequality, is not considered a central part of the proper transformative or revolutionary debate (Arendt, 1963 [1979]).

An answer to the social question nevertheless is implicit in classical totalitarian models. If this question should not be addressed by the political sphere, the invisible hand of the self-adjusting market necessarily returns. Even the welfare state becomes a threat to public freedom. But the answer to the social question in this resurrected totalitarian model is unclear. The classical liberalism of Hayek (1944) and Friedman (1962) has gained popularity in Poland, especially among the technical and young humanistic intelligentsia. Although the various economic-reform programs put forward during the Solidarity period owed much to Polish socialist economists like Oskar Lange, Michal Kalecki and Wlodzimierz Brus (Nuti, 1981 [1982]), after martial law, free-market theories have gained increasing currency among parts of the intelligentsia.[3] Friedman's leitmotif, that capitalism is the necessary but not sufficient condition of freedom, finds growing numbers of supporters in Polish "post-capitalist" society.[4]

Despite this wide interest in neo-classical economics and classical liberalism in 1980s Poland, the new totalitarian model's stance on the social question is ambiguous. The new model demands some kind of destatization of the economy, but it is unclear whether that means the restoration of capitalist production relations or some "third way", neither statist nor capitalist (Horvat, 1982; Šik, 1976). Indeed, it is unclear where in this struggle between totalitarian political authorities and the self-organized society the economy fits all (Judt, 1988). This silence on political economy is partially an artifact of the political focus of the original totalitarian model, but it also has strategic roots. The market reforms most programs promote are unlikely to receive mass support given the ways in which they undermine employee security. Thus opposition movements generally increase their appeal by avoiding the "social question" altogether.

The absence of a political–economic program is in some ways compensated for by the new model's emphasis on culture. Because totalitarianism in East Central Europe is culturally constructed as the representative of foreign interests, the independent society need have no explicit economic model upon which to base its resistance to domination. Instead, its struggle can be based on a *cultural identity*, not an alternative societal model or social utopia. In fact, resistance in Poland tends to remain more solidary when it relies on abstract values and symbolism linked to religion and nation, and less unified when it invokes specific political or economic programs. Identity is, of course, essential as a foundation for resistance, but it is not obvious that a praxis based on identity by itself is transformative (Touraine, 1984:75–82).

The totalitarian model thus raises several major problems for a critical sociology of Soviet-type society. The first major objection, that it offers no image of immanent change, is "solved" by the Polish transformation's limiting the totalitarian sphere to the political authorities. Totalitarianism is not, then, an accomplishment, but an ambition of the authorities, as society remains beyond their control. "Independent society", then, serves as both emancipatory agent and utopia. This concept of independent society contains potentially contradictory ingredients, however. Drawing on the romantic tradition, "society" can be presented as an alternative unified culture. The independent-society image has also suggested a naturalistic utilitarian model, where rational actors pursuing their self-interest in the framework of civil society realize the greatest good for the greatest number of people. In the former, struggle is based on an eternal conflict between antagonistic cultures; in the latter, rebellion is grounded in the "natural" goal of moral actors to seek freedom. Although many Western "post-Marxists" and Eastern European sociologists have relied on both notions of the independent society to make their case, there are reasons to believe that the cultural and the political foundations of the independent society are not mutually reinforcing, and that even if compatible with one another, together they *might be* antithetical to the general critical project. In the following sections of this chapter I elaborate these general problems and clarify their relevance to the critical sociology of Soviet-type society.

Cultural foundations of the independent society

Polish sociology is oriented far more toward researching values than is Western sociology. Florian Znaniecki's cultural sociology, Stanisław Ossowski's emphasis on the subjective dimension of stratification and Maria Ossowska's investigations of morality bequeath a strong tradition in researching the "subjective." Attitudinal surveys are also a well-developed research method in Polish sociology, reinforcing interest in the investigation of values. But the study of values has gained a new dynamic from the development of a critical spirit in Polish sociology. Solidarity inspired many Polish sociologists to redirect inquiry toward the conditions of domination and resistance. Because the Marxian tradition of class analysis lost much of its critical edge, many Polish sociologists turned to their own tradition in cultural analysis and to the cultural emphases of Western sociologists like Touraine to develop a suitable problematic.[5]

This problematic revolves around the notion of separate public and private cultures, or "social dimorphism" (Wnuk-Lipiński, 1982, 1987). All societies have these separate realms, but in Poland, Wnuk-Lipiński (1987) argues, they are more separate and more antagonistic because of the characters of the ruling group and society. The ruling group's public realm is culturally alien. This monocentric and statist ruling group, through its control of language, law and physical coercion, does not need social legitimacy to remain in power. It recruits its members on the basis of political criteria, not meritocracy, and denies the possibility that its rule could ever be replaced. Society, that which is outside the state, accepts that rule because it cannot imagine any viable alternative. Society nevertheless manages to retain a separate vitality. Social dimorphism, although it exists within a political framework, rests ultimately on cultural foundations. Cultural differences separate authorities from society, and cultural resources enable society's continued independent existence. Polish sociologists generally set up the cultural antagonism as a conflict between collectivism and individualism or between political manipulation and truth. According to Wnuk-Lipiński, the official value system is a collectivist ideology based on state ownership of the means of production, the leading role of the Communist Party, and a centralized system of the production and distribution of goods. The authorities grant themselves the right to suppress individual freedom and grant freedom only if it facilitates the construction of the "perfect" social system. "Truth" does not emerge from public debate but is revealed by the center according to its political utility. In contrast, Polish national culture is rooted in the cultures of the nobility[6] and of Christianity, with a resultant system of values that emphasizes above all else individual dignity and eternal standards of truth. National culture has adopted parts of the official system, as egalitarianism and justice, but because these are not realized in practice, state ideology is pushed further away from the population's embrace (Białecki, 1987; Koralewicz, 1987; Wnuk-Lipiński, 1982, 1987). In Hungary, there is a similar clash between the values of the authorities and society's values rooted in bourgeois–citoyen, Roman Catholic–humanist, and urban–populist traditions (Hankiss, 1988:27).

Eastern European societies, of course, have different national cultures (Brown and Gray, 1979), but the general model of cultural antagonism holds to the degree that official and private domains clash. This clash is especially apparent in the conflict between Eastern Central Europe (Poland, Hungary, Czechoslovakia and East Germany, as well as Croatia and Slovenia in Yugoslavia) and the political–economic system modelled on the Soviet Union. This very idea of "Central Europe" is one strategy for resistance led by intellectuals from Hungary and especially Czechoslovakia (Judt, 1988; Konrád, 1984; Kundera, 1982; Szporluk, 1982).[7]

"Mitteleuropa"[8] was a common geographical term before the political division of Europe between East and West. In the last decade, it has been promoted again in order to underscore the common culture of the Germanies, Austria, Hungary, Czechoslovakia and Poland, in opposition to the Soviet Union, and by extension, the incompatibility between Russia's political allies and the societies they rule in the Eastern Central European zone (Kundera, 1982; Szücs, 1988; Vajda,

1988).[9] Kundera (1982) argues that, in fact, political economy and political terminology are adequate to understanding the character of domination in these systems. Domination is a politically based domination by one retrograde *culture* over others. Russia, allied with a Marxism that reduces totally "the world to its political signification alone" (p. 20), has "colonized" the small nations of "Western" Europe. Indeed, it has colonized some nations that never committed the sins of colonization themselves (p.18). Nevertheless, the imported political system ultimately failed to dominate Czechoslovakia because its western history, its western culture, helped to break down the Russian system (p. 17).

Roman Szporluk (1982) elaborates this cultural domination with his discussion of the Russian/Soviet attempt to destroy other cultures in Eastern Europe, and how their experience might illustrate what Eastern Central Europeans fear. In the Ukrainian capital of Kiev, for example, Ukrainian schools are in the minority despite Ukrainians being the majority. In the Belorussian capital Minsk, no school uses Belorussian as the language of instruction. For Poland, the aim of official instruction, he charges, has been to erase national identity and historical memory. Although there is a difference between Soviet republics and the formally independent nations of the Warsaw Pact, there seems to be a long-term Russian/Soviet goal to integrate the entire "socialist community" linguistically (through Russian) and create new historical memories to facilitate this integration.

Szporluk raises an incompatible note in this otherwise culturalist account of nationality's significance. In this framework, all problems can be attributed to the "stupid Russian-speaking officialdom" and not to the system itself. Here Szporluk anticipates one of the principal problems of understanding emancipatory praxis on the basis of culture. *Cultural identification by itself provides no alternative systemic model.* Thus, it can potentially reproduce the system even while another language is spoken by the ruling group. To the extent this cultural model fills its identification with a political or political–economic program, it avoids this problem.

Politically speaking, the *Eastern Central* European cultural ambition is normally portrayed as democratic, based on the reconstruction of civil society (Ash, 1986:48). György Konrád (1984:54), for instance, writes

> We want that internal process with which East Central Europe is already pregnant; we want bourgeois civil liberties and an embour-geoisiement that is not hedged about with prohibitory decrees. We

don't want the authorities to have discretionary rights over us. We want constitutional guarantees; we want it clear that semifreedom is not freedom, half-truth is not truth, liberalization is not liberalism, democratization is not democracy. We want no less than what the most advanced democracies now have.

This Eastern Central European cultural affinity with democracy is usually said to be based on the cultural *heritage* of the region (Vajda, 1988). This is partially a myth, given the statist and racist aspects of that heritage. But this myth is useful if tempered with an acceptance of historical responsibilities for evils these nations must not deny (Ash, 1986:46). The myth can become a cultural resource that society uses to maintain independence from the authorities and reproduce social dimorphism. This identification of a democratic civil society with national culture is one foundation upon which the "democratic opposition" lies.

Sociological foundations of an independent culture

Despite the prevalence of this modern *Kulturkampf*, most Eastern Central Europeans are not likely to join the opposition. Individuals have other ways with which to deal with cultural tensions. Polish sociologists have identified several types of schizophrenic actors, labeling them "reformers with controlled courage," "opportunists" and "conformists." Those who try to resolve this split might proceed by abandoning traditional values and adapting completely to the system, or by withdrawing entirely from public life and escaping into the private sector or going abroad (Koralewicz, 1987a; Wnuk-Lipiński, 1987). Generally, Poles have engaged in some kind of active or passive acceptance of the system. They did not accord the system normative legitimacy, but they adjusted practically to it. This "collective sense," enabling an accord between authorities and society, rests on a symbolic rejection of the political order but its acceptance in action. Between the Solidarity period of 1980–81 and 1987, the collective sense tends to be based on a valuation of social peace and learned helplessness. Large portions of society act as if any social order is better than the lack of it, which a contest for power would inevitably bring. What is more, large parts of society have come to fear uncertainty and thus pass up the desire to assume greater responsibility for their own fate (Marody, 1987, 1988). We must wait to see how the political reforms of 1989 will affect this collective sense in the 1990s.

In the 1970s, instrumental conformism was the common sense.

Staniszkis (1979:178) notes that those who made careers were adept at participating in public facade rituals and imitating its vocabulary in such settings. Conformists sometimes rationalized their behavior with reference to higher goals like the good of their family or of socialism, but other justifications were also common at this time: desire for personal achievement; fear of punishment; the commonness of conformism; a sense of helplessness and resignation; and cynicism (Koralewicz, 1987:13–14). In particular, the political sphere was considered off limits for criticism; it was in this sphere that "fear" became an important factor in motivation (K. Nowak, 1988). In 1980–81, these cultural antagonisms were transformed into clear organizational expressions. Thanks to the visit of Pope John Paul II, the public realm was opened up and these divisions, formerly expressed through social schizophrenia and opportunism, were translated into contending social forces (Bakuniak and Nowak, 1987). Even after the declaration of martial law and the dissolution of its legal organizational forms, these opposing social forces were maintained on cultural foundations (Koralewicz, 1987a:25). From this perspective, Solidarity was essentially a consequence of the cultural conflicts between the Soviet-type system and Polish society. "We" and "they" were the principal forms of identification, and these were culturally constructed (Kuczyński, 1983). And inasmuch as the intelligentsia was one of the principal forces behind the creation of this meaningful cultural identity (Bauman, 1987), this national intelligentsia was split from the authorities and their drive to "command." According to cultural theorists, Szelényi's thesis of an interest-based alliance between state and intelligentsia is based on errant assumptions that relegate cultural identification to a subordinate role in the formation of actors (Frentzel-Zagórska and Zagórski, 1988).

There are two analytically distinct sociological foundations of this cultural conflict in Eastern Central Europe. First, there is a conflict at the level of structuring or organizational principles. The authorities seek to maintain "institutional legitimacy," where their policies are accepted by their allies and the organizational consequences of those policies fit the system identity, but social legitimacy remains unserved (Rychard, 1987a). These organizational principles can go beyond contradictory legitimacies and cluster into separate paradigms creating first and second societies in economy, public, culture, social consciousness and socio-political interactions (Hankiss, 1988). But noting systemic contradictions and describing how they are manifested does not explain how the "second" forms are maintained. The authorities must tolerate the existence of these second forms. Although an independent society has its own resources, which enable it to defend itself and decrease the fear of participation in the second society, by itself, an independent society cannot provide enough security against a state which is bent on instilling fear in the general population. This toleration is not, of course, based on the goodwill of authorities. It is based on their perceptions of their power's limits.

It can be argued that the second society rests on the foundations of a second economy, which has its roots in the system's functional needs. The authorities recognize the second economy's necessity for the continued functioning of the planned economy and thus tolerate the existence of these alternative exchange networks. Alternative communication networks, although not derived from systemic "needs," also rely on official tolerance; even family relations were historically not immune from the authorities' penetration in Stalinist times. Subcultures in some societies are integrated into the dominant, but in Eastern Europe the authorities have sometimes forced it into the second sphere by declaring it illegitimate (Hankiss, 1988). The second institutional dimension of this cultural conflict thus rests on the authorities' limited hegemony. In the terms of structuralist Marxism, the party fails to exert significant control over major ideological state apparatuses (Kennedy, 1987a). In Poland, universities have maintained some autonomy, but more important, the Church offers an institutional framework within which clerical and lay opponents to regimes remind churchgoers of the antagonism between state and nation. Religion too provides an alternative language with which to express resistance. Another equally important feature enabling reproduction of private society is, however, not formally organized. Informal social relations in kinship and friendship networks provide another foundation for an oppositional society. In fact, these informal ties were the basis for the organization of Solidarity on the Baltic coast (Latoszek, 1987).

Thus, the "private" sphere maintains its own separate existence from the public realm and maintains the possibility for resistance. This private sphere rests on cultural foundations: it is defined in terms of a set of symbols and myths that emphasize individual dignity and truth, against a state symbolically constructed as backward and repressive. These antagonisms are reproduced because the state must appeal for legitimacy to a systemic identity linked to a foreign power, the Soviet Union, rather than to the values of its own population. This "society" maintains its own values and distinctiveness through churches, but also on the basis of informal networks. In terms of power relations, individual autonomy from state domination is facilitated even in a system whose leaders harbour totalitarian ambitions, by reproducing the "social" in unpenetrated kinship and friendship networks whose contents are drawn from cultural models linked to symbols and myths antagonistic to communism as practiced.

Explaining domination and resistance does not meet the full set of criteria for critical sociology, however. These alternative value systems, while different, perhaps, from the authorities, do not automatically possess an emancipatory quality. Or do they? Touraine's problematic suggests so, as they reinforce freedom from the state. But this normative standard rejects any systematic analysis and any external standard for evaluating "progress". Indeed, this perspective fails to identify the structure of an alternative and not just "independent" society, even while such an alternative is the goal of these cultural movements. They do not seek freedom from the state, but another independent state with the opportunity to construct an alternative polity and economy. But how? The post-Marxists begin to address this question with their concern for the resurrection of "civil society."

Independent society as civil society

Some Western radicals have trouble understanding the disillusionment with Marxism of many of their Eastern counterparts (Fehér and Heller, 1987). Most Eastern dissidents or radicals have abandoned the use of the Marxist problematic to inform their vision of domination and its alternative. Bahro and Szelényi are notable exceptions, but even their work represents a significant overhaul of Marxism's conceptual apparatus, while retaining its preoccupation with class or classlessness. But are their overhauls of Marxism enough? In a critical sociology of Soviet-type society, does class deserve the theoretical centrality Marxists give it? Is class struggle the principal motor of social change? Is the classless society the best way of understanding utopia? These questions are central concerns of "post-Marxists."[10]

Jean Cohen's (1982) post-Marxist project is based on the claim that Marxism's overreliance on class analysis leads it to search for a subject that embodies the universal interest, which leads to the creation of a vanguard leader of the working class when workers fail to fulfill their imputed role. The vanguard, however, has failed to lead the workers to the promised land, and has rather instituted a new, probably worse, mode of repressing the development of human potential. Cohen favors a radicalization of civil society's institutions, in which the general interest would be attained through the independently negotiated compromise of particular interests. Such a notion of civil society is the principal alternative utopia for post-Marxist critics of Soviet-type society. When class-based critiques of Soviet-type society reject the Leninist vanguard solution,[11] a model of socialist civil society generally lies at the heart of their alternative vision. Luxemburg's critique of the Bolshevik project emphasized the lack of political institutions to develop mass initiative. Szelényi's analysis of the intelligentsia finds that their prospective class dominance will probably occur in "articulated conflict systems" between autonomously organized social groups. Even Bahro's analysis, though remaining committed to a Leninist vanguard, imposes his model on a civil society, albeit a theoretically underdeveloped one.

One of the major questions facing a critical sociology of Soviet-type society is *how a socialist civil society might be constructed* (Szelényi, 1979).[12] The major obstacle to an answer to this question is that modern civil society developed alongside of capitalism, and it is by no means obvious that it can exist outside of that context. One of the major challenges for a critical theory of Soviet-type society is to develop a theory of civil society[13] abstracted from its capitalist roots.

Civil society has meant many different things since Aristotle discussed it as a kind of society which contains and dominates others. Until the middle of the 1700s, civil society was generally understood to be the *polis*, the public sphere undifferentiated from the state itself. As the state posed greater threats to freedom, the concept of "civil society" was divorced from the state and civil society's associations became a means of defense against it. Ferguson anticipated this last possibility, but it was Paine and especially Tocqueville who elaborated it (Keane, 1988:35–71). Hegel, on the other hand, did not find a natural harmony in civil society and rather discovered internal conflicts and injustices into which the state must intervene in order to create the universal interest. In this, Hegel broke with natural-law theorists who found state intrusion a danger. Hegel also drew civil society more narrowly than his predecessors, excluding state and family, but including the system of needs (economy), a system of law and a system of pluralities including corporations and the police (Bobbio, 1988; Cohen, 1982:25; Keane, 1988). Marx's understanding of civil society was in large part based on Hegel's, although he drew the boundaries of civil society even narrower. He identified civil society mainly with Hegel's "system of needs" or economic relations (Avinieri, 1968:155; Bobbio, 1988). Cohen (1982) and Gouldner (1980) believe this understanding to be one of Marxism's major limitations as a critical sociology. Marxism leaves civil society to a supportive role to the capitalist mode of production, serving either as a "bourgeois institution housing production" (Cohen, 1982:48) or "the sum total of the material conditions of life" (Gouldner, 1980:357). Gouldner argues that Marx failed to recognize the organizational importance of civil society's institutions for protecting the nascent bourgeoisie from domination by a feudal class with state power. Cohen argues further that the emergence of authoritarianism in Soviet-type societies has theoretical roots in two principal points: (1) the overreliance on class as a mediating concept between system and action in social analysis; and (2) the perspective's rejection of civil society as a mediating instrument between state and society. For Cohen and Gouldner, then, civil society needs theoretical and actual resurrection.

John Keane (1988:14–29) identifies three basic ways in which the idea of civil society might be resurrected. As an analytical approach, civil society becomes an ideal type of relation between state and civil society, in which their division and interaction are explained. In particular, this analytical approach moves away from monistic "capitalism-centered" or "state-centered" approaches, and emphasizes a more complex picture of non-state and non-market organizations. Civil society is also involved directly as a tool in facilitating political calculation or emancipatory praxis. Although in Eastern Europe this is cast in terms of how to separate state and civil society, for the Italian Marxist Antonio Gramsci, civil society was mainly the terrain on which the cultural struggle to abolish the distinction between state and civil society was waged (Bobbio, 1988). Keane (1988:25) argues that a post-Gramscian approach to a praxis involving civil society is essential, as (1) the industrial proletariat no longer occupies *a priori* a privileged position; (2) the Leninist Party is antagonistic to a democratized civil society; and (3) Gramsci's interest in civil society is opportunistic, and sees in it no lasting quality (much as Trotsky's commitment to trade unions and formal democracy, see chapter 4). Nevertheless, Gramsci's ideas might be relevant to understanding the development of Polish Solidarity (Pełczyński, 1988). Finally, civil society is useful in reconstructing the normative dimension of social analysis. In particular, Agnes Heller (1988) argues that the distinction between these separate spheres is the *sine qua non* of democracy in advanced societies. Formal political democracy is also essential to its form. By this she means there must be "a relative (never complete) separation of state from society. Its democratic character is constituted by a fundamental document (mostly in the form of a constitution) which formulates the democratic civil liberties (the so called 'human rights'), pluralism, the system of contract, and the principle of representation" (Heller, 1988:130). Others have called these elements the essential ingredients of civil society as such, including (1) legality: complete equality of civil, political and social rights; (2) plurality: the existence and tolerance of self-organized voluntary organizations representing different interests; (3) publicity: the existence of public spaces in which different interests are articulated and contested with complete openness and without fear of political persecution (Arato, 1981; Cohen, 1982:225; M. Markus, 1985:57).

Civil society as a normative project, therefore, cannot be considered apart from the character of the state. The state cannot define what ought to be, and rather can only be the institution which enforces that which negotiation in civil society decides. Civil society in its advocacy of its separation from the state raises pluralism to the prominent place among the values structuring social life, for "in the selection of values all human beings are equally competent" (Heller, 1988:134). Although civil society cannot be separated from questions about the state and pluralism, it can, and does, avoid the questions about class and poverty. This is one of its greatest potential problems.[14]

Civil society and class in critical discourse

This emphasis on civil society is of course not new for those antagonistic to the Marxian project. Hannah Arendt, in *On Revolution* (1963[1979]), argued that freedom (civil society as *polis*) and not the end to poverty (a classless society) should be the object of revolution. Her ideal revolution was the American one, in which the institutionalization of a legal order through a constitution to establish freedom in the public sphere (read "political participation") was the central issue. Marx, she argued, transformed the idea of revolution from a struggle for freedom into the struggle for abundance or the end to poverty.

The post-Marxist emphasis on civil society is influenced by Arendt's work. Post-Marxists agree with Arendt that the ignorance of particular interests in favor of some postulated general interest is a serious danger to the genuine satisfaction of human need. But does this mean that they have abandoned their Marxist roots? The post-Marxists still embrace the Marxist concern for what Arendt calls the social condition, since the "citizen's right of access to the public realm" (Arendt, 1963[1979]:127) is influenced by the unequal conditions of material existence, and is not overcome simply by mastering life's necessities, as Arendt believes. As Karl-Otto Apel (1980:283) notes in his call for a general philosophical ethic based on the idea of unfettered communication: "it is evident that the task of realizing the ideal communication community also implies the transcendence of a class society, or – formulated in terms of communication theory – the elimination of all socially determined asymmetries of interpersonal dialogue." In their common concern for freedom in discussion, Arendt's public sphere corresponds to Apel's ideal communication community or to the post-Marxists' ideal civil society. Neither Apel nor the post-Marxists believe, however, that free communication is possible when material conditions are unequal. To say that revolution should limit itself to political change, and not social conditions of existence, is absurd.[15]

Thus, while post-Marxists agree with Arendt's concern for the foundations of freedom, rooted in a constitution in America or the construction of civil society in actual socialism, they hold on to their Marxist heritage by preserving the social question in debate. But the post-Marxists consider the focus on production relations too limited for purposes of emancipatory theory. When discussing actual socialism, post-Marxists emphasize instead the institutional and cultural constitution of civil society, not class analysis. The work of one of the foremost Western post-Marxist critics of Soviet-type society, Andrew Arato, exemplifies this shift.

Arato (1982b:201) believes that it is possible to establish the organizational principle of Soviet-type society on the basis of Jurgen Habermas's work: "state socialism is political-elitist class rule over a politically constituted but industrial system of social labor." The most significant difference with capitalist society is the absence of "free labour," the inability for workers to organize on their own. Following Offe's work, Arato (p. 202) defines state socialism as "the primacy of an administratively or bureaucratically conceived political domain over both the economy and the normative–cultural sphere." Arato considers this political element as a "prerogative state" or *Massnahmenstaat*, in which "the party–state . . . exercises an arbitrary mode of political action unchecked by any legal limits and guarantees." The primacy and intervention of the political sphere characterizes the party-led societies of the Soviet Union and Eastern Europe (excluding

Yugoslavia) from the 1930s through the early 1960s. After that a "process of partial yet significant depoliticization was initiated in some of the key social spheres" (p. 203). Arato's key problem is whether the maintenance of the political sphere's primacy can be maintained as the other social spheres evolve from being "positively" subordinated to being "negatively" subordinated to the political. Positive subordination occurs when the economic and cultural spheres are subordinated to the political directly and actively; negative subordination occurs when these non-political spheres gain relative independence while the political retains its "functional" primacy. This is a key problem, because the party–state's effort to dominate the economy with its plan has produced economic crisis. Planning rationality itself is self-contradictory, according to Arato (1982:206), because information is both super-abundant and yet inadequate. Planning rationality is self-contradictory also because it must incorporate too many kinds of rationalities – economic, social and political (pp. 206–7). The resolution of this economic crisis thus poses problems for the maintenance of the Soviet-type society's organizational principle. The resolution of economic crisis and the maintenance of the system itself necessitates economic reform, of which two types are possible. The first type of reform involves a "scientization" of the existing planning system, in which the centralized control of society by the party would be maintained and consolidated. The second is a decentralization of the economy and its transformation from a positive to negative subordination to the political sphere. Such a change poses the danger that economic decentralization could spill over into the creation of a civil society, which is incompatible with the organizational principle of the system (pp. 207–9). It is incompatible because the constitution of civil society would mean a legal reform that would eliminate the arbitrary nature of political interference into the activities of economic agents and citizens, which could lead to genuine interest groups, constituted and directed by group members themselves.

The constitution of civil society is not an inevitable result of the decentralization of the economy. While the economy could become formally rational, arbitrary political interference in culture and everyday life might remain; in this sense, a "dual state" of prerogative state over culture and normative state over economy would be constructed (pp. 209–10). The spillover of rights from the economic to social sphere only occurs when the autonomous logic of the cultural sphere, based on a society's history, pushes for the democratization of politics and liberalization of culture (p. 210). Arato (1981:24) finds that cultural logic with political consequence unites the Polish opposition: "the viewpoint of civil society against the state – the desire to institutionalize and preserve the new level of social independence." Zygmunt Bauman (1981:52) also sees the "campaign of 'depoliticization' waged by Polish workers . . . as an attempt to regain the lost autonomy for civil society." Indeed, especially for Solidarity advisors Adam Michnik and Jacek Kuroń, the desire to create a pluralistic civil society informed their political projects (Arato, 1981:38–39). As early as October 1976, Adam Michnik (1976[1985]:273) argued, "the only policy for dissidents in Eastern Europe is an unceasing struggle for reforms, in favour of evolution which will extend civil liberties and guarantee respect for human rights." Even Szelényi (1982), who strives to develop a new class analysis of Soviet-type society, argues that the alliance of society against the authorities in the struggle is chronologically, and logically, prior to any kind of struggle among classes. The constitution of civil society is therefore the most immediate utopia of post-Marxist analysis. But as utopia, it presents several problems especially if the restoration of capitalist production relations is out of the question.

Post-Marxists are distinct in the civil-society project through their raising questions about what a *socialist* civil society would look like. Arato (1981:46) suggests that the following possibilities need to be theorized:

> (1) the non-identity between private law and private property; (2) market without capital formation; (3) plurality without corporatism – indeed, syndicalist plurality of self managing entities; (4) critical publics in a world of mass consumption; (5) a structure of political compromise among particular independent units that encompass the universal; (6) the reduction of political and economic bureaucracy to purely technical, administrative functions under the control of democratic assemblies; and (7) a fruitful combination of direct and parliamentary democracy.[16]

These problems would not be raised were it not for the interest in the relationship between production relations and civil society. Although Arato finds in the praxis of Solidarity evidence of the possibility of another utopia, others find support for the restoration of capitalism. Generally, civil society as emancipatory agent contains no explicit program of political economy, but rather a program of social organization based on a revisionist totalitarian theory of the state.

Civil society as praxis incorporates several possibilities: (1) a self-organization of society based on self-defense and cultural autonomy, both used to exercise veto power over state policy; (2) a self-organization of society whose associations negotiate among themselves in order to find a common position with which to negotiate with the state; (3) a self-organization of society which not only negotiates with the state but actually formulates public policy; (4) finally, a self-organization of society which is used as a springboard for finally establishing national independence.

In each case, pluralism is found in societal self-organization; publicity is found to rest on that pluralism; and legality is to be assured through negotiation between self-organized society and a state ideally based on the characteristics of formal democracy (Heller, 1988). Although these positions were advocated by people with different perspectives in the opposition (Arato, 1981:38–39), Polish nationalist leader, Leszek Moczulski (1979, 1987), argues them to be incremental steps on the road to independence and the reconstitution of the Western-style parliamentary state and capitalist economy. Civil society as praxis moves, therefore, through a logic of increasing self-organization, based initially on self-defence from the state, but with a goal of self-management culminating in national independence.

Post-Marxist theorists of socialist civil society find themselves in a difficult position. They struggle to reconstruct another normative foundation on grounds beyond class and political economy. Indeed, their cultural and political formulation of utopia is adrift without an appropriate formulation of the mode of production. Without a political–economic foundation to their utopia, the praxis they deduce winds up uncomfortably close to the programs of those with radically different political ambitions. Of course, this theoretical difficulty reflects prevailing politics,[17] but it also suggests the problems of a critical sociology that is not based on class analysis.

The limits of civil society in social transformation

Civil society as emancipatory agent presents several major problems for a theory of social transformation, inasmuch as it fails to theorize the relationship of classes to political–economic transformations. This is especially relevant to the experience of Solidarity. According to sociologist and Solidarity advisor Jadwiga Staniszkis (1984b), Soviet-type society has incomplete and non-exclusive property rights. This characterization enables explanation of three important aspects of Soviet-type society: (1) why the state apparatus is located in the base, and not the superstructure; (2) how the pervading rationality of Soviet-type society differs from that which predominates in capitalism; and (3) why rebellion which is based on a "radical" dichotomous view of social structure actually leads to the system's reproduction.[18]

This convergence of factors eliminates concern for using the system's resources to enhance the efficiency of production. To substitute for a personally motivated interest in maximizing efficiency, the state institutes administrative mechanisms and moral/political appeals. But this substitute does not introduce real economic costs into decision making. Instead, the state's control over economy is motivated by concerns for control and not economic rationality. Even if the state had different motivations, groups are not, indeed cannot be, rewarded according to their contribution to economic efficiency, since the economic information or cost accounting necessary for such valuation is obscured by the non-correspondence of administrative and real costs. According to Staniszkis, these incomplete property rights make the Weberian notion of formal rationality impossible. Quantitative calculation based on the objective scarcity of resources is impossible. The most efficient means to reach a preselected goal cannot be established. The state selects, on the basis of *a priori* criteria, which means are allowed and which are not. Hence, even if economic growth would be the goal, certain means of obtaining that goal are excluded from the start. The means of reaching a goal take on the character of ends themselves. The most interesting consequence of these incomplete and non-exclusive property rights for Staniszkis is the "inert character of social structure" (*martwa struktura*). This does not mean the system is without conflict or contradiction, but rather that the contradiction-generated conflicts actually contribute to the reproduction of the structure itself. They are not transformative conflicts. Even when opponents in social conflict articulate very different normative pictures of how society should be constructed, they nevertheless invoke the same kind of moral economy "based on redistribution, and aprioric reasoning rejecting the 'Social Reality Principle.'" One reason conflict winds up reproducing the system is that economic interests have become relatively useless as an analytic concept. As in pre-capitalist societies, Staniszkis argues "political, legal, and social structures cannot be read off the economic base." Instead, there are two groups: one, that reserves to itself the right to determine and fulfill the needs of society with the help of a moral economy; and a second group that enjoys the care of the former, but without the right to articulate their own needs.[19] This structure is even reproduced in times of open rebellion. The map of allies and opponents thus is not based on the "real distribution of conflicts built into the network of economic activity," but on *a priori* reasoning rooted in moral categories. This was why Solidarity rejected the horizontalist movement in the party as an ally, even though both groups opposed the party apparatus.

This should not be surprising, as the first step of rebellion is to establish an alternative identity and alternative vision of what ought to be (Staniszkis, 1984b; Touraine, 1984). But when the alternative vision is only a variation on distributional rights, not a demand for alternative mechanisms of production and distribution, rebellion does not offer any possibility of systemic transformation. There are no lasting economic mechanisms that could organize lasting constellations of interests. The system in actual socialism is responsive to protest and distributional demands, and thus can manipulate alliances. As a consequence, alliances tend to form around political, and not economic categories. Staniszkis believes that the lack of alliances based on economic interests makes the possibility of system transformation through social conflict unlikely. A gap between alliances based on economic interaction and alliances based on self-identification in reference to the party tends to prevent the opposition from engaging in real politics (see also Walicki, 1988). It leads them to undertake "fundamentalist" moral positions, with little room for political negotiation, since such negotiation appears as moral compromise. And since the power of society is dwarfed by the state's power, the opposition's maximalist demands wind up having no chance of success, and can thus be fairly termed "pseudo-radicalist." Although Staniszkis argued such before the 1989 reforms, her argument remains sensible. The reforms took place only as maximalist demands were dropped in favour of "pragmatic" political ones.

Staniszkis finds that although the two sides were undoubtedly opposed in the Polish conflict of 1980–81, they reproduced the structure because both sides used an aprioric, deductive mode of reasoning based on doctrinal assumptions that ignored empirical realities. The ignorance was exemplified in the reproduction of the redistributive logic of the existing economic system through the workers' egalitarian challenge. Staniszkis believes that the level of egalitarian claims demanded by workers was not justified by criteria of economic rationality. The conflict revolved around who should have the right to make redistributive decisions: the apparatus based on its vanguard position or the workers based on their "productive work." The workers were not oriented toward a structural change in the system's political economy. Both sides rejected a change of the economic system to a market economy, since such a transformation would be too costly for both sides, although the economic crisis made such a solution imperative in social terms. Both sides were also unwilling to use the existing social surplus to recapitalize the economy, since both had come to rely on this reserve to limit the immediate social costs of economic crisis. Because of these issues, the system is preserved despite, and even through, conflict.

Staniszkis's interest in the material conditions of existence dominates her analysis and distinguishes hers from the cultural and political emphasis of other critical analysts of these societies. But both culturalists and post-Marxists treat these matters as subsidiary to the *Kulturkampf* and political struggle between Central Europe and Western Asia. They reject matters of political economy as they reject the Marxism of the Communist Parties. But Staniszkis's argument supports the general Marxist position that social transformation depends on theorizing existing and alternative political economies. She herself departs from what is generally regarded as *Marxist* political economy, however, as she makes a case for the rationality of systems with exclusive and complete property rights. This leads to one of the principal problems facing critical sociology of Soviet-type society. How does political economy fit into this intellectual program? And what type of political economy does not fit? There are two existing general political–economic strategies which can fit: (1) one based on classical liberalism; and (2) one based on self-managing socialism. In chapter 4, I have already discussed at length Horvat's version of the second option. It is also important at this point to consider the classical liberal position.

Classical liberalism as critical sociology

In Poland, those independent-society theorists who address political economy are increasingly likely to embrace classical liberal doctrine inspired by Hayek and Friedman. In turn, they have become more limited in their promotions of self-organization, arguing that it *should not* include the political sphere or workers' self-government. Instead, self-organization should refer only to increasing economic freedom for entrepreneurs first of all, and perhaps cultural groups secondarily, but not necessarily. Solidarity, therefore, was not perceived as the vehicle of emancipatory social transformation. In its promotion of democratization of the state and economic democracy within the workplace, it merely continued the collectivization so threatening to individual freedom and the rule of law. Liberalization, they argue, is a necessary precondition for political democratization; democratization without economic freedom would lead merely to a new kind of collectivest tyranny. Individual freedom, the rule of law and the market economy are the keystones of civilization, and social justice and equality its antithesis (Bronisław Lagowski in Walicki, 1988). Ironically, this classical liberalism finds support among sections of the authorities themselves. To the extent that Marxist ideology becomes irrelevant and the preservation of elite privilege paramount, the premises of classical liberalism become a desirable alternative to the continued economic decline associated with central planning. Classical liberal doctrine only calls for the extension of "economic freedom" for private entrepreneurs, and says nothing about transformations of political spheres or replacements of political elites. This transformation obviously challenges those bureaucrats who are empowered through the mechanisms of central planning, but party authorities might find an authoritarian politics with a new, revitalized, private sector a desirable alternative to another rebellion by Solidarity. Some of these Polish classical liberals also see the authorities as the only possible agents of this emancipatory transformation, as workers and Solidarity itself will not be the actors who bring the increased insecurity of a free market onto themselves (Walicki, 1988). Ironically, then, the Pinochet/Chicago/Virginia School transformation of Chile's political economy might find an appreciative audience among the authorities of Soviet-type society, discovering a new "Chilean road to socialism, *à la* Pinochet."

This strategy, argues Mirosław Dzielski, a member of the Kraków Industrial Association, is a "creative anti-Communism," while the militant uncompromising anti-communism of Reagan and the "true Poles" could lead only to a deepening economic, political and perhaps military crisis for Poland itself. Thus, emancipatory praxis involves strengthening the economy through entrepreneurial initiative and an alliance with communists who wish to strengthen the rule of law. Classical liberalist doctrine thereby acts as a "civilizing" influence on Polish communists. Dzielski claims to reject even the revised totalitarian model, arguing that the authorities no longer necessarily harbor these ambitions and represent potential allies for bringing civilization to Soviet-type society (Walicki, 1988).

This classical liberal model of praxis in Soviet-type society is not entirely incompatible with the revisionist totalitarian model, however. It is consistent with the latter in so far as both emphasize the importance of the detotalization of state power. Thus, the "alternative" to actual socialism is, in both cases, a restoration of civil society; except in this classical liberal model, the political economy of the transformation is spelled out as capitalist, or in less inflammatory terms, "market economy." The classical liberal model is incompatible, however, in its imagination of the agents of social transformation. The model no longer portrays the struggle as one between Soviet-backed authorities and Polish society, but rather enlightened Polish elites and the class of petty-bourgeois entrepreneurs vs the communist system. The "masses," the working class or Solidarity are not likely agents of this economic transformation, although they are likely beneficiaries of this creation of a rational system. Walicki (1988) concludes his article on liberalism in Poland by accepting the liberal view that the "government vs society dichotomy" picture of Poland has become even less tenable than it ever was. The classical liberal critique of Soviet-type society is easily dismissed by Marxists as an apologia for capitalism. But does that mean that it is a poor critical sociology of Soviet-type society? It certainly rejects important parts of the critical tradition itself, where emancipation should be carried out by the oppressed and that it should lead to a condition of greater equality and self-determination. On the other hand, the rhetoric of classical liberalism should not blind us to seeing its compatibilities with the other forms of critical sociology discussed previously. Most notable in this regard is that post-Marxist Szelényi, like the classical liberals, finds an emancipatory agent in the petty bourgeoisie. The major point which differentiates these perspectives is the ultimate political–economic telos of entrepreneurial empowerment: a mixed economy for Szelényi and a free market for the liberals. This difference is not inconsequential for critical sociology, as it shapes the research agenda.

Ultimately, Walicki (1988) argues, the classical agenda is to turn the petty bourgeoisie from a class in itself into a class for itself. This leads to the pluralism valued by civil society, as it creates an alternative elite to the political authorities. But critical sociology aims at self-actualization for all social actors including workers, and thus a wider pluralism and more substantive equality than classical liberalism has traditionally encouraged. This pluralism could be found only in a mixed economy, as Szelényi favors, or a self-managing socialism, as Horvat promotes. But this political economy of emancipatory praxis requires further work and debate, which can hardly be resolved here.

Classical liberalism thus is not entirely unsuited to a critical sociology of Soviet-type society. Instead it must be considered part of the debate, in so far as it does share some of the self-regulatory aims of the critical tradition. But not all independent-society theorists of culture acknowledge that legacy.

The limits of culture in emancipatory transformation

The emancipatory politics of civil society assumes that Central European culture embraces a commitment to democratic civil society. "Civil society" is not, however, an inherently "democratic" form of social organization. What is more, some theorists of civil society are rejecting important parts of the Enlightenment heritage, under which humans can be held responsible for their own existence and futures.

The old civil society was a consequence of the balance of powers between state, local lords, the emerging bourgeoisie and the compromise among them known as the *Standestaat*. This civil society was based on hierarchies of estates, not the more individualist principles and civil liberties now associated with a vibrant civil society. The Church was, of course, one estate in the old order, privileged to set guidelines for certain public practices. Its own internal organization reflects this etatist order more than it does universal suffrage and civil liberties. All elements of the society, including the state, were subject to the rule of law by an independent judiciary, but this did not require a multiparty system or acknowledgment of the supremacy of individual values. This corporatist civil society is what some Hungarian legal theorists consider the best next step in social transformation (Peter, 1988). This "civil society" associated with the old order of estate privilege and Church hierarchy is not the democratic civil society most post-Marxists identify as their goal today. The Church's participation in the opposition nevertheless helped make possible the very self-organization essential to the praxis of civil society. The Church's prominent position in the "democratic" opposition is thus ambiguous, but given its own internal structure and its historic relation to civil society, it seems to be biased towards a more authoritarian rather than democratic version of civil society in its vision of change (Arato, 1981:40–43), although this is a contentious point (Casanova, 1988).

Beyond the influence of pre-bourgeois social forms, there are additional reasons to be skeptical of the notion that the civil society to be introduced in Soviet-type society will resemble individualist democratic forms. As civil society is introduced from above, the "privilege" of participation in public discussion or public representation is likely to be granted to corporate groups rather than to the individuals which comprise them. The authorities are more likely to introduce this rather "feudal" form of civil society (Rev, 1984), because it allows the center to continue to control the terms of debate and the conditions of civil society's constitution. It is also likely that such a corporatist form will be introduced on pressure from below, however.

Pressure to introduce plurality, legality and publicity will be based on the collective self-organization of various groups. As these groups increase their influence over the authorities, and seek to defend themselves from being undermined by the authorities, they will be obliged to increase their organizational power. In this fashion, civil society will be based on power relations constituted by a balance of power among various corporate units. It is unlikely, therefore, that the equality sought by post-Marxist theorists could be conceived as developing on an individual basis. Instead, it will be an "equality" of organizational forms, with perhaps considerable inequality among individuals, depending on their organizational affiliations, and whether these affiliations are recognized by the authorities.

The corporatist civil society, based either on transformation from above or below, does not mean that other desirable aspects of civil society would not be introduced. Corporatism can be consistent with the mechanisms of formal democracy, a public sphere independent of organizational domination and pluralism as a fundamentally constitutive value. But, once again, this combination is dependent on the character of the organizations and groups whose compromise leads to the regeneration of civil society. It depends on the cultural constitution of these groups. Public-opinion polls from 1980–81 give reason to be skeptical of the democratic necessity of Polish culture, for instance. There is a clear division between the values of the authorities and of society, as the latter supported a greater role for the Church and limiting the influence of the party and central planning (Białecki, 1987). But even if the content is different, the political imaginations of workers and party are similar. Staniszkis (1984b) argues that both the working class and party apparatus have strong etatistic orientations, strong support for state ownership, a material and not procedural conception of justice, a low tolerance of the ambiguity of pluralism and an egalitarian orientation toward redistribution. On these issues, the working class is closer to the party apparatus than to their political allies among students and professionals (Kolarska and Rychard,

1982b). Thus, Staniszkis believes that "individuals (even in rebellion) actually hold on to beliefs that facilitate their own exploitation and repression."

Staniszkis's rejection of Solidarity's radicalism should not be exaggerated. If radicalism means a fundamental transformation of the status quo, in this case the construction of a socialist civil society, fundamentalist orientations might be truly radical when self-organization is prohibited. Elsewhere, Staniszkis (1984a) notes that it was the workers' very fundamentalism, their failure to recognize the significance of establishing an independent trade union, which enabled them to keep pushing for that which would undermine the party's claim to represent the working class. The nature of radicalism in Soviet-type society might therefore be dependent on the progress of society's self-organization. Once autonomous organizations are created, radicalism demands greater pragmatism. So long as geopolitical concerns and military might prevent unbridled revolution, reforms must be institutionalized through the politics of compromise, based on the social power of relatively autonomous agents. When each side has the power to exact compromise from the other, pragmatism carries the greater radicalism. Without autonomous organizations, fundamentalist demands for their creation are the more radical. My notion of "socialist pragmatism," a pragmatism based on the self-organization of workers, implies this very contingent understanding of radicalism. Culture may, of course, give to this self-organization very different political outcomes.

Those who are proponents of "Central Europe" or of Polish national culture recognize the divergent possibilities their cultural resources provide. As such, the cultural field becomes one of the most worn territories on which the struggle to define the "national" project is waged. There is no single project, and thus a common evaluation of the project is impossible. But it is important to note one opposition tendency which departs even further from the critical project inasmuch as it denies the foundation of critical inquiry. It denies that we, as humans, should even attempt to recreate our own social world.

Although most of the intellectual opposition is calling into question only certain aspects of the Enlightenment (Judt, 1988:235–40), Czech dissident Václav Havel (1988) is hinting at a complete break. He argues that the catastrophe of Eastern Europe is the consequence of rationalism, the belief that the world can be remade collectively. In our hubris, we have violated the "natural order" of the world which

God has wrought and have tried to play God with "cruel consequences" (Havel, 1988:386).

> To me, personally, the smokestack soiling the heavens is not just a regrettable lapse of a technology that failed to include the "ecological factor" in its calculation, one which can be corrected easily with the appropriate filter. To me it is more the symbol of an age which seeks to transcend the boundaries of the natural world and its norms and to make it into a merely private concern, a matter of subjective preference and private feeling, of the illusions, prejudices and whims of a "mere" individual. It is a symbol of an epoch which denies the binding importance of personal experience – including the experience of mystery and of the Absolute – and displaces the personally experienced Absolute as the measure of the world with a new, man-made absolute, devoid of mystery, free of the "whims" of subjectivity and, as such, impersonal and inhuman. It is the absolute of so-called objectivity: the objective, rational cognition of the scientific model of the world. (Havel, 1988:383)

Human reason and individual experience must be restored to a world in which impersonal structures and objective processes have rendered honest and free-thinking people both irrelevant and the ultimate threat. The modern world, both capitalist and most of all totalitarian, has sought to dehumanize the subject; the most fundamental challenge to this impersonal power is to drive totalitarianism from one's own soul, engage in anti-political politics by envisioning it as practical morality, and most of all, proclaiming the truth and acting on that basis. Such a person has far greater power than many impersonal dehumanized voters (Havel, 1988).

This challenge goes beyond what most oppositionists in Eastern Central Europe are prepared to grant, but it carries with it a common challenge to critical sociology embraced by most of the Eastern European opposition. Most, if not all, Eastern European oppositionists are prepared to reject the relevance of utopia. Most, if not all, are prepared to reject the idea that normative standards should be applied to systems at all. Most, if not all, are prepared to abandon the critical project to remake "society," and believe instead that critique should seek to protect individuals and their human rights and civil liberties. The search for civil society becomes, therefore, an admission that the utopian element of the critical project is unworkable, and that the best we should do is work to defend civil liberties and human rights. With this, even the structural sociological project becomes antithetical to practical morality, because the structural emphasis removes from the problematic the responsibility incumbent in individual morality.

With this move toward an emphasis on the "formal" requirements of civil society and move away from the substantive elements of the emancipated society, we approach the same dilemmas Max Weber outlined in the critique of formal rationality. If, as Heller suggests, the state possesses no capability for saying which uses of the mechanisms of civil society are better and which are worse, do we not abandon the critique Marxism and feminism have made of the substanceless norms of bourgeois–patriarchal society?

The optimistic Habermasian retort is that under conditions of increasingly free communication, facilitated by the institutions of civil society, communicative rationality will ultimately realize normatively superior outcomes. Although this non-gendered notion of the public sphere is itself suspect (Fraser, 1987; Markus, 1987), it becomes increasingly problematic in the transitory phase we are likely to see in the construction of civil society in Soviet-type society. To the degree that this civil society is constructed along corporatist lines and not the individualist ones ideally imagined, the internal relations comprising the corporate groups constituting civil society will set the tones for discussion. To the degree that these groups do not approach the communicative rationality some see in professional associations (Sciulli, 1986), the normatively desirable outcomes associated with civil society will not be realized. Indeed, the suppression of internal difference and conflict associated with the Solidarity movement in 1980–81 (Staniszkis, 1984a) makes Weberian pessimism seem all the more justified.

It therefore becomes obligatory for critical sociologists to consider the organizational forms which not only facilitate collective self-regulation at the societal level, but also individual self-regulation at the organizational level. To this extent, much work on the capacity of individuals to regulate themselves in accord with their own self-actualizing needs remains to be done.

Those who are post-Marxists and work on the socialist civil-society project obviously retain the self-regulatory aims of the Enlightenment and the sociological penchant to study systematically social relations, without putting individual conscience at its center. But the difficulty they have with finding an appropriate political economy for this civil society reflects the deeper theoretical misgivings this project represents. Admissions that the "good society" must be pluralist and that state and society cannot be unified reflect a deeper self-doubt as to whether we can engage, at all, in a project of *collective* emancipation. Even the political economy of self-managing socialism, although compatible with the model of civil society (Heller, 1988; Horvat, 1982), is not based on a praxis of collective emancipation but coordinated corporate freedoms. This partially derives from a loss of faith in systemic analysis and a return to the primacy of the really existing individual. This is suggested in Heller's (1988) point, that we cannot establish which values are superior. We can only support tolerance for their multiple expression through a commitment to pluralism. This, apparently, is the normative reaction to the tragedy of totalitarianism. But this reaction contains its own serious limitations.

Reflections on independent-society critiques of actual socialism

The independent-society model offers a basic alternative to those critical sociologies rooted in the Marxian project. The greatest virtue of the former is that it has allowed us to reconsider the utopia and normative foundations underlying the critique of Soviet-type society. Instead of equality or classlessness, it puts publicity, pluralism and legality to the center of the alternative. With that normative foundation, we need not search for the class behind the state, and can instead define the state as itself the principal source of repression. We need define no dominating interest other than the interest to dominate. Defining domination so, a new praxis is introduced whereby the establishment of organizations and activities outside of state control becomes a means through which transformation can be effected. The self-defense of self-organization can lead to self-management which might be the foundation for civil society.

Alternative perspectives within this general camp are less clear than are the alternative foci. Post-Marxists are generally interested in constructing an alternative utopia which can be called socialist civil society. Various Eastern European sociologists use the notion of independent society as a vehicle to investigate the separation of private and public cultures. Both tendencies draw on one another, however. The post-Marxists rely on national cultural commitments to democracy and freedom to explain why actors seek to create a rational civil society. The cultural sociologists identify the oppositional culture with the normative framework of pluralism and tolerance the post-Marxists elaborate. They achieve this unity by redefining the cultures of these independent societies as democratic and civil libertarian.

The combination of national culture and emancipatory civil society is tenuous. Although there is a gulf between public and private culture, the private culture itself is contradictory. In Hungary there is a rift in the opposition between populists and democratic opposition; in Poland between right-wing nationalists and social democrats. The "autonomous cultural logic" upon which some rely for emancipation is one which is not inherently emancipatory. Indeed, that logic can support repression within the system, as Moczar's anti-Semitic program allied party elements and workers against students and intellectuals in 1968 Poland. It also can be associated with the strict hierarchies and corporatism associated with feudal civil society, not its democratic civil libertarian descendant. This is obvious to those who study the culture of this region; but in the search for the motor which drives emancipation, cultural resistance to domination is too easily identified with only progressive elements of Western tradition.

The Marxist tradition is now rarely identified with such progressive elements in Eastern Central Europe. The perspectives which emphasize national cultures are almost universally disenchanted with Marxism. With that rejection, these perspectives avoid discussion of political economy and class, which, as Staniszkis suggests, lead to major problems when theorizing social transformation. Post-Marxists are among the few who attempt to synthesize their own Marxist backgrounds with these arguments from within actual socialism. But they too pay minimal attention to class and political economy and prefer to emphasize the cultural and political conditions of domination and resistance. This leads to similar problems as faced by those who abandon class entirely, but they do retain a predisposition for an examination of contradiction within apparently progressive developments. Post-Marxists remain most obviously within the Marxist field of discourse in their attempt to reconsider the utopias of emancipatory politics as *socialist* civil society. But this utopia is itself problematic for critical sociology, inasmuch as it recognizes that emancipation cannot be the product of a collective will, but rather the institutionalization of compromise among equally endowed actors. This transformation of utopia from classlessness to pluralism acknowledges the limits of social transformation. It also begins to accept, however, that the dream of collective self-regulation is a potentially dangerous utopia. It searches for barriers to emancipation not only in the resistance of existing repressive systems, but in the limits of human association itself. It opens itself up to functionalist questions which were recently dismissed as inherently conservative by critical sociologists. Indeed, by considering the *systemic* aspects of emancipation, functionalism restores to critical sociology its commitment to investigating the organizational forms enabling individual self-actualization.

As with functionalism, however, these independent-society accounts deemphasize those asymmetric power relations that are not part of the state/society dualism. Class relations are noticeably absent, as are gender and other forms of domination. In the struggle against the totalitarian state and for the establishment of pluralism, the egalitarian conditions of emancipation are minimized, and sometimes deliberately challenged on the grounds of political economy, as we have seen with the classical liberal alternative discussed above. Classical liberalism offers the most coherent alternative to the Marxist critique of Soviet-type society, in so far as the former provides both a model of political economy and a strong normative order built on its foundations. The virtues of petty-bourgeois class empowerment can also, however, be incorporated into a post-Marxist emphasis on an equalization of power relations among corporate groups, as Szelényi illustrates. Indeed, for the critical sociology of Soviet-type society to develop further, it must theorize the place of private ownership of the means of production in emancipatory social transformation.

There are, therefore, several currents of thought in the independent-society critique: a culturalist–romantic current; a post-Marxist tendency; and classical liberalism. One of the most important dialogues for critical sociology of Soviet-type society is to reconsider how their dialogue with Marxism and among themselves might reshape theory and research.

Theoretical foundations for a critical sociology of Soviet-type society

The central problem of critical sociology revolves around the conditions of social reproduction and emancipatory transformation. Both Marxist and totalitarian–independent-society critiques have this as their central problem. Based on my analysis of these two problematics in the last two chapters, the following represents theoretical foundations for the analysis of professionals, power and Solidarity to follow.

Marxists approach this central problem by establishing the conditions of class and group alliance, especially the conditions under which the working class establishes alliances with political bureaucracy, technocrats, intelligentsia or petty bourgeoisie. Classical liberals are also interested in class/group alliances, finding in the authorities the most likely allies for the restoration of a vigorous class of petty bourgeoisie. Although the normative commitments of these two groups clearly diverge, their common focus on the significance of class interest and alliance makes investigation of the relationship between political authorities, private enterprise, state managers, professionals, peasants and workers central to the critical sociological agenda. Critical sociology must ask, therefore, *how the class interests of various groups under different historical conditions lead to different kinds of alliances.*

Totalitarian/independent-society theorists focus instead on the cultural dynamics of the split between regime and society, and the foundations national cultures bequeath to the project of constructing a democratic civil society. They then search for the sociological conditions which enable these progressive cultural tendencies to develop. The independent-society theorists are correct to emphasize the significance of national cultures, and therewith the importance of parts of the intelligentsia to creating the emancipatory project. Cultural constructions can help unite groups in opposition, even when political economies lead class interests to support different programs for concrete reform. A critical interpretation of this alliance should, however, establish *how these cultural foundations relate to the class interests of various actors.* But a new critical sociology must avoid an *a priori* class or cultural reductionism in its analysis. Instead, both must be retained as potentially important factors shaping the conditions of class and group alliance.

Marxists and culturalists share a recognition of the centrality of the working class in effecting transformation. Their common ground rests on the power resources the working class possesses in terms of its numbers, concentration and capacity to strike to push for transformation. Classical liberals also recognize the potential power of an organized working class, but find their socialist tendencies antithetical to the construction of a liberal economy and society. It is not only important, therefore, to study class and group alliances, but also critical to make the working class central in any study of social transformation. In particular, *the degree of self-organization of the working class establishes the possibilities for all class or group alliances.*

One must therefore establish the conditions of self-organization for the working class and its relationship to social transformation. The independent-society theorists have been more detailed in their estimation of how this self-organization is related to social and political change, but they have been less than explicit on how economic reform would occur under this guise. Economic reform offers two principal alternatives: of the self-managing transformation of the state-owned means of production and of the establishment of a privately owned economic sector. Advocates of both types of reform have provided rough guidelines as to how the reform policies might be implemented, but they are generally weaker on how this relates to the organization of groups, especially workers, outside the policy process. Therefore any analysis of praxis must consider the *barriers and prospects for the translation of self-organization into self-management and how working-class self-organization and private entrepreneurial activity are related in social struggles.*

These analyses of praxis should not hold some essentialist identification between program and class, however. *Programs must be related not only to the "objective" class interest of the group it represents, but also to the conditions under which that program is constructed.* In this, the pragmatist critique of Marxism is important, for particular conjunctures with unusual alliances could make for unusual emancipatory, and repressive, alliances. At the same time, however, the Marxist critique of pragmatism is important, for without working-class self-organization, the possibility for emancipatory transformation is nil. Without this working-class resource, the only ally for reformers is Western capital and states.

This working-class self-organization is obviously related to the utopia behind analysis. All critiques of Soviet-type society have come to acknowledge that *pluralism is essential to the construction of an emancipatory alternative in Soviet-type society.* Marxists remain trapped in a cul-de-sac to the degree that they fail to transform their implicit recognition of the importance of pluralism into an acknowledgment that the "classless" society as utopia is potentially antagonistic to it. The traditional socialist utopia also does not capture the imagination of workers and others in Soviet-type society; especially in Poland, the rulers' Marxist rhetoric has contaminated this language of liberation. But even if the rhetoric is disposed of, commitments to classlessness also tend to push the analyst back to a Leninist problematic, which is part of the problem in Eastern Europe. Post-Marxists are right to search for a new utopia, and a "socialist civil society" may be desirable.

Without establishing the political–economic foundation of this alternative, analysts are leaving themselves open to problems in assessing praxis. Central planning is one means by which the authorities continue to rule; an alternative must be theorized that does not restore capitalism as a dominant mode of production. Market relations are obviously one part of this transformation, but they, by themselves, do not solve the political–economic dilemmas of transformation. Self-management theorists have an alternative, however, by posing socialism as neither statist nor capitalist, but based on a positive supersession of private property through self-governance. As Szelényi (1986–87) is right to emphasize, the emergence of a new petty bourgeoisie deserves as much consideration as schemes of self-management. Without theorizing this political–economic element, socialist civil society serves only to enhance imagination. It does not provide a solution to the class conflicts involved in transformation.

Civil-society theorists also face their own normative problems in the construction of their alternative. To the extent that the formal requirements of legality, publicity and plurality define the ethical conditions of an emancipatory alternative, civil-society theorists leave themselves without a vehicle for criticizing the informal structures of repression. This is especially problematic when civil society is constructed on the basis of corporate groups whose internal social relations suppress communicative rationality. To recall the feminist critique of Catholicism and Solidarity's own suppression of conflict is enough to point to the limits of the exclusively formalistic construction of utopia. *One of the central problems in the analysis of praxis is therefore the analysis of the internal constitution of emancipatory movements.* In particular, one should investigate their constitution in ways the movement activists themselves do not. In the case of Solidarity, that means questions of class and gender should come to the fore.

The level of theoretical discussion engaged in these last two chapters is important, as it serves to establish a metatheoretic dialogue among a wider range of critical sociologists. Polish Solidarity has contributed significantly to this dialogue by helping develop new critical models of Soviet-type society, most notably that of socialist civil society. A critical analysis of Solidarity also suggests, however, some of the greatest problems with these models, most notable of which is their failure to consider political economy and their avoidance of the movement's internal antagonisms. Obviously, no single research program can address all of the problems facing a new critical sociology, and I do not pretend to do so in this volume. I hope to have identified, however, some of the central problems facing the project. I also hope that the substantive analysis of professionals, power and Solidarity in the following chapters will at least clarify some of the dilemmas I have listed, so that future research and theory can make progress over my own work.

For substantive analysis to make headway within this general framework, more highly specified models of Soviet-type society must be elaborated which can help answer the questions of political economy, class alliance and culture we have established as central to the various traditions. On the one hand, we must study specific historical sequences of transformative praxis so that some of these issues can be clarified, as I attempted in part I of this volume. This is only one leg of the critical project, however.

Another aspect of critical sociology is to explain the character of domination emancipatory praxis seeks to overturn. Although certainly this domination has changed in style over the decades since World War II (Bruszt, 1988), its underlying structure through 1980 remained fundamentally the same. In the following chapter I propose a structural account of domination in Soviet-type society. Although control over the means of production and the prerogative/totalitarian state present the general picture of domination, the nature of social relations constituting the authorities and its relationship to society needs to be clarified. I focus on Poland, but the concepts I develop there are designed to be useful to similar regimes.

6 A theory of power relations in Soviet-type society

One of the fundamental concerns of critical sociology is the explanation of power relations as a dialectic of domination and resistance. In particular, what power resources enable domination and what power resources resistance? How are these resources used in the social relations which constitute this domination and resistance? And how are social groups constituted in this system of unequally distributed opportunities of action? In this chapter, I propose a theory of power relations in Soviet-type society that addresses these questions. In part III, I use this theory to explain the position of professionals in Soviet-type society generally, and to explain why Polish professionals participated in the Solidarity movement of 1980–81.

Domination in Soviet-type societies can be approached in generic terms, given that it is this common structure of domination which enables us to speak of different societies being of the same type. This structure of domination generates some common resources which enable resistance, but resistance does not take the same form in each setting. Resistance is also a consequence of agency and strategy, which has various outcomes that are not structurally determined. Thus, although Poland has been a Soviet-type society, Solidarity was not a structural outcome, even if its development was conditioned by the structure of the Soviet-type system.

To understand Solidarity's specificity, one must nevertheless recognize how both the movement and its opponents used generic resources of the Soviet-type system in their conflict with one another. This conflict in fact suggested greater opportunities for action by workers than previous theories expected. Greater limits in these opportunities can be found in the authorities' power also. And, as we shall see in part III, professionals, too, were dependent and autonomous in unexpected ways. In effect, Solidarity's emergence allows us to understand better the various power relations of Soviet-type society, because different opportunities for action were found in 1980–81. The theory of power relations advanced herein draws a great deal, therefore, from the analysis of Solidarity in part I.

This theory also draws on the discussion of Marxist and civil-society models of Soviet-type society in the previous two chapters. These accounts point to the importance of class alliances in shaping social reproduction and transformation. They suggest that workers are an important actor influencing conditions of social transformation, as relations between the political elite and the entrepreneurial and professional classes are shaped by the actions of these workers. But most of these theories depend on imputed interests or identities for establishing the conditions of alliances. In this chapter I propose to amend these accounts by introducing a distinctly social portrait of the relations which tie different actors to one another. I argue that the power elite holds considerable power over authoritative and allocative resources. But, while the power of the elite and their authorities is of broad scope, the exclusivity with which individuals use these resources is limited. The party, as a corporate body, is the collective ruler, basing its legitimacy on a perverted substantive rationality and defining its domination through organizational hegemony. Because all actors retain agency, this domination is incomplete, and even ineffective. The elite's vassals can resist, through passivity, the elite's direction. The agency of other actors can also distort the power of the authorities and elite. In the delegation of privilege, the authorities not only reward the loyal, but bribe the troublesome. The troublesome are those with autonomous power resources of considerable scope, as workers. Indeed other groups, like professionals, are dependent on either workers or the party for their own power and privilege. The elements of this theory are not all new. I do believe, however, that their combination represents a novel synthesis which can facilitate the critical sociological analysis of Soviet-type society.

Power resources

C. Wright Mills (1958:12–13) delimited the power resources available to his power elite as "facilities of industrial production and of military violence, of political administration and of the manipulation of opinion." More recent accounts generally stress two basic forms of domination in advanced societies: economic or allocative and executive or authoritative. These forms of domination are based primarily on the resources which enable that domination: control over material goods and control over individuals (Blau, 1977; Giddens, 1981, 1987). These two categories also serve analytically to distinguish instruments of domination in Soviet-type societies. The authorities in Soviet-type society have extensive allocative power. Through the central economic plan, they decide where, when and how the major means of production are to be developed. They allocate virtually all resources for collective consumption, from streetcars to sewage treatment and hospitals. The authorities also directly influence individual consumption, as they assign incomes and benefits to various categories of state employees and impose taxes on non-state employees. Of course, they allocate these resources neither arbitrarily nor capriciously, but in response to their own designs and the pressures exerted on them from different sectors. Most significantly, market forces play a comparatively small role, if any, in deciding how resources should be allocated. Other factors are more important.

Those who rule also have extensive authoritative power. With its control over the means of violence associated with state power, the party can command individuals in military and police units to use physical coercion against individuals and groups. Indeed, as in other modern states, a considerable proportion of the resources of the coercive apparatus is devoted to instruments useful only for repressing domestic populations, as are water cannons and riot shields. As Max Weber noted, however, even though physical repression is the ultimate form of power, and has become significantly more violent in this century, it is also the most costly. When domination by a group or individual over a collectivity is based on authority (non-questioning compliance with the wishes of the powerful), the powerful are freed from the obligation of ensuring that their wishes are being followed (Weber, 1978:53) and can divert their resources to other purposes and expand the scope of their power. Authoritative control over information can make the use of physical coercion more cost-effective by relying less on sanction and more on manipulation. Through surveillance, the authorities also can supervise activities and learn which individuals to coerce selectively rather than engage in random demonstrations of terror. It can document individuals' activities and generally restrict their autonomy by restricting the sphere which is private (Giddens, 1987a). In this, Soviet-type societies have become more similar to democratic capitalist ones by moving away from the mass terror that characterized Stalinism in the 1930s and towards a more selective and demonstrative persecution of individuals who challenge seriously the collective wisdom of those who rule. Control over information also involves controlling its distribution. This is not just a matter of using symbols and ideas to instil values that will buttress the authorities' legitimacy. Equally, if not more significant in this context, is the authorities' capacity to control the fields of discourse, thereby shaping the categories with which individuals consider themselves and their relation to the authorities, as Michel Foucault has suggested. This also allows the authorities to control the information with which individuals fill categories.

The authorities also exert considerable control over formal organization. They exert this power through their control over the administrative structure of the state and economy. They also have the power to approve or deny the formation of formal organizations outside of these spheres. Even as more groups become "self-organized," they do so as a "privilege," with permission granted from the center. The authorities directly control appointments to significant hierarchical positions in these organizations through *nomenklatura*. *Nomenklatura* is a list of key positions in various organizations, whose occupants must first be approved by some committee of the party. Other positions not falling under the official *nomenklatura* can be influenced by the party too. Promotions can be held up through the intervention of a local party committee if an individual does not meet expectations. Usually, however, the party need not intervene directly, since it can rely on those selected through *nomenklatura* to use good judgment.[1]

In summary, the authorities of Soviet-type societies have considerable power resources at their disposal ensuring their capacity to dominate. They have varying degrees of influence over forms of allocative power in their control over (1) the means of production; (2) the means of collective consumption; (3) the means of personal consumption; as well as varying degrees of control over authoritative resources in (4) the means of violence; (5) surveillance and the distribution of information; (6) the structure of formal organization; and (7) the appointment of individuals to that formal organization.

While we can make analytical distinctions between executive and economic power resources in Soviet-type societies, they are not as important to a discussion of power relations in Poland as they are in the United States. The distinction between executive and economic power has greater relevance in democratic capitalist societies because (1) these different kinds of power potentially have different groups with different goals exercising them; and (2) these different groups tend to define the basic structure of conflict. Democratic capitalist societies have multiple centers of organizational power, the most obvious being the power in the private economic world and the power centered in the state. Hence, the executive and economic, or the allocative and authoritative, can be (but are not necessarily) empirically distinct, facilitating their analytical distinction. More importantly, the distinction between these kinds of power makes sense because the executive and the economic also can be at odds with one another. The resources and interests of each center differ, at least to the extent that workers are organized in trade unions and political parties (Korpi, 1985:38–39). Although the manager and politician are both employees of organizations, their tenure depends on employing different resources to pursue different aims. The important distinction between kinds of power in democratic capitalist societies rests in the interests and resources the wielder of power possesses, what motivates and enables that power holder to exercise power. If executive and economic power are used by the same people toward the same ends, the significance of the distinction between these power resources is reduced. Thus the distinction is less valuable in Soviet-type societies. The same organization controls both executive and economic power resources. Although this distinction illustrates different forms of domination, the distinction reveals neither different power centers nor goals, except perhaps in late 1981 in Poland (chapter 3). If the distinction between executive and economic resources is less significant in Soviet-type society, what variations in types of power resources are important?

It is important to understand power from two points of view: from the viewpoint of *possibilities*, as the degree to which the possession of various resources enables the achievement of goals; and from the viewpoint of *constraints*, as the degree to which one must take into account the actions of others in the use of power resources. Both viewpoints are influenced by the autonomy/dependency interpretation of power and both come down to the analysis of the character of control over resources, in terms of the *scope* of resources under control and *exclusivity* in the determination of their use.[2]

If power is of broad scope, that means that both many others and a wide range of their activities are dependent upon one's decisions. That need not mean, however, that the executors of power themselves are relatively autonomous. They are to some degree dependent on those whose lives they influence, since power relations are always two-way. But they can also be dependent on others whose lives they scarcely influence. Power of broad scope can be wielded by people with limited control over how that power is to be executed. In Soviet-type societies, this observation is critical to defining domination. In non-exceptional historical periods most power resources are delegated by the party itself. In one sense, one can even say that the power resources of the various Eastern European communist parties are to some degree delegated by the Communist Party of the Soviet Union. No matter the scope of resources at one's disposal, therefore, the exclusivity in their employment is always subject to limitation by the center, be that a center in the periphery like Warsaw, or the empire's center in Moscow. Hence, in order to achieve power of broad scope within core or periphery, it is necessary to be close to the centers of power in the party in order to influence what the party accepts as reasonable. It is not surprising, therefore, that many conflicts are characterized by revisionist struggles over who is to lead the party and what program the party shall follow. The scope and exclusivity of power resources clarify the power relations characterizing domination in Soviet-type society when they are used to construct two basic concepts: organizational hegemony and delegated power. Organizational hegemony is most useful for clarifying the corporate dimension of domination in terms of both culture and economic development. Delegated power is most useful for clarifying the social relations among the authorities and between "them" and "society."

The party has been meaningfully interpreted as a collective ruler in Soviet-type society (Bauman, 1972:142). It is an absolute ruler, intolerant of any contenders to its hegemony. It constitutes a one-party system,[3] meaning the exclusion of all potentially rival organizations "with essentially alternative programmes in the field of politics, culture, economy, etc. and with it also the possibility to propose such alternatives. It excludes at the same time contractual relations among individuals and collectives independently of the state" (Fehér, Heller and Markus, 1983:157). Although the party is a collective ruler, party members are not the political rulers themselves. They do not constitute a ruling political class. Party members can be purged on the command of leading party organs. Rank-and-file challenges of the top have never been successful. The centralization of power in the upper organs of the party is the enduring characteristic of these systems. The balance of powers within the party leadership may change, the organs which emanate power may change, the ways in which the power is executed may change, or the reaction of the rest of society to that power may change, but that the party leadership is the center of power in the system is what constitutes the system's essence and cannot therefore change without the system itself changing (Fehér, Heller and Markus, 1983:167).[4] The bottom line for the party leadership is the maintenance of organizational hegemony over politics, economy and society. This principle dominates the field of power relations, as it does its logic of economic development and even the discourse of its self-justification.

Organizational hegemony and substantive rationality

Hegemony must be understood not only in terms of the absence of alternative organizations but also in terms of the meaning that absence embodies (Kennedy, 1987a). The meaningful principle which underlies organizational hegemony in Soviet-type society is substantive rationality. According to the constitutions of Soviet-type societies, the goal of social organization is the construction of communism. This goal of Communist Party power is unlike the bourgeoisie's goal to accumulate capital, because the latter has some possible measures in the market against which to evaluate success. There is no outside indicator against which to measure party success in communism's construction. The definition of the goal and means by which that goal is attained are subject to the interpretation of the party itself. Thus, "substantive rationality" is the principle which defines Communist Party domination, much as the sanctity of private property defines the domination of the bourgeoisie in capitalist society (Fehér, Heller and Markus, 1983:143–66). Max Weber used substantive rationality mainly to clarify the meanings of value and formal rationality. Fehér, Heller and Markus (1983) elaborate that discussion to identify substantive rationality as the absence of clearly defined goals or predefined values for the determination of appropriate behavior. Instead, the goals and means toward those goals are subject to the interpretation and reinterpretation of the dominant group. Rationality comes to be identified with the group itself. The party's self-ascribed supreme ability to interpret what is best for all, but without any yardstick against which to measure success, enables continued self-justification with no capacity for outside agents to define failure. Indeed, it is inherently illegitimate for anyone outside the party to define what is an accomplishment or what is a failure (Bauman, 1972:137).

Substantive rationality allows the party to see the merit of its ways when few others do, even by criteria the party itself previously established. Universally declining rates of economic growth would suggest that the original vision of superior economic development is unfulfilled. Even the demand by Polish workers for their own independent organizations is insufficient to challenge the party's claim to substantive rationality. These "failures" do not violate the notion that the party embodies substantive rationality, because its claim is based on its identification with the sacred, not with its actual behavior. The sacred status of the Communist Party of the Soviet Union derived from its position as the incarnation of the hierophantic October Revolution. Eastern European parties gained their initially sacred status by conference from that incarnation (Jowitt, 1987). This sacred status of the party means that loyalty to it becomes a higher principle than any other moral guidelines (Fehér, Heller and Markus, 1983:208–17). Julia Minc, former chief editor of the Polish press agency and wife of one of Stalinist Poland's ruling troika, responded in an interview to a question about party infallibility:

> if you have to choose between the party and an individual, you choose the party, because the party has a general aim, the good of many people, but one person is just one person. (Can he be killed?) The questions you ask! The party isn't a Christian sect that takes pity on every individual, with a vision of a heavenly tsardom; the party struggles for a better life for all mankind. (Can you rebel against the party?) You can rebel against particular people, but not against the party, because that would mean you were rebelling against socialism, which aims to better the living standards of the working class. (Torańska, 1987:23)

The Komsomol slogan of "the party is our reason, honor and conscience" means that individual conscience is completely estranged and embodied in the "mythical will of the organization" (Fehér, Heller and Markus, 1983:208). In 1968, Poland's Communist Party even formally rejected the challenge made by Leszek Kołakowski and others that individual conscience should take precedence over party dictates for deciding morality (Kuroń, 1973 [1983]). Substantive rationality thus enables all mistakes made by the party to be attributed to individual error, and all accomplishments by the party to the group's collective infallibility.

Substantive rationality thus has a meaningful root in the assignation of virtually divine status to the party. But this refers only to historical origins. The party need not retain its sacred status in order for it to retain a claim to substantive rationality. There is sociological justification for relying on substantive rationality to legitimate the party as the embodiment of socialism or morality. Reliance on empirical yardsticks to evaluate the degree of party success in socialist construction is bound to lead one to conclude the party does not represent socialism. But this is because the authorities come to be blamed for all that is wrong because they are directly involved in the economic administration of society and are perceived as the antagonist in all frustrated aims (Wesołowski, 1966a [1979]:129). The authorities become the antagonist because they try to assume responsibility for the whole range of society's values.

Organizational hegemony thus relies on substantive rationality to justify loyalty to the party as a supreme value. It also uses this principle to justify its organizational hegemony to those outside the party, but the degree to which this self-justification contributes to popular legitimacy in Soviet-type societies varies. To the degree that this substantive rationality is buttressed by other forms of legitimacy, especially "traditional" forms, substantive rationality can work to confer greater authority. Traditional authority and authority in "etatist" society have many common elements (Horvat, 1982; chapter 4). As discussed in chapter 5, the identification of an "Eastern European" culture rests on its "difference" with "West Asia": its move beyond the servility characteristic of traditional society and its participation in the Enlightenment and democracy. On these grounds Central Europeans propose that their culture is incompatible with party claims to substantive rationality. Agnes Heller (Fehér, Heller and Markus, 1983:153), for instance, finds the power of substantive rationality greater in the USSR because of the submissive character of Russian popular culture.

By contrast, the Polish national tradition shaped by centuries of resistance to foreign occupation is identified with a rejection of authority. Rather than reinforcing the party's claims to substantive legitimacy, national tradition helps to undermine it (Opara, 1982). Cultural factors thus influence the relationship between substantive rationality and popular legitimacy, but they are only relevant in the structural context of a Communist Party legitimation crisis.

Eastern European communist parties must appeal both to their own societies and to the Communist Party of the Soviet Union for legitimacy (Rychard, 1987a). The CPSU does not have this internal/external combination, and thus does not generate the tension which makes a crisis out of the relationship between substantive rationality and popular legitimacy. But the non-Russian republics of the USSR have the same internal/external combination as the Eastern European states. The structural roots for the crisis may even be greater in these republics. To the degree the contradiction between social and CPSU legitimacy is accentuated, the greater the possible appeal to a perverted form of substantive legitimacy.

Among the Eastern European states, this antagonism of legitimation principles grants to communist parties their substantive rationality. The Hungarian Communist Party's self-justification is based on its relative tolerance of dissent in comparison to Czechoslovakia and its economic success versus Poland. The Czechoslovak party can point to Polish economic crisis as an indicator of the former's rationality. In Romania, the party can point to its relative independence in foreign policy compared with other Warsaw Pact states. In Poland, the party can rely on its comparative tolerance for independent culture and religious expression, if not its economic management skills. At root in all of these cases, however, is the final appeal to a substantive rationality based on the claim that a communist party is the only alternative to Soviet occupation. Independence under the tutelage of a communist party is the only kind of independence possible. In each case, the Communist Party presents itself as the only leadership which can guarantee what the society already has. These are not themselves independent yardsticks of accomplishment, however. If these gains were to be lost, they would be lost because it could not be otherwise. No other group could do more, given the Soviet Union's military position and its preferential treatment of communist parties. All accomplishments are the consequence of the party, not because of its infallibility, but because of its special relationship to the Communist Party of the Soviet Union. On the other hand, these parties need not assume responsibility for the worst aspects of these societies. Any party can point to other societies where the CPSU's substantive rationality has legitimated even greater suffering, be that in economic crisis, political repression or loss of national independence. The better the relative position of the society or republic in contrast to other systems in the Soviet sphere of influence, the greater its accomplishments and its right to claim substantive rationality. It is in this sense that the non-Russian republics of the USSR have a stronger foundation for legitimation crisis, if national independence is a greater claim to social legitimacy than is political tolerance or economic security.

In this discourse, whatever the party provides to the population is a privilege bestowed from those with substantive rationality, not a right inherent in social association. The identification of this society as a "dictatorship over needs" by Fehér, Heller and Markus (1983) is based on their characterization of the regime as inherently "paternalistic."

As the patriarch, the "source of all power and the source of all virtues are identical" (Fehér, Heller and Markus, 1983:213). As such, the "subjects of the Soviet-type state have just two rights: ius supplicationis (the ancient feudal right of asking for favours) and the right of denunciation" (pp. 175–76). The party therefore becomes much like an ideal sovereign whose wisdom and benevolence is all that the population need seek. Likewise, the substantive rationality of the Eastern European parties consists in their greater ability to win favors for their peoples from the CPSU. They can beseech the Soviet Union to permit market experimentation, religious freedoms and greater national autonomy. Were societies to reject their Communist Parties' claims to rule, the Soviet Union would rule instead. Thus, not only is paternalism the foundation for rule within societies, it is also the international factor which bestows on Eastern European parties the right to make their own claims to substantive rationality. This use of substantive rationality in Eastern European popular legitimacy depends on the constant uncertainty of the threat of repression by the center. Because this factor is kept out of direct discussion even as it is referred to constantly, it remains the basic factor guaranteeing the national party's substantive rationality and claim to rule. Without that threat, party rule is unlikely to survive. The substantive rationality which underlies organizational hegemony is justified ultimately in terms of potential coercion from the center. Thus, one need not have a national tradition of "servility" for substantive rationality to legitimize organizational hegemony. National traditions which emphasize resistance do, however, make the appeal to coercion more central as a factor justifying this perverted rationality.

To the degree that substantive rationality is accepted "voluntarily," without the threat of coercion, organizational hegemony can be more complete as it is perceived to be more legitimate. To the degree that organizational hegemony is complete, patterns of social reproduction and transformation are shaped by developments within the authorities. "Political" models which focus on conflicts among elites become more adequate under these conditions. But where substantive rationality is perverted and based on coercion and its threat, political models are limited, as Polish Solidarity has illustrated. To the degree people cease to fear the authorities, appeals to the party's substantive rationality decline and the possibility for organizational hegemony recedes. To the degree that organizational hegemony is limited, the authorities are more defensive, reactive and coercive than they are prescriptive and leading in their policy. Under these conditions, a "political" model of Soviet-type society becomes especially inadequate, as the dynamics of change are established within civil society. Most notions of civil society include the economy in its constitution. In Soviet-type society, however, the economy is one terrain of struggle between civil society and the authorities. In this system, the economy has a different logic of production and distribution.

Organizational hegemony and economic development

Soviet-type societies differ from democratic capitalist ones by virtue of the former's goal function (Marx's *Zweck der Produktion*), which suggests that economic development is first and foremost subordinated to the extension or maintenance of party control. In Leninist ideology, industrialization is linked to the construction of socialism. Lenin thought that socialism and eventually communism would be constructed by the development of the productive forces under proletarian state power (Sirianni, 1983:252–60). The rapid initial industrialization of all Soviet-type societies seems to attest to the importance technological advance had in the ideology. Decades later, Khrushchev also relied on grand economic claims to buttress party claims to substantive rationality (Fehér, Heller and Markus, 1983:150–51). But technological development cannot be held to be the goal by itself, given the universal decline in rates of growth in all Soviet-type societies as they shift to an intensive from an extensive mode of accumulation. Something about their methods of development is more important than the goal of development itself. A broad array of critical sociologists from Soviet-type societies are in general agreement about the goal function of economic activities in Soviet-type societies. The basic arguments of Kuroń and Modzelewski (1966), Markus (in Fehér, Heller and Markus, 1983:65), Voslensky (1984:125) and Szelényi (1982:318) are in keeping with Fehér's (Fehér, Heller and Markus, 1983:243) position: "The objective 'goal of production' [in a centrally planned economy] implies, on the one hand, a constant effort to increase the material wealth of society . . . while on the other hand, this can only happen in ways which ensure the increasing power of disposition of the apparatus over this material wealth."

In this view, economic development and its consequences are desirable but only so long as they remain under the control of the authorities. This goal function explains the apparent irrationality of many economic decisions by the authorities. Indeed, this "irrationality" is one reason why there was a Veblenian-type rebellion of Polish engineers against the irrationality of the communist captains of industry (Kennedy and Sadkowski, 1990). The drive for party control over use values, be it out of a genuine belief in its own superior rationality or pragmatic acceptance of the need for its own control, leads to selectivity in industrialization.

Although this perspective may be useful for understanding the purpose of power in the pre-Gorbachevian USSR, its utility appears to be diminished in this period of reform, where the authorities apparently seek to reduce their control over the production of value. The Hungarian economy is in the vanguard, where contracting is taking place more and more outside the auspices of state supervision. Gorbachev has viewed the Hungarian New Economic Mechanism and its descendants as something of a model for *perestroika*. Do these reforms mean that this postulated goal function of Soviet-type societies is inaccurate now? Indeed, has it ever been?

Throughout the postwar history of Eastern Europe, there have been retreats from the party's commitment to control the production of value. The most notable retreat was in the failure to collectivize agriculture in Poland. Even from 1948, Polish leaders resisted Stalin's directive to impose a Soviet-type collectivization. They resisted this not because of their personal preference for private farms, but because, as one leader from that time said, they "recognized the true distribution of power and the resistance there was in the countryside" (Torańska, 1987:296). This goal function is but a tendency and not an "iron law." The tendency can be blocked when it is perceived by the authorities that increased control over the production of use values will not lead to a more secure role for the party and rather increase a social instability that endangers organizational hegemony. This tendency is more easily blocked when the authorities are limiting an extension of their power, however, and not when they are trying to divest themselves of it.

The normal response to a crisis in production by the authorities is to try to overcome the problem without relinquishing any control. When there is greater organizational hegemony, as in the USSR, the authorities are more likely to deal with a crisis this way. But even in Eastern Europe, strategies for dealing with crises have usually been sought that do not diminish the hegemony of the party. Gierek's economic reform, for example, did not relinquish control over the economy. Tellenbeck (1978:448) argues that the economic crisis of the late 1960s forced the Polish political elite to undertake an economic reform, but the political elite opted for a reform in which they had to share their privileged position with the "technocrats," but not give anything up.

The party seeks to retain its hegemonic position in all parts of social organization, but some reformist communists have begun to believe that if the party is going to be able to retain its political and social hegemony, it must somehow delegate away much of its direct responsibility for the economic health of society. Bogdan Denitch (1977) argued that one reason the Yugoslav League of Communists retained considerable legitimacy through the mid-1970s is because it managed to separate economic administration from direct party responsibility. Renata Siemińska (1985) noted that the Catholic Church continued to enjoy legitimacy in Polish society through 1985 partially because it never tried to claim responsibility for the country's economic health, unlike the party or Solidarity. Divestiture of the authorities' power resources in the economy nevertheless faces major barriers because of the social relations which have constituted the power resources enabling domination.

This propensity or goal function of organizational hegemony over the economy can easily be associated with the "values" of the authorities, at least until Gorbachev. Gorbachev has expressly encouraged a devolution of responsibility for the economy, even to the point of encouraging economic "self-sufficiency" in the Baltic republics (Kahk, 1988). But even Gorbachev faces considerable resistance to reform, as Jaruzelski, Kádár and others before him. This is because this economic goal function is rooted structurally and not just dependent on the ideology or values of the society's leaders. These roots are in the social relations which constitute the authorities. To explain these social relations, we must clarify the meaning of delegated power and the social groups constituted by it: the power elite and vassals. Before that relationship can be clarified, however, the nature of "autonomous" resources must be elaborated. Delegated power acquires its distinctive quality only in relation to the existence of autonomous resources.

Delegated and autonomous power resources

Power resources in Soviet-type societies are usefully distinguished as *delegated* and *autonomous*. The distinction is important because it outlines (1) the most significant differences in power resource bases and (2) the likely structure of conflict. Delegated power resources have always been very important in Soviet-type society, but autonomous power resources are growing in importance. Delegated power resources tend to be of broader scope but more limited exclusivity. Autonomous resources tend to be of lesser scope but greater exclusivity.

"Autonomous power resources" do not refer to power resources which are completely at the control of an individual. All power resources of any scope involve some measure of dependency on those who are affected by their execution. I use the term only to refer to those power resources which do not inhere in a position delegated by the party, but are rather substantially controlled, or "owned," by groups outside of the party or by individuals. Autonomous power ultimately inheres in individual agency. Agency has been defined variously, but here I mean to refer to it only as the capacity to do otherwise (Giddens, 1984). This is the basis for resistance to any form of domination. When this basis is taken away, we can no longer speak of power *relations*, and only of total control by one of another.

Agency is not easily conceived within sociological discourse, since its presence implies the improbability of sociological generalization or of the meaningfulness of causal regularities. It is nevertheless a useful corrective to the potentially demeaning consequences of certain socio-logical world views which, by ridding explanatory schema of agency, simultaneously rid its subjects of responsibility. Theorizing agency reintroduces individual responsibility not only for individual morality, but for macrosocial collective decisions.

Some oppositionists in Eastern European societies elevate the per-sistence of agency to a central place in resistance. Havel in Czecho-slovakia, Michnik in Poland and Konrád in Hungary all emphasize that the basis for social transformation in these societies lies with individuals living "as if they were free," speaking the truth, refusing to compromise and retaining their prerogative to live as they deem rather than as those who dominate society demand. This emphasis on individual agency and responsibility poses a sharp contrast to the emphasis on the party's substantive rationality and organizational hegemony which constitute the essential features of Soviet-type society. Although these collective vs individual and impersonal vs personal contrasts capture the basic antagonism in Soviet-type society, they are inadequate by themselves for explaining social transformation, or even social reproduction.

Agency expresses only one dimension of power: its exclusivity. Individual dignity refers only to a person's control over one's own action, and thus agency requires only the minimal scope of power resources. Given that emancipatory praxis requires power resources of both broad scope and relative exclusivity, agency is only the first step toward the possibility of transformation. But it is an important step. Isolated individuals refusing to compromise are the foundation upon which resistance to and transformation of all systems are built, but this is especially true in Soviet-type societies. To wield power of broad scope in this system, one must act through the party, given its organizational hegemony. The only viable means to remain independent, according to the Hungarian dissident Mihály Vajda (1981:137), is to become "apolitical," to withdraw into private life and to forfeit all collective goals. This action, especially if pursued *en masse*, is, however, a collective action in itself, even if it is not explicitly coordinated. It is also considered by many, especially Hungarians, the most effective kind of movement against organizational hegemony precisely because it establishes more autonomous power resources in the system (Róna-Tas, 1990).

The scope of power resources available to persons acting according to individual conscience and to groups unbound by the system's mono-organizational logic must be increased for transformation in Soviet-type society to occur. Thus, a principal aim in a critical sociology of Soviet-type society is to examine the character of autonomous power resources and their relationship to social transformation. Agency, the capacity for doing otherwise, also helps to reproduce Soviet-type society, however. Indeed, its pervasiveness among vassals is that which effectively limits social transformation from above. Thus, the relationship between autonomous and delegated power resources shapes the conditions of social transformation. A consideration of agency is central to the revisionist theory of social transformation, as well as to the limits of this form of transformative praxis. Alternatively, generating autonomous power resources of increasingly broad scope is central to the self-organizational transformative strategy.

Power resources of broad scope are delegated to individuals by the party, but the *party* cannot delegate resources. The party cannot act. Although it is a collective ruler, it is itself composed of social relations connecting individuals which enable it to act collectively. The only way in which the party can be seen as a single actor is in its ideological claim to substantive rationality and infallible action. Individuals can act in the name of the party, however, and thereby delegate resources to other individuals to carry out the intentions of the collective ruler. In order to understand the social relations which constitute domination in Soviet-type society, we must understand the relations enabling the use of delegated power resources by the authorities. Because power resources are delegated, we should not think of the occupants of *nomenklatura* positions as members of a ruling class, at least if we are to use that term in the Marxian sense. In Soviet-type societies, there is no private ownership of the means of production. Certainly, individuals are granted control over economic resources, but their control is based on appointment by the party. The party can also dismiss these individuals, and thus deprive them of their power. The power of the occupants of *nomenklatura* positions originates in their appointment and not their control over the means of production. Thus, while their power may be of broad scope, the exclusivity in its application is potentially quite limited.

The power elite

C. Wright Mills (1956:18) defined the power elite as "those political, economic and military circles which as an intricate set of overlapping cliques share decisions having at least national consequences. In so far as national events are decided, the power elite are those that decide them." The power elite is thus defined in terms of where power of the broadest scope and greatest exclusivity is concentrated. The "mono-organizational" (Rigby, 1964) quality of Soviet-type societies enables an "easy" answer to the question of concentrated power's location in this system. Kremlinology's search for who stands next to whom on the dais overlooking the October Revolution anniversary parade indicates this "obviousness" of where to look for the power elite, and who is ranked where within it. As Mills (1956:11) emphasized, "to have power requires access to major institutions, for the institutional positions men occupy determine in large part their chances to have and to hold these (power, wealth and celebrity) valued experiences." Given organizational hegemony, the major institution is self-evident in Soviet-type society. We can say without much debate, therefore, that power is concentrated in the center of the party in the center of the empire. Those in this center establish the rules and resources which guide the behavior of others in the official hierarchy of power. Power of more limited, but still broad, scope and relative exclusivity is concentrated in the centers of republican or national communist parties. Individuals who hold such broad power at the center of the empire or in any of the regional centers may be called the ruling group or "power elite." But this power elite is very different from the one Mills analyzed in the USA.

Mills (1956:18) found that defining the boundaries of the power elite is to some degree an arbitrary task. Nevertheless, he identified the elite as the very rich, the chief executives of the largest companies, admirals and generals, and some fifty-odd men in the political directorate. There is also an "inner core" of the power elite, who "interchange roles at the top of one dominant institutional order with those in another," as well as those legal and financial experts who are the go-betweens between these institutional orders (Mills, 1956:288–89). The outer fringe of the power elite passes imperceptibly into the middle levels of power, whose decisions might not bear national weight, but whom the elite must take into consideration. There are hundreds of people who are part of the power elite in the USA, and tens of people who compose its inner core.

There are different institutional orders in Soviet-type society too, but the distinctions among them are not as significant as those in capitalist societies. For Mills, coordination of the elite was *accomplished* through mechanisms of recruitment and socialization, intermingling of elites from different sectors, as well as explicit coordination. This explicit coordination peaks in the mono-organizational control exerted over these institutions by the party. Its organizational hegemony is a finer expression of explicit coordination than that which can be accomplished in societies with relatively autonomous institutions of domination. As such, membership in this power elite can be restricted to very few people at the top of the party hierarchy. At the height of Stalin's power, he may have constituted the power elite alone. Stalin's lesson suggested to subsequent generations a "first man" principle, in which one person dominates the rest of the ruling group. In subsequent times and places, most ruling groups are composed of at least two or three persons. During Poland's Stalinist period, for instance, Bolesław Bierut, Hilary Minc and Jakub Berman constituted a ruling troika, where the "first man," Bierut, rarely failed to follow the advice of his colleagues (Torańska, 1987:309–11). Lowit (1979:845) estimates that in Czechoslovakia about eight to ten people at any one time work out the political line of the party and state, and therefore guide the plans and policies addressing fundamental questions.

To decide who are members of this elite at any given time is extremely difficult, however. Membership in the ruling group is both fluid and hidden from the public. Formal responsibilities rarely indicate true influence. While we can be reasonably sure that the first secretary of the Communist Party has been the most powerful individual in Soviet-type societies, the extent of even his power is difficult to estimate. Other powerful persons could include the prime minister of the government, the minister of internal affairs, or even a Politburo member who holds no governmental title at all. PZPR politburo member Zenon Kliszko was supposedly the second most powerful Pole in Poland in the 1960s, even though his only official governmental position was the largely ceremonial position of speaker of the Sejm. During the 1970s, the second most powerful figure in Poland was reputedly Prime Minister Piotr Jaroszewicz. More recently, the most powerful man after Jaruzelski is assumed to be Minister of Internal Affairs Czesław Kiszczak.[5] The composition of the ruling group is informally constituted and therefore bears little relation to the formal organization of power. The public therefore does not know with certainty who belongs to the power elite. This contributes to the uncertainty characteristic of power relations in Soviet-type society, and is one more aspect of the general set of conditions underlying vassalage (Kennedy and Białecki, 1989). Given the concentration of power in Soviet-type society, it would appear that the ruling group in Soviet-type society is the ultimate expression of what Mills (1956) understood as a power elite. Their decisions certainly have national consequence, they are recruited and socialized through the same organization, and they can move among the various institutions with ease. And also as Mills (1956:11) emphasizes, their power depends on their access to this major institution. Power does not inhere in their persons.

Revisionist strategies of social transformation place great stock in this kind of elite theory. As Mills (1956) argues, this group more than any other has the capacity to make the roles they follow, rather than follow the roles made for them. Thus, the "agency" of the power elite, and therefore the individuals who constitute its membership, establish the possibilities for social transformation. Domination and repression also can be understood in this elite theory as a consequence of the rule and role makers' distinctiveness. Stalinism, for instance, resulted from "perversions that Stalin introduced into the theory and practice of the Communist movement" (Medvedev, 1971:565). If others had led the USSR after Lenin's death, the system would not be as "pseudocommunist" as it became, according to Medvedev. Likewise, the hopes engendered by change in leadership at the top of the Soviet Union today, from Brezhnev's gerontocracy to Gorbachev's movement for *perestroika*, rely on the notion that the power elite possesses power of both broad scope and great exclusivity.

The power elite of Soviet-type society differs from Mills's elite not only in terms of its size and institutional concentration, however. The alienability of power resources in Soviet-type society is much greater than that in capitalist society, with psychological consequences that ultimately reduce the exclusivity of those power resources. This difference is obvious in a comparison of the power elite in Soviet-type society with a true capitalist who owns means of production. Her right of ownership is legally guaranteed, even if market forces could push her to sell her property rights. But does the chief executive officer of a large corporation, or even a national president or leading cabinet officer in the West, not possess the same exclusivity in regard to power of broad scope? Institutional differentiation in capitalist society not only allows intermingling, but it also allows those who are endangered personally in one institution to retreat to another institution. The revolving door of elites not only allows an integration of these elites, but it also allows greater boldness in decision-making, because "survival" does not depend on success in a single institution with a single set of expectations. Because elites in Soviet-type society must survive in a single institution, and there are no other institutions to which they can escape, they impose greater self-restrictions on how to use their power, so as to assure greater chances of survival.

This caution reduces the collective power of the elite, because elites are more hesitant to make decisions that might introduce instability and endanger their own personal survival, as the collective leadership will sacrifice individuals in order to assure the survival of organizational hegemony. This means, therefore, that while the power of any member of the power elite in Soviet-type society is of greater scope than a member of the power elite in capitalism, it is of more limited exclusivity. Access to institutional power in Soviet-type society is more precarious than it is in capitalism, and therefore the autonomy with which leaders exercise that power is more limited. The power elite's caution is not the only reason for its limited prescriptive power. The instruments of the elite's power, vassals, also engage in behavior which maximizes their capacity for survival and with that limit their ability to be used by the elite for its own ends.

Vassalage

Employees of the state administration, the party apparatus, the military and civil militia, plus managers in the economy and those working for mass media and propaganda are most directly affected by this concentration of power in the power elite. They are the power elite's vassals, because they act in the name of the ruling group in seeking to control the major features of everyday life.[6] They derive their power from the ruling group and their activity is informed by a concern for the reaction of the ruling group and even their more immediate superiors. Every vassal has masters to obey, but the vassal also has his own subordinates to control. But vassals do not always seek to impress their superiors; rather, they hope to avoid their superiors' displeasure. Vassals are thus those people whose occupational careers depend on their expressions of loyalty and obedience to their superiors and ultimately to the power elite.

Vassalage is best conceived as a role played by individuals rather than something attached to a given position within an organization. Vassalage is, then, analytically distinct from the formal organizational structure of actual socialism, even though the formal rule which underlies its organization is *nomenklatura*. Vassalage proper is based on more informal relationships of fealty that only sometimes coincides with formal organizational structure. Sometimes a vassal's patron can be one's immediate organizational superior, but it is more effective to have a patron located higher in the official hierarchy who can intervene with the vassal's formal superior on the vassal's behalf. The more occupational appointment and performance are dependent on expressions of loyalty and obedience to superiors and ultimately to the ruling group, the more the vassal role characterizes the individual's position in the power relations of Soviet-type society (Kennedy and Białecki, 1989).[7]

This set of vassals is under the ruling group's direct control, but the group's control indirectly embraces a much larger proportion of the labor force. Other positions, not falling under the official *nomenklatura* of the central committee, can be influenced by the ruling group and its vassals. Promotions, for instance, can be held up through the intervention of a local party committee if an individual does not meet party expectations. Usually, however, the center need not officially intervene, since it can rely on those selected by *nomenklatura* to use good judgment.

It is difficult to estimate the proportion of the labor force who are vassals, because loyalty does not only vary according to occupation; it also varies by society, period, institution, individual occupant of a position and even over the life-course of that individual. The main factors establishing the depth and breadth of vassalage over time are the strength of the power elite and the predominant form of its "operative ideology." Since Ceausescu consolidated his power, the strength of the Romanian ruling group is perhaps the greatest in

Eastern Europe as Poland's ruling group has been historically the weakest (Norgaard and Sampson, 1984). But this difference might be more one of depth rather than breadth, since in both cases major institutions have not won formal autonomy and *nomenklatura* has endured in most institutions. The Hungarian case represents another alternative to the Polish and Romanian, where through reform the breadth of vassalage has been reduced as some major institutions have acquired relative autonomy from the party.

Although the breadth of vassalage may not have varied significantly over time in Poland, the depth of the ruling group's control has varied considerably, peaking in the Stalinist period and reaching a new low in the Solidarity period. The operative ideology of the party varies along with these changes. In the Stalinist period, the authorities emphasized the importance of political criteria among its vassals, therewith reinforcing the vassalage system. In the Gierek era, the authorities emphasized more professional criteria, and thus limited the depth of its vassalizing penetration (Taras, 1984).

Within these societal and periodic variations, there is considerable possibility for institutional and individual differences. Vassals tend to predominate among those who hold directing positions in institutions which are important for the reproduction of power relations. This necessarily includes (a) managers of large factories, who enable the party to control the economy; (b) those who occupy key positions in the mass media; (c) those who hold important positions in state and party administration; and (d) all professional members of the coercive apparatus, including the army and militia. In periods when the influence of the ruling group is limited and the operative ideology emphasizes professional qualification, academic and research institutions, for example, have considerable potential for autonomy from the ruling group and its vassalage. To a considerable degree, this autonomy is established through replacements of directors or changes in the behavior of those who manage to remain in supervisory positions. The personal resources and intentions of directors vary, and with it the extent of vassalage within institutions. In this sense, in Poland, the Solidarity period has had a tremendous influence in that some managers have helped to establish working conditions which minimize the importance of the vassalage system. Although vassals can be found everywhere in the society, they are concentrated among managers who are also party members (Białecki, 1985). Filling key managerial positions with vassals is a means by which the ruling group exerts its control over society, but individuals need not always fulfill the role assigned to them.

Uncertainty and inertia

Although uncertainty exists in every society, it characterizes the power relations that define the system in Soviet-type society. I have discussed above the uncertainty of who actually constitutes the power elite, but uncertainty also reigns in the power relations of vassaldom. The party has the capacity to delegate power through its appointments; it also has the capacity to take power away. Thus, while an individual may enjoy power of great scope, that person is also dependent on the organization. She has power so long as she is useful to it. Hence, the exclusivity in the employment of power resources is limited and one's use of delegated power resources is guided according to how one can best ensure continued employment in that position or higher. A fall from grace can have serious consequences. After the 1968 invasion of Czechoslovakia, many prominent leaders of the Prague Spring were reduced to driving taxi cabs. As a result of the turmoil in Poland in that same year, party officials like Roman Zambrowski were removed from their positions of power and lost many of their accompanying perquisites (Smolar, 1983:48). That pattern was also repeated in the 1980s, although more selectively. Those who turned in their party memberships shortly after martial law were not punished much, if at all, but those who did so later were punished by withdrawing most of their professional privileges.

Jadwiga Staniszkis believes that after the December 1970 crisis, the party elite was beginning to develop a "crisis-oriented philosophy" to compensate for this uncertainty. Because the elite was beginning to believe that crises were inevitable, they wanted to assure that their own future fall from grace would not be as damaging as it had been to others in the past. In a sense, they wanted to provide for themselves the same "golden parachutes" that Western corporate executives receive when they are dismissed by their own companies. The Polish authorities issued two decrees, which had the effect of issuing guarantees to the political elite that "their privileged financial position would be preserved even if they had to serve as scapegoats during the political crisis" (Staniszkis, 1984a:106). Financial privileges would be guaranteed to ex-members of the elite as well as to their children. If they were to be dismissed from one *nomenklatura* post, the law implied that they would be assigned to another. Often those who were domestically embarrassing to the party were reassigned to foreign posts (Staniszkis, 1984a:151; for the USSR, see Voslensky, 1984:81–88).

Thus, while the power and privilege of the authorities are circumscribed by organizational imperative, common fear can result in the creation of a culture that attempts to mute the harshest edges of the uncertainty that organizational dependency generates. This is especially likely in a situation where there are frequent falls from power. Poland's "gentlemanly agreement" does not reduce the importance of survival for vassals, however. It only cushions their fall, should it occur. While vassals may not be executed (as in the Soviet Union in the 1930s) or lose their apartment, a fall from grace continues to mean a reduction in personal power and privilege. Because of the continuing importance of survival, vassals are not ideal servants to the power elite.

The occupational and social milieu of vassals is shaped by uncertainty. Since vassals are always appointed, the opinions of their subordinates do not matter and the main criterion for a vassal's success is meeting the expectations of his superiors. But because the share of power among his superiors are constantly changing and vassal responsibilities are imprecise, vassals can only guess about what their superiors expect. In addition, the formally determined scope of a vassal's responsibilities typically exceeds the resources at his disposal, and he is therefore often unable to rise to the situation even if he so wished. Centralized planning also increases uncertainty. Alec Nove (1983b:71–73) argues that scarcity is a consequence of centralized planning, one of the instruments of the ruling group's power. Scarcity increases uncertainty because resources essential to the fulfillment of responsibilities are often unavailable through normal channels.

The most profitable strategy for a vassal in such a milieu of uncertainty is to avoid decision-making for as long as possible. One commonly employed managerial strategy when a decision of consequence has to be made is to pick up one's briefcase and leave. When vassals are dismissed or demoted, their record is blighted. Rather than risk blame by making a bad decision, they prefer to avoid responsibilities to survive. Even as reforms promising self-management, self-financing and independence are promoted by the power elite, Polish vassal–managers resist. Kozek (1986) compared managers with non-managerial professionals, workers and political activists in four factories on their desire for increasing responsibility in work. Managers were, as workers, less interested than professionals in increasing their responsibility in work. Indeed, managers who had the most upward mobility were those least interested in increasing responsibility. Passivity is a strategy for a vassal's survival. The individual vassal's strategy for survival overrides the manipulation possible in vassal loyalty and makes vassals collectively an inert body that even the ruling group cannot steer or manipulate. Thus, while individual vassals are subject to vast control, as a group they are not. Vassals also understand this logic of collective action: that it is hard, if not impossible, to fire or dismiss a whole group of people for their strategy of survival; some can be fired but the whole group cannot be dismissed.

The vassal's successful career does not, therefore, depend on doing efficient work. Although today in Poland it is uncommon, in some other centrally planned economies and not long ago in Poland itself it was common to come upon retail stores that displayed a picture of the first party secretary in their front windows instead of the store's best products for sale. This was rational managerial behavior, because the manager's career did not depend on how many goods were sold but rather on how loyal the manager seemed to his superior. This condition exemplifies how on the one hand the vassal's orientation toward superiors and his uncertainty on how best to meet their expectations pushes power and responsibilities upward, but on the other hand makes it more difficult for the top to exercise power, especially to introduce changes into the system. The top is powerful because the organization of the system leads vassals to reject and return responsibilities upward, but the top is also powerless because it has to implement its power through an inert and passive instrument. Vassals are efficient in only one way: their passive resistance to any changes that could damage their interests. This often determines their collective behavior. The many examples of failed economic reforms in the history of Soviet-type societies is testimony to the power of vassal passivity.

This passivity has structural roots in the power relations of Soviet-type society. Both vassalage and passivity are the rational responses of those who seek to increase their own individual security in positions which contain power resources of broad scope but limited exclusivity. The domination of this type of power resources in the system creates greater uncertainty by making it unclear who actually wields power and what the rules for exercising that power are. In this sense, we can say that while *nomenklatura* might be the structural basis for vassaldom, uncertainty is the existential foundation of both vassaldom and passivity, which ultimately reduces the collective power of the authorities by diminishing the responsiveness of the instrument through which the ruling group exercises its power (see figure 6.1).

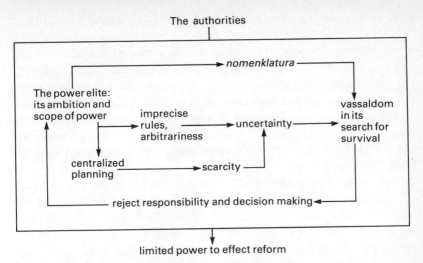

The authorities

The power elite: its ambition and scope of power

imprecise rules, arbitrariness

nomenklatura

uncertainty

vassaldom in its search for survival

centralized planning

scarcity

reject responsibility and decision making

limited power to effect reform

Figure 6.1   Power relations in the authorities

The limited corporate effectiveness of this system of power relations can only be explained, however, by the interaction between delegated and autonomous power resources. Vassals acquire power of broad scope when the collective sovereign delegates them the capacity to use economic resources or to order individuals to particular tasks. But vassals always retain their agency, or their capacity to do otherwise. And, indeed, vassals will often avoid the responsibilities their position demands in order not to make the wrong decision and risk punishment. In this case, the system is reproduced by the existence of the autonomous power resources of vassals, as they restrict the action of a power elite which might effect systemic transformation if it had better instruments with which to implement reformist policies.

Power and privilege in Soviet-type society

The organizational hegemony of the Communist Party and the internal social relations which constitute the authorities help to explain the peculiar character of domination in Soviet-type society. There are considerable power resources at the disposal of the authorities, in both allocative and authoritative forms. No other set of authorities in the history of humankind has had as many resources at its direct command. This concentration of power is both obliged by and legitimated by the substantive rationality party members confer onto the collective sovereign, the party. This substantive rationality is analogous to paternalism, and likewise ultimately based on the threat of coercion. The concentration of power also is illustrated by the goal function of production in these societies: to increase the amount of use value under the control of the authorities. Economic development, too, reflects the contradictions of this concentration of power. Development has proceeded unevenly, very rapidly at first and then quite slowly in the intensive phase of development to the point of economic crisis. This is an example of the more general problem of how this tremendous concentration of power resources is associated with its limited effectiveness.

The social relations which constitute the field for the use of these domination resources are characterized by vassalage. Because vassals use their own power resources to ensure their own security rather than act as their superiors wish, they limit their usefulness to the power elite. Domination in Soviet-type society is less a case where one group achieves its will despite the aims of another group; it is more a case where the limited exclusivity of all power resources of broad scope effectively limits the ability of any group to realize collective aims. This is especially relevant to the hopes placed in revisionist strategies of social transformation. If the power elite continues to rely on vassals to effect reform, transformation is unlikely and stalemate will continue. This stalemate can proceed indefinitely until sufficient autonomous resources of relatively broad scope are generated. Thus, we might best conceive resistance in the field of Soviet-type society's power relations as a struggle to generate autonomous power resources that are of increasingly broad scope and available to those who are not vassals of the authorities.

This examination of the relationship between delegated and autonomous power resources also is useful to explaining the distribution of privilege in Soviet-type society. Domination is facilitated by the authorities' control over the logic of distribution. One form of resistance to this control is the redistribution of privilege independent of the authorities' supervision. An examination of the relationship between power and privilege is helpful, therefore, to understanding the relation between domination and resistance in Soviet-type society. In periods free from economic crisis or social challenge, privilege tends to be allocated from the center in patterns shaped by power relations within the party hierarchy. In periods of economic crisis and social challenge, however, autonomous power resources distort the delegated distribution of privilege. Thus, in order to explain the opportunities for action by social groups in Polish society, one must first establish their relationship to delegated power and second their possibility for accumulating autonomous power resources.

One opportunity for action which power resources enable is the acquisition of privilege. Lenski (1966:44) argues that "power will determine the distribution of nearly all the surplus in a society." Because he understands privilege as "the possession or control of a portion of the surplus produced by a society," he comes to identify the distribution of power with the distribution of privilege, after the basic needs of society are addressed. The conceptions of power and privilege which underlie this identification are based on the assumption that they can be possessed by groups or individuals. In the terms of power we have considered so far, it assumes that power might vary in scope, but is essentially the same in terms of exclusivity. This is a problematic assumption for the character of the power resources available to the power elite and vassals. Although power resources of narrow scope might be relatively invariant in their exclusivity (as in the philosophical assumption of agency, or each individual's capacity to do otherwise), resources of broad scope in Soviet-type society are characterized by their limited exclusivity. This means that the use of these latter power resources cannot be identified with individual aims. Individuals do not "own" power resources of broad scope, although they might "own" privilege. Lenski's definition of privilege can be indistinguishable from allocative power resources, and thus cannot be identified with ownership in any meaningful sense in Soviet-type society. If we do, however, restrict privilege to that part of the societal surplus *consumed* by individuals or groups, we can say that privilege is owned or controlled by those individuals or groups because consumption implies exclusive use of that surplus product. We might even extend the notion of privilege to include those things which are not necessarily part of an economic surplus, and rather are the consequence of the control the authorities retain over information and civil liberties. In this case, privilege can include the right to travel abroad, the right to form an organization and the right to obtain or distribute information. These are not part of the surplus product of a society, but they are made artificially "scarce" by the requirements that they be consumed only with the permission of the authorities. Thus, not only is the possibility of consuming privilege generated by the production of surplus, but it is also created by the formal restriction of rights. Indeed, to the extent we identify the only rights in Soviet-type society as "ius supplicationis and denunciation" (Fehér, Heller and Markus, 1983:175–76), all other "rights" are "privileges." Thus, both the production of surplus and the restriction of rights are part of the general pattern of domination in which the distribution of privilege is central.

The officially recognized basis for the distribution of privilege is "to each according to his work." The other basis is an egalitarian principle in which basic needs should be satisfied. But neither is the main principle guiding the logic of distribution. The principal tendency guiding that logic by the authorities is "to each according to his/her significance in the reproduction of power relations" (Kennedy and Białecki, 1989). The party does not only allocate privilege to vassaldom. The authorities allocate privilege in both collective and individual consumption to all parts of the society in line with its quest to maintain organizational hegemony.

In both democratic capitalist and Soviet-type societies job location is sometimes more important than job type for explaining variations in income, but the rationales behind this variation differ. High wages in the American monopoly sector are a result of the pressure workers can exert through unions, and the ability of corporations to pass off those higher costs to consumers. While there are definitely more and less privileged sectors in the Soviet-type economy, the reasons for their variation differ. Communist Party leaders promise that in the stage of developed socialism, each is compensated according to his or her work contribution. At the organizational level, there *should be* a correlation between the level and dynamics of wages and enterprise efficiency (Misiak, 1984). Enterprise efficiency or productivity is notoriously difficult to compute in these societies, however. One of the greatest problems concerns the real value of inputs and outputs. The prices of some goods and services, notably coal, electrical energy and transportation, are provided at a cost significantly lower than the real cost of production, and, as a result, some enterprises attain much higher rates of accumulation because the costs of their inputs are artificially low (Misiak, 1984). Despite the problems, Rychard (1981) compares net wages and net output per employee in four different Polish industries: coal, machine construction, chemical and clothing. The average wage is highest in the coal industry, at 8,307 złotys per month. The average wage in the chemical industry is slightly less than half the coal industry's average, despite its productivity being 1.42 times higher. This favoring of certain sectors, particularly heavy industry and mineral extraction, exists throughout Soviet-type societies. More recent data at the enterprise level shows that wages are indeed not very closely tied to productivity. In 1984, Polish authorities for the first time published their own "Fortune 500" list of the top economic enterprises in the country (excluding mining and energy) according to total sales. Unfortunately, the whole list of 500 enterprises was not published, and there are other limitations in the data they provide, but it is nevertheless informative. It was originally published in the managers' journal *Zarządzanie* in order to provide more and better information about economic conditions to the country's managers. But other periodicals have also published the data, since, in the words of one observer, "if we have to lead the economy to rationality, to ensure the real socialization of economic processes, all of the activities of the economy must be conducted behind open curtains, in the public's eye" (*Polityka*, July 7, 1984).

The data in table 6.1 show that, at least in the fifty enterprises with the greatest sales, the magnitude of average wages has very little to do with profits, sales, financial results or even size. The places with the best enterprise performances, at least in terms of contributions to the whole economy, are the POLMOS vodka factories, the petrochemical factory in Płock, the car factory in Warsaw, the car factory in Bielsko Biała, the refinery in Warsaw, and the URSUS tractor factory. The best-paying places to work are in the steel factories without exception, even though their position in the profit hierarchy ranges from number 282 to number 451 out of 500! Although the vodka factories had the highest rate of accumulation and the second-best financial results, and the meat factories were in fifty-second place in financial results, their employees were among the worst paid in Poland's Fortune 500, ranking number 316 and number 444 respectively. Explanations for these patterns of favoritism usually rest on how critical the activities of an enterprise are to the economy, but that only captures part of the explanation. Steel is crucial to any newly industrialized country, but the foundries' preferential treatment goes beyond that to factors associated with the command economy. Nove (1983b:97) claims that in Soviet-type societies, "in the competition for resources, victory is likely to go to the sector which has the biggest 'pull', the best hierarchical connections, the most senior and influential boss . . . So instead of bias toward anticipated profitability, one has a bias in favor of the already big and powerful." The Polish group, *Doświadczenie i Przyszłość*, argues similarly: "the power of a particular (industrial) lobby is not determined by the real value and importance it has in the economy as a whole, but by the reigning dogma, or the current notions of the party and state leadership about what constitutes modernity and progress, or finally, by incidental personal connections" (DiP,1981:12).

Table 6.1   *Position according to various economic indicators for selected enterprises in Poland's "Fortune 500"*

Enterprise, its 1982 rank according to total sales and product	A	B	C	D	E
1. Polmos Warszawa (vodka)	1	2	115	25	316
2. Petrochemia Płock (petrochemicals)	2	1	200	24	138
3. Huta im. Lenina Kraków (steel)	7	6	282	1	1
4. Huta Katowice (steel)	452	8	404	3	2
5. Polskie Gorn. Naftowe i Gaz. Warszawa (coal, oil and gas)	6	5	179	495	7
6. FSM Bielsko-Biała (small cars)	4	3	75	2	137
7. Z-dy Rafineryjne Gdańsk (refinery)	3	10	170	345	52
8. Komb. FSO Warszawa (autos)	5	4	55	6	223
9. Okr. Przeds. Przem. Miesn. Katowice (meat)	469	52	470	19	444
10. Zrzeszenie Ursus Warszawa (tractors)	9	9	218	4	92
16. Huta Warszawa (steel)	29	18	226	20	6
25. H. Celgielski Poznań (machinery)	94	47	345	10	115
26. Z-dy Metalurg. Trzebinia (metallurgy)	187	109	431	360	3
38. Huta Batory Chorzów (steel)	280	184	449	36	10
41. Huta Kościuszko Chorzów (steel)	283	203	451	64	9
46. Huta Florian Świętochlowice (steel)	89	65	309	105	8

A = accumulation from all activities; B = financial results; C = net profit; D = total employment; E = average monthly earnings.

Lobbying is one of the possible forms establishing the official distribution of privilege. "Incidental" connections are those established by the informal ties of vassaldom. It is the presence of these strong lobbies where the anarchy characteristic of feudal vassaldom is most nearly imitated, as various fiefdoms compete against one another for their share of the resources of the system. At the same time, this lobbying illustrates the centralization of power in the system. Lobbying can change which sectors are defined as central, but this is all done with an eye toward redefining what the power elite considers most important for the reproduction of power relations. This "importance" is understood in a dual sense. They use resources to reward those, their vassals, who help them maintain their influence. This delegation of privilege by the authorities thus reflects the pattern of power relations within the authorities, among the vassals and their various fiefdoms. They also use this capacity to distribute privilege to "buy off" potential threats to their organizational hegemony, reflecting again the significance of "autonomous" power resources in the use of delegated power.

In his discussion of power relations, Anthony Giddens (1981:63) emphasized that control is never complete, that "however wide ranging the control which actors may have over others, the weak nevertheless always have some capabilities of turning resources back against the strong." And thus, no matter how nearly total the party's control over force, economy and information, the non-party population has other resources at their disposal. The degree to which they have influence varies, however. In Soviet-type societies, strikes and organizations independent of party control are illegal. The major exception to that generalization is, of course, the 1980–81 Solidarity period in Poland. Workers, in order to exercise power, are for the most part forced to act in an atomized fashion. Jones (1981) and Sabel and Stark (1982) argue that the planned economy, by its very nature, creates a precondition for shopfloor power: tight labor markets. Given the manpower shortage, workers typically improve their socio-economic status by changing sites of employment. And also, given the need to hoard labor, managers cannot be too demanding about work norms and productivity. Thus, the threat to leave work gives the unorganized worker power over the pay packet she receives and the pace of work she is expected to maintain. Strikes and work stoppages can also be a way of influencing the distribution of privilege. Jones (1981) showed that even in the USSR strikes for higher wages and better working conditions occasionally occur, and the demands of the workers are typically met. But their frequency in the USSR is minuscule in comparison to that which exists in Poland. Between 1976 and 1980 at least 1,000 strikes occurred, even though they were officially illegal. Staniszkis (1984a:185–86) argues that the Gierek regime sought to deal with these work stoppages on a case-by-case basis; rather than challenge the strikers, the regime would simply buy them off with promises of more wages or better supplies. It was a strategy to buy off strategic and powerful groups. Thus, in the late 1970s, certain groups of workers, especially skilled workers in heavy industry, began to accumulate more privilege. The greater the potential of actual threat to continued production of goods, the greater the privilege bestowed from the center. After the establishment of Solidarity, and even since the declaration of martial law, this favoritism of potentially disruptive groups remains. Although the data in table 6.1 do not allow us to assess the independent effect of militancy on earnings, it is worthwhile to note that Huta im. LENINA (Nowa Huta), Huta KATOWICE, URSUS, Huta WARSZAWA, and H. CELGIELSKI, were all Solidarity strongholds. Their prior preferential treatment in allocated privilege is augmented by their militancy.

The interaction between delegated power and autonomous power resources therefore shapes the official distribution of privilege in Soviet-type society. The greater the power resources of each type available to a group, the greater the potential for privilege delegated by the center. The distribution of privilege is not only influenced by the preferences of the power center, but also the threats perceived by the power center. Greater privilege is delegated to those who are perceived as loyal, valuable, but also potentially troublesome. The distribution of privilege is thus a consequence of the interaction between the delegated power of the authorities and the autonomous power resources of workers to leave their jobs, or to organize collectively. Lobbying and the threat of social protest can go hand in hand in increasing the share of resources delegated by the center. Through this coordination of militancy and vassalage, the logic of distribution set by the authorities, "to each according to their significance in the reproduction of organizational hegemony," continues. This interaction continues to privilege the authorities in their organizational hegemony as they continue to shape patterns of privilege, even if they do not do so with impunity.

Although this is the intention of the authorities, this distribution of privilege is not guaranteed to reproduce power relations. To the degree that the authorities retain the economic resources to maintain this logic of distribution, they can reproduce the system. But this logic also can contribute to an economic crisis if the allocation diverges too much from principles of "economic rationality." One response to such an economic crisis would be for the authorities to relinquish control over the economy. Were this the outcome, the economic irrationality of such a logic of distribution could be understood as unintentionally producing social transformation, much as the systemic contradictions of capitalism have produced various transformations designed to overcome its crisis tendencies. But as we have seen, the stated intentions of the ruling group to reform the economy are not always realizable, given the character of delegated power in the system. To the extent the authorities must rely on delegated power to transform the system, reform is likely to fail.

"To be free and secure is to have an effective control over that upon which one is dependent," wrote C. Wright Mills in *White Collar* (1951:58). The centralization of political and economic power in the USA moved Mills (1956) to argue that the march of history is increasingly subject to control by the power elite. Although centralization has not led to such elite direction in Soviet-type society, the necessity of effective control over resources upon which individuals depend is essential to the prospects for social transformation. To a large extent, therefore, transformation depends on the proliferation of autonomous power resources. In particular, the way in which delegated power and privilege interact with autonomous power resources shapes the conditions for alliances between groups and therefore the reproduction and transformation of the system.

There are several kinds of autonomous power resources, each with a different relationship to the delegated power of the authorities. Autonomous power derives from the amount of occupational control over scarce goods and values. It can be derived from the ownership of a scarce skill or personal resource like prestige or even time to stand in lines. It can also come from the networks of informal social relations in which one lives. Although analytically distinct and occasionally empirically separable, these conditions frequently converge. But it is most useful to consider them separately.

In Soviet-type societies, shortages of goods and services are commonplace. Classical Marxist theory assumed that socialism would be constructed in a condition of resource abundance. Conflict over the unequal distribution of goods and services would not exist because there would be enough for all. But that assumption of resource abundance was made because socialist revolution was to occur in the most advanced societies, where Marx thought the problems of production had already been fundamentally solved (Nove, 1983b:15). Since the revolutions occurred in agrarian or relatively underdeveloped industrial societies, the mistaken assumptions of Marxism are compounded by the empirical difficulties endemic to the initial stages of industrialization. But even in the "developed socialisms," shortages are still common features of everyday life. Nove (1983b:71–73) in fact argues that they are endemic to planned economies. Macro planning cannot anticipate all changes in micro demand. Thus, even if the individual has the money for the goods needed, it does not mean one can get those goods. The problem extends from the lowly individual consumer to the factory manager. Never knowing when supplies will be adequate, the consumer is led to stock up when things are available. Even the factory manager must rely on informal relationships for supplies of goods. His success is sometimes derived from the quality of his relations with other managers (Tarkowski, 1983).

Whatever the source of the system's endemic shortages, a crisis economy magnifies the problem. Shortages are both broader and deeper. More goods are unobtainable through official channels, and the unofficial channels are harder to work. Those people who have control over these scarce resources gain power because they have some degree of discretion as to whom they "sell" their resource. Hraba (1985:398–99) describes how clerks would inform their "favorite" customers about when special deliveries arrive and even set items aside for them. In return, the customers would drop off an occasional bottle of vodka, take care of the clerk's children or even entertain the clerks themselves. Wojciech Zaborowski asked 330 inhabitants of Warsaw in 1979 how they imagined the shape of the social structure. According to these Varsovians, "access" to "distribution points" of scarce goods and services has become a new dimension of the Polish hierarchy of power (Zaborowski, 1983). It was clearly distinguished from the hierarchies associated with education or position in the official hierarchy. This power is particularly obvious in places where goods are rationed. The customer's lack of rationing coupons might be overlooked if he has something equally handy to exchange. People who are otherwise not very powerful, those who do not have high education, are not high in the official hierarchy or do not even belong to privileged sectors of the economy, have as much of this potential power as some people who are otherwise powerful. Butchers, gas-station attendants, shoe makers and others who have control over the distribution of goods have the potential for using that occupational control to enhance their own position. For example, in 1983, an advertisement in Życie Warszawy read: "Female manager of meat store wants to rent a comfortable but inexpensive apartment." The understanding of this advertisement was that the renter of the apartment would provide better or more meat for the person who would provide her with what she wanted (Białecki, 1985). This kind of power is more directly translated into the consumption of privilege than the power of broader scope wielded by highly ranked party members. It reflects the greater exclusivity inherent in control over scarcity.

Indirect but more systematic proof for the increasing power of this kind of occupational control can be found in the data on the relative wealth of private artisans and shopkeepers. Given the system goal to place as many use values under state control as is economically feasible, the very existence of private artisans and shopkeepers suggests the perceived necessity of their action to economic functioning. Polish policy requires that private markets "complement and not compete with the socialised sector over supplies, labour, and markets" (Aslund, 1984:431). Since their prices are invariably higher than those in the state stores, their economic success is a good proxy for the shortage of goods in the state sector and the potential power of those who control the distribution of goods in that state sector. A large part of the private sector's supplies comes from paying state store-people bribes (Aslund, 1984:432). In 1972, technical and non-technical specialists and managers had the highest monthly income, averaging about 2.1 thousand złotys per month. Owners of productive and service establishments made on average 1.6 thousand złotys per month, less than technicians, and the same as low-level non-manual employees. In 1982, however, their income was by far the greatest of any occupational group, exceeding even the highly educated specialists and managers by 1.14 times (Pohoski, 1984). Aslund's (1984:434) data suggest that entrepreneurs would not engage in the business for anything less than three times the national average wage.

These data probably underestimate the actual privilege enjoyed by these private entrepreneurs. It nevertheless indicates something very important: privilege (at least in the form of higher incomes, and probably much more) escapes the control of the party most in time of economic crisis. The party seems to be forced to allow some degree of "entrepreneurial" initiative in order to assure some minimum level of economic rationality. Their tolerance also serves a second function: if the party can point to individuals making out very well in the crisis, it can shift some of the blame for poor living conditions from itself to these individuals. In 1984, Polish newspapers were filled with accounts of the party cracking down on private tradesmen gouging the public. This propagandistic attempt to make scapegoats of the private sector in order to show the party in a good light only makes my point stronger: crisis breeds opportunity for autonomous hierarchies of power and privilege.

Non-delegated privilege is also common in Hungary, but there it may be less a manifestation of crisis and more a consequence of systemic reforms that reduced the power of the center over the delegation of privilege. David Stark (1986) analyzes one dimension of this market reform, in the development of subcontracting within the firm. But inequalities are also created outside this innovation. Self-interests are promoted through various informal ties in addition to ones derived from political position, position on the labor market and the position in the social pattern of the working place (Kolosi, 1984:60). According to a 1981–82 survey of a representative sample of Hungarian adults, this dimension of the Hungarian status hierarchy is the most dissimilar from the other dimensions of status: housing, settlement location, consumption, culture, financial and place in the division of labor. It also has the strongest independent effect on overall status and contributes substantially to explaining about 15 percent of its variation (Kolosi, 1984:74–75). Data collected in Poland in 1982 show that between 11 and 14 percent of the goods and services consumed by families headed by state employees (intelligentsia and workers) came from outside the "market" proper, and between 20 and 25 percent more came from the private sector. The figures for private producers and those connected with agriculture are considerably higher (Sikorska, 1987:104).

There are an increasing number of "currencies" which enable the acquisition of privilege which are not distributed by the authorities. Huge incomes from private initiatives, access to Western currencies, time to stand in queues for scarce goods, prestige and personal connections and control over scarce goods all contribute to one's "wealth" and possibility for consumption (Hankiss, 1988:30). These autonomous power resources could contribute to systemic transformation, as the authorities lose their ability to integrate and steer social action into patterns which reproduce organizational hegemony. To the extent that these other currencies are not controlled by the authorities, the system is transformed, as organizational hegemony is gradually undermined in this "generalized market" (Kennedy and Białecki, 1989).

Conclusions

I have developed the preceding concepts and relationships in order to improve upon existing frameworks for the analysis of power relations in Soviet-type society. I have argued that the party is usefully understood as a collective sovereign. Its position is legitimated with reference to its "substantive rationality," and on that basis the party maintains organizational hegemony in the system. This hegemony extends even to the economy, where the goal of production is the extension of use values under the control of the Communist Party. The power elite draws upon the party's sacred status in substantive rationality to delegate powers of fairly broad scope to other party members. As such, most power of broad scope in the system is derived from an appointment, not from real control over resources. Nevertheless, given the capacity of actors to do otherwise, those with delegated power can use these resources in their own interests. Very often, this interest can be defined as the preservation of personal position. The power elite therefore has a very unwieldy instrument with which to exercise its power. Vassals are unreliable because the uncertainty of the system leads them to avoid responsibility and avoid decision-making. This leads to considerable inertia in the system, even when the power elite wishes to introduce reform. Reform, therefore, depends on initiatives from outside vassaldom.

Social transformation thus depends on the proliferation of autonomous power resources. Without this proliferation, the relationship between elite and vassals will define the course of social change, and therefore lead to the reproduction of the status quo. This proliferation depends on the more active assertion of individual agency, but by itself "living as if one is free" does not introduce institutional change. Power of broader scope, in combination with this greater exclusivity, is essential. Working-class self-organization and militancy is one of the most important examples of this generation of autonomous power resources. Solidarity is the greatest example here, where, through self-organization and eventually self-management, the movement promised to create a civil society out of Soviet-type society. This is also exemplified earlier, in the workers' ability to redirect the authorities' delegation of privilege, so that those who are not only loyal but also those who are troublesome are rewarded better.

There are other forms of autonomous power resources to which other social groups have access. In general, to understand the relationship between delegated and autonomous power resources enables us to understand better the place of different social groups in the power relations of the Soviet-type system. This is especially true for professionals.

Professionals are themselves internally differentiated in terms of their access to delegated and autonomous power resources. Separate occupations ought, then, to be considered separately. They do share one autonomous resource, however, which makes their common discussion meaningful: in the next chapter, I consider how professional prestige is useful as an autonomous power resource in Soviet-type society. In the following chapters, I explain how the participation by engineers and physicians in Solidarity might also be understood in these very terms of autonomy and dependency.

Part III

Professionals and Solidarity

7   Professionals, power and prestige

The principal aim of this chapter is to examine the power relations enabling and constraining professional action in Poland especially and Soviet-type society generally. Because the authorities control opportunities for professional work in this system, professionalism depends to some degree on political qualifications. Professionals also control resources, especially through their monopoly over forms of specialized knowledge. But their power in dealing both with authorities and with other social groups comes in the prestige associated with that monopoly. In Soviet-type society, this prestige can influence the authorities' delegation of power and privilege, but under conditions of economic and social crisis, professionals are likely to lose some of their perquisites. Professionals thus are normally "dependent" on the authorities, but in exceptional periods they can transfer their allegiance and become "dependent" on other social groups. In the Solidarity period, professionals were dependent on the self-organized working class.

When one writes of the highly educated in Eastern Europe, one normally writes of the intelligentsia, not of professionals. To use "professionals" in the title of this volume therefore suggests a distance from the normal Eastern European discourse. My terminological alteration reflects an intentional departure from this portion of the Eastern European analytical framework. Use of the term "intelligentsia" would divert me from my principal concern with the Soviet-type system of power relations, and direct me toward questions of the cultural identity and moral evaluation of one group. While these concerns are certainly important for the questions of social transformation, use of the intelligentsia as concept obliges the analyst to put the intelligentsia as a group at the center of politics and society. The major assumption of part III is that the highly educated do not deserve such centrality because their position is shaped more by the interaction between authorities and working class than the activities of an intelligentsia shape it. But, as most residents of and experts on Eastern Europe might balk at my use of professionals instead of intelligentsia, I begin this chapter with a discussion of the difference between concepts, and the analytical consequences of their uses.

Intelligentsia and professionals

Use of the term "intelligentsia" begins with a controversy over what the term includes. It obliges some acknowledgment of the long and many debates over what is and what is not the intelligentsia, and what is and is not an intellectual. Of course, this is not only a Polish debate. Journals including *Daedelus* (summer 1972) and *Salmagundi* (spring–summer 1986), for instance, have devoted whole issues to defining and identifying the intellectual in the contemporary world. Post-structuralist thought also makes a great deal of the intellectual, given the "political economy of truth" and the place of intellectuals in formulating categories and defining truth's relationship to power (Foucault, 1977 [1984]). But in Eastern Central Europe, and especially Poland, these debates take on a special importance.

Intellectuals and words seem to matter a great deal in this region. At least, political authorities and many in civil society pay attention to what intellectuals say. In part, this has a historical legacy. When the West was consolidating its capitalist economies, Eastern Europe was still dominated by a royal imperialism. Many intellectuals, instead of being recruited as professionals, state apparatchiks or cultural authorities, were made into political vanguards of dispossessed groups, especially of their nations. But because these nations were themselves untransformed by capitalism, it became the intelligentsia's obligation to define how modernity should be faced by the nation. This definition obliged the intelligentsia to use state power, not defend civil society from state power as in the West (Barańczak, 1986–87; Bauman, 1987).

Although Eastern Central Europe is now industrialized, the nineteenth-century Eastern Central European intelligentsia is similar to the intelligentsia of the Soviet-type system, which in turn is quite different from the Western "professional" (Bauman, 1987; Szelényi, 1982). Both professionals and members of the intelligentsia are part of a speech community defined by its secular and theoretical discourse (Gouldner, 1979), a community Szelényi (1982: 307) calls intellectuals. But he identifies professionals as those intellectuals whose "know-how" of this secular and theoretical knowledge dominates the teleological component of knowledge. Where the latter is dominant, we have an intelligentsia. Professionals provide the means for others, and the intelligentsia sets the goals. In this goal-setting responsibility, the intelligentsia and Communist Party share much (Szeleńyi, 1982; chapter 4). But the Communist Party, not the intelligentsia, controls the intelligentsia's constitutive functions in Soviet-type society. There is, then, a foundation for conflict between the party and those parts of the intelligentsia who struggle for the right to define the future and the role played by intellectuals in it (Bauman, 1987: 178). The massive modernizing experiment undertaken by the Communist Party has, however, meant that a smaller and smaller portion of the intelligentsia contest the party for that right to constitute itself as more intellectuals passively fill the positions created in the new order.

In 1939 Poland, non-manual workers constituted little over 5 percent of the population (Davies, 1984: 406; Żarnowski, 1964: 135). About 40 percent of this group were the "true intelligentsia," including doctors, dentists, pharmacists, lawyers, teachers and engineers (Żarnowski, 1964: 321). But in 1933 only about 11 percent of the broadly defined intelligentsia had completed higher education (Żarnowski, 1973: 202). In the academic year 1938–39, there were approximately 50,000 students of higher education, with about 15 percent of them in technical studies (J. Tymowski, 1980: 23). The highly educated in Poland before World War II were an elite, but the war destroyed between one-third and one-half of this group (Hoser, 1970; Lukas, 1985). Poland's Communist Party sought to replenish the educated ranks of its nation by expanding educational opportunities considerably. The amount of time required for winning degrees was reduced; fields of expertise for degrees were narrowed; in addition to day schools, more evening schools for working people were established; in addition to universities, the number of secondary occupational schools was increased; the participation of youth from working-class and peasant backgrounds was encouraged; and emphasis was given to practical and technical subjects (Szczepański, 1980; J. Tymowski, 1980). Already in 1945–46, 55,980 people were enrolled in higher education; five years later, that number more than doubled (to 125,096 persons) (J. Tymowski, 1980: 96). Since the early 1950s, between one-third and two-fifths of the nation's students in higher education were in technical studies (J. Tymowski, 1980: 96). By 1980, over 8 percent of the labor force had higher educations (Rocznik Statystyczny, 1983: 59). Over one-third of this group has been engineers since the 1960s (Spis Kadrowy, 1977: 32). An expansion of this sort had to change the fundamental character of Poland's intelligentsia.

Jan Szczepański (1962: 419) wrote that this new Polish intelligentsia has "no common institutions, no common economic interests, and no common ideology or social consciousness." In effect, it ceased to be a social group and became merely a statistical category that social researchers called *specjaliści z wyższym wykształceniem*, or "specialists with higher education". But to transform the intelligentsia so meant to rob it of its teleological, and moral, power. Segments of the Polish intelligentsia resisted this. At the end of the 1970s, Polish intellectuals, especially around KOR, sought to reestablish the intelligentsia as the "moral government" of the nation (Hirszowicz, 1980). In part, this was to be achieved with words. To pursue only professional matters and fail to recognize political responsibilities in one's work might define one as merely an *inteligent*, and not an *intelektualista*. Although both terms are translated into English as intellectual, the former implies mere membership in the highly educated stratum of the intelligentsia, while the latter was reserved for creative and, by necessity in Poland, politically responsible individuals (see Barańczak, 1986–87). The debate in the pages of *Aneks* over Walicki's (1984) discussion of Solidarity, the intelligentsia and the authorities reinforces this moral understanding of the *intelektualista*. The principal focus is one of the intelligentsia's strategic options and moral responsibilities, not of how the intelligentsia is itself formed by systems or social struggles.

This turn of phrase and its associated debates represent the significance of the transformation of Poland's highly educated stratum. As Gella (1971) defined the old Polish intelligentsia to be culturally homogeneous and united by charismatic feelings and values, the new intelligentsia became heterogeneous and not well distinguished from the laboring classes from which many came. This new intelligentsia was integrated into the state, even if not perfectly, as Bahro's discussion of *reservatio mentalis* (see chapter 4) suggests. As the intelligentsia surrendered its teleological function to work for the authorities' bureaucracy, it also surrendered its old moral identity. To distinguish between the highly educated and those who were the true inheritors of Poland's intelligentsia legacy became, therefore, a matter of considerable political consequence for intellectuals. But was it so important for Poland as a whole? Is this invocation to speak the truth in the face of power, as Foucault (1977 [1984]) would have it, so important for the reproduction and transformation of Soviet-type society?

To use the term intelligentsia necessarily obliges one to consider such questions. For example, was KOR or the working class ultimately responsible for Solidarity's formation (as Laba, forthcoming, debates)? I do not propose to resolve such questions of the intellectuals' potency in general or in Solidarity. For the latter, one should investigate the role of "experts" in Solidarity, and the role of the highly educated in Solidarity's leadership. This is another set of questions. I am more interested here in the "rank-and-file intelligentsia." And to be assured that I am not accused of betraying the historical legacy and moral role linked to the idea of the intelligentsia, I choose to call the highly educated of my study "professionals." In the choice of this label, I do not by any means wish to argue that the "intelligentsia" is irrelevant to understanding the rank and file of this group. Indeed, many of the highly educated have an affinity with this historical intelligentsia. And this leads more Polish professionals to assume a political role in social struggles than professionals in systems without a comparable historical legacy. It also leads professionals to regret their own diminished status more. Professionals are well aware of the considerably higher status of the intelligentsia in Poland before communism. This memory also lays the foundation for the professional to regain the status group identity associated with the intelligentsia. Thus, the rank and file are likely to be influenced by the debate over the meaning of the intelligentsia and that identity can be important in the structuring of power relations. But I am less interested in clarifying this controversy over the meaning of this group in contemporary Poland, given other efforts in this area (Babiuch, 1988). I am more interested in establishing the relationship of professionals to different kinds of power resources. But "professionals" is not itself an uncontroversial term.

The sociological literature also is replete with questions of who is and who is not a professional. This debate too reflects questions of power and morality. Talcott Parsons (1939) argued the professional was distinguished by the application of highly generalized esoteric knowledge. But part of his definition was that professionals controlled themselves, and put their clients' or the public interest ahead of their own self-interest. This latter understanding of professionalism is extremely useful, of course, in enhancing a group's self-interest. As such, many groups in capitalist society are led to acquire a "professional" standing for their occupation, so that they can police their own affairs and define their clients' needs (see Wilensky, 1964). This affirmative understanding of professions led many critical and conflict theorists to challenge the use of the very term "profession" (Klegon, 1978; Roth, 1974). Larson (1977), for instance, redefined the professional project from being an altruistic endeavor to an occupational strategy of collective upward mobility. To apply the term "professional" to social groups in Soviet-type society reflects many problems, therefore. One of the most prominent problems, of course, is that these groups typically do not have the self-regulatory functions associated with an occupation's professional status. Nevertheless, many of the struggles by Polish engineers and physicians in 1980–81 could be seen as an attempt to establish the professional project in the Soviet-type system (Kennedy and Sadkowski, 1990). Also, Polish intellectuals in the post-martial law period have found their "old world" status as those who define change replaced by a more professional consulting status, as workers and political authorities define the directions of change and employ professionals as advisors (Curry, 1989).

Physicians, engineers, lawyers, economists, teachers and journalists in Soviet-type systems can be classified as professionals for several reasons, therefore. First, these occupations have the same knowledge bases as those groups defined as professional in the West. Second, they do not reproduce the teleological functions of the intelligentsia in that system of knowledge. Finally, as the political authorities and working class come to define the parameters of change, the actual role of these professionals is increasingly that of consultant rather than of intelligentsia. I use the term professional therefore to refer to occupations whose base is organized around a systematized esoteric body of knowledge that is transmitted through institutions of higher education, and whose practice is to offer advice to others on that basis. By and large, this common information base and increasingly common role enables us to speak of physicians, engineers and other professions as being of the same type across political–economic systems, even if their organizational capacities and consequent power resources are quite different.

The power resources of professionals in Soviet-type society are much more limited than in most capitalist societies (Duran-Arenas and Kennedy, forthcoming). Although employment has been guaranteed in Soviet-type systems, one's choice of employment and adequate wages are not (Burawoy, 1985: 171). Highly qualified workers are frequently employed in jobs that do not correspond to their professional qualifications (Bahro, 1978: 176; Fehér, Heller and Markus, 1983: 73). Access to professional work depends, therefore, on political and not just professional qualifications. Thus, while full employment provides the less-qualified worker with some measure of personal discretion in behavior, given that less-skilled employment can be found elsewhere, the professional must be more cautious if a career is to be advanced. As Maria Hirszowicz (1980: 192) notes, "Political conformism has to be accepted as the price paid by professionals if they want to carry out their proper functions effectively." Professional work enables some measure of intrinsic fulfillment and can translate into a relatively privileged lifestyle under certain conditions. In part, that depends on how successfully professional prestige operates as a power resource in the system. Prestige is a power resource generally available to professionals across systems. It is on this foundation that other measures of professional power are established. As such, an analysis of the prestige of Polish professionals is an important place to begin understanding their place in the power relations of Soviet-type society.

Professional prestige

Professionals in all industrial societies enjoy high prestige (Treiman, 1977), but the prestige of Polish professionals is especially significant among Soviet-type societies because there is more variation in occupational prestige in Poland than elsewhere in the Soviet bloc, especially in comparison to the Soviet Union and Czechoslovakia (Connor, 1979: 92). Professional prestige is the principal power resource upon which Polish professionals depend in obtaining delegated privilege from the authorities. Prestige becomes all the more important as professionals increasingly approximate the ideal type of status group. But prestige is a particularly weak power resource, since it has little force behind it.

The distribution of prestige in Polish society is not very different from that found in other industrial societies. Except for the absence of large capitalists and the presence of "apparatchiks," the most significant difference between Poland's occupational prestige hierarchy and prestige hierarchies in capitalist societies is the higher position of Polish skilled workers (Wesołowski, 1978: 107–40). As in other industrial societies the Polish professional/managerial stratum tends to cluster at the upper end of the prestige scale (see table 7.1). Physicians are particularly prestigious, although engineers, journalists, lawyers and teachers are also among the most esteemed occupations. Polish public opinion on the broad outlines of occupational prestige has been consistent over time too (Pohoski, Słomczyński and Wesołowski,

Table 7.1. *Prestige hierarchy of occupations in Poland, 1975*

1. University professor
2. Doctor
3. Minister of the national government
4. Teacher
5. Chief manager in a factory
6. Engineer
7. Miner
8. Journalist
9. Priest
10. Agronomist
11. Army officer
12. Lawyer
13. Nurse
14. Supervisor on state farm
15. Office supervisor
16. Factory foreman
17. Accountant
18. Lathe turner
19. Electrical technician
20. Small farmer
21. Private locksmith
22. Private tailor
23. Truck driver
24. Shopkeeper
25. Sales clerk
26. Office clerk
27. Typist
28. Unskilled construction worker
29. Unskilled farm laborer on state farm
30. Cleaning woman

Source: adapted from Pohoski, Słomczyński and Wesołowski (1975: 75).

1975). The self evaluation of professionals' prestige for the most part reflects the population's evaluation, although physicians rank themselves lower than the general population ranks them (Łabanowska, 1978).

Prestige has been considered both as a reward for power and an additional dimension in a multidimensional hierarchy of inequality. The rationale for the latter conceptualization is the recognition that power in society can come from the possession of different resources: from control over the market, political power in the state or from the esteem of others (Weber, 1978: 926–40). The distribution of social honor, the status order, is affected by the economic order and political order, but not necessarily determined by them. For instance, in the feudal order, status honor, rather than military proficiency *per se*, was often the basis for the distribution of fiefdoms (Weber, 1978: 1081). Prestige can act as a resource for augmenting power or accumulating privilege on two levels: in interpersonal relations; and on the scale of collectivities. On both levels, voluntary homage (Simmel, 1908, [1971]: 100) or voluntary submission to the will of others enhances the power of those exerting it (Blau, 1964: 321). Though esteem is usually augmenting other power resources, power can also be based almost exclusively on esteem.

Prestige or status can be a more or less autonomous resource for facilitating access to powerful positions. Membership in a prestigious social group is sometimes a necessary, though not sufficient, condition for attaining a powerful position. Membership in the pre-revolutionary Russian aristocracy, for instance, facilitated access to powerful positions in the state. Educational titles in the modern world also play such a role. While the training received in formal education may not be necessary to job performance, it often serves as a screening device for gaining access to powerful occupations (Collins, 1979).

In inter-personal relations, prestige is based on many factors other than place in an occupational prestige hierarchy, although among macrosocial properties, occupational role is among the most significant entitlements to deference by others (Shils, 1968: 107). At this level, prestige, deference or esteem can be consumed as a reward in itself or used as a basis for exchange, as a kind of power resource (Eisenstadt, 1968: 65). Blau (1964: 127), for instance, sees prestige accumulated when the esteemed provide some kind of instrumental assistance to those of lower status, who in turn provide respect and compliance to their superiors. In this sense, esteem is given as a *reward* for something exchanged; possession of esteem is not used as a power *resource*. But prestige can be, at least theoretically, a relatively autonomous power resource in interpersonal relations. Blau (1964: 132–40) considers "superior status" as something akin to capital, which can be drawn upon to obtain advantages and is expended in use. A prestigious person can request something of a subordinate, but in so doing, some of the obligation the subordinate feels to the superior can be discharged in the performance of a task (p. 133). Of course, the degree and security of prestige affects the likelihood of its being used up. If the prestige is securely anchored in some other power resource, there is little danger of dissipating it (p. 134). But if it is an isolated resource, it is easily expended in use, unless the politically or economically powerful themselves lack esteem and seek to accumulate it by associating with those who may have prestige and little else (Eisenstadt, 1968: 71). Prestige is thus not only a reward for activities, but also a *potential* power resource itself. It can act as that resource at different levels, in interpersonal relations and relations between groups. Charismatic authority is the strongest example of prestige's power in domination (Shils, 1968).

Culture, prestige and power

Poland has different power hierarchies corresponding to the different resources available. Certainly, there is pure economic or market power, held by those successful in taking advantage of the space for private initiative. Political power is based on position in the official hierarchy. Prestige is not perfectly derived from either category, although, of course, one form of power can be at least partially translated into others. Some directions are easier. The successful private entrepreneur has had very little chance of achieving significant political power.[1] The prestigious doctor is not as likely as the less prestigious engineer to attain significant political power, given occupational recruitment patterns in the party. The highly placed political activist has the potentially greatest universalizable power, in that political strength can be converted into economic power and privilege. This was especially true in the mid-1970s (Smolar, 1983), but the economically successful do not automatically earn prestige, since material success is often viewed suspiciously. The assumption has frequently been made that it was accomplished illegally (Reszke, 1984: 21–22). Of course, too, when political power is held with such low legitimacy as it is held in Poland (Lewis, 1982), high political power translates into prestige very poorly. According to Irena Reszke (1984:

Table 7.2. *Criteria of occupational prestige (in %*) (N = 823)*

Criteria	Esteem of respondent	Esteem in society
Social value of the occupation	58.7	60.6
Usefulness, service to people	34.1	41.5
Importance of occupation, indispensability	26.3	22.3
Creative, progressive occupation	0.7	3.0
Measurable effects	2.5	0.9
Social power of the occupation	1.8	5.7
Qualifications	24.7	20.7
Education, difficult studies	11.5	11.7
Professional know-how	8.7	4.9
Personal qualifications	7.2	4.8
Talents	4.4	4.6
Expenditures	47.9	20.3
Strenuousness of work	33.1	11.1
Responsibility, risk	15.9	7.4
Generosity, sacrifice	12.9	6.0
Unappreciated work	7.4	0.5
Rewards	4.9	21.9
Material benefits	2.5	12.4
Non-material benefits	1.9	4.8
Work attractiveness	0.2	3.9
High occupational position	0.2	1.9
Popularity, fame	–	1.8
Traditional respect for occupation, esteem and occupational authority	0.7	1.6
Authority/power	0.2	0.7
Personal and other criteria	7.4	1.8

* Percentages exceed 100 percent because respondents could cite more than one category.
Source: adapted from Reszke (1984: 79).

79–80), the most important criteria of an occupation's prestige in the eyes of Polish survey respondents are the social value of the occupation, its expenditures and its qualifications. The prestige accorded that occupation in the society, according to these respondents, is similar, although rewards become more influential and expenditures less so (table 7.2).

The criteria which influence an individual's ascription of prestige to an occupation do not include economic rewards or political power to a very great degree. This is exceptional in the general portrait of the relation between power and prestige (Treiman, 1977). The effective cause for this disjuncture is cultural, although the condition for it is systemic.

Professional success in Soviet-type society requires some measure of vassalage. Even in Poland, where Marxist–Leninist ideology is the most bankrupt, loyalty to the authorities has been crucial for professional success. Loyalty, in and of itself, is not problematic for professionals. It only becomes problematic when there is a contradiction between it and cultural values. In Eastern Central Europe, there is just such a contradiction between national culture and *"partinost'"* (chapter 5). To the degree that professionals identify with this national culture, it is likely that vassalage and professional competence will be defined as antagonistic principles. There are two basic consequences for power relations. Those who are professionally successful can be identified as having allowed "loyalty" to define their career trajectory more than professional competence. This allows a discourse to emerge which separates professional competence from the "normal" indicators of professional success. Thus, Poles have discussed their system of promotion as one based on "negative selection" (A. Tymowski, 1982). This "negative selection" can be used by professionals to define the incompetent and non-professional character of the authorities and thus introduce a rupture between "them" and professionalism. Alternatively, professionals can use this divergence of competence and loyalty as a resource with which they can influence the party. In exchange for greater influence and prestige in the system, "competent" and prestigious professionals might exchange their cooperation. Prestige, to the degree that it is relatively independent of political or economic power, can then operate as an independent power resource.

While prestige seems to be relatively autonomous from political or economic power in Poland, this does not necessarily mean that prestige plays an autonomous role in power relations or in shaping the distribution of privilege in Polish society. Various macrosocial conditions influence the likelihood of prestige acting as an independent power resource. Patriarchy is one of the most powerful of these conditions even while it is one of the most invisible to Poles.

Gender, professionals and power

One common indicator of institutional sexism is uneven labor-force participation by gender. But the gender differences in

Polish labor-force participation are not exceptionally uneven, even among the highly educated. In 1980, approximately 44.5 percent of the state-sector labor force were women, and 44.6 percent of those with higher education were women (Rocznik Statystyczny, 1982: 60). Women are, however, unevenly concentrated. Engineering, for instance, is an overwhelmingly male occupation. Only 19.9 percent of engineers in technical occupations are women. Among physicians, however, women are a majority with 51.6 percent. They are even more prominent among dentists: here, 82.3 percent are female (Rocznik Statystyczny, 1982: 121). But, as in the West, the feminization of an occupation is associated with declines in material privilege. Unlike the West, argues Irena Reszke (1984), feminization does not seem to diminish directly an occupation's prestige. Poorer wages pull the prestige of an occupation down, but the gender associated with that occupation seems to have no effect. That suggests that women might be able to use prestige less effectively as a resource than men in pressuring the authorities to redistribute privilege. This is probably rooted in the sexism of the Polish cultural system.

According to a survey of 566 Warsaw inhabitants in May–June 1980, the social standing of both women and men is most often evaluated in terms of gender-neutral qualities like education, financial conditions, occupation and honesty. But women are also evaluated in terms that men are not, as in their marital status, the social standing of their spouse and their appearance (Reszke, 1984:90–98). Evaluations of esteem based on inter-personal relations tend to avoid these questions of social standing, but women are again evaluated differently than men. Here their homemaker abilities are added to the gender-biased list, while men are more frequently understood in terms of their professional skills, wage earning abilities and courage (Reszke, 1984: 64–71). Some occupations are also considered unsuitable for women, especially those which require physical strength or are dangerous. When women are employed in those "unsuitable occupations," they also are likely to be less esteemed than men would be (Reszke, 1984: 121).

Polish women, if they are married, are therefore more likely to depend on the professional prestige of their husband in the macrosocial allocation of privilege. In the use of prestige as power in interpersonal relations, women are more likely to have to rely on their appearance or traits associated with their gender, while men rely more on power associated with their job. It is common to speak of professionals in a gender-neutral fashion. But given the very unequal conditions of their work, and the very different understandings the Polish population has of the capacities and proclivities of women and men in work and family relations, the gender of a professional, and of a profession, has much to do with the conditions of professional power. If professionals can approximate the status of the historic intelligentsia, for instance, it is likely that their own professional power and privilege can be augmented. But because the public realm is generally understood more as a male than female arena, the status group will likely be constructed by men. For example, the leadership of the Solidarity movement in 1980–81, even in the feminized occupational sector, was overwhelmingly male. Sexism is not something that Poles will identify about their culture, as a gender-based division of labor is quite "natural" for them. Less than 20 percent of Reszke's (1984: 113) Warsaw sample found all occupations suitable for women. Patriarchy is thus one of the most powerful structures shaping Polish life and professional power. Status-group formation is another.

Male professionals as a status group

Weber (1978: 306) defines a status group as "a plurality of persons who, within a larger group, successfully claim (a) a special social esteem, and possibly also (b) status monopolies" and argues that they come into being "(a) in the first instance by virtue of their own style of life, particularly the type of vocation: 'self styled' or occupational status groups, (b) in the second instance, through hereditary charisma, by virtue of special claims to higher ranking descent: hereditary status groups, or (c) through monopolistic appropriation or hierocratic powers: political or hierocratic status groups." The traditionally dominant *status* group in Polish and other Eastern European societies in the nineteenth and early twentieth centuries was the intelligentsia. But, given the changes in their status produced by communist modernization, the late twentieth-century Eastern European intelligentsia has little in common with the status group of decades past. Their economic situation, narrowly construed, is not as favorable as the inter-war intelligentsia's (Wesołowski, 1966b). The professions are also far more heterogeneous in lifestyle. The inter-war intelligentsia had behavior patterns based on the traditions of Polish nobility (*szlachta*) that set them apart from the masses. They had their own salons in smaller towns for informal association. They also were strongly self-conscious. They secured a strong position in society by their common recognition of one another as an essential part of the

Polish nation, its moral government, so to speak (Chałasiński, 1946). Their ethos to a large extent dominated inter-war Poland. It is fair to say that they were the dominant status group, and that they had very high prestige.

Communist modernization directly attacked this old-world intelligentsia. It aimed to elevate labor and the laboring classes in popular culture and attack the aristocratic ethos represented by the intelligentsia. Changes in prestige hierarchies suggest that this attempt was partially successful. Occupations that are part of the contemporary intelligentsia (those usually filled by people with higher educations), that are traditionally part of the petty bourgeoisie, or that are part of state military or security, tend to have declined in relative prestige, while occupations of the working or peasant classes have risen in relative prestige. Thus, in comparison to the inter-war period, the intelligentsia seems to have suffered a loss of prestige (table 7.3).[2]

Before World War II, the intelligentsia also tended to reproduce itself. After World War II, the party undertook a concerted effort to create a "socialist intelligentsia," that would not be antagonistic to the development of Polish socialism, as the pre-war intelligentsia seemed to be. Children from worker and peasant backgrounds were encouraged to enter higher education, and learn occupations that would place them in the intelligentsia. Initially, then, Poland had a genuinely new intelligentsia, produced from the ranks of the laboring classes. The portrait of inter-generational mobility is changing, however, as the intelligentsia reproduces itself more and more. One investigation of social mobility shows that, between 1972 and 1982, the proportion increased of those upper non-manual job holders whose fathers held the same kind of occupation. In 1972 only 18.6 percent of those people who held an upper non-manual job had fathers from the same socio-economic group, but by 1982 28.6 percent of professionals and semi-professionals had fathers who were also professionals or semi-professionals (Pohoski, 1984). Thus, although it is true that contemporary professionals have relatively heterogeneous backgrounds, they are being recruited from their own strata more and more. In comparison to the pre World War II intelligentsia, of course, contemporary Polish professionals are not nearly so homogeneous in social origin. But apparently, with declining rates of social mobility, they are becoming more homogeneous. They *could* thus develop more of the characteristics of a status group. While contemporary professionals have relatively lower prestige than their inter-war counterparts, they still have more prestige than other occupational groups, which could

Table 7.3. *Pre-war and contemporary esteem rankings of occupations by Warsaw inhabitants aged sixty and over (average score on a scale of 1 to 5, with 1 being very high esteem, 5 being very low, N = 70)*

Occupation	1938	1974	1938–74
University professor	1.10	1.31	−0.21
Physician	1.46	1.96	−0.50
Cabinet minister	1.54	1.86	−0.32
Architect	1.75	1.86	−0.11
Electrical engineer	1.83	1.98	−0.15
Army officer	1.85	2.73	−0.88
Director of manufacturing plant	1.96	1.98	−0.02
Catholic priest	1.98	2.94	−0.96
Grade-school teacher	2.46	2.65	−0.19
Journalist	2.31	2.25	0.06
Clerk in state administration	2.53	3.10	−0.57
Factory foreman	2.61	2.33	0.28
Technician in construction	2.77	2.55	0.22
Coal miner	2.78	1.73	1.05
Nurse	2.78	2.60	0.18
Printer	2.87	2.50	0.37
Craftsman (owner)	2.92	3.22	−0.30
Factory locksmith	2.96	2.60	−0.36
Policeman	3.22	3.52	−0.30
Farm owner	3.45	2.80	0.65
Home worker	3.95	3.52	0.43
Farm-worker	4.14	3.22	0.92
Unskilled worker in construction	4.38	3.74	0.64
Domestic servant, maid	4.40	3.42	0.98

serve as one resource for the construction of a status group. Other constituent features of a status group, although less prominent than in the inter-war period, also exist.

Contemporary professionals exhibit different patterns of consumption from the working classes and peasantry. Those with higher education spend more of their income on cultural goods and transportation, and less on alcohol than strata with less formal education (Sikorska, 1979: 112). Friendship networks also show a coherence of occupationally based status groups. Approximately 91 percent of professionals and semi-professionals have as their best friend someone also of white-collar status (Jaakkola and Markarczyk, 1980: 342). Members of the intelligentsia in Łódź surveyed in 1973 reported that approximately 82.9 percent of their three closest friends were also highly educated (Wojtysiak, 1980: 143). If the respondents came from social backgrounds other than the intelligentsia, they were much more likely to report that their closest friends came from working or peasant classes (Wojtysiak, 1980: 145). Thus, as rates of social mobility decline, it is reasonable to believe that friendship networks or personal relations will become more homogeneous.

A common set of values is probably one of the weakest status-group features among professionals. S. Nowak (1981) has shown that the distribution of values in Polish society is remarkably homogeneous, meaning that a professional is as likely to have the same view as a worker on social affairs as he is to have the same view as another professional. Still, on some issues, professionals are different. Professionals tend to have the least egalitarian economic views. When a national sample was asked whether they favor equal incomes, only 49 percent of professionals indicated their support, in contrast to 78 percent of farmers, and 77 percent of mixed manual and white-collar workers; in regard to full employment, only 68.5 percent of professionals were in favor, while 91 percent of unskilled workers indicated their support for the position. Professionals are also much more likely to be in favor of the decentralization of power. Increased control over society by the authorities is most often accepted by unskilled workers and farmers (59 percent) and least often by professionals (35 percent) (Kolarska and Rychard, 1982b: 217).

The difference between professionals and other groups in society is probably less important for defining their quality as a status group than the difference between their values and the official ideology of the system. The contradiction between official ideology and national culture is most extreme in Eastern Central Europe. This national culture is reproduced in various ways and different places, from informal social relations to Church practices. But it is also reproduced by the humanistic intelligentsia in their literature, art and history. To the extent that the non-humanistic intelligentsia are consumers of this culture, they are likely to belong to a status group which is distinct from the authorities, if not so distinct from the rest of society. Given that professionals in Poland do identify with the nineteenth-century intelligentsia and its claim to be the "moral government of the nation," they share values which are different from the authorities which delegate power. Given this, professionals have an even stronger basis for using their prestige as a power resource in either strengthening the cultural power of those who are opposed to the authorities or exchanging that prestige to the authorities for greater delegated power and privilege. Polish professionals have pursued both strategies.

Given these patterns of prestige, mobility, consumption, friendships and values, it is reasonable to believe that professionals are a status group in Polish society, although, of course, a much more poorly defined status group than the intelligentsia in pre-communist Poland. They are also better distinguished from the authorities than they are from the rest of society in their status.

Prestige and status as power

Although professionals exhibit characteristics of a status group, this does not necessarily mean that status influences power relations and the distribution of privilege in Polish society. Weber (1978: 938) argued that status groups were important when "the acquisition and distribution of goods are relatively stable." When economic and technological transformation is rapid, the role of status groups becomes less important. The market also respects no prestige, no honor (Weber, 1978: 936). A market-dominated society diminishes the importance of status groups in the struggle for power and privilege. In *The Philosophy of Money* (1978), Simmel also attributed great significance to the role of money in universalizing transactions and making other bases for exchange obsolete. Of course, Weber and Simmel had traditional societies in mind when they wrote of the impact of economic growth and market-based universalization on status groups. But, in some ways, Soviet-type society reflects some of these same conditions. Not only is Poland not experiencing rapid economic growth, but between 1979 and 1982 there was a *negative* rate of growth. Furthermore, while there have been reforms offered to strengthen the role of the market in major economic transactions, reform has been unsuccessful through the end of the 1980s. The Polish economy has remained in essence a shortage-ridden command economy. And, as Weber and Simmel observed for traditional societies, these conditions also enhance the autonomous importance of prestige in power relations and in the distribution of privilege.

In Polish society, as in other Soviet-type societies, goods are not distributed according to market relations. Goods are distributed according to a plan, and redistributed through personal networks in the "generalized market." Money plays only a supporting role in this distribution. Official prices are set by administrative fiat, and price setting is only partially influenced by any market or even cost

Table 7.4. *Income, housing conditions and socio-occupational groups in 1972 and 1982*

Socio-occupational group	Income*		Housing**	
	1972	1982	1972	1982
Technical and non-technical specialists and managers	4.4	12.0	1.3	1.5
Technicians and administrative– bureaucratic specialists	3.6	11.6	1.4	1.6
Other non-manual workers	2.9	10.0	1.6	1.7
Physical–mental workers	2.6	11.2	1.9	2.1
Owners of productive and service establishments	4.1	19.6	1.7	1.6
Foremen and skilled workers	3.5	11.4	1.8	2.1
Semi-skilled and unskilled workers	2.6	9.4	2.1	3.2
Individual farmers	–	–	1.9	2.5
Agricultural employees	2.8	10.9	2.2	3.0

* Average monthly income from main work in thousands of złotys.
** Average number of persons per room.
Source: adapted from Pohoski (1984).

considerations. Income poorly predicts actual consumption levels, since so many goods are provided through collective consumption or administrative connections. Nevertheless, professionals are advantaged in consumption, especially housing (table 7.4). As with Szelényi's (1978) findings in Hungary, professionals (the first category) enjoyed the highest wages in 1972 and best living conditions in both 1972 and 1982. In 1982, however, owners of private establishments had the highest incomes, which is probably attributable to the economic crisis. In any case, professionals do seem more favourably situated than other groups within the state sector, although the difference between groups is not very great.

These data also suggest interesting differences over time. In 1972, the ratio of professionals' income to skilled workers' income was 1.3 and to unskilled workers' income 1.7. In 1982, those ratios were 1.05 and 1.27 respectively. I do not believe these differences reflect a natural trend of increasing Polish equality, but are more a reflection of changes in the way in which the party elite allocates privilege. As the economy becomes more crisis-ridden and workers more militant, the party is forced to use its resources to buy off challenges to its rule. In order to assure, or at least better protect, organizational hegemony, the party has to respond to the demands of workers for higher wages and better consumption. Professionals are less of a threat, and thus their wages can be raised at lower rates, while workers' wages are raised at greater rates. But why would a party, supposedly of the working class, favor professionals in the first place? Szelényi's theory of class alliance based on rational redistribution is one possibility, but another explanation can be based on this discussion of prestige.

Daniel Bell (1973) argues that theoretical knowledge has become the axial principle of post-industrial society. Randall Collins (1979) finds the same importance attributed to higher education, but because the credential system has just become a kind of status ranking. Whatever the rationale for their prominence, professionals are a prestigious ingredient to an industrial society. Gierek's Poland was a case of professional prominence *par excellence*.

Gierek and his lieutenants in the 1970s were fascinated by the professional image. That fascination was reflected in both their politics and in their personal behavior. In politics, Gierek attempted to create the impression that politics was being based on "rational foundations," by giving a prominent place to professionals and experts in the formulation of policy (Sokołowska, 1974: 443). The "professionalization" of governance is reflected in the behavior of the authorities themselves, too. Maria Hirszowicz (1980: 192) wrote, "Professional titles, ranks, symbols of occupational status and scientific degrees are among the most coveted and valued social commodities; even ministers and high military and police commanders try to raise their prestige by studying for a respectable degree." Reflecting the fashion, regime members went so far as to award themselves professional titles in spite of questionable credentials ("Jak Edward Gierek Został Inżynierem?" *Wiadomość Dnia* 1981). The alliance between engineers and the Gierek regime was symbolized in the appointment of Jan Kaczmarek as the minister of higher education and the general secretary of the Polish Academy of Sciences. Kaczmarek is one of Poland's leading technocratic experts, and is the elected president of the Supreme Technical Organization (*Naczelna Organizacja Techniczna*, or NOT).

In People's Poland, neither political nor economic power translate into prestige very well. By "professionalizing" themselves, the Gierek regime sought to enhance its own prestige and, in addition, enhance the legitimacy of its domination. In exchange for mingling with the authorities and acknowledging their professionalism, professionals and especially engineers were compensated with privilege, as in better apartments, trips to the West and so on. But when organizational hegemony was threatened, as it was in the late 1970s and 1980s, the party was forced to return to more egalitarian policies favored by the more autonomously powerful workers. The elite's quest for prestige had to be put off until organizational hegemony could be restored.

Conclusions

Professionals are the most prestigious socio-occupational group in Soviet-type society. Of course, various professionals have different amounts of prestige and even different specializations within a single profession are differently endowed. In Poland, professional prestige does not flow from economic or political power and does not depend on the gender of its occupant. It rather depends on the social value, qualifications and expenditures involved in the occupation. In theory, prestige can act as a power resource, supplementary to or autonomous from other power resources. But prestige is not like other kinds of power resources such as economic or political power, since, divorced from other kinds of resources, it cannot force people to do things against their wishes. It can, however, serve as a resource for accumulating privileges in certain times and places. Professional prestige is a more effective power resource when held by men. Although women are nearly as likely to be professional as men, women are clustered in professions that are paid more poorly. Their occupational success is also less important for establishing personal esteem and social status than men's professional accomplishments. Women are still more likely to be evaluated in terms of their appearance, their spouse, and their abilities as a homemaker. Professional prestige as power is more likely to be used by men than women.

The Communist Party can be influenced by this prestige and sometimes allocates goods and services to prestigious individuals or institutions, as to professionals at the beginning of the 1970s in Poland. It seems reasonable to say that as Soviet-type societies become more highly developed economically, and especially in periods of economic growth and social stability, a preferential allocation of privilege for the professional is likely, because party leaders increasingly tend to identify themselves as technocratic leaders. They are especially driven to this identification in Poland because the prestige associated with political leadership is so low. By associating themselves with professionals, they accumulate some prestige. But when a challenge from the working class emerges, especially in conjunction with economic crisis, more egalitarian policies are implemented under the pressures of ideology and the autonomous power of the working class. The importance of prestige in direct party allocations of privilege thus declines.

In inter-personal relations, prestige can also influence the distribution of privilege, but it is even more limited at this level. If that prestige is associated with control over some scarce good or service, such as those which physicians can control, privilege acquired on the basis of status or prestige can continue. But as Blau suggests, status is like capital and is exhausted in its use if not replenished. If prestige is not associated with another power resource, it will not serve as a lasting power resource, and only be of occasional use in inter-personal relations. The professional's membership in a status group, the intelligentsia, is of more lasting value. It gives him more frequent access to people who are in privilege-endowing positions. Since friendships or family ties likely diminish the stock of favors to which someone is entitled less rapidly than relations based solely on status-based deference, membership in the intelligentsia may be one of the most valuable independent power resources a Polish professional has.

While professional privilege generated through autonomous resources on the generalized market may not be endangered by economic and social crisis, professional privilege delegated on the basis of prestige is likely to dry up in these times. When that delegated privilege disappears, there is less reason for professionals to remain allied with the authorities, especially when there are cultural pressures that move them against the regime. As we shall see in the next two chapters, this decline in the significance of delegated power and the rise of autonomous power resources is the structural foundation for the alliance between professionals and workers in Solidarity. At the same time, the cultural contradiction between competence and *partinost'* facilitates the shift in allegiances.

8   Engineers in Solidarity

In Soviet-type societies, engineers and other professionals constitute a pivotal class for social reproduction and transformation. They are between the elite, which allocates economic surplus, and the working class, which creates the surplus but has little say in how it is allocated. Although some consider professionals to be potentially a class for itself, the limited autonomous power resources professionals have at their disposal make it more likely that they will have to serve somebody in Soviet-type society. If professionals can acquire and use in their interests the political and bureaucratic power of the authorities, then they could become a class for itself. So long as *political* criteria overwhelm professional-class criteria in the distribution of power and privilege, however, professionals remain "dependent" on political authorities. It is difficult, therefore, to imagine professionals *en masse* acting in opposition to the authorities of Soviet-type society. But this limited imagination depends on a failure to identify the sources of dependence.

The attribute of Soviet-type society which makes professionals dependent on political authorities is organizational hegemony. The greater the limitation in this hegemony, the greater the opportunity for professionals to choose other alliances. The relative independence of the Catholic Church in pre-Solidarity Poland, for instance, gave some journalists alternative outlets for their work. But the Church's independence does not help to reshape the range of alliances for all professionals, especially for engineers. Opportunities for alternative engineer alliances arrive under two conditions. First, the restoration of private enterprise affords some engineers new possibilities. The computer revolution in technology has made specially trained engineers part of the emergent class of entrepreneurs reshaping the class structure of Soviet-type societies. But even here private enterprise remains dependent on political tolerance, and therefore explicit oppo-

259

sition by those who profit from this arrangement is unlikely. Professionals remain indirectly dependent on the authorities, even with the emergence of a new, private sector.

The more fundamental challenge to organizational hegemony comes with the self-organization of the working class. The second possibility for alternative alliances rests in worker self-organization. This working-class self-organization need not move professionals to their side, however. There are, after all, potentially contradictory class interests between professionals and workers, as well as social antagonisms which lie on top of these opposed interests. It is an important sociological problem to establish the conditions under which professionals will ally with a self-organized working class. In this chapter, I propose to delimit the conditions which facilitated Polish engineers' participation in the 1980–81 Solidarity movement.

This account will be primarily "structural," meaning that I try to establish an explanation for the considerable participation of engineers in Solidarity with reference to the conditions of their work and consumption at the end of the 1970s and the ideological structure of their alliance in 1981. I do not rely heavily on the engineers' own self-understandings of why they do what they do, although, of course, this cannot be avoided completely. But it is my intention to demonstrate that important insights into the conditions of cross-class alliance can be generated by an examination of the set of macrostructural power relations in which that alliance is formed.

Engineers' alliances

Konrád and Szelényi (1979) find grounds for an alliance between political elite and professionals in their common support for a knowledge-based legitimation of control over the distribution of surplus. Professionals have little use for a legitimation of control grounded in a notion that those who create wealth should also decide its allocation. The preferential living standard professionals enjoy is the final cement which secures an alliance of professional strata to the political elite (Szelényi, 1978, 1982). Connor (1980) and Kostecki and Mreła (1984) also observe a disjunction between professionals and workers, except their interpretations emphasize the strategic value for the party in keeping professionals and workers apart, or society "divided and pulverized." All of these perspectives agree that for the political elite to be dislodged from its contemporary dominant position, an alliance of professionals and workers is necessary.

Although these scholars emphasize the importance of the professional–worker alliance, earlier theorists emphasized the conflict between political elites and professionals in the technocratic threat engineers ("experts") pose to political domination ("reds"). Engineers bear a technocratic rationality that challenges the bureaucratic domination exercised by political elites (Mallet, 1974; Parkin, 1971; Parry, 1966; White, 1974). These authors use a line of reasoning similar to that used by Thorstein Veblen (1965) and his followers. They are also guilty of the same wishful thinking.

Veblen thought that the technical training of engineers filled them with an appreciation for technical efficiency in production. Inspired by the examples of early twentieth-century engineer–reformers like Morris Cooke, Veblen thought it was possible that engineers could be driven to revolt against the captains of industry because the businessman's preoccupation with profit in organizing production precluded the organization of a more thoroughly rational system of production. Of course, the revolt of the engineers never occurred in capitalist societies. Veblen himself recognized that revolution was not in the offing in his day because engineers had become so "commercialized." He nevertheless thought revolution a possibility if engineers came to recognize just how irrational capitalist production was. Subsequent analysts of US engineering see similar tensions in the engineering profession. Layton (1971) finds, like Veblen, potential sources of conflict between the engineer as scientist and the engineer as businessman, but concludes that the coexistence of orientations is part and parcel of the profession in the modern world. Layton argues that large corporations or bureaucracies are the only worksites with sufficient scale that make an engineer's services profitable, and hence they provide the major sources of engineers' employment. Today, the high-technology microelectronics industry may afford engineers greater entrepreneurial opportunities, but Layton's point is well taken: engineers historically have been *salaried* professionals.

The predominance of engineers' salaried employment need not mean that engineers identify with management, however. David Noble (1977:40) observes that there were at least three theoretical possibilities for the relationship between engineers and corporations in the beginnings of America's corporate development: engineers could have emphasized the "business leadership function of engineering," which would facilitate the creation of engineers' business associations; they could have emphasized their status as employees, and developed a trade-union mentality; and finally, engineers could have focused on the professional character of their occupation, and formed strong professional associations. The fact that engineers *did* eventually identify with the first role was the result of the corporate engineers' triumph in the definition of the profession, both culturally and physically (Noble, 1977:243, 310). Research on contemporary engineers in America (Zussman, 1984) and in France and England (Whalley and Crawford, 1984) also find minimal engineering solidarity with labor and practical commitment to business or managerial interests. Engineers' identification with management is derived from their career structures, often culminating in management even when starting off at lower levels in the enterprise. Thus, in capitalist societies, engineers' solidarity with labor seems to be blunted by engineers' integration into management.

Discussions of the engineers' place in Soviet-type societies have followed the same logic as that of Veblen and his descendants. It was fashionable to talk of the technocratic challenge in Soviet-type society shortly before, during and immediately after the failed Prague Spring of 1968. After the ousting of the Novotny regime in Czechoslovakia by more liberal Dubček forces, technocratic reformers like Ota Šik were given the responsibility of reconstituting the economic structure of Czechoslovak society. The theories posited that if Soviet-type societies were to progress economically, policy-making was going to have to become the province of experts and not of the politically orthodox (White, 1974:41). Sten Tellenbeck (1978), for instance, sees the cooptation of technocratic strata into the ruling elite as a necessary move to both maintain the existing power structure and save the Polish economy from collapse. The struggle between technocrats and political hardliners also seems to explain the political rhythms of Hungarian developments since the New Economic Mechanism was initiated in 1968 (Rakovski, 1978). This dynamic of technocratic–bureaucratic conflict, and especially its resolution in the cooptation of the technocrats, led some theorists to speculate that a new dominant class of the intelligentsia, or at least the technical intelligentsia, is being created and is the likely future for the class relations of these societies (Giddens, 1973; Gouldner, 1979; Konrád and Szelényi, 1979; Tellenbeck, 1978).

Like the challenge posed to businessmen by engineers that Veblen described, political elites in Soviet-type societies appeared to face the same threat from their own engineers. And it appeared that they found the same solution. By the mid-1970s, in Hungary and Poland at least, it appeared that the technocratic challenge was weathered best by "professionalizing" the party and enterprise management. Through this, necessary economic reforms could take place and the cooptation of technocratic challengers could ensure the continued reproduction of party domination. The participation by engineers and other professionals in Solidarity suggests a fly in the theories' ointments. The analysts of the 1970s seem to have been overoptimistic about the party's professionalization and technocratic takeover. This was prompted by two issues: a focus on the wrong variables and a misinterpretation of the transformations in power relations.

Consistent with the emphases of modernization theory, analysts focused on changes in rhetoric and the educational background of political and economic elites rather than examining the professionals' position in overall power relations. Tellenbeck (1978:445), for instance, points to new phrases like "the right person for the right job" (*właściwy człowiek na właściwym miejscu*) as evidence of the predominance professional competence gained over ideological commitment. He also points to the supposed "professionalization of the party," indicated by the growth in non-manual workers and highly educated people in the party, which would in turn be accompanied by a change in its internal value system (1978:443).

These modernization accounts track important trends, but the emphasis given these changes is unjustified. They achieve importance only in the modernization framework. Industrialization mandates professionalization and thus modernization theorists search for evidence of its occurrence. The theory's uncritical assessment of power relations fails to take into account the autonomous power of the working class and the delegated character of power within the apparatus. Engineers and other professionals are left then with a role to play larger than their power resources allow. Without an alliance with workers, engineers and other professionals remain dependent on the political authorities whatever the prominence of professionals in the party. The conditions of alliance between professionals and workers in a single opposition organization is therefore of tremendous theoretical interest.

It is of substantial historical interest too. Until the mid-1970s, professionals and workers were not coordinated in their opposition. There have, of course, been instances of coterminous opposition, as in Poland in 1956, but these classes did not actively support one another. The seeds of new class alliances were sown in Poland in the mid-1970s (chapter 1). The "moral responsibility" of Poland's intellectuals to act in the national interest in fact became a "cultural phenomenon of some political significance" (Hirszowicz, 1980:193), and on this foundation intellectuals were encouraged to participate in oppositional (KOR) and reformist groups (*Doświadczenie i Przyszłość*). Although a cultural basis for moral opposition to the system was thus regenerated in the mid-1970s, powerful mechanisms continued to ensure the integration of citizens into the political and economic system. This is especially true for professionals. The dependency on authorities described in chapter 7 is especially appropriate to engineers.

Engineers[1] are the dominant professionals in Soviet-type societies. In Poland, they constitute over one-third of all highly educated workers (Spis Kadrowy, 1977:32). They have joined Poland's Communist Party in considerable numbers; engineers, technicians and technical supervisors constituted slightly over 10 percent of party candidates and members in 1970 and 1982. There were approximately twice as many engineers and technicians in the party than teachers or economists and accountants (Rocznik Statystyczny, 1983:28). Engineers also predominate among highly educated managers. Although their prevalence has decreased over time, one study found in 1974 that managers with higher educations were more than twice as likely to have technical education than any other form of higher education (Najduchowska, 1974). Among engineers with more than twenty years at work, over half hold management positions (J. Tymowski, 1984). Engineers' access to these management positions offers them opportunities for considerable privilege. If any professionals should be integrated into the status quo, engineers should be. If any group of professionals should resist the opposition, engineers should. Engineers apparently have more to lose than their political chains.

Growing professional membership in upper-level positions in the hierarchy does not necessarily pose a challenge to basic power relations within the society. Technocratic challenge can be absorbed into the extant power relations much like engineers can be coopted into capitalist relations of production by management opportunities. In Soviet-type society, professionals, as with less educated members of the hierarchy, are dependent on the ruling group for their preferential position. Their power and privilege remain delegated and as such engineers possess insufficient resources to challenge the reproduction of the status quo by themselves. This dependence can also assure the normal alliance of engineers with the ruling group in opposition to workers. Serious and sustained challenge depends on the self-organization of the working class, but even the emergence of an autonomously organized working class in Soviet-type society does not by itself suggest that professionals would ally with workers. In capitalism, engineers are most often allied with management, despite the existence of independent labor unions, because of engineers' managerial possibilities. The alliance of Polish engineers with workers in Solidarity was enabled by a special conjuncture which weakened the dependent relationship of engineers on the ruling group. I attempt to establish those conditions in the following sections. Before I do, I reestimate the extent of participation by engineers in the independent trade union, Solidarity.

Solidarity and engineers

Membership in Solidarity cut across occupations. Although skilled workers were the union's strongest base of support, both the most highly educated and the least skilled state employees tended to be members. Before martial law was declared on December 13, 1981, a nationwide sample of the population was asked about their union affiliation. The occupational group most likely to belong to Solidarity was skilled workers in heavy industry; 86.7 percent of that group belonged to the union. Only 3.3 percent belonged to the government-supported branch unions. Over two-thirds of the following groups also belonged to Solidarity: skilled workers in light industry, foremen, technicians, semi-skilled and unskilled workers, doctors and other highly educated people (excluding engineers and economists), and middle-level management, many of whom were engineers. Apart from teachers (see chapter 3), among the occupational groups working in the socialized sector of the economy, engineers and higher management were the least likely to belong to Solidarity and most likely to belong to the government-sponsored trade unions. Over half of this category belonged to Solidarity and nearly a third belonged to the government-sponsored trade unions (see table 3.1).

The figures presented on union membership across occupations are not entirely reliable for representing engineers' membership in Solidarity. Upper management is only partially composed of those with engineering backgrounds, although they are in the majority among the highly educated. University-educated engineers are also present among middle-level personnel and even occasionally among foremen. A more recent study of engineers' social self-identification, attitudes and past and present organizational memberships undertaken after the declaration of martial law can help clarify levels of engineers' participation. In this survey of 399 engineers, approximately 63 percent of the respondents reported their past membership in Solidarity (Mach, 1987).

How do we interpret these levels of participation? Should we seek to explain why so *few* engineers participated in Solidarity, given what great proportions of other occupations participated? Or should we seek to explain why so *many* engineers participated, given the risks that participating in an independent trade union presented to engineers? These are not contradictory questions. Certain new characteristics of the engineering profession in Poland pushed engineers to participate in Solidarity, while other features, more typical of the past, inhibited participation. Further data from Mach's analysis clarify the problem.

Mach (1987) presents data on the responses of workers, engineers and a national sample of Poles to the following question: "Please imagine people who are in a similar life situation to you. How would you name this group of people?" These self-constructed identification groups have obvious intrinsic interest, but I restrain my observations to the different levels of membership among different identification groups. Engineers were more likely than the general population and much more likely than workers to report that they were "well adjusted." They were also, however, quite likely to report that they were "unable to manage" (table 8.1). Those engineers who were well adjusted were most likely to mention their good material situation (45 percent) and their general optimism (41 percent), while those engineers who reported their inability to manage mentioned most often their pessimism (55 percent) (Mach, 1987). The range of subjective inequality present in the general population is thus replicated *within* the engineering profession. Although these data on self-identification were collected after decisions to join Solidarity were made, they are nevertheless useful in helping us to understand the variable engineer response to the union. If being "well-adjusted" limits support for Solidarity, and if being "unable to manage" encourages support as one might expect, something about the Polish engineering profession is at the same time encouraging and discouraging support for Solidarity.

Past membership in Solidarity is indeed related to the group with which the engineer identifies. Those who are well adjusted have a membership rate of "only" 50 percent; 75.8 percent of those who are unable to manage belong to Solidarity. Not surprisingly, those engineers who claim to belong to the group which is "deprived of power and influence" (according to Mach, the most "political" of any of the

Table 8.1. *Kind of social self-identification among workers, engineers and a national sample of Poles, plus percentage of engineers' membership in Solidarity by category (in percentages)*

Kind of self-identification	National sample	Workers	Engineers	Engineers' Solidarity membership
Working in occupation	15.0	7.6	9.0	69.4
Well adjusted	20.4	12.9	21.6	50.0
Deprived of power and influence	5.2	13.2	6.0	87.5
Honest/hardworking	5.5	10.7	11.0	59.1
Regular, normal	18.1	21.1	18.6	66.2
Unable to manage	25.8	22.3	22.8	75.8
Other	8.0	10.4	8.0	59.4
Lack of data	2.0	1.8	3.0	–
Total	100	100	100	–
N	834	394	399	399

Source: adapted from Mach (1987).

identifications) are the most likely to belong to Solidarity with 87.5 percent of their ranks belonging.

Politically minded engineers were not only the most likely to become members of Solidarity, but they were also very often in prominent positions in the union leadership. Twelve of the union's top thirty-three activist officials had higher educations. Of these, four were engineers (Pakulski, 1986:72). Engineers were also prominent in the regional commissions of the union; in Upper Silesia, for instance, 15 of 62 commission members were engineers, and 13 were "semi-professional" technicians ("Wybory," 1981). Given the greater prominence of national and political concerns among leading activists, it is likely that political commitments or cultural orientations moved these engineers to leadership, regardless of their professional interests. Although Wałęsa is an electrician, two of the other best-known activists were engineers: the "radical" Andrzej Gwiazda and the "true Pole" Jan Rulewski. Using Touraine's tripartite identification of the movement, their motivations were apparently more democratic and national than trade unionist (Touraine, 1983:146–49).

Cultural or political accounts are thus helpful in establishing reasons for why a few engineers might become "organic" intellectuals for and activists among the working class, but it does not explain why the mass of engineers allied with Solidarity. And the available data do not allow us to discover occupational or structural features that might explain who is in what group. One might presume, however, given the distribution of reward based on proximity to or inclusion in *nomenklatura* (chapter 6), that those higher in management are most likely to be found among the "well-adjusted," and those engineers working in non-managerial poorly paid work on the production line or in research to be those without influence or unable to manage.

With that assumption, in what follows I should like to do three things that can help account for the cross-class engineer–worker alliance in Solidarity. First, I wish to explain why such a large proportion of engineers (22.8 percent according to this sample and probably much larger for reasons I document below) is "unable to manage." Because this is such a large group and the second most likely to participate in the union, to explain how they came to form such a large group within engineering could help explain why so many engineers ultimately joined Solidarity. Second, I wish to explain why such a substantial proportion of "well-adjusted" engineers belonged to Solidarity. For that, I examine the working conditions of managerial engineers and suggest why approximately half of those whom we would not expect to join the union, did. Third, I argue that the second stage of Solidarity's evolution, the stage in which "self-management" was central (chapter 6), was determined not only by the structure of conflict between movement and authorities, but was also ideologically necessary to preserve the alliance of engineers and workers, given their potentially contradictory class interests.

It is tempting to say that Solidarity was such a powerful social movement that it merely swept away the Polish nation in a frenzied optimism. Therefore, to look for factors in the engineer's professional milieu enabling alliance with workers is unnecessary and one need only note that engineers are as patriotic, if not more so, than the rest of the nation. That is important, and as my discussion of managerial engineers illustrates, a critical aspect of the account. But part of Solidarity's power came from the readiness with which so many different sectors embraced the trade union. It seems advantageous to look at the movement as dialectically constituted, gaining strength from the readiness of different sectors to join it, but using that very strength to press more hesitant sectors into joining it. It is in that spirit that I present the following structural account of the alliance of engineers and workers.

Non-managerial engineers

Engineers who identify themselves as lacking power would seem to need little pressure to join a union promising to empower those disenfranchised by the authorities. Those unable to manage have little to lose by joining a movement promising to change their plight. The task I set for this section is to explain how this group came to be constituted.

Poland's communist authorities expanded educational opportunities, especially in technical studies, dramatically after World War II. Expanding educational opportunity can cause an inflation of education's instrumental value in times of economic decline, however. In practical terms, this means that (1) the same position is filled by increasingly highly educated people; and (2) the chance that educational advance leads to a higher socio-economic position is decreased. This is especially true for the value of a middle-level general education. It is also true to some degree for the highly educated, or those who have completed university or polytechnical training. Although a higher university education is increasingly necessary for upper-level positions, the highly educated appear more frequently in lower-level positions too. Białecki compares the three cohorts who began their first work in 1945–59, 1960–70 and 1971–82 and finds that the highly educated in the last cohort are more likely to work in positions not requiring their credentials. For instance, in the first cohort, 13 percent of people whose first job was a technician had a higher education; 5.3 percent in the second cohort had such a degree; but in the youngest cohort 22.2 percent had a higher education. The same trend is true for clerks; 4.0 percent of the oldest generation of people who became clerks in their first job had a higher education, and 4.8 percent of the middle-aged cohort clerks were so educated. In the youngest cohort, 11.1 percent were so educated (Białecki, 1986). The Polish economy was able to absorb the increase in highly educated workers when the economy was expanding in the early 1970s. When economic growth began to slow down, and especially when that growth turned negative in 1979, the value of an educational degree also declined. As engineer scholars like Janusz Tymowski suggest, there was an overproduction of highly educated people, especially of engineers. J. Tymowski (1982a) argued that the number of engineers trained has to be cut by about 20–25 percent in relation to those currently employed. The fault not only lies in oversupply, but a decline in demand, of course, given Poland's economic crisis of the late 1970s.

Of what consequence was this for engineers? That decade was a period of rising expectations and crushed hopes. One Polish journalist described the period this way: "the fascination of technical progress, an opening to the West, great programs of investment, purchases, great careers. All of that crumbled in a few years, and we found ourselves in the opposite extreme" (Baczyński, 1983). This affected the engineering profession in four principal ways: (1) competition for the most desirable spots became more intense; (2) available work became more frustrating; (3) engineers' wages and their general socio-economic status declined; and (4) more and more engineers took work outside the profession.

Engineers in Poland prefer research work, especially in comparison to work on the line (Grzelak, 1965). Once on the line, however, engineers are anxious to escape it into management (Jaśkiewicz, 1977). This has a consequence of a shortage of production engineers and an oversupply of those in research. Wojciech Kubicki (1983), writing for the Warsaw daily *Życie Warszawy*, lamented "We have then more and more of the universal theoretical engineers, consciously or instinctively escaping from close contact with production, whose problems they have neither learned nor understood." Preference for research and secondarily management is not surprising, given the frustration in production in a crisis economy. Beyond problems of labor control characteristic of state socialism (Sabel and Stark, 1982), shortages in the crisis economy make production work even more difficult. Although shortages also may be endemic to the centrally planned Soviet-type economies (Nove, 1983b:71–73), the frequency and intensity of the shortages are augmented during a crisis. Often, due to shortages, ingredients called for in the production of goods are not available. The engineer linked to production therefore has to figure out some kind of substitute part. Ingenuity in the face of these difficulties was sometimes remarkable. In the mid-1970s, rubber gaskets (*uszczelki*) were in very short supply. Substitutes were sought and finally found in the form of condoms. This, of course, demanded new ingenuity in contraceptive strategies. Nevertheless, this "round-about technology" characterized much of production in the late 1970s; fully one-third of all production in this period was so characterized (Białecki, 1982:115–16). Apparently there was an occasional sense of triumph when an engineer could find the appropriate substitute, but there were enough unsuccessful forages to make work on the whole frustrating. Stanisław Klimaszewski (1981), writing in the Solidarity newsweekly, *Tygodnik Solidarność*, reported that many engineers preferred to work at other things rather than in their learned profession. One engineer reportedly said, "I'd rather raise pigs"; others with doctoral degrees in engineering preferred to work in privately run booths selling sausage sandwiches. To what extent these exits from engineering are reported truthfully or with tongue in cheek is not apparent, but the frustration is.

In the same article, Klimaszewski (1981) criticized the leadership of the Supreme Technical Organization for its complicity in the inept investment decisions of the early 1970s, especially for the purchasing of foreign licenses to manufacture Western products. Polish plants often required *komponenci dewizowe* (components that must be purchased with hard currency) to operate. When economic crisis came, and hard currency was scarce for purchasing replacement parts, factories sometimes had to shut down for the lack of those very parts, which were occasionally very small and inexpensive. Klimaszewski (1981) writes that "we are not able to produce oxygenated water without western components." This frustration derived from the crisis was thus compounded by the reliance on scarce and expensive Western produced goods. The fact that the policy of buying Western licenses for manufacture was devised without the involvement of Poland's engineers also led to engineers' frustration. NOT did nothing to oppose the authorities and went along with their game (Klimaszewski, 1981). Klimaszewski is not alone in resenting the investment decisions of the 1970s. Kazimierz Kłoc (1981), in the engineering journal *Przegląd Techniczny*, argued that one reason the authorities picked the strategy of industrialization that involved Western licensed goods was in order to avoid giving professional groups, like engineers, too much bargaining power. If Polish engineers developed a Polish technology, their control over the development of technology would give them a power base too close to the heart of Gierek's legitimacy, the drive to modernize industry. Rather than depend on Polish engineers, the authorities preferred to rely on Western capitalists. One Polish engineer with whom I talked also suggested this. He said that the authorities preferred to develop the country in a way that objectively limited the power of engineers and technical rationalists (e.g. by importing licenses for production rather than allocating capital to domestic technological innovation). Economist Dominico Nuti

(1981 [1982]:34) estimates that 10 percent of all the licenses purchased were unjustified, given the existence of domestic alternatives.

These accounts were constructed, however, in the Solidarity period and after. It is difficult to say, therefore, how accurately they convey the feelings of the 1970s. Indeed, some of my consultants suggest that these indictments of the authorities are inconsistent with the dominant engineering mood of the 1970s, where engineers praised Gierek's import strategy. It allowed, after all, some engineers to go abroad and enjoy the benefits foreign travels provide. It might be useful to consider these critiques of NOT and of the Gierek investment strategy as cultural accounts which can help justify the shift in engineers' alliances from the Gierek regime to the Solidarity movement. They were useful in absolving the majority of the profession from responsibility for the economic crisis. Instead, they heaped blame on the political authorities and a small group of compromised engineers. It also showed why engineers should ally with Solidarity, since an *independent* technical organization is essential for replacing the Supreme Technical Organization. Nevertheless, we might understand this new ideology as the product of the shift in power relations occasioned by the emergence of Solidarity and the simultaneous failure of vassalage. Evidence for the latter can be found in the engineers' decline in standard of living.

In the initial stages of post-war industrialization, engineering wages were among the highest of any socio-occupational group. Differentials between the wages of engineers and workers grew in the 1960s, as the party sought to make the economy more efficient (Kolankiewicz, 1973). The difference reached a peak in the mid-1960s, as table 8.2 indicates. These data combine the income of technicians and engineers, however. When the wages of engineers are considered separately, the decline in status from the mid-1960s is even more dramatic. In the mid-1960s the average monthly wage for a mechanical engineer was 2.09 times the average wage in industry, but by 1980 the engineer's wage stood only 1.3 times that figure and by 1982 the mechanical engineer's wage was nearly identical to the industrial wage average (Rocznik Statystyczny, 1970; 1981; 1983). Of course, engineers' wages, as all other wages in Poland, differ dramatically by economic sector and branch of industry in which they are employed. A survey of engineers by NOT (J. Tymowski, 1983) found the best situations for *magister* engineers in transportation and industry, and within industry, mining is the best. Management offers the best wages among different engineering activities, with operations and pro-

Table 8.2. *Ratio of engineering/technician wages to workers' wages in industry over time*

	1955	1960	1965	1970	1975[*]	1980
Ratio	1.56	1.59	1.64	1.50	1.29/1.37	1.23

[*] After 1970, a new basis for enumeration was introduced, and ratios from old and new methods are presented in the table.
Source: adapted from J. Tymowski (1983:4).

duction coming in second and third respectively. The lowest wages came in those positions with the greatest intrinsic desirability: research, construction projects and education.

Although engineers' wages vary across activities, branches of industry and economic sector, the more important point for this analysis is that the relative status of all engineers declined over time, and reached an all time low in the late 1970s and early 1980s. This is not only objectively apparent, but also of considerable subjective import-ance for engineers themselves. A survey of members of the intelli-gentsia in Łódź taken in 1973 illustrates this (Święcicka, 1980). They were asked to evaluate their social position on the basis of whatever factor they consider most important. As table 8.3 indicates, engineers had the lowest self-evaluation of any of the occupations surveyed, even when controlling for social origins. Income is the most important factor explaining engineers' poor self-evaluations. It is also more important for engineers than for any other occupational group, as the correlation between the engineers' self-evaluation and evaluation of wages suggests. Research conducted on a national sample of engi-neers in 1974 and 1975 confirms the importance of wages in engineers' self-evaluation. Krzysztof Hirszel (1983) found that engineers were more dissatisfied with their work than were workers, and the issue that disturbed engineers most was their material condition.

Given the fact that engineers' wages suffered such a dramatic decline in the second half of the 1970s and 1980s, engineers' support for Solidarity is none too surprising. One of the factors integrating engineers into the system was their opportunity for professional specialization and relatively higher wages. As professional work became more difficult to find and more frustrating when found, and as wages declined, the mechanisms ensuring many engineers' depend-ence on the authorities were diluted.

Table 8.3. *Social origin, occupation and self-evaluation of social position and wages in the intelligentsia (in percentages)*

Occupation	Self-evaluation of social position				
Social origin	High	Low	C*	C**	N
Physicians	84.3	15.2	0.1	0.24	46
Intelligentsia	87.5	12.5			24
Other	81.8	18.2			22
Engineers	56.3	43.7	0.04	0.44	48
Intelligentsia	60.0	40.0			10
Other	55.3	44.7			38
Economists	75.0	25.0	0.1	0.31	48
Intelligentsia	66.7	33.3			9
Other	76.9	23.1			39
Humanists	70.3	29.7	0.02	0.30	37
Intelligentsia	71.4	28.6			14
Other	69.6	30.4			23

* Pearson's correlation coefficient between origins and status evaluation.
** Pearson's correlation coefficient between status evaluation and evaluation of wages.
Source: adapted from Święcicka (1980:81, 94).

Managerial engineers

This observation of engineers' relative impoverishment does not seem to square with most observations about Poland in the 1970s. Jadwiga Koralewicz-Zębik (1984a) notes that while in the 1960s people were generally optimistic about reductions in the levels of inequality, by the end of the 1970s people thought that inequalities were on the rise. In 1961 only 10.7 percent of an urban sample thought inequalities were greater than those before 1939, and 49.3 percent expected that inequalities would decline in the future. By 1980, however, 67 percent of a national sample thought that inequalities in Poland had actually risen during the 1970s.

Inequalities were exacerbated during the 1970s, but they did not grow along educational lines. Education no longer guaranteed a well-paying job, but as we have seen, frequently led to jobs not requiring higher education at all. Two groups fared especially well in the 1970s and early 1980s: managers and private entrepreneurs. Although the flourishing of private enterprise in Poland is of considerable interest, I do not pursue the matter here. The manager's lot is, however, of considerable interest to the principal concern of this chapter.

If managers are highly educated, most often they are engineers. Since the Stalinist era, managers have increasingly received higher educations in technical studies. But while the managerial definition of engineering professionalism has blunted union sympathies in capitalist societies (Noble, 1977; Whalley and Crawford, 1984; Zussman, 1984) its impact in Poland seems to be more limited. Table 3.1 shows that upper-level managers were more often members of Solidarity than of the government-sponsored trade unions and table 8.1 shows that one out of two "well-adjusted" engineers were members of Solidarity. Why would such successful engineers be interested in becoming members of a worker-dominated trade union? This is especially interesting, given the common perception of their materially privileged status. The ratio of income between the factory manager and average worker is small, in 1981 only about 2.29 to 1 (Rocznik Statystczny, 1982:132), but that is only a tiny part of the story. There are various bonuses and premiums that the official statistics do not include. While the general population must wait to obtain automobiles and apartments, managers can obtain nicer ones more directly and more quickly. Gifts, obtained at state expense, are regularly exchanged between political authorities and managers. Facilities built ostensibly for factory use, like regal and expensive clubhouses, are used for private affairs by managers and other elites (Smolar, 1983). While the most extreme abuses occurred during the 1970s, privilege is still a fact of life for top managers. Relying on interviews conducted with nine experts on Polish society, Janusz Hryniewicz (1983) was able to estimate that enterprise managers and their assistants benefit privately from their official position about five times more than technicians benefit from theirs (see table 8.4). Though this does not seem large in American terms, in the comparatively egalitarian structure of Polish society this is quite significant. Among socio-occupational groups, only managers of larger factory consortiums and political secretaries of these consortiums and factories have more privileges than managers. The possibility for engineers' advance into the managerial ranks helps account for the substantial proportion of engineers reporting their membership among the "well-adjusted" in Polish society. But why would half of their ranks belong to Solidarity?

Table 8.4. *Upper-level occupational groups and possibilities for personal profit from workplace (100 is an average score in the entire economy)*

Occupational group	Possibilities in points
1. Permanent secretaries of factory party committees	650
2. Secretaries of provincial party committees	583
3. Directors of consortiums	533
4. Directors and their assistants in industry	483
5. Permanent president of factory trade union	433
6. Institute director	316
7. Departmental director	275
8. Chief engineer	266
9. Chief accountant	258
10. Departmental director in consortium	241
11. Foreman	186
12. Salespersons and cashiers	183
13. Storekeepers	181
14. Non-managerial engineer	151
15. Non-managerial economist	133
16. Lower foreman	118
17. Secretary or typist	101
18. Technician in industrial specialization	100

Source: adapted from Janusz Hryniewicz (1983).

The answer does not lie in privilege. One answer lies in the political domination of promotion.

To advance in management one must be prepared to demonstrate one's party loyalty. Wasilewski (1981) studied the occupational careers of directors in the Warsaw area and found that there were several different types of career patterns: technical, administrative, political and their combinations. This meant that some managers advanced to their positions more or less on the basis of professional qualifications, while some advanced to the top on the basis of their political quali- fications or connections. These data are useful to show that political factors alone no longer determine most promotions. But despite the difference in career patterns, even the technical career managers had to be members and activists in socio-political organizations; about two-thirds of them were active in politics at the beginning of their careers (see table 8.5).

Solidarity sought to eliminate political influence on promotions. The most obvious attack on party domination was the union's call for an

Table 8.5. *Socio-political activity of managers at different stages of their careers (in percentages of persons in a given type of career)*

Stage of career	Type of occupational career					
	T	A	T–A	M–E	P	Together
Activists in unions or self-management organizations						
First job	43.9	49.4	50.9	75.0	59.6	54.8
First supervisory job	43.9	43.2	50.9	45.5	36.2	44.1
First management job	46.3	48.1	50.9	45.5	42.6	47.0
Current job	46.3	48.1	52.6	45.5	51.1	48.9
PUWP, Peasant Party, Democratic Party or Union of Socialist Youth Member or Activist						
First job	46.3	54.3	56.1	56.8	74.5	57.4
First supervisory job	24.4	64.2	50.9	40.9	97.9	56.7
First management job	82.9	85.2	86.0	77.3	97.9	85.9
Current job	90.2	95.1	91.2	84.1	100.0	92.6

T=technical A=administrative
T–A=technical–administrative
M–E=managerial–expert P=political
Source: adapted from Wasilewski (1981:186).

end to *nomenklatura*. Solidarity's congress in September–October 1981 produced a program of which the following was one of its propositions:

> The authoritarian direction of the economy, which makes rational development impossible, must be brought to an end. In this system, enormous economic power is concentrated in the party apparatus and the state bureaucracy. The structure of economic organization serving the command system must be broken up. It is necessary to separate the apparatus of economic administration from political power. Enterprise managers should no longer be dependent upon the ministry, and nor should important appointments fall under the party nomenklatura. (Persky and Flam, 1982:208)

Solidarity thus sought to eliminate the procedure by which all top managers were appointed, and in that way to weaken the influence of the party over managerial appointments. It also sought to eliminate the unseen but well-known privileges the managers held. It thus seems incredible that any managerial engineer successful in this system would be willing to cooperate with Solidarity, much less become a member. Managerial engineers cooperated with Solidarity for at least two reasons: (1) Solidarity became so powerful that at least surface cooperation was necessary to keep production going; and (2) the attack by Solidarity on the political domination of promotion and production was supported by sections of management.

In Soviet-type societies, outward behavior reveals little of one's true feelings. That is probably true in most societies, but in Poland it is more extreme. Communism is necessary for geo-political reasons, but it is not widely accepted by the general population. Social schizo-phrenia exists: a conflict in spheres of values between that dominated by the Polish United Workers' Party and that influenced by Polish historical traditions and culture (Wnuk-Lipiński, 1982; chapter 5). But in order to advance in hierarchies controlled by the party, one must at least feign political loyalty. One has to join the party or belong to other socio-political organizations like official trade unions, attend the May Day Parade or write for party newspapers. It is not necessary, however, to really believe in one's political activity to advance. Staniszkis (1979:178) notes, "to make a career one must be able to participate in 'facade' rituals and to imitate facade vocabulary in public situations." She further argues that the middle class is most adept at using this ideological language in brackets, making it possible to look like a conformist yet feel clean and honest inside. This inconsistency in thought and behavior among engineers seems to be something con-sistent across Soviet-type societies. Rudolph Bahro (1978:317) des-cribes this process as one of *reservatio mentalis*. Despite that attempt to salvage authenticity, Staniszkis (1979) believes this costs the actor his ability to articulate his own needs and desires; it creates inner disintegration and a crisis in self-esteem. Research on the distribution of stress and self-esteem among social groups in Poland shows that engineers have among the highest levels of stress and they have the lowest self-confidence (Koralewicz-Zębik, 1987a). The only group to have higher stress than engineers are highly educated humanists in management positions.

The Solidarity period allowed more freedom of expression than ever before. Facades crumbled. Workers demanded the removal of poli-tically appointed, corrupt, and incompetent managers. Their replacements, behoven to Solidarity, were also more likely to be professionally qualified and committed to the reform of the economy. Of course, as the data on membership indicate, there were also still very many managers who remained loyal to the authorities and stayed in the branch unions. If the manager won his position because of his political loyalty, that was necessary; but if he held his position because he was professionally competent, and political loyalty was a distasteful but pragmatic necessity, the manager finally had a choice when Solidarity gained power. It even became less legitimate to act one way and believe another. The non-authenticity of some engineers' loyalty explains why it was possible for many engineers, even in management, to abandon the party for Solidarity.

Professionally oriented managers were not only frustrated by the charades they were forced to play but also by the political domination of the higher positions and of decision-making. The highest managerial post outside of the ministry of a branch was to be a manager of a *zjednoczenie*, a consortium or association of different enterprises. In the late 1970s out of 111 *zjednoczenies*, 68 directors had less than complete secondary education; ten thousand enterprise directors had that same low level of education (Karas, 1981). For the professionally minded engineer, subordination to what were obviously political appointments was objectionable. It was even more objectionable since these political appointments were perceived to have been the results of a negative selection (A. Tymowski, 1982). The political appointments would not have been so bad had they not so obviously contributed to the economic crisis. As I noted previously, professional engineers frequently complain about the investment policy of the apparatus in the early 1970s. The political domination of management was not only objectionable to the professional engineer because it kept him in lower positions, but also because it contributed to an inept investment strategy. The engineer's ideology of "rationality" was thus offended by the political domination of production and of distribution.

Although some managerial engineers may have liked what Solidarity tried to do, this is not sufficient reason for them to join the trade union. After all, it was risky to join a group that was such an obvious challenge to party power. If Solidarity would lose, as it eventually did in 1981, those managers who supported the independent trade union would probably be demoted. The final reason that managerial engineers joined Solidarity was that the union became so strong, production depended on having good relations with it. Good relations were best ensured through membership or in support for the union.

The strength of the union and managerial participation in it varied across the country. Although Solidarity had gained the support of most foremen, Silesian foremen tended to remain with the official trade unions while managers in Warsaw often joined Solidarity. Alliances were thus determined by local struggles for power (Drążkiewicz and Rychard, 1981; chapter 3). Diversity among higher levels of management became more apparent over time too. In Nowa Huta for instance, the party factory committee sought to block the signing of an agreement between the director and personnel; in Ursus, a party representative introduced a sharp and primitive propaganda struggle against the strikers, without the support of the management. Management sought to deal with the strikers "pragmatically," and the party dealt with the problem "doctrinally." Because of these different approaches to the strikes, one can see the roots of differences among managerial engineers in their union membership. It became increasingly obvious that Solidarity was a force to reckon with, and a legitimate negotiating partner from the economic point of view. Those engineers whose positions depended most on their professional competence, rather than political allegiance, would be more inclined to join or cooperate with Solidarity. Those engineers whose positions depended on demonstrations of political loyalty would more likely stay with the old unions, and oppose the independent trade union as an "anti-socialist" force. The degree to which appointments were professional or political varied from factory to factory; the level at which appointments were politically made also varied.

Andrzej Rychard (1984) argues that, as the strikes progressed and Solidarity became better organized, the lines of the struggle shifted. The popular view that this was a struggle between authorities and society is only partially accurate, and relevant to the earlier stages of struggle. By summer 1981, it appeared that there was a struggle between "supporters of the old order" and the "world of work." Rychard even believes this to be one reason why martial law was introduced. The unity of the authorities in the face of Solidarity was crumbling. Rychard (1984) suggests two reasons for this fragmentation: (1) the necessity of cooperation in the organization of work; (2) the greater importance of support by workers than support by political authorities for production to continue. Thus, managerial engineers were forced into cooperating with Solidarity for the sake of continuing production. In certain factories, the very strength of the union and its importance in continued production induced support or at least a tacit alliance between the union and management.

Although the world of work had a common enemy in the "supporters of the old order," they also had their own internal differences. In order to construct an alliance between engineers and workers, and indeed to maintain the unity of the "world of work," an ideology was necessary to cement the tactical alliance. Self-management proved suitable.

Engineers and self-management

The initial stages of the Solidarity movement were dominated by the struggle for self-organization. Engineers were part of this movement, although they placed far less priority on the establishment of a new independent professional association than did other groups. In August 1981 an appeal for the formation of a new professional association appeared in *Tygodnik Solidarność* and *Przegląd Techniczny*. This text emphasized the need for an organization that would defend occupational interests. The old NOT (*Naczelna Organizacja Techniczna* or Supreme Technical Organization) was inadequate from this point of view, given that it was "owned" by the authorities. A new NOT (*Niezależna Organizacja Techniczna* or Independent Technical Organization) was necessary.

This appeal only appeared in August when the "stage" of self-organization had passed the movement by. Engineers were already self-organized around their workplace. A new professional association would have been attractive, but it was less essential, given that engineering interests and occupational concerns were closely tied to the plants and ministries to which engineers belonged, and less relevant to system-wide professional concerns. Engineers' immediate interests were more similar to those of workers in the same workplace than to those of other engineers. But this does not mean that there were no contradictions between class interests in the workplace.

The dire straits of the Polish economy and the hostility of the authorities forced Solidarity to become more than a self-organizing trade union and try to take control of its field of action (chapter 3). The only apparent option for this was "self-management." But why was this such an obvious move? Self-management was more compatible with the official ideology of the system than many other alternatives. Self-management could not be called a return to capitalism, although it might be called revisionist or anarcho-syndicalist. Nevertheless, this reform was easier for the Soviet-type system to digest, ideologically speaking, than opening up the private sector.

But there is another reason for self-management's attraction from the point of view of Solidarity's own construction of internal alliances. Self-management proved an excellent strategy for smoothing over potential antagonisms between professionals and workers within Solidarity. It enabled professionals and workers to focus on their common enemy rather than address tough choices that other economic reforms would raise. Much as I described Horvat's (1982) account of the struggle for self-management as one of "classless praxis" (chapter 4), the "classlessness" of Solidarity's struggle for self-management was ideal for maintaining the unity of the alliance between professionals and workers, even if it did not, and could not, address the basic problems of economic reform. Solidarity experts knew as much, but their voices were largely lost in the wind as both workers and professionals pinned their hopes on self-management as something which could realize everyone's interests.

Self-management is usually promoted as a democratization of industrial relations. At the same time, however, most employee councils have been composed of engineers and technicians. This was even the case in Czechoslovakia in 1968 and seemed to be the case in Poland in 1981 (Touraine *et al.*, 1983:30, 85). Self-management has a dual character as an economically "rational" form of industrial management and as a more democratic form of industrial relations. This dual character was ideal to constructing an alliance between efficiency-minded engineers and democratically oriented workers. One article in *Przegląd Techniczny* (June 28, 1981) illustrates this discourse, and the attempts to find an organizational form allowing the alliances of interests and of classes to form.

Six representatives[2] from a machine-tool factory discussed some of the difficulties of self-management. They agreed that self-management can go too far when not only enterprise directors but also directors of departments are hired and fired by councils (as it was in Ursus). It also can go too far when the council interferes in the daily decisions of the enterprise manager. The general strategy for the enterprise should be a matter of discussion for the whole enterprise, but the decisions bearing on execution should be the province of the manager. There must be a division of labor to assure efficiency, but there must be supervision to assure democracy. This is certainly a reasonable compromise, and one that in broad strokes proved uncontroversial.

The group recognized also the likelihood of conflicts between the trade unions and the factory council, but did not consider them problematic. The self-management secretary argued: "I see the economy like an organism, in which there are employee councils and trade unions, but in which roles are clearly divided. Trade unions will defend the interests of workers, and instead the council should defend the interests of the factory." This does not mean that there will be constant conflict, for each group will act responsibly, even if there may be occasional disagreements. The metalworker representative elaborated: "We are aware of how important accumulation is and how consumption depends on it. On the other hand, what will be the proportion between accumulation and consumption? Here there may be a difference of opinions and we will reckon with them." They will reckon with these differences by having the personnel of the factory decide what is in their best interests. If they decide poorly, they must suffer the consequences of bad decisions. If the personnel is not held responsible, he argues, that is not real self-management.

These discussants recognized that self-management was no panacea. The problems before them were too great. Economic and energy crises, insufficient data and general demoralization are considerable barriers to recovery. Self-management nevertheless offers them an opportunity to challenge this fate. Enterprise democratization meant that real experts could be selected, and if not sufficiently competent, fired by the personnel. Democracy and efficiency went hand in hand. Democratic control would become useful, however, only if the enterprise were truly "free." The real question was the need for establishing enterprise independence from the state. Only when there is this independence does the question of self-management even become relevant, they argued. And only then can tough questions be addressed ("*Samorządni, samodzielni, i . . .*"). Thus, economic rationality depended on the establishment of independence. All sectors could ally in this quest.

Even with enterprise independence, however, the tough questions were not answered automatically. One of the most difficult challenges was the mechanism for the reallocation of resources. Stankiewicz (1981), for instance, argued that Solidarity was not challenging the authorities' hold on the economy, and rather was reproducing statism. The very same places that were Solidarity strongholds were also places that received resources because of strong lobbies, not for their efficiency or economic sense. Solidarity thus engages in a contradictory project, he argues: it wants ministries so weak that they accede to the union's demands, but at the same time wants them strong enough to reform the economy. An even tougher challenge to Solidarity was made by Kazimierz Kopecki (1981), an engineering professor from Gdańsk Polytechnical Institute. The economy is consuming far too much energy given its production levels, he argues. Not only is a price reform necessary so that the real costs of energy can be reflected, but those enterprises, or even branches of the economy, that waste the most energy must be liquidated. Poland must close down the least effective cement factories, and modernize or close down steel factories like Huta Katowice. All of this must be done with the minimum cost to society, but it would mean that Solidarity would have to seek the closure of many of the very factories which were so important to its political strength. Although this interview appeared in *Tygodnik Solidarność*, and therefore reflected the very serious discussion in which Solidarity engaged, it also showed the difficulty of establishing an effective reform program that also kept Solidarity by ameliorating potentially contradictory interests.

Where professionals might advocate the restructuring of the mechanism of allocation and the elimination of "inefficient" plants, most workers, and especially the politically powerful workers in those plants, would resist. "Self-management" was a desirable alternative, for it promised both workers' democracy and capitalist efficiency. It did not answer the tough questions, but it did promise a move in that direction by way of encouraging enterprise independence and financial responsibility. In *Tygodnik Solidarność*, Pawel Kozlowski (1981) portrayed the unity of this self-management elegantly. He argued that an economic reform based on the increasing independence of the firm will lead to greater managerial influence, even if many managers will probably resist this increase in their responsibility (as we would expect given the structure of power relations, chapter 6). At the same time, the state will also have to retain considerable power in the first stage of economic recovery in order that energy, raw materials and credits be allocated to the most promising sectors. Thus, the manager will be constrained quite severely by shortages and the centralized state, and that is not all. In this self-managing reform, the manager will be constrained by his/her own personnel. If this personnel is empowered by their own trade unions, they too will be quite demanding in their consumption needs. The only way then, that the director will be able to succeed in such an environment is to be one of "us" and not one of "them." The director must be elected in order to have the moral authority to enable a success based on management–workforce cooperation. Solidarity is therefore not against hierarchy *per se*, just a hierarchy that is based on force. A democratically constructed hierarchy would resolve potentially contradictory interests.

Tygodnik Solidarność also provided a step-by-step example of how a Wrocław factory undertook just such a search for a director (Koziński *et al.* 1981). A factory commission composed of Solidarity activists and representatives from the PZPR factory committee, branch unions and management established a competition. They provided a list of various psychological and professional qualifications, of which one was having a higher education. After the candidates were evaluated on this basis, a discussion took place and finally a secret ballot to decide this manager's election. In this case, there were 23 candidates of whom 19 were engineers, 3 lawyers and 1 economist. Clearly, those managers more professionally competent would win in this electoral process, and political appointees would fail. For Koziński *et al.* (1981), this was but an example of the way in which a director could be chosen "objectively." It was also a lesson in how engineers would not lose, even in a workers' self-management scheme. "Objective" elections defined their field of eligible candidates in strictly "professional" terms.

There was considerable discussion in the Solidarity press about how democratic these councils should be, nevertheless. Although there was little dissent about letting a manager "manage," some Solidarity activists (Jakubowicz, 1981) warned that these councils not be confused with "boards of trustees" (*rady nadzórcze*) composed of representatives from central and regional bodies, banks, suppliers and customers, consumer groups, etc. These may exist alongside of employees' councils (*rady pracownicze*), but they have nothing to do with the conditions of trust and participation that self-management represents.

Self-management thus allowed both engineers and workers to cooperate in plans for economic reform. They could identify their common interest in this scheme, where in other plans their interests might appear more antagonistic. In self-management, workers would realize their concerns for greater workplace democracy, while the form this democracy would take emphasized above all the "professionalization" of management. The "destatization" of the economy was not only necessary from the point of view of Solidarity's struggle to control its field of action (chapter 3), but self-management was the particular strategy necessary for the movement to retain the cross-class alliance defining Solidarity's peculiarity.

Self-management is therefore a "classless" praxis, inasmuch as no group in "etatist" society has ontological priority in the struggle for it (chapter 4). Self-management appears to be equally in the interests of workers and of engineers, given that democracy and technical rationality are wedded in their mutual subordination to economic necessities everyone comes to recognize. Professional know-how presents the enterprise personnel with the choices that expand their chances for success, and the personnel, in the most democratic fashion, hold their directors to the highest standards of competence.

Indeed, this is what self-management is designed to do – to find an organizational innovation which makes the interests of otherwise disparate groups similar. But self-management is only a reform of the enterprise level of power relations – it says little about macrosocial power relations or about an alternative logic of distribution. What is to replace the mono-organizational state and central planning? Clearly, there was a search for some kind of market-like mechanism that would allocate goods on the basis of their real costs and reward producers more on the basis of the exchange value of their product. For those who had the skills and knowledge that this new economy might reward, for example engineers, such a distributional transformation might have proved appealing; but for those who would lose security in the elimination of large plants and the restoration of unemployment, as skilled workers, the existing distributional logic seemed more reassuring. Thus, reform of the macroeconomy raises questions of class alliance neatly hidden in the self-managing transformation of actually existing socialism.

One of self-management's greatest contributions is, however, the promise of an organizational form that makes imputed class interests merely transient. It acknowledges the possibility for difference among groups, but finds a mechanism for adjudicating the difference. Self-management can only solve the problem at the level of the organization itself, however. It cannot solve the problems of macroeconomic reform, nor can it address the socio-political transformation of socialism *per se*. It does suggest, however, that questions of the social organization of utopia must be brought to the center of critical sociology. Not only must we explain the historical accidents and strategic developments that enable potentially antagonistic groups to ally in common struggle, but we must also theorize how these groups might retain an egalitarian cooperative spirit once the initial barriers to their success are torn down.

Conclusions

The copresence of professionals and workers in Solidarity was one of the union's constitutive features. It is historically significant in Soviet-type societies, because this was the first time large numbers of professionals and workers cooperated in the same opposition organization. It is also theoretically significant, because it has been assumed that the gulf between the interests of professionals and workers is one thing ensuring the reproduction of the status quo. Hence, to explain how this class alliance between workers and professionals was constructed is important.

Class alliances do not appear out of thin air. Divisions between classes have to be overcome or overlooked in order for alliances to form. In the case of Polish engineers, both happened. A substantial proportion of engineers suffered declines in socio-economic status. Higher numbers of engineers were forced to work outside their profession. When they found engineering work, it was often more poorly paid than workers. The status gulf formerly separating engineers from workers had been partially dissolved. The mechanism which reproduced professional dependence on the authorities was partially dissolved.

Economic crisis did not dissolve the dependence of managerial engineers on the authorities, however. The goals and strength of the Solidarity movement were sometimes able to override that dependence. The goals reflected the interests of some professionally oriented managers, and the movement was strong enough to force the transformation of some interest-based sympathies into support. Theirs was a strategic alliance, one in which their differences derived from their different places in the organization of production were overlooked temporarily.

The strategic innovation on the part of Solidarity which allowed both non-managerial and managerial engineers to form a more enduring alliance with workers was the emphasis on the self-managing transformation of the enterprise. Self-management claimed to embrace both technical rationality and democratic organization, thus fulfilling the "class interests" of both engineers and workers in the field of production. But this convergence of interest ended at the emancipation of the enterprise from the state. Questions of the reorganization of the logic of distribution and other macrosocial and economic matters could not be addressed adequately under the self-management rubric. Indeed, there was no rubric with a program for the social transformation of power relations and political economy that professionals and workers equally could support. The project which comes closest is the struggle for "civil society," but even it offered no theory of political economy upon which to base its pluralism, legality and publicity. The absence of an imagined political–economic and social alternative representing all class interests is thus one of the great barriers facing a transformation initiated from below.

A transformation resisted from above and pressured from below depends on the unity and solidarity of popular forces. Without that unity, authorities can suppress grass roots initiatives with far greater ease by playing one popular force against another. But even the possibilities for replicating the conditional unity we witnessed in Solidarity in 1980–81 have considerable limitations. Solidarity itself could not move beyond an agenda for self-management transformation because there was no program available that could ameliorate contending class interests and simultaneously restore "economic rationality." Even more, the conditions which enabled Solidarity's level of cross-class alliance were themselves exceptional.

The common interest among political elites and professionals in maintaining a system where distribution is guided by experts rather than those who create wealth is one basis for their political alliance. Further cement for this alliance is provided when political elites grant professionals preferential privilege. When the political elite deals with economic crisis in such a way as to reduce the privileges of professionals, the mass of professionals is more likely to become susceptible to the overtures of anti-systemic forces. Economic crisis led the Polish authorities to generate such an alliance at the turn of the 1970s by squeezing professionals and appeasing, without integrating, workers' opposition. The authorities broke their vassalage contract with professionals and also forced workers to become increasingly militant and self-organized by their refusal to negotiate in good faith with a new self-organized force. But this is only one way for the authorities to deal with economic crisis in Soviet-type society.

To the degree that relative impoverishment can be addressed individually rather than collectively, the possibilities for professional alliance with a militant working class decline. A repetition of the Polish experience was quite unlikely in Hungarian society, for instance, because the latter's "hidden economy" enables individual solutions to financial problems, and makes collective ones less likely (Manchin and Szelényi, 1985). To the degree the elite allows professionals access to this sector, professionals in Soviet-type societies will be less inclined to endanger their privileges and dissolve their alliance with the elite. And of course to the extent that workers have access to this sector, they are much less likely to become self-organized (Burawoy, 1985). And finally, to the extent that the authorities find a way to make independent unions compatible with the party's substantive rationality and thus coopt legalized unions into the reproduction of power relations, the reasons for professional alliance with an anti-systemic force also fade away.

This first oppositional engineer–worker alliance in Soviet-type society derived from a particular combination of conditions: limited regime repressiveness, a militant working class, economic crisis and declines in professional socio-economic status and limited opportunities for individual solutions to those declines. The translation of common resistance into a program for social transformation depended on an ideologically informed plan: the construction of a "classless" agenda for economic reform, reflecting the cross-class alliance itself.

It is unlikely that these events will be replayed. The authorities have analyzed their mistakes, and therefore will probably do all they can to prevent another nationwide Solidarity trade union and movement for democracy and independence to form in its old mold. But social movements also can learn. One example of movement innovation in the face of structural constraints was that of Polish physicians in the 1980–81 struggle. They had no heritage of social protest or cross-class alliance, but their struggle to transform health care led them to find a new emancipatory cross-class praxis.

9 Physicians in Solidarity

Critics of the class analysis of Soviet-type society emphasize the internal heterogeneities of the working class and the intelligentsia. They argue that there are more significant lines of division within each class than there are between them. There are considerably different conditions of life and work even within professions, as the analysis of engineers suggests. Engineers are nevertheless commonly dependent on the authorities for both delegated power and privilege. Physicians occupy a different niche in Polish power relations. They are also professionals, and might be considered part of Konrád and Szelényi's ruling class *in statu nascendi*. But if we are to consider their place in a power relations defined in terms of autonomy and dependency, physicians are different from either skilled workers in large factories or engineers. Their extensive participation in Solidarity also has different structural roots, derived from their continued dependence on the authorities for power of broader scope despite a capacity for a relatively autonomous individual power.

Physicians and other medical personnel were very active in this independent trade union and social movement for democracy and independence. For the August 31, 1980, agreement which led to Solidarity, physicians and other medical personnel compiled an extraordinary list of thirty points delineating the demands of the health sector. A separate medical section of Solidarity was subsequently established, which continued and broadened the activism of the original health-sector activists. According to physicians whom I interviewed, between 80 and 90 percent of all physicians belonged to the union and about 20 percent of the profession were activists in it.[1]

In what follows, I wish to establish in greater detail the character and conditions of Polish physicians' participation in Solidarity. This account will be more hermeneutically informed than the previous exploration of engineers' participation as I rely heavily on physicians' own accounts of why they did what they did in 1980–81. At the same time, however, this is also a *critical* hermeneutics, as I examine the meaning of their movement participation in a context of a power relations which may shape action in ways physicians themselves do not acknowledge or emphasize in their own accounts of why they acted as they did. Nevertheless, fuller acknowledgment of the conditions and consequences of action ought to lead to a greater capacity for the self-regulation and fulfillment of future social movements. At least, that is my hope.

Professional authority and consumers' markets

A physician's knowledge and skills provide a base for power and privilege. Starr (1982: 3–29) calls this base "professional authority," by which he means that professionals hold power over clients by virtue of the latter's voluntary dependence on the knowledge and competence of the former. Whether this professional authority is transformed into a broader power resource depends on the social context in which physicians work. Professionals have the greatest power when their own profession is unified by a single organization which controls the reproduction of their ranks and the market for their services (Johnson, 1972). The transformation of physicians into the USA's most privileged occupational group was a product of their growing professional organization and control over the market for their services (Larson, 1977; Starr, 1982). Engineers never achieved that control because the consumers of their services were large and powerful organizations in the economy and the state.

The organizational hegemony of the Communist Party in Soviet-type societies obviously has implications for this kind of professional power. Professionals in Soviet-type societies cannot have the same kind of power as physicians enjoy in the United States. Professionals in Soviet-type societies can accumulate power of broad scope only if they are closely linked to the organizational source of power of broad scope, to the party. I have discussed already the thesis that engineers have that very kind of power, and concluded that while *some* engineers might be so endowed, the profession as a whole is definitely not.

The Polish medical profession never had the chance of attaining power similar to that realized by engineers. Physicians' power comes from their professional prestige, occupational control over scarce goods and services, and informal networks including those who have such control. These power resources are of relatively exclusive jurisdiction but also of limited scope. They insulate physicians from the same kind of socio-economic decline engineers suffer in times of crisis, but they do little to alter the allocation of resources to the society's medical sector. Physicians' participation in Solidarity should be understood, then, in terms of the place of the health sector in the power relations constituting Polish society.

The development of socialist health care

Polish physicians were formally organized in 1921 after Poland regained sovereignty.[2] The Polish parliament, the Sejm, legislated forty-nine articles on the medical profession and established the *Izba Lekarska*, or Physicians' Chamber, a professional body with control over the practice of medicine. This body was consciously modelled on the organization of health care in the Austro-Hungarian empire. Each province had its own *Izba Lekarska* and a central chamber negotiated with the government (Hornowski, 1981). This association was autonomous and self-governing, and was the only organization that could grant or withdraw the right to practice medicine. It is now commonly believed that the considerable professional authority enjoyed by Polish physicians before World War II was in part a consequence of the monitoring and controlling activities of the *Izba Lekarska* (consultant 19).

After World War II, the promise of generally free and easily accessible health care for all, especially for those whose class before the war denied them health care, contributed substantially to the legitimacy of communist authorities. In the years 1945–46, the pre-war model of health care was maintained while a broad discussion took place over how to realize health and social needs, and associated with that, how physicians were to be remunerated for their contributions. Health care was placed under the jurisdiction of the Ministry of Health and Social Welfare. Early discussions emphasized that health care was to be universally accessible, but the new constitution of the Polish People's Republic guaranteed this only to state employees. Individual farmers were not to benefit from officially free and universal health care until 1973.[3] Instead, socialized health care focused on the proletariat's leading forces in mining and heavy industry (Sokołowska, 1982: 92–93).

As in other sectors, the medical sector was the scene of class conflict. The struggle against "imperialist medicine" began in 1949. Poland withdrew from the World Health Organization and the selection of candidates for medical school came to be based more on their social consciousness and social origins than on traditional academic qualifications. A struggle was also launched to eliminate nuns from medical care. Whether physicians were allied in this struggle for socialism was an apparently debatable question.

Sokołowska (1982: 91) writes that the new model was favored by physicians because they understood their work as a public service rather than as a free profession. Although the universalization of care was supported by many physicians, the concomitant lowering of the physician's social and economic status was not so eagerly embraced. Even Marcin Kacprzak, the leading advocate of public health care in Poland before World War II (Kirschner, 1988), stated simply in the journal *Zdrowie Publiczne* (1947, cited in Łabanowska, 1978): "It is not possible to send the physician out on a badly paid position." The daily press responded to such protests with attacks on physicians' privileged lifestyles. Consistent with this attack on privilege was the authorities' opposition to the *Izba Lekarska*.

In 1946, the Trade Union of Health-Care Employees (*Związek Zawodowy Pracowników Służby Zdrowia* or ZZPSZ) was founded as the principal health-care organization. The *Izba Lekarska* was charged with being hostile to the socialization of health care. In 1952 it was eliminated and its responsibilities were transferred to the ministry. The ministry created the Commission of Occupational Control (*Komisja Kontroli Zawodowej*) to oversee physicians' ethical practices. Unlike the *Izba*, this commission played no defensive role for the profession. Non-physicians also have been part of the commission (consultant 19). On the other hand, the Polish Physicians' Association (*Polskie Towarzystwo Lekarskie*) has been an exclusive body of physicians, but it has served mainly as a clearing house for information and presentations of professional papers (consultant 17). The PTL has had neither control over the medical profession, nor has it acted as any kind of advocacy organization for the profession (Hornowski, 1981).

When Polish Stalinism was being dismantled in 1956–57 and a more open public discussion developed, the dissatisfaction of physicians with their fallen status reappeared. Physician A. Wilczyński wrote in *Zdrowie Stolicy* (1956, no. 19),

> The treatment of the question of physicians' and nurses' wages is [to this time] scandalous ... Physicians work twelve to fourteen hours per day in order to have humane [living] conditions ... bureaucratism and the administration of the physician's functions, overly high physicians' work norms, an insufficient number of medical person-

nel, and the substitution of them with medical students and surgeon's assistants, what with bad local conditions and a lack of
indispensable equipment lowers the quality of services and undermines the physician's authority.

The difficulties of physicians' work and their frustrated status
prompted doctors to call for greater occupational autonomy and their
own organization that would represent their own interests, modelled
on the pre-war *Izba Lekarska*. Gomułka disappointed the physicians, as
their hopes for a major reform of health care were never realized
during his tenure. Health care and social policy generally were not
even matters for public debate or discussion at that time. According to
Sokołowska (1974: 441), the very terms, "social policy" and "social
planning," only entered the government's vocabulary after Gomułka's
overthrow. At the Sixth Party Congress in 1971 health care and reform
became an important point in Gierek's new social contract with Polish
society.

The major elements of this reform in Polish health care were the
inclusion of private farmers in the system of free public health care; an
increase in funds for the health sector's services from the state budget,
voluntary contributions by enterprises and new taxes on alcoholic
beverages; an increase in investment funds to expand the capacity of
Poland's medical infrastructure, especially in hospitals and rural
centers; the reorganization of health services into integrated units
called Teams of Health Care (*Zespoły Opieki Zdrowotnej* or ZOZy), where
territorial units each had their own hospital complexes, specialist facilities and local care centers; the liquidation of small local pharmaceutical
enterprises in favor of huge specialized chemical consortia; an increase
in the number of physicians per 10,000 population and the utilization of
their expertise more efficiently; and an increase in wages for health
sector employees (Badanie Społecznego Komitetu Nauki i Społecznej
Komisji Zdrowia, 1986; Biednota, 1986; DiP, 1983; Kaser, 1976; Russell-
Hodgson, 1982; Sokołowska and Moskalewicz 1986; Webster, 1982).

Despite these reforms, the health of the Polish population and the
efficacy of the health service appeared to have deteriorated over the
1970s. Although in some ways the gap between the rhetoric of free and
universal health care and the reality of its practice diminished (as in
opening to individual farmers the socialized health sector), in many
more ways the disparity grew. The only way in which individuals
could recognize the gap between rhetoric and reality was, however,
through their own personal experiences. There were no critical studies
published in the general press assessing the seriousness of problems

with health care, even though systematic research was conducted as early as 1967–69 (see Rychard, 1987b). A public sphere first had to be created for the problem to be addressed openly.

The development of a health crisis

In May of 1979, a group of doctors, whose names are still not publicly known, wrote a report for KSS–KOR on the state of hospital care. The report was designed to move the authorities to devote more resources to health care. It was made available in KOR publications and sent to leading figures who could have an impact on changing national priorities (Lipski, 1985: 293–99). This report also indicted the increasingly apparent stratification of health care, with the elite enjoying their own special health-care facilities. The most notable of these elite centers was the government clinic in Anin, near Warsaw. The investment cost of one hospital bed in this privileged center cost nearly thirteen times more than that for a bed in a more common hospital (Lipski, 1985: 295). Not only was there an elite level of health care, but an increasingly impoverished one too. The supply of drugs available to the public was so poor that doctors had to ask patients' families to find drugs on their own (Lipski, 1985: 295).

KSS-KOR wrote to Marian Śliwiński, minister of health and social services, urging him to arrange for better medical supplies. If not, KSS-KOR would arrange, in alliance with the Church, help from abroad and distribute medicines independently of the authorities. KOR never managed to secure this alternative distribution network due to the rush of events that shortly followed. Lipski (1985: 299) is generally skeptical about what KSS-KOR accomplished with its activities, suggesting that it was "next to nothing in this area, apart from alarming public opinion."

Some medical experts believe that the KOR report overstated the crisis and underemphasized the significant accomplishments of the socialized health sector (consultants 5, 22). It was, in the words of one, "hysterical, not accurate." But the alarm of public opinion that this account inspired contributed to the mobilization of other experts to provide more accurate information for public discussion. One important informational source on health conditions in Poland came from the Experience and the Future group (DiP).

DiP was mainly a professional "think tank" advocating rational public discussion of policy questions. Discussion ideally would lead to cooperation among various sectors of society and the authorities in order to resolve social problems (Świdlicki, 1982: 150). Essentially, DiP sought to create a public sphere without initiating political opposition. One of its working groups was devoted to health problems.[4]

In Soviet-type societies, the initial stages of any kind of self-organization rely on personal networks established from work and private life. Personal trust, not common class interest or organizational affiliation, provides the initial basis for independent organization, as the formation of the DiP health commission illustrates. This group was formed between October and December of 1980.[5] Jerzy Zieliński, a journalist who edited the science section in the periodical *Problemy*, contacted several people in 1979, but not until after Solidarity's formation did the group organize formally. Several members were reportedly "skeptical" that any independent group could be effective. The formation of Solidarity changed their mind. The self-organization of workers appeared to be an essential prerequisite to the public organization of independent medical experts. Zieliński contacted Piotr Krasucki, a physician expert in industrial medicine, and Magdalena Sokołowska, trained as a physician but then a medical sociologist. Both were active in medical research and policy analysis and knew each other from the 1950s, when they worked together in Łódź. They in turn relied on their own personal contacts to invite other prominent physicians and medical researchers to join the group. The Solidarity experience would leave a legacy of far larger informal networks, but in the initial stages of self-organization, networks remained very small and local. The common element of membership in this commission, besides some specific professional expertise, was Warsaw residence and personal acquaintance acquired in work or friendship networks. Otherwise, their identifications were quite different. Sokołowska, for instance, belonged both to the party and to Solidarity; Krasucki belonged to neither; other group members illustrate the diversity in identity further.

Henryk Kirschner and Jan Kopczyński, two epidemiologists from the Warsaw Medical Academy Institute for Social Medicine, were known for their scientific independence and expertise, not their militance. Kirschner even belonged to the party until the declaration of martial law. Bacteriologist Kazimierz Piekacz was also a member of the party and identified most closely with it within the group. Jerzy Serejski was a specialist on adolescent health in the Department of Occupational Health, and a member of the official organization Association of Friends of Children (*Towarzystwo Przyjaciół Dzieci*). He also had worked with Sokołowska in Łódź in the 1950s. Zbigniew

Religia would later become the first surgeon to perform a heart transplant in Poland. Despite recognition of his expertise in the field, his activism and outspokenness on medical matters had prevented him from finding a position in Warsaw altogether. Stefan Klonowicz, a demographer and editor of the journal *Zdrowie Publiczne*, was originally trained as a physiologist and physician in the army. He had been interned by the Russians for eight years, and in 1968 was prohibited from finding work in medicine on the basis of his Jewish origins. At that time he turned to demography. Marian Miśkiewicz, the closest of the group to the Catholic Church, and in 1988 vice director of the Institute of Cardiology, in 1980 worked in the Ministry of Health and played a central role in obtaining important data for their study. Mariusz Stopczyk, a cardiologist specializing in technical equipment, was also an activist in Solidarity.

The DiP Health Commission was therefore somewhere in between Solidarity and the authorities. Some of its members belonged neither to the party nor to the union; some belonged only to the party or only to the union; some belonged both to the party and the independent union. Most in this health commission were members of the union, but officially there was no connection. The authorities were nevertheless suspicious of the group. Although Solidarity's very existence contributed to the organization of all independent groups, the authorities kept surveillance on this commission; the same consultant who noted this also emphasized that nobody ever was punished for their participation in this group.

This commission's experience is illustrative of the character of self-organization in Soviet-type society generally. Self-organization must begin with personal networks united around some socially identifiable issue. Self-organization is thus fragile, given its size, but resilient, given the strength of the bonds uniting the group. The very existence of self-organization suggests the limitation of official organization, however, and therefore exists as a criticism of official practices. Any kind of self-organization is thus risky. Self-organization might be tolerated, but it will be subject to surveillance and arbitrary repression if there are no power resources or formal recourse with which self-organizers might defend themselves.

The final product of the commission's work, "Health and Health Protection of the Polish population," was the only DiP report to have been published officially in Poland. It was published in April 1981 in the *Życie i Nowoczesność* section of the Warsaw daily, *Życie Warszawy* (DiP, 1983). This was the first time such a report appeared in a legal public press, and not in a medical journal or underground publication. This publication was made possible also because of personal networks: one of DiP's leaders, Stefan Bratkowski, was still editor of that section of the paper.

The KOR and DiP reports were the beginnings of new levels of medical information in the country. Shortly before martial law, the Ministry of Health through Janusz Indulski published its own critical piece in the journal *Zdrowie Publiczne*. The 1980–81 alternative press also carried more impressionistic reports on the medical crisis in the country. Even after martial law, the underground press has continued to disseminate information on the country's state of health. Two publications stand out: part IV of *"Pięć Lat po Porozumienia – Raport Stan Kraju"* (Five Years after the Agreement – Report on the State of the Country) by *Niezależnej Samorządony Związek Zawodowy "Solidarność"* (NSZZ *Solidarność* = Independent Self-governing Trade Union – Solidarity) and the periodical *"Zeszyty Niezależnej Myśli Lekarskiej"* (Notes of Independent Medical Thought).

These publications show how the "publicity" of civil society was extended in the health sector. These publics were to a considerable degree local, however. One of my Gdańsk consultants (no. 24) stated that at least half of his physician colleagues never heard of the DiP report. Instead, relying on less systematic data, local physicians issued publications to discuss their problems in and proposals for health care. For the first time, they were able to acknowledge publicly shortages of medicines. They thus began to create a public sphere in which "private" medical problems were made public. Without such publications we could not understand the severity of the health crisis that faced Polish society at the end of the 1970s. This nationwide medical emergency, and its public discussion, provides an essential context for understanding the relationship of physicians to Solidarity.

Although Gierek's reform of the Polish economy and health-care system theoretically was designed to improve the health of the population, the consequences of this transformation contributed to the mobilization of health-care workers against the authorities. One of the first paragraphs of DiP's (1983: 488) analysis sums it up: "Theoretically, Poland should be a healthy society: our health was to be secured by a free of charge and universally accessible health service concerned with both treatment and prevention. But we came to feel long ago that such was not the case: neither the health of the population is good, nor does the health service function properly."

According to the DiP report, while the latest economic crisis began in the mid-1970s, the crisis in health care began long before that. The socio-economic crisis, of course, magnified health-care difficulties, but, there were already problems because

> (1) nearly 6 million peasants became covered by free medical care while the health service budget remained at its previous level; (2) the administrative division of the country was changed, annihilating many organizational structures of the health service; and (3) the health service was reorganized (so-called Integrated Teams for Health Care were introduced), perhaps with the intention to counter-act the effect of the first two factors. (DiP, 1983: 489)

Funding levels have always been a problem, but adding to the caseload put added stress on an already overworked system. This was especially obvious in terms of investments. Hospital construction was especially inadequate: about 60–70 percent of all medical and social institutions were constructed before World War II (DiP, 1983: 498). Mental hospitals were particularly archaic, with only 15 percent of them constructed after World War II (Sokołowska and Moskalewicz, 1986). The amount of time it takes to construct hospitals is illuminat-ing: the 1985 Solidarity report (p. 102) stated that the average time of hospital construction in Poland is 10 to 15 years, while in England only 2.5 to 4 years. For obvious reasons, therefore, the Gierek reforms highlighted the increase in number of beds. Most of the increases in the number of hospital beds resulted from the reorganization of existing facilities either through renovation or simple increased crow-ding, however. Because of the lack of new investment, the space allocated each bed was reduced in this period; "the 'official' bed includes six square meters of space per patient, but in reality only three or four square meters are allocated – so that there are three beds where there are supposed to be two. The corridors of provincial hospitals are so crowded with beds that it is difficult to move trolleys through" (Russell-Hodgson, 1982: 186).

In 1981, one doctor wrote to the ministry to complain that in the town of Gliwice in Silesia the hospital conditions made it impossible to treat patients: the hospital was over 100 years old; there were only 300 beds for an average of 550 sick people, necessitating that the ill wait two or three months for a bed; the sick were even lying in corridors, moved from place to place as required. The doctor estimated that there was a shortage of 1,200 beds (Choina, 1981). In Warsaw, it was estimated that there was a shortage of 5,000 hospital beds. In Gdańsk, the ratio of beds to the population had declined to 1945 levels by 1981 (Sokołowska and Moskalewicz, 1986). In one of the hospitals I visited, two physicians (13, 14) complained that Poland's hospitals were more like "medical museums" than modern health care centers. Heat and air conditioning were poor, if they existed at all. But it was not just a matter of comfort. Hygiene levels were inadequate, and overcrowding was just one reason. Their most poignant example was that the same elevator was used to carry food, the sick and the dead, thus enhancing the chance for infection.

The horrendous state of medical care was a frequent theme in the press during 1980–81. One article in *Tygodnik Solidarność* presents a particularly powerful example of this crisis in hospitals. In a small 20,000-person town, the size of the local hospital was far from adequate – for several thousand women of child-bearing age the maternity ward had only twenty-seven beds, and only one bathroom. But what is worse, in the course of a day, the water worked on average for only ten minutes. Often after operations, one could not wash one's hands because there was no water. Through these conditions, fourteen children died in June 1981 alone. The authorities kept on putting off closing the hospital with promises that there would soon be enough water for hospital use (Wywrich, 1981). Medical supplies were also drastically inadequate, including everything from bedpans to artificial kidneys. Drugs were in very short supply as well; in 1977, about 280 drugs were in short supply, and 68 of those were completely unavailable (DiP, 1983: 500); by 1982, there were shortages of about one-fourth (500–600 items) of the items covered by Polish Pharmacopoeia (Sokołowska and Moskalewicz, 1986).

Not surprisingly, these adverse conditions in health care have had an impact on the nation's health. Mortality rates for adult males deteriorated between 1965 and 1981, increasing by 15 percent for those in the 23–43 age group, by 35.3 percent for those in the 35–44 age group and by 34.7 percent for those in the 45–54 age group. In the second half of the 1970s, the average chance for women's survival even worsened: in 1976 by 0.1 years, and in 1977–79 by increments of 0.4 years in each year (DiP, 1983: 490–91).

Although all physicians have been distressed by the trends in the population's health, and universally dissatisfied with the existing allocation of resources, several problems in health-care delivery are a result of the behavior of physicians themselves. For instance, physicians prefer to live in cities than in the countryside. As a consequence, the allocation of physicians per 10,000 population is geographically distorted and some areas suffer for it. The city of Szczecin, for instance, has about 42.3 physicians per 10,000 population, but in the most rural province of Siedlice, there are only 9.0 physicians per 10,000 population (Sokołowska and Moskalewicz, 1986). Of course, this is not a problem peculiar to Poland, but common to industrial and industrializing societies alike. Nevertheless, in this period several physicians asociated with Solidarity proposed to both national and rural local governments changes in their activities that could attract more physicians to the countryside (Mackiewicz and Skrzypek, 1981). Another problem derived from physicians' behavior is their "technical" orientation toward health care. Polish physicians, as physicians in other industrial societies, accord the greatest prestige to those working in the most complex worksites and employing the most sophisticated equipment. In 1980, 70 percent of all Polish physicians had advanced medical degrees (Webster, 1982: 310). As a consequence, not only do rural health-care centers suffer, but so do primary health-care centers in cities. There is a shortage of about 5,500 physicians in these units. Given the working conditions, it is not surprising that it is difficult to attract physicians to work in these places. On the average, a physician attends eight patients per hour, while each patient must wait on average two hours to see the doctor. As a result of understaffing in these settings, physicians must devote approximately half of their time to non-professional activities (Sokołowska and Moskalewicz, 1986). Thus, while the declining health-care facilities and health standards of the Polish population inspired many physicians to anti-systemic activity, the answers to the problems were by no means simple nor universally recognized. In the following discussion of physicians' relationship to Solidarity, this will become readily apparent.

There is one additional contextual feature essential to understanding the relationship of physicians and health care to Solidarity: their place in the power relations and logic of distribution of Polish society. Although improved wages for health-care workers were supposed to be part of Gierek's reform of health care, and the crisis in health care was a central reason for the rebellion of the health sector, the personal privilege allocated Polish physicians, and indeed all health-care employees, remains at the bottom of the wage scale and a central part of the story.

Physicians, power and privilege

Official statistics for personal income are misleading. This is not because they are intentionally falsified, but because (1) goods in a shortage economy are allocated on the basis of administrative distribution as much as on the basis of actual purchase; and (2) individuals acquire purchasing power through means other than official wages. Physicians in particular have other possibilities for acquiring personal privilege. It is, nevertheless, a valuable exercise to consider official income for two reasons. First, some physicians, like radiologists and anesthetists, rather than surgeons, do not have much occupational control over scarce goods and services which they could exchange for their desired goods and services. Hence, for these physicians, income is a relatively good indicator of the consumption potential. Secondly, officially reported income statistics are social facts on which public discussion and discontent are focused. When representatives of an occupation complain about the social status of their constituency, they will refer frequently to income statistics.

The official wages for postwar Polish physicians have always been low. Even at the beginning, the authorities assumed that physicians would be compensated for their services by their clients beyond the earnings provided in the state sector (consultant 17). The physician's administration of health care in the countryside before World War II was conducted on an informal basis in which peasants compensated doctors with agricultural products. This is at least how it is perceived today. In addition, the model for pre-war Polish physicians was the hero of Stefan Żeromski's 1901 novel *Ludzie Bezdomni* (Homeless People), Dr Judym. He was the model of selfless sacrifice for the health of his patients. The combination of these factors, the assumption that medical treatment would be "tipped" and that the model physician was a self-sacrificing missionary rather than privileged professional, helped justify giving physicians low wages.

In the 1970s, despite the reform, physicians still suffered relatively low wages. Although physicians' earnings are higher than the average, and exceed the wages of middle-level personnel like nurses substantially, they do not exceed the average in the nationalized economy substantially, and especially the industrial-sector average. Without supplements, they earn about the same as a mechanical engineer. But while they earn about the same as a mechanical engineer, they do not have the same possibilities for bureaucratic advance to especially privileged positions that engineers do. The physician in 1980 earned on average only 38.5 percent of the 1979 average wage of a factory director in industry (table 9.1). But while the physician's possibilities are limited that way, the physician always has the possibility of taking on extra work. That possibility is not always

Table 9.1. *Average net monthly earnings of physicians, middle-level health-care personnel, mechanical engineers and the average in the national economy and industry (in złotys)*

Occupation	1975	1980
Physicians	6443	8774
(without supplements)	5539	7529
Middle-level personnel	2904	4260
(without supplement)	2848	4211
Mechanical engineers		7832 (in January)
Average	3783	5789
in industry	3981	6181

Sources: Rocznik Statystyczny Ochrony Zdrowia (1981: 190–91); Rocznik Statystyczny (1981: 163, 170).

appreciated, of course, as Wilczyński's comments above showed. Despite the possible resentment, as table 9.1 indicates, doctors rely substantially on extra wages from overnight duties, assistance and overtime. Most physicians also hold more than one job. According to surveys of physicians' opinion conducted in 1976 and 1977, only 37.4 percent of physicians attending a special course in Warsaw held just one job; 48.9 percent of that sample worked in two places and 11.7 percent worked in three or more places (Łabanowska, 1978: 135). If we consider the potential for earning extra income, it seems that physicians are potentially a rather privileged lot, despite the statistical data.

Indeed, that is the way the Polish population saw it before the Solidarity movement, too. When a sample of the Polish population was asked in 1969 why young people decide to become physicians, 66 percent believed it was the material benefits accompanying the position and 27.2 percent mentioned authority, while only 16.6 percent thought it a calling, 9.2 percent a sense of generosity or social service, and 3.1 percent because of the work being interesting (Kurczewski and Solarz, 1972:9). When this same sample was asked about what profession they would like their son to pursue, most chose physician (23.8 percent). The only other occupation to even come close was the engineer, with 20.1 percent. Their reason for selecting a physician's career? Over half of them mentioned the social benefits for society, but 47.9 percent also mentioned a physician's earnings (Kurczewski and Solarz, 1972: 39).

While the population seemed to think physicians live quite well, the

Table 9.2. *Proportions of physicians reporting financial difficulties,
according to age and bureaucratic rank (in percentages)*

	Age			Rank		
	<35	36–45	>45	A	B	C
Financial difficulties	58.2	41.9	36.6	44.1	43.3	47.2
of these serious difficulties	35.2	22.2	17.5	19.7	24.5	28.9
Total	91	203	114	114	157	142

A = Kierownik w organizacji i zarządzeniu służba zdrowia (director in
organization and management of health care)
B = Kierownik lekarskie (medical director)
C = Non-managerial
Source: Łabanowska, 1978: 196.

physicians themselves do not. According to Łabanowska's data,
physicians, especially younger physicians, evaluate their material
situation rather negatively. Of those physicians under thirty-five years
of age, 58.2 percent reported having financial difficulties, and 35.2
percent of that group reported those difficulties serious (Łabanowska,
1978: 195–96). The proportion reporting difficulties with their finances
declined with age, but it did not decline substantially with attaining
higher bureaucratic rank, thus supporting my previous argument that
bureaucratic advance is not as important for improving financial
standing among physicians as it is among engineers (table 9.2).

Earnings also differ substantially depending on the sector in which
the physician works. Salaries are as much as 1.25 times greater in the
countryside in order to encourage more physicians to work there
(Webster, 1982: 311). Employment in factory health-care services is
also better paid and entitles the physician to the perquisites of
productive-sector employment. The best money is to be obtained in
private practice. It is impossible to estimate just how many physicians
have private practices out of their homes, but cooperatives are better
documented: in 1981, cooperatives employed about 3,000 physicians
and provided about 4–6 percent of all outpatient specialized services
(Sokołowska and Moskalewicz). Although there are no systematic
data detailing the number of physicians in private practice or their
incomes from it, some research on private practice suggests both that
private medical practice is frequently used by the public and can be
prohibitively expensive.

Indulski and Rzepka-Koniarek (1982) found that nearly 70 percent of those employed by the state used a variety of health services in the past two years, including regional clinics and workplace health facilities. Over half of this group saw private physicians. Only 12.2 percent of the employed find socialized health care good enough, and only 1 percent say private medical care is worse than the socialized sector. But nearly two-thirds of the employed report that private health care is too expensive. Given this widespread use of private health care, and the fact that it can be prohibitively expensive, it is reasonable to argue that some physicians make out quite well in the logic of distribution. One of my consultants (no. 24) was a member of such a private cooperative in 1988; for each housecall, the physician received 2,300 złoty and the manager of the cooperative 450 złoty for coordinating it. This fee is greater than the bonus received by physicians for night duty at the hospital and about 7.5 percent the hospital physician's monthly salary. The lucrativeness of private medical practice affects only that group of physicians who belong to a private practice. We have no idea what proportion of physicians do this and thus no idea as to how well, in general, physicians fare in the logic of distribution. It seems that the general public suspects that physicians are quite well off, while many physicians find themselves to be inappropriately compensated.

The gap between interesting and highly paid work is one of the frustrations that frequently recurred in my interviews. All of the Polish physicians with whom I spoke were familiar with the privileged status of American physicians in which interesting and well-paid work are combined. Polish physicians took that as their point of reference. Not surprisingly, Polish physicians feel relatively deprived, even if the public is skeptical of their deprivation.

Physicians' participation in Solidarity reflects these problems of privilege. While physicians were at least partially motivated to join the union out of frustration with their material compensation, they could not put their own demands for better compensation to the forefront of their protests for two reasons. First, they were not organized as a professional group, but as a corporate body including nurses and other medical staff in the union's medical section. Because physicians enjoyed much greater levels of privilege than nurses and others, they could hardly press for the same wage increases as those who made a fraction of what physicians did. Secondly, since the population viewed physicians as a rather privileged profession already, if physicians' wages demands were put to the forefront of their proposals, they would have lost the support of workers and others whose allegiance was necessary to the medical section's success in bargaining with the authorities. The health levels of the population had to be put to the forefront in negotiations if the medical section was to achieve any success in their other demands.

The particular place of physicians in Polish power relations also clarifies their activities in Solidarity. Among professionals, the authority of physicians is least easily usurped by political or bureaucratic elites, and the independence of physicians from political controversies relatively greatest. One of my respondents (no. 6) stated that one reason she went into medicine was for its independence from politics: "whether dictatorship or democracy, the work will be the same." Although *nomenklatura* exists at various levels, in that the local party exercises veto power over the selection of docents and professors in academies and chiefs of clinics and departments in hospitals, the degree of negative selection for promotions is less extreme here than in other places.

Physicians are nevertheless highly dependent on the authorities for the fulfillment of their professional projects, unlike journalists, writers, actors and other intellectuals. The physician needs the cooperation of the state sector to provide for medical equipment and medicines (consultant 11). Indeed, the relationship between the Ministry of Health and physicians can be quite a cooperative one (consultants 1, 5, 17). But it can also be quite threatening: there are boundaries of acceptable behavior which, should physicians cross them, could put them and their clinics in serious jeopardy. The consequences range from a lack of cooperation to dismissal to the elimination of whole clinics. This general picture can be clarified with a consideration of the problems associated with one physician activist (no. 18).

In 1980–81, this activist was chair of a regional branch of the Solidarity health commission in Warsaw. After martial law, she remained on the Church Health Commission sponsored by Primate Józef Glemp. In 1983, she and a team of physicians tried to visit twenty political prisoners in Kwidzyn whom they heard were beaten. The prison authorities refused to allow the physicians into the prison. The doctor learned, however, that some of the prisoners were so badly beaten that they were in a local hospital. She went to the hospital on her own and not as a member of the commission, and subsequently published findings on these prisoners. In response to her activities, the authorities closed down her ninety-bed ward in a regional hospital. Shortly after, they reopened the ward and invited her staff, but not her, to return. In solidarity, her staff of ten physicians refused to return without her. One thousand physicians signed a petition of protest; 5,000 signatures were collected in that region on one Sunday morning on another petition. All of this was to no avail: she was now on the blacklist for *nomenklatura* positions. This was confirmed when she applied for an advertised position as head of a department at the Warsaw Medical Academy. Not only did she receive the support of the physicians there, but she was also the only applicant. The authorities, rather than hire her, decided to cancel the opening of this clinic. Instead, at the time of the interview, she worked in an outpatient clinic.

These developments took place after the imposition of martial law; they are, however, illustrative of the place of physicians in the power relations of Polish society. There are real boundaries which physicians cannot cross if they want to continue to be "successful" in their medical practice. And, more often, they are too tired to cross those boundaries anyway, because they are frequently working more than one job.

The health section of Solidarity organized around these occupational concerns, as well as the more general problems with health care. Individually, physicians and other health-care personnel could do little to challenge the system, given their place in the system of power relations. They had to organize in alliance with workers in Solidarity. Physicians recognized that an alliance with the self-organized working class was necessary to minimize their dependence on the authorities. Power relations are thus prominent in the discursive consciousness of physicians. But some power relations are more prominent than others.

There is limited gender consciousness in Polish society despite the fact that women are doubly exploited: by the state in their workplace and in the disproportionate responsibility women have for work at home. Women are reluctant to discuss their domination by men. The feminist question is considered something "typically American" and not relevant to the struggle that Solidarity waged. Health care and the health section in Solidarity illustrate patriarchal relations very well, but must be understood in the context of the health sector's feminization.

There are more women employed in Polish health care than men. This is especially true among pharmacists, dentists and lower-level personnel (table 9.3). There are so few men among nurses that the number of male nurses is not even reported in official statistical

Table 9.3. *Registered health-care personnel, and gender*

Occupation	1960	1970	1980
Physicians	28708	49283	67780
Proportion women	38.4%	47.6%	51.9%
Dentists	9316	13611	17879
Proportion women	78.0%	81.3%	81.4%
Pharmacists	7924	12298	16359
Proportion women	73.9%	80.7%	85.0%

Source: Rocznik Statystczny Ochrony Zdrowia (1981: 181).

yearbooks. The dental profession was already a feminized occupation before World War II, with over half of dentists being women in 1921. But pharmacists were not overwhelmingly female before the war; in 1921, only 16 percent of them were women (Sokołowska and Moskalewicz, 1986). The feminization of the pharmaceutical profession has been, therefore, quite dramatic (Dziecielska-Machnikowska, 1966). Because more women apply to medical schools than do men, the proportion of physicians who are women would be even greater were it not for the legal requirement that equal numbers of men and women be admitted. In 1982, 7,267 women applied to medical schools, while only 4,372 men applied (Sokołowska and Moskalewicz, 1986). Despite this feminization and the sector's low wages, the prestige of physicians remains considerable (chapter 7). But how is this relevant to physicians in Solidarity?

More women played a leading role in the Solidarity medical section than in any other branch of the movement. Its principal leader was a woman, Alina Pieńkowska; women were among its leading activists; one-third of those who signed the final agreement between the government and the health section of Solidarity were women. Despite this representation, this was not the "feminist" section of the Solidarity movement. There was a systematic silence on feminist questions in 1980–81 reflected even in the organization of the health section itself. To the extent possible, I shall make this theme prominent in the narrative account of the health-care section's activities that follows. But this is a difficult theme to raise, precisely because most activists claimed it to be a "non-issue."

Solidarity and the health sector

A 24-year-old nurse and Free Trades Union activist named Alina Pieńkowska was the leading figure of the Solidarity health-care movement. She was one of those who convinced Wałęsa to reject the initial agreement between the strike committee and shipyard management and to declare the solidarity strike that laid the foundations for independent trade unions (Singer, 1981:219). Pieńkowska, along with the Gdańsk physician, Barbara Przedwojska, composed the comprehensive set of demands for health care that was included in the original twenty-one point Gdańsk agreement (consultant 12). Pieńkowska was also one of three women on the original eighteen-member Gdańsk inter-enterprise strike committee and was later elected to the coastal regional board of Solidarity (Jancar, 1985: 174). She eventually chaired the medical section of Solidarity.

The Gdańsk agreement was a substantial document. Its twenty-one demands covered many of the grievances of the Polish population, but none were so detailed and informed as demand number 16 concerning health care. This set of demands is all the more incredible, given the speed with which it was composed and the conditions in which it was produced. The general demand was "to improve working conditions and the health services so as to ensure better medical protection for the workers," and it was agreed that

> It is necessary to increase immediately the resources put into the sphere of the health services, to improve medical supplies through the import of basic materials where these are lacking, to increase the salaries of all health workers, and with the utmost urgency on the part of the government and the ministries, to prepare programs for improving the health of the population. (See Brumberg, 1983: 291–92)

These demands, as well as the later activities of the health section of Solidarity itself, illustrate the particular position of the health-sector workers. Demands for their own benefits were always linked to improvements in health care. The thirty points of the sixteenth demand in the Gdańsk agreement concerned improvements in the working conditions and remuneration of health-service workers as well as the improvement of the health-care delivery system itself. This linkage of personal demands to universal goals is, of course, not peculiar to these health-sector employees. Most groups couch aims in universal terms, but this strategy becomes more important to the degree a group is dependent on others to help realize its goals. In what follows, I should like to illustrate the dependency of health-care employees on workers in Solidarity.

In August, health-care units organized their own enterprise committees and registered with and sent delegates to the inter-enterprise strike committee in Gdańsk. The Gdańsk Medical Academy, Cefarm (a pharmaceutical enterprise) and the Joint Provincial Hospital all registered and sent delegates. Both the Integrated Health-care Complex no. 2 and Regional Railway Hospital were without delegates, but they too registered with the inter-enterprise strike commission. Interviews conducted by Gdańsk sociologist Marek Latoszek and other researchers in 1980 shed further light on the composition of these groups.

Many of the nurses in the affiliated health units were married to the striking shipyard workers, thus reinforcing organizational solidarity on the basis of primary social relations formed through kinship networks. Nurses were always present on enterprise committees, although physicians were in the majority. Together, physicians and nurses comprised 68 percent of the enterprise committees for the Regional Railway Hospital, Provincial Hospital and Integrated Health-care Complex; just over one-quarter of the enterprise committees were nurses and 40 percent were physicians. Women held a comfortable majority (nineteen of twenty-five) on these committees. The mean age of all committee members was 34.9, higher than the typical factory activist. Only one person in this group had belonged to the Polish United Workers' Party, although every person but one had belonged to the old trade union. Only three of these unionists held any official position in the old union. None of the six delegates sent to the inter-enterprise strike committee by the Provincial Hospital and Medical Academy were party members, and only half of them had been members of the old trade union. Four of this group of six were physicians and four were male. These delegates were also older than those on the enterprise committees, with a mean age of 43.7 (table 9.4).

From the beginning of the Solidarity movement, therefore, it appears that both physicians and nurses were prominent in self-organization. Women were more likely to appear on enterprise committees, but they were underrepresented, given their overwhelming numbers in health care. Although organized, health-care sector strikes were virtually non-existent. Throughout the sixteen months of Solidarity's existence, the only mass strikes of workers in the health sector were very brief strikes in the pharmaceutical industry and among workers who transported blood and medicine. Even during the strikes in the tri-city area in August, health-care workers functioned as usual

Table 9.4. *Occupation, age, gender, party and old union membership and officialdom in the health-care committees*

Occupation	Age	Gender	Party	Old union	Official in old union
The Regional Railway Hospital:					
Enterprise committees:					
Lab. technician	43	w	no	yes	no
Physician	40	m	no	yes	no
Nurse	25	w	no	yes	no
Chef	47	m	no	yes	yes
Physician	29	w	yes	yes	yes
Attendant	35	w	no	yes	no
Physician	28	w	no	yes	no
Physician	29	w	no	yes	no
Nurse	35	w	no	yes	no
Provincial Hospital:					
Physician	53	m	no	yes	yes
Physician	38	m	no	yes	no
Physician	50	w	no	yes	no
Nurse	45	w	no	yes	no
Statistician	45	w	no	yes	no
Physician	43	w	no	yes	no
Technician	30	w	no	yes	no
Nurse	23	w	no	yes	no
Nurse	28	w	no	yes	no
Integrated Health-Care Complex no. 2:					
Nurse	29	w	no	no	no
Physician	28	m	no	yes	no
Technician	36	w	no	yes	no
Nurse	46	w	no	yes	no
Pediatrician	28	m	no	yes	no
Not employed	?	w	?	?	?
Technician	39	w	no	yes	no
Delegates to inter-factory strike commission:					
From provincial hospital:					
Physician	52	m	no	yes	yes until 3/80
Physician	45	m	no	yes	no
Midwife	45	w	no	yes	no
From medical academy:					
Docent physician	55	w	no	no	no
Asst. physician	29	m	no	no	no
Technical writer	36	m	no	no	no

Source: unpublished research by Marek Latoszek.

except in the occupied plants where health personnel were on round-the-clock duty. In this period, as well as later, health-care workers in virtually all units showed their solidarity with the strikes by hanging state flags in their workplaces and wearing ribbons and armbands with Poland's national colors. Later they wore Solidarity badges. This resistance to strikes is one important source of health-care workers' dependency on the working class, however, and can be illuminated by a more detailed consideration of the developments in health-care politics in 1980–81.

At the signing of the Gdańsk agreement, it was announced that a meeting between health-service workers and the government would take place in September.[6] Before negotiations were to take place, the medical section of the union had to be organized in order to ensure proper representation. Further, a more complete and specified list of demands from all the sectors of the health services had to be formulated. Organizing and discussions took place throughout the country. Each medical organization had its own enterprise commission (*komisja zakładowa*); these organizations in turn would elect a regional body (*terenowa komisja zakładowa*); a nationwide presidium would be elected from this to serve as an executive body (consultants 25, 26). In Gdańsk, for instance, 300 representatives of various medical institutions from the province met at the Gdańsk Medical Academy in the first week of September (consultant 24).

On September 13, Vice-minister of Health and Social Services Józef Grenda came to the coast and met with representatives of these health-care workers. About 400 postulates were assembled and presented to him (Gmaj, 1980). Later that month, the first national meeting of medical-section activists took place in Gdańsk, at the club "Ster." At that meeting, a thirty-person committee was elected to conduct negotiations with the minister of health and social services. Various working groups were established to deal with alcoholism, self-government, the *Izba Lekarska*, basic health care and other issues. From the discussions throughout the country, some 4,000 demands and postulates were assembled. The negotiators for the health section requested a meeting with the ministry. They waited through the end of the month without a reply.

On September 16, the Gdańsk inter-enterprise strike committee had already protested the delays of implementing the wage increases already negotiated. They were especially slow in the smaller enterprises and service sectors. On the 29th of the month, the new National Coordinating Commission of Solidarity declared that there would be a warning strike on October 3. They struck at noon in solidarity with the demands expressed by the employees of the health sector, transport, internal trade, fire protection and the gas industry (Holzer, 1984: 116–18). On October 7, the second national meeting of health service workers was held in Gdańsk. After the session was opened by Wałęsa, Alina Pieńkowska chaired the discussions. The activities of the Gdańsk leadership and implications of the strike were discussed. Most of the discussion, however, centered on the health legislation suggested by the Ministry of Health and Social Services. They decided that it was unreasonable and not fulfilling the intentions of the original agreement. Especially objectionable were the wage increases the bill offered.

The bill (resolution 81/80 in the Council of Ministers) offered a 700 złoty per month raise for health-service workers after October 1. That was objectionable for three reasons. As the free Saturday issue for the larger union, the size of the raise was decided without negotiating with the health-sector representatives of Solidarity, symbolically rejecting their representative capacity. Secondly, the wage hike was inadequate, since even with the wage hike the average health-service worker's wage was still less than the national average. Thirdly, it offered those who earned least in the health service the same as those who earned the most. When talks were finally held in Gdańsk and Szczecin with representatives of the ministry on October 16–17, the medical section made the following offer: for workers making up to 5,000 złotys per month, there should be a 2,000-złoty raise; for those earning 5,000–8,000 złotys per month, a 1,500-złoty raise; and for those over 8,000 złotys per month, a 1,200-złoty raise.

The authorities' representative in Gdańsk, Vice-minister Grenda, was authorized to agree only to wage increases as stipulated in the original bill. In Gdańsk, therefore, the negotiations were postponed. In Szczecin, at the request of the authorities' representative, Minister of Health and Social Services Marian Śliwiński, the wage demands were left to the end of the negotiations. The unionists agreed, and one after another representative of the various branches of the medical section presented their very specific demands. Finally, they came to the issue of wage demands. Szczecin activists had been in contact with Gdańsk people, and were prepared to press for the same wage demands. They pressed for the same, and got the same answer as Gdańsk the day before: even the minister of their department could not sign any agreement that had wage demands that exceeded those allowed by resolution 81/80. He said that to change that agreement was beyond his responsibility. No agreement was reached, but they agreed to continue talks at a later date, this time, however, with one government body and one union committee. The health sector would no longer be regionally separated in their negotiations.

Wages were the chief stumbling block in negotiations, and one of the central concerns among health-care workers. But they also enjoyed support outside their occupational circles. One technician from the Szczecin shipyard said after the October 16–17 meetings,

> We in the shipyards are aware of the situation in which the whole health service finds itself . . . The nurse has enough wages only for the price of food, and about the ward attendant's salaries, there is nothing more to say. Then I ask: how could it be in a socialist state where the highest value is the person? When the ironworker arrives to work in the hospital and gets 16 złotys per hour, while he can earn in industry at least 22 złotys, there is a practical reason for the difference: the hospital cannot strike. We workers, we know what is necessary in order for the health workers to work well. (Semprich, 1980)

In the next round of negotiations, such support from workers in large industrial complexes would be critical to negotiations. For the moment, it was mostly symbolic and reassuring.

On November 5, a meeting of delegates from health-service groups from throughout the country was held in Gdańsk. Negotiations with the government began on November 6. Vice-minister Grenda represented the authorities, and the thirty-member presidium of the union represented the health-care workers. Alina Pieńkowska was their chairperson. Before the talks could even begin, the unionists demanded that three doctors, unjustly fired, be allowed to return to work. Grenda signed a letter authorizing their rehiring. The next thing they moved to was wages. Again, Grenda was not authorized to negotiate, and requested that they wait until the next day for Minister Śliwiński to arrive. Discussions were resumed the next day at ten o'clock in *Herbowa Urzędu Wojewódzkiego*, the office of the provincial governor in Gdańsk. The talks began with an appeal by J. Wasilewska, whose eloquence was amplified by a one-hour solidarity strike by transportation workers in the tri-city area as well as in Slupsk and Lublin (Holzer, 1984: 131). The following is a fragment of what she said,

> We want to be spokesmen of all citizens in our country, whom in our daily work we accompany in their births, lives, and deaths. We want to speak in the interests of: the youngest members of our society who

are often given birth on hospital carts or stretchers because there are not enough hospital beds for women in childbirth, and who are threatened by death or dangerous diseases because of the disastrous epidemiological conditions prevailing in our hospitals; all those patients who are not admitted to the hospital for a shortage of hospital beds despite the fact that they suffer from diseases dangerous to their lives; those who are incurably ill and cannot find a place where they can die with dignity; all those patients who are crowded in corridors and halls and have to lie on carts, mattresses spread on the floor, and broken canvas chairs in our hospitals; those patients who are exposed to death because of a shortage of cardiac drugs, drugs necessary to cure dangerous infections and drugs which prevent sudden cerebral hemorrhage; those who are old, lonely, crippled or invalid, dependent upon social welfare; all the members of our society who are being systematically intoxicated as a result of the pollution of the natural environment; the middle rank and lower personnel in our national health service, who are the worst paid employees in our country, and have to work under extremely bad conditions, with a permanent shortage of personnel, often without the essential things they need to perform their duties; finally on behalf of those who are burdened with a great responsibility for the health of their patients and who are helpless in their justified protest against so miserable working and living conditions (translated in Sokołowska, 1982: 102–3)

Before the discussions even began, the unionists asked Śliwiński what he was empowered to offer them in terms of wages. The workers had learned that the scope of the negotiators' authority was key to successful negotiations. Śliwiński replied that all he could offer them was an increase to 790 złotys, a 90-złoty-per-month wage increase ("Telefonogram z Gdańska" 1980). With that news, talks were called off again.

The unionists faced a dilemma. On the one hand, it appeared necessary that some kind of collective action would have to be pursued to pressure the government to move. On the other hand, a strike by the health workers posed several dilemmas. According to Magdalena Sokołowska (1982: 99–100), "health workers did not consider a strike (of theirs) to be a proper form of protest. In Polish social consciousness, health service is a public service of a humanitarian nature and its people cannot stop working regardless of their motives." The only time in the entire postwar history of Poland that medical workers struck was the Warsaw nurses' strike in 1963, when they struck for "higher pay, better working conditions, and a higher vocational status." Morality is not the only factor discouraging a strike by health-care workers. Such a strike would only hurt and alienate their patients who are, as producers, the critical allies of the health-care workers. A strike certainly could not hurt the authorities, since they had their own health-care facilities and personnel, and these personnel were not organized by Solidarity. A survey conducted by the *Ośrodek Badanii Społecznej* (OBS) found that most (77 percent) of the Mazowsze region too felt that health-care workers directly caring for the sick should not have the right to strike ("Z Prac OBSu," 1981). A strike by health-care workers would not only go against the wishes of society, but it could endanger an already tenuous relationship. This relationship between society and the health service was not entirely positive. Health-care personnel were not the most qualified workers in Poland. In a communiqué, Alina Pieńkowska (1980) wrote, "For years there have been discriminatory payments to the health service, leading to the degradation of the health professions, negative selection of cadre, and a general decline in the quality of health care." The authorities tried to exploit this problem with personnel by associating it with the decline in health care (Kulerski, 1980). Another communiqué (Moskwa, Tymowska and Dębicka, 1980) noted as much: "The government has been disrespectful of the Gdańsk accords; workers in the health sector have been the lowest paid in all of the PRL [*Polska Rzeczpospolita Ludowa* or Polish People's Republic] for 35 years and they work in unusually difficult circumstances; the government constantly tries to manipulate public opinion so as to make the terrible state of health care the sole responsibility of the employees of the health sector. We are not responsible for this. Simple adherence to our occupational ethic will not solve problems."

The health-care section in Solidarity thus faced twin problems: it had to force the authorities to move on this question of wages, and it appeared that they would not move without some kind of organizational challenge. At the same time, the health-care workers had to be sure to preserve a good relationship with "society," for without its support, the health section's cause would certainly be lost. To strike would be risky, because the government would take this action as a perfect illustration of how health-care workers are not committed to their occupational ethic, thus demonstrating the true source of the health crisis. Thus, the health-sector workers' movement was, and indeed *had to be* one which moved first against the deteriorating conditions of health care in the society. It also had to appear that way, which would be no small feat, since one of the main problems in negotiations was over conflicting wage demands. In addition to the

Table 9.5. *Health-care strike-committee representatives*

Alina Pieńkowska	Gdańsk	Lidia Lukasik	Walbrzych
Jerzy Nowak	Poznań	Anna Grędziak	Warsaw
Henryk Marek	Gdańsk	Piotr Gmaj	Gdańsk
Michał Kmach	Bydgoszcz	Władysław Sodulski	Wrocław
Tomasz Janas	Katowice	Krzysztof Musiałek	Poznań
Maria Referowska	Gdańsk	Michał Kurowski	Szczecin
Ryszard Zając	Gdańsk	Marek Balicki	Labork

Source: "Pomost," *Biuletyn Informacyny*, 5 (November 10–11, 1980), p. 10.

problems of negotiation, therefore, there was also an active campaign in the public sphere to assure that society would support the demands of the health-care workers.

On November 7, 120 health-care representatives, along with eleven education delegates and eleven culture and art employees, initiated an occupation strike of the very building in which the negotiations were supposed to have taken place (Holzer, 1984: 131). A strike committee was formed with representatives from around the country. Only five of the fourteen committee members were from Gdańsk. Pieńkowska again served as chair of the committee, although ten of the fourteen were men (table 9.5).

On November 10, the strikers received an invitation to talk in Warsaw on the next day with Vice-minister Stanisław Mach, the person, the authorities claimed, who could negotiate the wages issue. As other workers' strikes had shown them, however, to leave the site of occupation is to assure defeat. As with the workers in Szczecin ten years earlier, the striking health-care workers wanted the authorities to come to them. One striker said, "if we were invited here to negotiations, then it is only here that we can conclude them." The strikers sent letters to the minister of health, the Sejm Committee on Health and Physical Culture, and the president of the Council of Ministers informing them of the strike and the demands. These letters, as Wasilewska's appeal, illustrated the character of the movement: (1) the wage dilemma was downplayed; (2) the threat against the government was made on the basis of solidarity strikes by workers; and (3) the unionists wanted to be sure that the country would not misunderstand their commitment to health care.

Marek Latoszek's interviews with some of the strikers addressed the issue of wages. One striker said, "[The matter of] wages for us does not mean destitution of personnel, but their presence. In order to be able to function normally we must be able to have a wage raise, which draws people to work." Another said, "the Solidarity commission dealt with wages not as a factor of the discrimination of health service workers among other trades, but as one of the important elements of personnel policy, holding back the employment of highly qualified personnel in health care." And still another said, "We treat wages as a mechanism of the quality of personnel and work, which in health services demand a cure." Their defense in pursuing this wage increase was that it would improve the personnel working in health care. But this reasoning shows why the unionists were apprehensive about society's support. They knew how society viewed the quality of the existing cadre. They worried whether society would understand that improved wages would improve health-care delivery, and not just reward incompetents.

Immediate support for the strike came from its frequent visitors. Lech Wałęsa and a team of transport workers came as early as November 8. In the following days more people came: Anna Walenty-nowicz, Jacek Kuroń, representatives from the medical academy, a group of actors, children from the State Home of Social Help, coal miners, students, and workers from the FSO car factory, the Ursus tractor plant and the Warsaw steel works. There was also international attention from journalists and a team of Japanese trade unionists. Elsewhere in the country, health workers wanted to strike to protest against the intransigence of the authorities. The union representatives remained in the building over the weekend, and on Monday issued a communiqué asking health workers throughout the country to keep working, as their representatives were striking in their name. Non-strikers could demonstrate their support symbolically, however, through wearing armbands and buttons (see *Biuletyn Informacyny "Pomost,"* no. 5).

One of the principal concerns of the unionists was that society would neither understand nor support their strike. As it turned out, no pharmacies, hospitals, clinics, or ambulances went on strike. Students in medical academies did strike, however, since they felt their inactivity did not endanger the health of the population. The authorities tried to paint it otherwise, however.

On November 7 at 2.00 p.m. in the "Old Anatomy" Building's lecture hall at the Gdańsk Medical Academy, a text in support of the strike was read to approximately 400 students. By acclamation, they decided to support the health-care commission's actions and declare an occupational strike. By 8.00 p.m. 1,200 students had occupied the building. A strike committee with representatives of various student organizations was formed. They decided that this would be a pure solidarity strike – they would not demand higher stipends, changes in curriculum or address other university matters. Given that point 16 of the Gdańsk agreement was still not realized, the students believed their strike was essential; one striker recalled that "without such pressure, 'they' [meaning the authorities] will do nothing." The students understood that their senior colleagues could not strike. The strike committee therefore decided on November 9 to continue their occupational strike until an agreement between health-care representatives and authorities would be signed (consultant 24). This was the first medical-student strike in Poland, but it soon spread.

The threat of a student strike was probably less significant than the informative role the students played in this struggle over health care's future. Students were concerned that the demands for higher wages might appear "egotistical" or selfish to the population. Tens of students from the Gdańsk Medical Academy went out to publicize the strike. They generally found support. Nevertheless, they also tried to promote the general demands of the strike, and deemphasize the demand for the increase in wages (consultant 24). Some fliers from the period did not mention the wage question, for instance; instead, the major theme, which could be found at the conclusion of most fliers, was "We want medicines and hospitals for you" ("Oświadczenia Komitet Strajkowy Studentów Pomorskiej Akademii Medycynej" 1980).

It was important to take direct initiative to inform the public about the strike. Contrary to the request in the initial strike letter, the government refused to allow the media to feature the strike in their publications. The local paper just had a small piece. As they tried to break the industrial union, the authorities also tried to undermine the independent health section. Although nobody who struck endangered the health of the population, the editor of the Szczecin paper, *Głos Szczecinskie*, admonished the students that they could help health care more by studying rather than striking. They replied that their help was essential, and that they were studying anyway ("Odpowiedni na Notatki Prasowe," 1980). The press also maliciously portrayed the students as unethical ("Obywateli i Studenci PAM-u Informują," 1980). Rumors were circulated that students were behaving "immorally" and abusing alcohol, which the students felt compelled to deny in print ("Studenci PAM-u Informują," 1980). Even more unsettling to the strikers, however, was the rumor that the authorities were going to imprison them upon the conclusion of the strike (consultant 24).

From the beginning, the authorities also tried to make the old unions more attractive. The ZZPSZ reorganized itself in September, declared its independence from the authorities and demanded a raise for its members, that it won almost immediately. Solidarity health-section activist Piotr Gmaj (1980) ridiculed the union, calling it an "old union in new clothing." The words changed, but the union did not. The proof of the pudding for him was that this "new" union declared its autonomy on orders from the authorities! The "new" union also declared that health-care workers had the right to strike if it would not endanger moral, ethical or humanitarian norms. Gmaj also found this ridiculous. How could a strike take place in health care that would not endanger these norms?

The provincial president also tried to break the strike initially, by threatening "extensive consequences" if the strikers did not leave the building. Perhaps if the strikers had not had the active support of the leading workers, what happened in Bydgoszcz later that spring could have taken place in Gdańsk. Realizing the breadth of support they enjoyed, the governor changed his obstructionist tactics and eventually allowed them the use of telephones and even offered secretarial assistance!

On November 12, Vice-minister Grenda visited the strikers. The strikers told him that they would not budge. They would hold talks only in Gdańsk. They also insisted that he arrange a nationwide broadcast of the strike and its demands. On November 13 they received a telex from the authorities stating that talks in Gdańsk could be held. Pressure on the authorities had been building. Students at more medical academies throughout the country were beginning to occupy lecture halls. By the 14th, 1,600 students were striking in other medical academies in Warsaw, Kraków, Łódź, Poznań, Białystok and Bydgoszcz ("Studenci PAM-u Informują," 1980). Workers in the Lenin shipyards and Warsaw steelworks also announced that they would begin solidarity strikes if an agreement were not reached by November 17. Finally, the appropriate authorities flew to Gdańsk and began negotiations with the strikers on November 15. By November 16, an agreement was reached, and at 7.35 the next morning, the strike was called off.

The final agreement met many of the demands of the striking workers. Retroactive raises beginning on October 1 treated workers with different salaries unequally, as the union wanted. Those earning less than 4,000 złotys per month were to receive a 1,300-złoty raise; those earning 4,000–6,000 złotys were to get 1,000 złotys; those earning 6,000–8,000 złotys, 800 złotys; and those earning above 8,000 złotys, 400 złotys. These raises were lower than what the union sought, but were nevertheless much higher than what the government had originally been prepared to offer. These wages were to be in effect until October 31, 1981, and, beginning November 1, new wage scales were to be enacted.

The agreement also settled other issues. Special raises were also to be considered for certain kinds of work. Medical academies and their employees were guaranteed additional funds. New consultations were to take place from April 30, 1981, to June 30, 1981, to meet whatever new demands over wages are formulated in the interim. Points 4, 5, 6, 7, 10, 13, 21 and 24 from demand 16 of the Gdańsk agreement were to be included in a new wage framework by November 1, 1981. It was also agreed that 5 percent of the national income was to be allocated to health-care services and 2 percent of national investment would be spent on health services, beginning in 1981. Further consultations between the Ministry of Health and Social Services and Solidarity would decide the rate at which these proportions would be increased in following years. The remaining specific propositions were to be negotiated by the two sides on and after November 25. The final agreements, concluded on January 23, 1981, created an elaborate document, entailing twenty-five additional appendices that addressed subjects including the regulation of pharmacies, conditions of employment in outpatient clinics, control over the distribution of drugs and so on.

The Solidarity negotiating team for this agreement included people from throughout the country, although only eight of the signatories were from outside the tri-city area on the coast. Given that these negotiations were taking place over an extended period of time, it was important that the negotiators be able also to fulfill their job responsibilities, hence the majority from Gdańsk (consultant 25). Pieńkowska continued as the principal representative for the health section, but Michał Kurowski from Szczecin and Tomasz Janas from Upper Silesia were also regular negotiators for the union. Two-thirds of the signatories were men (table 9.6).

Most health-service workers were satisfied with the initial agreement, but also were skeptical as to what would come of it. The most concrete and immediate achievement was, of course, the wage settle-

Table 9.6. *Solidarity signatories to the final agreement*

1. Alina Pieńkowska, Gdańsk	14. Janusz Andruszkiewicz, Gdańsk
2. Michał Kurowski. Szczecin	
3. Tomasz Janas, Region Gornoslaski	15. Bernard Hazuka, Gdańsk
	16. Władysław Milewski, Gdańsk
4. Dr. farm. Wojciech Kuźmierkiewicz, Gdańsk	17. Anna Jabłonska, Gdańsk
	18. Marek Balicki, Gdańsk
5. Barbara Przedwojksa, Gdańsk	19. Ewa Brandt, Gdańsk
6. Andrzej Rink, WKTS Bydgoszcz	20. Danuta Słomczyńska, Gdańsk
7. Andrzej Skibiński, WKTS Wrocław	21. Janina Idzińska, Sopot
	22. Małgorzata Malinowska, Szczecin
8. Ryszard Piotrowski, WKTS Gdańsk	
	23. Jerzy Makowiecki, Wrocław
9. Iwona Bielawska, Gdańsk	24. Henryk Wojciechowski, Gdańsk
10. Anna Sokołowska, Gdańsk	25. Ryszard Zając, Gdańsk
11. Artur Odrosek, Slupsk	26. Andrzej Świtek, Region Gornoslaski
12. Piotr Gmaj, Gdańsk	
13. Wojciech Kazimierkiewicz, Gdańsk	27. Marek Doraciak, Radom

Source: *Protokol Porozumienia zawartego między Komisją Rządową a delegacją pracowników Służby Zdrowia nszz Solidarność* (Protocol of Agreement concluded between the Government Commission and the delegation of workers of Health Care NSZZ Solidarity)

ment. Nurses most often mentioned this as one of the most important accomplishments of the agreement, while doctors were more interested in the re-creation of some kind of independent body, like *Izba Lekarska*, that would allow autonomous control over the practice of the profession (consultant 1).

This account of the struggle to win the agreement enables several observations on the place of the health sector in Polish power relations. The authorities were not interested in negotiating with an independent organization of health-care workers, and tried to avoid having to meet with them. They might have succeeded, too, since health-care workers were averse to striking. Had not other sectors, especially skilled workers in large factories, supported the demands of the health section, their occupational strike could have been ignored, or broken with minimal controversy. Since that support was so necessary, the health-care workers had to have good public relations, which was not automatic. Because health care had become so poor, it was conceivable that the public would not be interested in supporting a strike of "incompetent" employees. Since the health-care workers were able to conduct the strike and issue even personal wage demands in a context of trying to improve the quality of health care for the country, they were able to avoid the antagonisms between them and society that were always possible. This narrative primarily clarifies the dependency of the health sector in Polish power relations, not the position of physicians. Were many physicians organized in Solidarity? Did they form their own professional association? What led doctors to activism?

Physicians and Solidarity

The material on health-care organization and negotiations discussed above confirm that some physicians were active in the Solidarity movement. There are no nationwide data that can tell us the general extent of their participation, however. The only primary investigation during 1980–81 that addressed Polish physicians' socio-political activity was conducted by Marek Latoszek in the summer and early fall of 1980. I have relied heavily on that investigation as well as on a 1981 reanalysis of that and other material by Warsaw medical sociologist Danuta Duch. In order to elaborate upon these investigations, I also consulted physicians in 1983–84, 1987 and 1988 about those sixteen months.

The activists I consulted represented most specialities: industrial health, radiology, anesthesiology, hematology, internal medicine, pediatrics, various kinds of surgery, psychiatry, orthopedics, medical research and those who worked in outpatient clinics. Seven were men, nine women. Some of these physicians had been members of the party from the beginnings of their careers, while others had always maintained a critical distance from it. Those who joined the party (in this group universally medical researchers, consultants 1, 17, 22) presented their membership as a means for genuinely improving the health care of the system. They had worked with a revisionist model to change the priorities of the system. Every one of my consultants who belonged to the party left it, however, either in the fall of 1981 or after martial law, when it became apparent to them that the party was not interested in reaching social accord. But even those antagonistic to the party found themselves cooperating more than they would politically prefer, especially after martial law. Physicians are not in a privileged position like actors or writers, said one activist (consultant 11). They cannot boycott cooperation with the government, because it is only in cooperation with the government that physicians can perform their professional duties. Of course, they can also perform their duties outside of official boundaries. Two Warsaw activists described how in their free time they would go to a church in Old Town and administer treatment to those who had been beaten by the police (consultants 15, 16). They and others emphasized, too, how they would try to influence immoral doctors in prisons who would help engage in torture or forced feeding of political prisoners (consultant 18).

Consultants generally estimated that about 20 percent of the profession were activists and that between 80 and 90 percent of the profession belonged to the union. For, example, at the Psychoneurological Institute, 600 of 800 staff members joined the union (Webster, 1982: 312). In one medical research clinic in Lublin, about 140 out of 170 were union members, and about half of the party members belonged (consultant 1). At a factory hospital on the outskirts of Warsaw, 37 of 40 physicians belonged to Solidarity (consultant 20). In a large Warsaw hospital, about 900 employees were members of Solidarity and only about 30 stayed in the old union (consultants 7, 8, 9, 10). In both the Central Medical Academy Hospital in Warsaw and in a specialist branch of that academy outside the city, about 80 percent of the physicians joined (consultants 3, 21). In a small neighbourhood hospital in Warsaw, 13 of 15 physicians in one consultant's department belonged to Solidarity. Those who did not join the union, she (no. 23) said, were either party members or simply afraid. Why were so many physicians involved? Given the structure of the wage raises, their relative position was minimally improved even with Solidarity. Why, then, were physicians part of the union? Why did they not remain in the old union, or why did they not create their own professional association?

The "new" but old branch union tried to maintain its membership by competing with Solidarity directly. They charged that Solidarity would neglect the occupational and branch concerns of groups. In response, the health section activists responded that Solidarity won more for the health sector in the Gdańsk agreement than the branch unions won in thirty-six years ("Solidarność a Interesy Zawodowe i Branżowe," 1980). The contest between these unions became especially clear in two interviews conducted by Andrzej Mozolowski in the November 29, 1980, issue of *Polityka*. Mozolowski asked Solidarity activist and pediatric-anethesiologist Marek Kulerski and Janusz Biernacik, director of the National Commission of the "new" old union, *Związek Zawodowy Służby Zdrowia*, about their unions and the potential for cooperation between them. Biernacik believed that there could be cooperation, but charged that Solidarity did not want it. What is more, there were essential differences between the groups. His union wanted the raises to be provided in installments and to be provided across the board. Unequal wages would break down the structure of earnings and worsen health-care provision. Kulerski did not note these differences, but noted instead the hostility of the branch union toward Solidarity from the beginning. In some places they cooperate, he said, but in others the official unions try to sabotage the independent union; Solidarity naturally has to defend itself. But he did not find this challenge too surprising. The old union lost 70 to 80 percent of their membership to Solidarity.

An exclusively professional union also existed at this time, the Warsaw-based Trade Union of Polish Physicians (*Związek Zawodowy Lekarzy Polskich* or ZZLP), also called the Polish Physicians' Union (*Polski Związek Lekarski* or PZL). The character of this union and numbers involved in it are controversial. To some of my consultants, this was an honest union, filled with people who believed that the affairs of physicians could only be taken care of by physicians themselves. To others, whether its members were honest or not, the support offered to it by the authorities made the ZZLP an illegitimate means for pressing forward the needs of the profession. In practice, the ZZLP divided the opposition. The exchange between Kulerski and Biernacik clarifies this unusual response by a physician to an exclusively professional group.

For Biernacik, the ZZLP was a significant group, counting among its members some 9,000 physicians, or about 12 percent of those eligible. He emphasized further the good relations his union had with the doctors' group. Kulerski noted that Solidarity also had good relations with the union, but ultimately Solidarity was the "only one that counts" in health care. All of the physicians whom I interviewed either knew nothing about this union or found it to be elitist, irrelevant or collaborationist. Given that Solidarity was the union with whom the government negotiated the main health-care settlement, Kulerski's evaluation rings most true. But why would physicians belong to any union?

Solidarity was, of course, more than a trade union; it was also a movement for democracy and independence (Touraine *et al.*, 1983). To many of my respondents, the explanation for physicians' participation in Solidarity was simple: it was a means to express one's opposition to the system and its authorities. This kind of answer was provided both by those who were merely members of the union and by those who were its leading activists. One of the latter said: "What is the problem? It is this system, being the artificial creation of the minds of a few men, not the result of natural conditions as capitalism is. People don't work because they like their work; they work for money. This needs to be understood. The system exists simply because it is imposed by the Soviets, and that is why it remains" (consultant 12).

For all of these physicians, such a question about why one would participate in Solidarity seemed painfully obvious. At the same time, however, physicians were never before involved *en masse* in a political opposition. Indeed, physicians often enter medicine so they can avoid politics (consultant 7). But a commitment to occupational concerns forced them back to the politics of health care in 1980–81. Both the general crisis in health care and the organization of the health system moved many physicians to oppositional politics. Much as for engineers, it is useful to see this section of the Solidarity movement as dialectically constituted, gaining strength from the readiness of some politically minded physicians to join the movement, but using their own conviction and the solidarity of health-care organization to press the cautious into joining.

Declining health conditions in the country certainly made physicians sympathetic to any movement that promised to challenge the status quo. Inadequate medical supplies and poor working conditions often made it impossible to fulfill their professional responsibilities. Physicians with whom I spoke were frustrated with the deteriorating health of the population. One physician, when I asked him what the greatest satisfaction in his work is, replied simply that it was necessary. The greatest frustration? When he could not do his work (consultant 5). Physicians refuse to take responsibility for their inability to perform. Several physicians told me that they were just as good as American physicians, maybe even better, but they could not do their job because they did not have the material means to do it (consultants 3, 4, 13, 14). Given the emphasis on improving health-care delivery in Solidarity's negotiations, inability to treat the sick adequately seems to have motivated many physicians to support the union.

The solidarity in the medical system itself also encouraged membership. It was universally held by activists that those physicians who worked in hospitals were the most likely to join the union. The support and encouragement from activist colleagues would shame even the most apolitical physician into at least passive support by joining the union. Physicians in outpatient clinics, or especially in the country, where they were isolated and poorly informed of the union's progress, were much less likely to join. Morality and informal peer-group pressure thus generated the professional solidarity underlying the health sector's organization.

This solidarity within the health profession has carried forward after martial law. Very few, if any, physicians belong to the new unions (consultant 21). At a 1987 meeting of the Society for Internal Medicine, a party member said in a speech that only about 150 out of a potential pool of over 70,000 physicians belonged to the post-martial law trade unions (consultant 18). Moral solidarity apparently lasts longer than its formal organization, and has remained intact in the medical community. Those who would form Solidarity belonged to government-sponsored unions before 1980; after 1980–81, even apolitical physicians boycott official organizations.

In 1980–81, activists came from different corners of the medical field, but according to some (consultants 8, 9, 10, 15 , 16, 28) they were most likely to be found among anesthesiologists, radiologists and pediatricians. The first two have the least chance to be successful in private practices, while the latter tend to have the greatest sense of a social mission. They agreed that opportunities for private-sector profits distract physicians from more public activities. Gynecologists, for example, were especially unlikely to be active in Solidarity. Internists, dermatologists and surgeons were also less likely, for similar reasons. Another suggested that lower-ranked hospital physicians, rather than chiefs or professors, were the most active (consultant 18). Family doctors were often active, but it was more difficult for them, given their longer hours (consultant 11). Another suggested that many younger physicians active in this struggle cut their teeth on independent organizing when they arranged for a visit, independent of the authorities, by the British faith healer, Clive Harris, in 1978 (consultant 17).

Most physicians preferred to emphasize morality, courage or political perspective as the decisive reason for variations in their profession's participation in the movement, however. Indeed, much like those who portrayed their struggle as one for civil society, physician activists sought to emphasize their activism as part of a larger cultural project to restore democracy and human rights to an arbitrary and inefficient system. Most of the respondents were uncomfortable with sociological generalizations differentiating across specialties. They in general rejected any demographic differentiation of the movement, reflecting the ideology of solidarism underlying Solidarity. They were especially uncomfortable with questions of gender.

The significance of gender was never raised spontaneously by any of my consultants among physicians or indeed by any of the Polish social scientists with whom I discussed the relationship of professionals to workers in Solidarity. When I asked one physician–activist (no. 25) about the significance of women's participation in the movement, she replied hastily, "what a typically American question. It is not important. It is all the same whether it is a man or woman," and so the matter was dropped in that interview. I suggested to a medical researcher more familiar with Western feminist discourse that the health section, given its overwhelmingly female constituency and the compatibility of its demands with feminism's critique of productivism and instrumentalist logic, was a pseudo-feminist movement. She replied:

> the health sector had nothing to do with feminism; the old model of the Polish woman was a professional or working woman, but in the Solidarity period the new ideal was that of Wałęsa's wife, who never worked and stayed at home with children. Solidarity was a very Catholic movement and so it was antagonistic to many feminist elements. In the Solidarity movement, and in 1980–81, all of the public meetings were filled with men, and women were standing in the lines [for food, etc.] (consultant 17).

Asked directly about gender, another consultant (no. 27) noted that as one moved up the organizational ladder of Solidarity, the representation of women declined. If we compare the strike committees of summer 1980 with the strike and negotiating teams in the subsequent six months, we find a drop-off in women's representation: in the former, women were over 70 percent of the committees, and in the latter, less than one-third. Jancar (1985: 169–70) also notes a similar pattern in Solidarity as a whole: only 7.8 percent of the 881 delegates to the fall congress of Solidarity were women. Consultant 27 acknowledged that there was some discrimination in this health-care organization, but these patterns of representation derive from the *political* evolution of Solidarity. Women are, she said, more "pro-social," while men are "political"; also, these tendencies are reinforced by the fact that men have more time: women have to take care of their children, after all. Another physician–activist (no. 28), identifying herself with "KOR," acknowledged that men were in the health section's leading positions, but justified it because women have so many other responsibilities as wife and mother. She also said that this is as it should be – women should be able to stay at home with children, and men should be able to make enough money to enable that. This gendered division of labor into domestic and public life was based primarily, therefore, on some essentialist notion of female and male character. When women became activists, this was something made "necessary" by the moment and occupation, not something that fulfilled them or enabled them to realize their aims.

A non-discriminatory self-organized movement in the health sector would have to be predominantly female, given that this sector is overwhelmingly feminized. Any movement of nurses would have to be female, given its virtually complete feminization as an occupation. Participation by physicians with certain medical specializations, as pediatrics and dentistry, would necessarily involve more women. But there was no commitment to ensuring women's representation. Women were less underrepresented at the lowest levels, but as one ascended the organizational hierarchy, the rate of woman's participation declined. This can be understood in light of the antipathy to feminism and the valuation of family above individual or professional identity for women in Polish everyday life.

The Polish authorities had tried to promote certain aspects of women's emancipation, in particular their employment outside the home. Feminism therefore came to be identified with leftist or communist politics. It was perceived to be in opposition to the Catholic Church's teachings that valued the family and motherhood as women's particular responsibilities. As such, "feminist" politics has been delegitimized in those circles which have elements of either anti-communist, Catholic or nationalist ideology, which virtually all informal groups do. But it is not just beliefs which undermine the feminist agenda in Polish life: the struggles against the authorities and to maintain a standard of living both undermine the possibilities for gender consciousness. The principal opponent against which most Poles struggle politically is the "authorities." To the extent that patriarchy is so deeply rooted in Polish everyday life, a struggle against sexism would undermine the solidarity that enables the self-organization of society to proceed. Thus, some female activists have told me that the "divisive" character of gender consciousness makes a feminist agenda impossible, given the current nature of struggle between state and society. Secondly, the family acquires a far more important role in Polish life, given the dependence on family networks to satisfy daily needs. Shopping, for example, occupies so much time that those who are retired from work shop for their children's families, saving them important time and energy. Women, as grandmothers and mothers, play the central role in this family network.

Thus, although women did not promote a feminist politics in the health section, their greater prominence in this section of the movement presumably had some impact on their organization and aims. Its impact was limited, however, by the suppression of any gender consciousness and the failure to make gender a significant criterion in the promotion of personnel to leading roles in the Solidarity section. Future research should consider the significance of this female participation in the health section, how it reflected the gendered character of social life in Polish society, and most importantly, how it might potentially undermine that patriarchy.

In sum, physicians were very likely to be members of Solidarity and viewed membership as opposition to a system which does not enable the fulfillment of their occupational ethic. Extensive female participation in this section derived from the sector's feminization, and not from gender consciousness. Women were active despite traditional ideology. Activists came from all corners of the profession and had various relations with the authorities previously. Some had tried to work with the authorities in the view that together they could build a better health system, while others performed their work in spite of the authorities' irresponsibility. Nearly everyone saw Solidarity as a means by which the health-care crisis might be overcome. But the answers were not so easy, despite the obviousness of their membership in Solidarity.

Solidarity health-section activities during 1981

Although an agreement was reached in January of 1981, the health section had not won all of its struggles. *Tygodnik Solidarność* continued to publicize the irresponsibilities of the authorities in health care, both as articles and letters (Kuratowska, 1981; "Nieczynny Szpital," 1981; Rosner and Krasucki, 1981; Słabisz, 1981; Wywrich, 1981). They also discussed the importance of bringing religious sisters back into the hospitals (Pajdak, 1981). They published appeals to the public, too, asking them to engage in more healthy behaviour, by drinking less alcohol, smoking fewer cigarettes, exercising more and eating better diets. Of course, they acknowledged, the health-care system is inadequate, but healthier behavior among citizens themselves could drastically improve living conditions ("Apel Lekarzy

Polskich" 1981, reprinted in DiP, 1983). The health section also sponsored several nationwide discussion forums. In Bydgoszcz on May 16, 1981, for instance, along with members of the Polish Physicians' Union, they discussed the merits of a proposal by the *Polskie Towarzystwo Lekarskie* for the reestablishment of the *Izba Lekarska* (*Tygodnik Solidarność*, 1981). There were also several other major activities undertaken by the health section.

The health section established a medicine bank (*bank leków*), which would obtain medicines independently of the government and provide them to union members. Churches sometimes distributed medicines independently or in concert with the union, but in the Mazowsze region, a central bank was located at the Warsaw Solidarity headquarters. Individuals would come to the bank with a prescription from a doctor and would receive that medicine without charge if it were available (consultant 28). The medicines that were available changed frequently (Grędziak, August 28, 1981) which sometimes led to charges of inefficiency (Bulczak, July 19, 1981). The importance of this alternative distribution network was contested, with some (consultants 21, 26) believing it insignificant and others (23, 28) finding it central. Its empirical consequence is certainly debatable, but its symbolical importance is not. This bank represented another stage of self-organization, where there would be popular social control over the import of medicines, not the authorities whose public responsibility could not be trusted.

Another major activity undertaken by Solidarity was to force the authorities to hand over existing government buildings for health-service use and to build new ones for hospitals. This occurred throughout the country. In Jelenia Góra, a ten-day occupation strike that began on January 27, 1981, demanded that a sanitorium reserved for employees of the Interior Ministry, mostly security forces, be turned over to the public health service (Ash, 1983: 142). In Warsaw, the health section found several buildings eligible for transformation: the Army Polyclinic, a Provincial Committee building, a Ministry of Health infirmary and a building operated by the Central Council of Trade Unions. The authorities replied that new buildings were sought, but military buildings could not be converted for fear of endangering the defense of the country ("Lokale dla służby zdrowia," 1981). But the union was anxious to convert buildings and even complexes designed for use by the repressive arm of the authorities. This was especially obvious in Warsaw, where they sought, ultimately without success, to transfer a complex operated by the Zomo, the special internal riot police, into use for public health (Kuratowska, 1981). The buildings chosen by the union for transfer carried a symbolic message more than a pragmatic one. Most of the activists with whom I spoke considered these building transfers relatively unimportant from a medical point of view; one even called it "desperate activity" (consultant 25). There are too many technical problems in such transfers and the construction of new hospitals and medical facilities would have been far better (consultants 24, 26). Nevertheless, the symbolic protest against a logic of distribution favoring the authorities and the coercive apparatus at the expense of public health was enough to merit the activity in many activists' eyes.

Finally, the health section was a part of the larger union, and supported its activities. Peculiar to their profession, they played a special role in potential strikes. For example, in connection with preparations for the March 1981 general strike, the Coordinating Commission of the Solidarity Health Section called on all physicians to prepare for working twelve-hour shifts ("Lekarze pracują 12 godzin," 1981).

These activities led to some important changes in the internal social relations of medicine. Some elites were replaced, notably in those places, like the Gdańsk Medical Academy, where elections replaced the government-appointed director with someone broadly popular (consultant 24). In other places, however, there was virtually no organizational consequence of Solidarity's formation (consultant 21). More important than the circulation of elites was the generation of new social ties. One consultant (no. 24) noted that as a consequence of Solidarity's very organization, he gained contact with people in other institutions whom he could not have met otherwise, enabling him now to organize letter campaigns or petitions much more quickly.

This change in internal social relations means too that the relationship of physicians to the public sphere and social conflict has changed. In 1979 physicians were afraid to acknowledge their authorship of a critical report (KOR); by the conclusion of 1981, physicians had built a network of activist physicians which has led to the creation of a new independent public sphere for medical information. The small network that enabled the formation of groups like DiP has now been replaced with much larger, heterogeneous networks that reflect the civil society organized from below. This new civil society is not of terrific intrinsic importance to the medical world, however. Civil society offers no answers by itself; it offers only the means through which answers might be found. Its significance for medicine lies primarily in the ways in which public information and coordinated pressure can be used to discover the kind of institutional transformation of health care Poland needs. This was by no means obvious.

The transformation of socialist health care

In Marek Kulerski's 1980 interview, Andrzej Mozolowski asked him what Solidarity wanted. The list included higher wages, better professional ethics, a reorganization of health care through its debureaucratization and the restoration of the *Izba Lekarska*, greater attention to ecological matters, and better public information about the national state of health. The 1985 Solidarity report also called for the elimination of inequalities in health care, the elimination of the material and social–psychological conditions which are bad for the health of society and a general improvement in the quality of health care. Health care had to become a priority in and of itself, and workers should not be treated merely as factors of production. Toward that end, they advocated higher wages, the end to *nomenklatura* in the appointments of directors, better information on medicines and a reorganization of the profession, emphasizing the free election of doctors and an *Izba Lekarska* (p. 106). Zofia Kuratowska (1987) also published in the Paris-based *Kultura* as well as in *Zeszyty Niezależnej Medycyny Lekarskiej* a similar critique of health care. These are the dominant themes in the discourse of health-care reform, but there are others too.

One of the greatest problems facing the health-delivery systems in Poland was the inadequate staffing of basic health-care facilities in cities and especially in the countryside. Many of the union activists were interested in improving these measures that had suffered such a relative deterioration over the years. Whatever its other drawbacks, Stalinist dictatorship reassigned doctors in the "broad social interest." Before Gomułka came to power, physicians were assigned to a shortage area for three to five years (Webster, 1982: 311). Now, doctors in the outpatient clinics and countryside are in especially short supply. Even preferential wages are not enough to draw them there. Some of the union activists were interested in trying to change the "specialist" culture dominating the medical profession by reversing the hierarchies of prestige in which specialist hospital work was the most desired profession in order to offset this maldistribution. Mackiewicz and Skrzypek (1981), for instance, advocated that not only should national and local authorities provide better apartments, workplaces and incomes for the rural health-care workers, but they should also promote greater occupational prestige for them, facilitate their further education and even develop a rural ideology which would make the non-urban scene more appealing. This set them at odds with most medical-academy professors, who taught their students that specialist work was the best way in which physicians could fulfill their medical callings. Essentially, the question of the renewal of basic health care was by no means a simple problem and did not enjoy a universally supported solution within Solidarity. In fact, the divisions on this issue cut across the lines separating authorities from society, with medical academy personnel on one side and the Ministry of Health and basic health-care proponents on the other (consultant 1).

Another theme, enjoying support from both Solidarity and the Ministry of Health, is the question of "free choice" of physicians. But this also presents problems and also finds its supporters on both sides of the political divide. Before Solidarity, an individual was assigned a physician based on residence and workplace. Activists in the union wanted to reform the selection of physicians so that patients would be able to choose the physician they wanted. This was attractive, since for them it was simply a "human right" to be able to choose one's own physician (consultant 18). This would also reduce the huge black market for private physicians' services, and severely limit one of the physician's main power resources. Thus, this kind of reform faced resistance from those who were making out quite well in the private sector (consultant 1). It also faced resistance by physicians who thought that it would simply overburden the caseloads of good physicians, without compensating them sufficiently for their extra time. One physician told me that it would just not be financially worth her while treating more patients if she were only to get 20 złotys per patient, as was being considered then. Certainly, that would be more than the average 7 złotys per patient physicians were receiving then without free choice, but the additional 13 złotys per patient would still not be worth her extra effort (consultant 4). The reform was still being examined after martial law, but in an almost Orwellian fashion the name has been changed from "free choice" (*wolny wybór*) to "efficient choice" (*skuteczny wybór*).

For both experts who identify with the authorities and those with society, free choice is understood in terms of the extension of medical cooperatives and even private practice. Maria Znana (1985) and Ryszard Płoński (1985) both advocate the extension of these cooperatives where physicians are both members and coowners of the establishment. More money has to be provided, however, if they are not going to go bankrupt. An extension of private practice is also being considered. One public-opinion survey found that the population is split over whether private medicine should be developed: among the employed, 31.2 percent want it to be developed further, 24.1 percent want it to be more limited, 23.2 percent want it to stay the same (Indulski and Rzpeka-Koniarek 1982). In the opinions of some physicians, free medical care was itself a problem, since people wind up abusing the system. They seek professional help for too many minor reasons. Free drugs for certain groups is also a problem, some of my interviewees suggested, especially for a poor country. People use them when they are not warranted. It was argued that the union's pressing for free drugs for all health-care employees would only aggravate the problem, and was something pressed for by nurses, and not doctors (consultant 3). For Solidarity activists, however, this was not the problem with medicines, and was another ploy used by the authorities to place the blame for inadequate medical supplies on the shoulders of nurses and doctors.

Nurses and physicians also differed over the creation of special professional groupings. One of the things some physicians wanted to create was a new *Izba Lekarska* which would govern the profession. During 1980–81, nurses objected to this, and argued that if physicians should have their own professional control group, so should they. Not even all physicians were in favor of this body, however. Some physicians were indifferent, as they saw little difference between the *Izba* and the existing Commission of Professional Control (20, 24). Others were more hostile. Another activist told me that it would simply become another elite body reinforcing the "specialist" culture in medicine and would therefore contribute to the problems in basic health care and not help them. Furthermore, it would probably be limited in its self-organizing effects, since the elite who would dominate such an organization are themselves tied closely to the party elite (consultant 1). Others supported the *Izba* on the grounds that an independent and self-governing chamber would promote greater morality in the system (consultant 25). The decline in professional ethics, one activist argues, is particularly dangerous, and thus the *Izba* is particularly important. But if it is not independent, it could become a powerful political tool for getting rid of troublesome physicians. If it is not democratic, it will become boring as all other institutions are, and anybody will want to participate (consultant 18). To the degree that it is independent, another consultant (no. 17) found it attractive in so far as it offers an opportunity for "decolonizing" the system through the creation of more autonomous groups. In 1983, the *Polskie Towarzystwo Lekarskie* submitted to the Sejm a plan for the restoration of the *Izba Lekarska*. This plan is supported by physician–activists, but one noted two drawbacks: (1) physicians working in the prisons, military and secret services are not subject to the chamber's authority; and (2) the Ministry of Health can still change the head of the *Izba* under special conditions, but cannot affect elections. On the whole, however, she recognizes these to be probably necessary compromises (consultant 18).

By and large, these differences were only matters of priority. Most supported physicians' self-organization as well as their greater influence over the administration of health care. There were differences over how that self-organization should proceed, and what the institutional transformation of health-care delivery might look like, but virtually every consultant was in favor of "decolonizing" health-care from the state. There was, however, one consultant who challenged the whole framework.

That framework was one which identified the interests of the patient with those of the physician. Solidarity activists all agreed that increasing the wages of the health sector would be good for the patient because it would improve the quality of health-care personnel and their performance at work. They also argued that reducing the work week of health-care personnel would be better for the patient because it would enable them to perform better at work. On the contrary, consultant 5 challenged, these demands were "only for themselves." Higher wages would not mean better health care – "they would work the same even if they earned 100,000 złotys per month" (three to five times their present wage). Already, he charged, physicians in Poland do not work as hard as those in the West – in the USA, he charged, they work over forty hours per week, but in Poland they work thirty-five hours at most. At one Solidarity meeting, a physician stood up and said he deserved 200,000 złotys per month because Western doctors earn similar wages, but would continue to work fewer than thirty-five hours per week. What is more, physicians escape direct contact with patients; far too many prefer research or administrative work. The problem, claimed consultant 5, was not so much that physicians do not have enough control over health care; instead, the organization of health care is irrational and physicians are not sufficiently concerned for the welfare of their patients to take the tough steps. Most physicians recognize that there are too many of their number outside of direct contact with patients. Consultant 26 noted, for instance, that only 40–50 percent of Warsaw physicians have any contact with the sick. At the same time, however, to say there is a disparity of interests between physician and patient is absolutely wrong. The reason so many escape patient care to go into research is precisely the fault of the system. If physicians were paid more, they would not be obliged to take on extra jobs and would not seek work in administration. Indeed, he suggested that perhaps Solidarity was wrong to give the greatest wages to those who were paid the least. It is "absolutely crazy" that some doctors earn even less than nurses.

While such matters of institutional reform are beyond the scope of the present work, the debates around the appropriate transformation of health care are essential to understanding the character of the alliance between professionals and workers in Solidarity. The place of physicians in the Solidarity movement illustrates, perhaps better than any other group, the sociological construction of the unity which identified this independent trade-union and social movement.

Conclusions

Much like general portraits of the Solidarity movement, most physicians portrayed their participation in the independent trade union as completely unproblematic. It was "obvious" given their common cultural commitments to a democratic and independent Poland. This strong moral community was quite real and necessary to the 500-day survival of Solidarity as a legal entity and the subsequent survival of Solidarity as a counter-culture. But alternative cultural identities are not enough to transform anti-systemic movements into agents of social transformation. Part of that self-understanding requires that the movement identify with some alternative social organization so that institutional transformation can proceed in a purposeful manner. And that alternative social organization must be connected, via some theory of praxis, with the existing system of power relations.

When moved to go beyond the ideology of solidarism, most physician–activists with whom I spoke had just such a theory of identity and social transformation. With near unanimity they supported a model of health care where physicians would be self-organized and through that have greater control over the organization of health-care delivery. Their theory of praxis required that they ally with self-organized workers in large factories because by themselves the health-care workers, much less physicians alone, would not have the resources to effect any consequential transformation. This required, therefore, the construction of an ideology suitable to the alliance, even if this ideology bore an uncertain relationship with the alternative system they sought.

Engineers' professional ambitions depended, too, on their alliance with workers. Engineers and workers were able to overlook potentially antagonistic interests by their construction of an ideology of self-management. This vision was especially powerful given that it was developed through a negotiation between professional and working classes. Health-care workers also depended on workers in large factories, but they constructed their vision of transformation without as much consultation with workers themselves. Health-care reform was a producers' prerogative. It was not the result of any informal negotiation between patients' organizations and health-care employees. It had, therefore, greater potential for reflecting one sector's interests, but could not appear that way, given the structure of power relations. Physicians could not organize into their own professional body, for this would undermine the alliance with Solidarity they needed to succeed. The health sector itself could not strike, since it had to convince workers in Solidarity that it was worthy of their support, and not itself responsible for the health-care crisis that all recognized. It had to paint its efforts as being primarily for the benefit of society's health, not for the benefit of health-care employees. The Bank of Medicine was, for example, an excellent means of demonstrating how society and health-care workers had common interests in establishing extra-state control over the distribution of medicine. Attempts to wrest buildings from the coercive apparatus for health care were also symbolically useful for emphasizing the common interests of health-care sector workers and society in opposition to the state. But the "state" was not so uniformly opposed to health-sector needs as it might be to democracy or national independence.

The Ministry of Health was perceived by several activists as an ally in certain struggles for greater resources and improved basic health care. The minister of health was a major proponent of this emphasis in health-care reform (consultant 1). In fact, according to one activist (no.17), his ministry was one of the few that seemed to be genuinely interested in trying to resolve the crisis. The institutional transformation of health care was therefore not identified so neatly with the dichotomy of society vs the authorities. "Society" was not so homogeneous, and neither was the state. But the structure of power relations was such that these cross-cutting interests could not be acknowledged. Potentially contradictory interests between patients and physicians, or elite and rank-and-file physicians, were suppressed with an effective vision that posed society against the state. This was useful for the preservation of a defensive movement, but less useful for the institutionalization of the social transformation of medicine. Of course, time was too short to evaluate empirically the possibilities of an institutional transformation of medicine from below, but, given the conflicts suggested in my interviews, there is good reason for more skepticism than a solidaristic discourse would allow. Whatever the doubts raised by this critical inquiry into the alliance between physicians and Solidarity, there was one aspect of the struggle upon which all activists could agree, and which, too, was antagonistic to the definitive character of the authorities.

All activists noted that without Solidarity, a relatively free and open discourse about the conditions of health care in Poland could not have been launched. Without the pluralism created by the workers' self-organization, the publicity of a civil society could not have been approximated. Without this openness, no adequate social transformation of medicine could be realized. But at the same time, without a field of discourse that could recognize antagonistic interests beyond those between state and society, the most difficult problems will tend to be suppressed in favor of the reproduction of an ideology fundamentally antagonistic to the principles of civil society Solidarity sought to recreate. Instead of a pluralism that recognizes the right to conflict, a solidarism which recognizes only one conflict will flourish. For civil society to be institutionalized, therefore, the state has to be brought in as a different kind of actor. The health sector's struggle for a transformation of medicine reveals the power of society united, but the impotence for the institutional transformation of a society without a state.

Part IV

Conclusion

10 Critical sociology and Soviet-type society

The Solidarity movement of 1980–81 initiated a decade of social transformation in Poland and Eastern Europe. In this volume, I have presented a sociological account of the movement at three levels: the movement in its conflict with the authorities and the system; the movement in its implications for the systemic theory of Soviet-type society; and the internal constitution of the movement in its gender, but especially its class, alliance between professionals and workers. Proper explanation of each level required some elaboration of the other levels. In this concluding chapter, I begin with a brief summary of the book's main themes in order to demonstrate their mutual dependence. I then consider what theory and research might follow this analysis, and more importantly, how that analysis might be related to the transformations of Soviet-type society yet to come. I follow the summary of the book's main themes with a brief comparison of Solidarity's 1980–81 struggle for civil society with the *perestroika* of the Soviet Union. I then consider the implications of the Soviet and Polish experience for reformulating the critical sociology of Soviet-type society. In particular, I consider how Marxism, cultural and civil-society theories, and feminist theory might approach the problems raised by this volume. I conclude with an argument for socialist–feminist pragmatism as the most useful approach for developing the critical sociology of Soviet-type society.

Professionals, power and Solidarity in Poland

Solidarity was a recent episode in a long history of conflict between Poles and communism. This is not to say, however, that Polish culture and socialism are intrinsically antagonistic. But at nearly each moment of historical alternativity, Polish cultural identity and the socialism represented by the Communist Party grew more antagonistic, from the Polish–Soviet War of 1920, to the Soviet invasion of Poland in 1939, to the Stalinization of Poland's postwar system, to the failure of Gomułka to maintain a properly Polish road to socialism, to Gierek's failed technocratic and consumerist socialism. The antagonism between nationalism and communism was finally cemented with religion. When the nation was given a new basis for self-organization, self-understanding and mutual recognition in the elevation of Karol Wojtyła to Pope, the "truth" of the Polish nation became the basis for establishing the independence of the Polish life world from the Soviet-type system. The product of that separation was Solidarity.

Solidarity can be understood in a myriad of ways. One approach builds on essentialist readings of Polish culture and Marxism–Leninism to establish Solidarity's virtual inevitability. Solidarity also can be understood as an expression of class struggle, where workers sought to gain greater control over the means of both production and consumption. The self-understanding of Solidarity activists was based on these elements too, as its own tripartite identity as trade union and movement for democracy and national independence suggests. But Solidarity should also be understood critically, not only in terms of what Solidarity supporters understood and believed, but also in terms of what they did not recognize or could not anticipate.

Such a critical sociology that recognizes these unanticipated conditions and unexpected consequences of action can be found in the Marxist interpretations of the period. In this, Marxist accounts also integrate both structural and action accounts of the movement, clarifying not only what Solidarity activists understood but also perhaps what they did not. One of the most important problems facing Solidarity was its class composition. Its base was overwhelmingly working class, but professionals were also significant participants in the movement. This alliance could have been "non-problematic" if a new emancipatory class had been formed that transcended the different positions of these groups in production. Such an argument certainly amplifies the solidaristic ideology of the movement, but it probably does not prepare the movement very well for the strains it is likely to face in the ultimately necessary move beyond self-defense to institutional transformation.

Indeed, Solidarity faced its own logic of evolution, which was established in part by the strategic decisions made by its activists and opponents. Solidarity's cross-class nationwide organization was made in response to the authorities' unwillingness to deal with self-organized actors. The party's traditional organizational hegemony and commitment to a perverted substantive rationality made Solidarity's one big union virtually essential to the movement's initial survival. But self-organization could not guarantee the movement's continued existence, given the basic antagonism retained by the authorities. In order for Solidarity to counter this aggression, it had to gain control of its milieu. For students, this meant self-management of the university; but for the Solidarity movement, whose self-organization of the working class enabled all other efforts, this meant wresting control of the economy from the authorities.

Enterprise self-management was the main form in which this effort to gain societal control over the economy was made. But it was initiated too late and in too severe economic conditions for it to provide an answer to the growing crisis both Solidarity and the authorities faced. Solidarity was obliged to move to a more political strategy, but with that the possibility for non-violent transformation ended. The authorities were not willing, nor were they able, given the constraints imposed by the Soviet Union, to tolerate a significant political change. Martial law became virtually inevitable when economic crisis could not be overcome with the self-managing transformation of Poland's economy. This does not mean, however, that Solidarity's only choices were revolution or cooptation. The very fact of their existence and survival for 500 days represents the significance of pragmatism, of strategy and learning, in the social transformation of Soviet-type society.

What lessons does the Solidarity movement provide for a theory of Soviet-type society, therefore? It suggests, first of all, that systemic change in these societies cannot be counterposed as a struggle between the "old" and the "new." The Solidarity movement was not seeking to make their society "modern" in their attempt to weaken central planning. They were attempting to establish an order more humane and more just that incorporated not only economic rationality but also greater social equality. It is appealing to think that the "new" incorporates rationality and justice, but most modernization perspectives emphasize functional inevitabilities that deny the legitimacy of what Solidarity strove to realize.

Classical liberalism recognizes this. Classical liberals did not see in Solidarity an emancipatory agent, but yet another potential barrier to the free-market system that would realize the greatest good for the greatest number of people. The self-organization of workers into trade unions violates the principles of market rationality identified by these liberals. As such, the systemic transformation they see most feasible in the 1990s is one where the state and a new class of entrepreneurs ally in the creation of another economy, one where workers can provide decent standards of living for their families only by escaping their class, or by exploiting themselves even more by working harder and in more jobs.

It is difficult for the authorities to make this transformation by themselves. Ideology certainly poses one barrier, as the postures of East German and Czechoslovak leaders through mid-1989 attest. But ideology is not all. Central planning and *nomenklatura* are fundamental instruments giving the elite their power. The vassals of these authorities also see little reason why they should risk their positions, too. As such, they resist any reform which reduces the authorities' control over the economy by doing what they do normally, avoiding decisions of consequence. This means, then, that reform becomes impossible if pursued by the authorities alone. They need an alliance with other sectors in society. One likely alliance for change is an alliance with the emergent petty bourgeoisie. Assuring resources to vassals in this new economy was one way Hungarians were able to construct an alternative to the old system after Solidarity's initial failure (Róna-Tas, 1990).

This is not the alliance most Poles think of, however. In Poland, civil society is organized on a cultural foundation where the Polish life world and the Soviet-type system are clearly at odds. When this cultural antagonism is translated into contending organizations, as it was in 1980–81, we can speak very easily of a cultural foundation for the struggle of civil society against the state, or even against the empire. This cultural foundation, while it certainly reinforces the identities of opponents, does not provide a systemic alternative in political economy, however. Nor does it assure that the cultural characteristics associated with an emancipatory civil society, especially one that assures legality, publicity and pluralism on an individually egalitarian basis, will be realized. Civil-society theories are prepared to acknowledge that a social transformation creating civil society involves cultural struggle to define the character of that alternative, but the theory is not well prepared to address the difficult political–economic questions that restoration of civil society involves.

Classical liberal economic theory is one obvious solution, especially as it is an ideological formation that arose with bourgeois civil society itself. But this theory is problematic, especially in Poland, as it offers little to the self-organized working class. Self-management Marxism is more appealing, especially in so far as it emphasizes that this form of political–economic organization addresses both concerns of economic rationality and workplace democracy. Indeed, self-management becomes the only feasible strategy for economic reform when the working class is organized and militant. Professionals recognized this too.

Professionals are normally dependent on the political authorities in Soviet-type society for their power and privilege. And these professionals can be rewarded quite well to the degree they are esteemed by their political supporters. But they are not very powerful by themselves, especially when it comes to power of relatively broad scope. Engineers in particular are obliged to the political authorities in normal times. Physicians need not be so politically supplicant, given their greater professional authority and prestige, but they are also dependent on the authorities for the delegation of medical resources. In 1980–81, however, alliances were different, as Polish engineers and physicians sided with Solidarity. While there are cultural foundations for this, the alliance was also the consequence of a change in power relations. This shift made the professional–worker alliance not only desirable but necessary, at least from the professionals' point of view.

Engineers could not make the economy more rational, nor increase their own professional autonomy from the authorities, without the alliance with workers. This was especially obvious in the move toward self-management. Engineers were among the most active in this movement and they were the ones who would be elected to new managerial positions. But this self-management was not a technocratic dream, because engineers could lead only in so far as they could convince workers, through enterprise elections, of their right to lead. Self-management is the perfect expression of this class alliance.

Physicians were also dependent on workers for the institutional reform of the medical system, but the alliance they established was less interactive than the self-management alternative promoted by engineers. Physicians and nurses designed an institutional transformation, but depended on workers' support to push the authorities to negotiate with them. The symbolic representation of this alliance could be found in the slogan "We want medicines and hospitals for you," and in the health-care workers' refusal to strike. Health-sector activists claimed to act on behalf of Solidarity and the nation, not of themselves, even though they managed to suggest a program that provided both for the interests of personnel and clients.

In both cases, self-organization could not proceed along professional lines, even while it was apparent that engineers and physicians had different concerns than workers and nurses. In both cases, professionals and workers managed to construct an organization that recognized their mutual necessity to the aims of each. Indeed, it was their own lived experience which made these actors search for a new form with which to articulate their demands for a better life. But this alliance *within* the social movement was not enough for the institutional transformations necessary to the emancipatory struggle self-organization began.

Both the self-managing transformation of the economy and the reform of health care demonstrated the importance of the state and the role of the authorities in institutional transformation. Self-management was eviscerated by the authorities in their attempt to preserve their power over the economy. The reform of health care was not eviscerated, but the struggles over its direction suggested that the state and the advocates of basic health care had more in common with each other, and perhaps with patient needs, than some influential physicians in the academy. Both attempts at institutional transformation suggested that the social movement could not succeed without some kind of alliance with the state. This, of course, is not peculiar to economic or medical reform. The state must be an active player in the creation of civil society itself.

Solidarity suggests that the cultural foundations for a civil society can be constructed from below by social movements. It also suggests that civil society can be defended in its cultural and social relations from the state by self-organization. But the *institutions* of civil society cannot be made without state intervention. Ultimately, a democratic polity, the rule of law based on civil liberties, and an independent judiciary can be made only with transformative gestures from above and below, by authorities and society. Because this civil society is constructed in a system with a socialist legacy, the economy also must be reformed with this state–society alliance.

Poland in 1989 began to move down this road, where social self-organization is combined with the institutional transformation of the state and economy. It is too early to offer a scholarly account of this transformation, although I shall conclude this volume with some observations of the summer of 1989. Because the Soviet Union under Gorbachev has been on this road of reform for a longer period, a brief look at *perestroika* might help us understand better the tasks facing the critical sociology of Soviet-type society.

Civil society in the USSR and Poland

The first valuable contrast between Eastern Europe and the USSR for critical sociology can be found in the putative origins of civil society. Soviet scholars find civil society not in historical traditions but in the modernization of Soviet society itself (Lewin, 1988). If an embryonic civil society exists in the USSR, much of the Central Europeans' historical virtue argument loses power. Instead, it reveals the very praxis Central European cultural determinism expresses. Central Europeans could not attribute civil society to the "emancipatory modernization" (Ash, September 29, 1988) the communist authorities brought them without according those authorities a greater legitimacy than the pre-war traditions the idea of Central Europe promotes.

Secondly, in contrast to Hungary and Poland, the leading force for the constitution of civil society in the USSR is in the power elite. Although there is debate about the "sincerity" of his initiatives, there is no doubt that Gorbachev is pushing for radical changes in Soviet society. The nature of those transformations is more difficult to determine, because it does not seem that Gorbachev himself knows what he is struggling for. Gorbachev is above all pragmatic, since the aims of *perestroika* change as the conditions of struggle change. A list of slogans associated with *perestroika* nonetheless includes "*glasnost'* or publicity, democratization, self-government in the workplace, social justice, human rights and respect for human individuality," as well as intensification of economic development or *uskorenie* (Lewin, 1988:112–21). Lewin finds that these slogans and the reforms they represent are but the sensible response of authorities to a nascent civil society within an outmoded statism. There have always been, he argues, autonomous groups; but, given the urbanization and professionalization of the population, they are more difficult to resist than ever.

Like those who focus on Eastern Central Europe, Lewin (1988:80) understands civil society in the USSR to be that sphere independent or relatively autonomous of the state. But, unlike in Poland, civil society is not posed in opposition to the authorities. It is linked to it by the necessity of the very institutional reforms mentioned above. The flourishing of civil society even depends on these government-sponsored reforms. With the exception of the Baltic states and perhaps the Caucusus, there are few organized forces within the civil society that could force the state to institutionalize reform, as Solidarity has. Instead, the authorities argue that they must pull back from dominating society to allow it to operate according to its own "systemic" laws.

Another important difference from Poland comes with the class motor generating civil society. Although the official discourse suggests that "everyone" must support the changes, professionals are treated as the class which must initiate the transformation in the USSR. They are the ones who have been most interested in *glasnost'* (Brown, 1987:793). Intellectuals are the ones who, through political institutions, translate the pluralism of the nascent civil society into the requisite institutional transformations (Titma, 1989). They are the ones who are most important, given the "modern scientific, technological, administrative and intellectual tasks of the reform" (Lewin, 1988:124). To this end, Gorbachev has even encouraged greater professional participation in the Communist Party (Lewin, 1988:131). Workers must also "participate" if the reform is to succeed, but their role had appeared to be acquiescence, not initiative or self-organization (Bova, 1987).

The first major step away from this working-class passivity is the strikes by miners in Western Siberia, the Ukraine and elsewhere. These workers even state interest in the experience of Solidarity, suggesting that independent trade unions are not impossible within the Soviet framework. But one major difference between settings lies in the initial Soviet and Polish reactions to independent trade unions. Where they posed only a threat to the authorities in Poland in 1980–81, Gorbachev managed to construct them as an ally in his struggle for reform. He cannot do this in each circumstance if strikes spread, however. One leading Soviet sociologist argues that such strikes are counter-productive to *perestroika*, as they involve the use of force to establish change, are "egoistic" and could spark reactionary backlash (Titma, 1989). Whatever the case, while transformation in Poland has depended on the self-organization of workers, in the USSR leading reformers argue that transformation depends on workers' willingness to participate in new political institutions. Soviet reform involves the tolerance of only some autonomous forces, therefore. But in contrast to the early days of Solidarity, it focuses on institutional transformations.

Also unlike the Polish case, Lewin (1988:133) believes these political transformations cannot involve the establishment of a multiparty democracy, or even the appearance that the party is being weakened. There should be a restoration of debate and the destatization of the party, he argues, but there cannot be the elimination of the party's leading role in Soviet society. Of course, Lewin wrote this before the establishment of the People's Congress and the constitution of the new Supreme Soviet, where independent legislators are forming a faction that is challenging the old party regulars. It seems, therefore, that even in the Soviet Union the establishment of a multiparty system cannot be ruled out. Indeed, with the establishment of civil society it becomes ever more likely.

The party sacrifices its main power resources in the creation of civil society. It reduces its control over the economy through central planning, and it loses its organizational hegemony and its claim to substantive rationality. Despite the contrary appearance, this does not mean that the party itself is being weakened. There is no question that the bureaucrats who delegate power to factory managers and to chairs of official organizations as well as those intellectual hacks who decide what is ideologically correct for the moment lose power in civil society. Factories and organizations elect their own managers and ideologies emerge from self-organization. But the party's corporate power and real substantive rationality can also grow if the economy it oversees has greater formal rationality. The party's authority can grow if its leading role is respected and legitimated, not merely tolerated for the lack of alternatives. But this transformation of the meaning of party power means an attack on the character of the ruling party itself.

Lewin (1988:132) notes this very factor as the reason why there must be pressure from both above and below on these middle levels of management and power. Vassals' own inertia is quite a considerable barrier to any institutional change. But can there be pressure from below when initiative is from above? Can civil society be formed when the members of civil society are themselves constrained from without? The answer to that question is unclear, but the point of the question is not. Most argue that the authorities *must* limit workers' autonomy so as to not stand in the way of economic reform. Others argue likewise that the authorities must limit national movements so as to avoid threats to the empire and the return of right-wing nationalists and militarists. But these alternatives also show how easy it is to get stuck in an elitism where the only way in which genuine transformation is possible is through the suppression of mass initiative.

Solidarity's experience suggested just the opposite. The more the "masses" could be involved in negotiation, the more they were able to see the reasons for compromise and caution. The "self-limiting" revolution was not imposed by the intelligentsia of Wałęsa; it was a grass-roots initiative. The breakdown of the formula came when the rank and file could see no fruits in self-limitation (chapter 3). This has important lessons for the Soviet authorities. Pressure from below cannot emerge without society's own self-organization and initiative. That self-organization must take place under conditions of complete openness and publicity, however, so that these groups themselves can understand why they must be bold sometimes and cautious at other times. Limited and distorted information produces uncertainty, which in turn increases frustration and maximizes the chance for violent conflict. The authorities must also be ready to compromise with these self-organized groups. The Polish authorities did not have sufficient autonomy for that; the Soviet authorities do.

The objection rings clear: such pragmatic learning through social movements might succeed among workers in economic reform, but it cannot succeed when if comes to such an emotional and enduring problem as conflict among nations. Civil society is itself a national project, and its promotion necessarily undermines the imperial struc- ture of the Soviet state itself. The structural divisions of civil society combined with the emotive power of national identity in Soviet society make any Soviet reform promising civil society virtually impossible (e.g. Brzezinski, 1989; Szporluk, 1988a).

I am not a specialist on Soviet nationalities, but the Poles field nearly as great an animosity for Russians as any one nationality for another. They were nevertheless able to proceed with caution for a remarkably long time. Poles' self-limitation was predicated, of course, on the threat of Soviet invasion. This limitation on emancipatory praxis, too, might be a practical limit that nationalities within the USSR use to guide their action. But the central authorities also must show to these nationalities the wisdom of self-limitation by providing the opportuni- ties for increasing autonomy within a Soviet framework.

Above all, the Soviet authorities cannot treat civil society as an instrument of state policy; rather, civil society must itself acquire the power resources that allow the state to become its instrument. Scanlon (1988) is skeptical that a civil society with one political party would enable much effective social control over the state. He is also critical of the way Soviet thinking on civil society still treats individual rights as contingent on their social relationships and the fulfillment of social duties. Finally, he argues, individual interests are so far treated as mechanisms of social control and economic development, not as ends in themselves. It is difficult to avoid such an instrumentalist character to civil society when it is not being pressured from below.

Civil society is, however, being developed from below in some

Soviet regions where nationality provides an identity for opposition. The Soviet authorities therefore face a great dilemma. If they wish reform to proceed, they must allow and indeed encourage this self-organization, based perhaps on nationality, from below. And if they want to assure that this identity contributes to a program that does not undermine reform by provoking violence, they must treat the rights and interests of civil society as intrinsically valuable. The Soviet authorities are obliged to develop an entirely new political–economic framework, in which various national civil societies are united in a federative socialist association. This, of course, will be new, but that part of the world has not been a stranger to social experimentation in this century.

Civil society is the specter haunting Eastern Europe. Whether civil society will appear is unclear. It is, however, apparent that if civil society is to form and survive, there must be a responsible state legislating institutional transformation in response to the original initiatives of self-organized social forces. It is also apparent that the particular nature of that legal compromise between state and civil society will reflect the social movements pressuring for transformation.

Different theoretical perspectives emphasize different movements. Marxists focus on class movements, feminists look toward women's movements and culturalists emphasize national movements. Although these different traditions are not sealed off from one another, they do tend to develop within their own spheres. The most fruitful kind of development normally occurs when traditions are counterposed to one another. This volume has been one such attempt to bring together these different concerns. In this conclusion, I wish to return to their separate concerns so that the implications of this study can be considered for the development of each tradition. In the final section, I bring them together again in order to consider the prospects for a socialist–feminist pragmatism.

Western Marxism

For Western Marxism, the realization of emancipatory alternatives in Soviet-type society is central to the restoration of socialism as a desirable alternative future elsewhere. Gorbachev's transformation of Soviet society, for instance, is seen as the means by which a socialist vision might regain legitimacy in Western public discourse (Shanin, 1988). Simultaneously, a production- or class-based Marxism and a real workers' socialism might also find a more vital prospect in the class struggles of Eastern Europe, because there the difference between socialism's promise and the reality of existing society is most clearly drawn (Burawoy, 1989). The class struggles in Soviet-type society might be more important to the socialist project than class struggles in capitalism. Is this the only transformation of Marxism Eastern European changes mandate?

One of the central arguments of this book has been that civil liberties cannot be treated as ancillary to the emancipatory alternative that critical sociology seeks to foster. Civil society, although founded within capitalist logic, should not be negated in socialist trans-formation. The rights of self-organization and open discourse as well as a law to which even the authorities are subject are central to the emancipatory alternative in Eastern Europe. This argument is not new, of course, and derives from the work of some Eastern European intellectuals and Western post-Marxists. But do those origins contri-bute further to the delegitimation of civil society as socialism's equal in utopia's construction? For Marxists, the origins of ideas partly define their meaning. Because these ideas have been promoted by those with more limited commitments, if not downright antagonism, to Marxism, the ideas themselves have been cast by some Marxists as reviving the bourgeois project or fostering an agenda desired by Eastern European intellectuals but irrelevant to workers and peasants.

These kinds of objections are easily dismissed by many Eastern European intellectuals. They acknowledge readily the different inter-ests and experiences of workers, peasants and intellectuals, but see their promotion of civil society as somehow transcending class differ-ences. Intellectuals, they claim, are promoting the universal interests of the nation in this new emancipatory project, for this project is different from past projects where some claimed to speak for others. Civil society theorists aim only to establish the framework which will allow other voices, including those of workers and peasants, to be heard.

Marxists counter, with justification, that formal equality in the public sphere does not make social justice. The Marxist critique of bourgeois civil society remains relevant to the project undertaken in Eastern Europe. We must ask what civil society offers to those in whose name its banner is waved. We need not, however, assume that those who articulate alternatives are themselves acting autonomously, in their "own" interests. One of Gramsci's major contributions was to emphasize how in capitalism intellectuals could but serve other classes. In Soviet-type society we have a new option, if Gouldner and Szelényi are right. Intellectuals might now speak on their own behalf. But does this mean that their wishes are inconsistent with the needs and interests of other groups or classes in Soviet-type society? Or that the vision they articulate *must* be their own class vision? This question cannot be answered *a priori*, for the universality of visions depends on the sociological conditions under which they are constructed. This is especially true for the construction of civil society.

The struggle for civil society, although typically articulated by intellectuals, might be premised on their alliance with workers. To the extent that the struggle is so defined, as it was in the case of 1980–81 Solidarity, the character of the civil society sought would presumably look quite different from a civil society that is not constructed in alliance with the self-organized working class. One of the most important components of such a civil society, as we saw in chapter 3, was the working-class right to self-organization and self-management. These are by no means necessary ingredients in constructing civil society in Eastern Europe, especially when this construction does not reflect any cross-class popular alliance. These components are, however, likely in a civil society constructed by a professional–working-class alliance.

Instead, the social construction of civil society might very well reflect classical liberalism's intellectual construct. Instead of a civil society premised on organized labor, one might have a civil society based on free markets everywhere, even in labor. This alternative, although seemingly unlikely in states formally identifying with socialism, is on some groups' agendas. Eastern European liberals have identified the alliance between entrepreneur and state as the only feasible means for escaping economic crisis. Some parts of the ruling elite seem, too, to recognize that their own survival might be premised on such an alliance (Ash, September 29, 1988), especially as Western capital and states pressure for an Eastern European transformation that legitimates their own form as the best of all possible worlds, and opens up Eastern European markets for capitalist penetration.

Although in Poland workers' self-organization makes this liberal form of civil society less likely, the Hungarian political–economic landscape suggests more immediate possibilities. Contemporary struggles to reconstitute civil society in Hungary find workers notably absent from efforts in self-organization and pressure for pluralism's reconstruction. Workers are significant as they escape from the statist system of production to other sectors (Róna-Tas, 1990), but they are not the co-forgers of an alternative vision for Hungary. Instead, intellectuals (in the Democratic Union of Scientific Workers, for example) and students (in the League of Young Democrats most notably) lead in constructing civil society by taking advantage of the openings statist liberalization generates.

Presumably, the liberal kind of civil society sought by Hungarian reformers will be advantageous to workers and peasants too, as they can benefit from the pluralism, legality and publicity this should represent. But at the same time, workers and peasants will likely not see this as something they helped to construct, nor will the construction have identified the concerns of laboring classes very well. All constitutions bear the imprint of the consensus which brought them into being (Fehér and Heller, 1983:102). To the degree civil society is constructed from above, workers and peasants will identify less with this system, and those above will consider them less important to the system. This is not only a problem of moral significance, but also of practical consequence.

One of the most important questions facing the emancipatory alternative for Soviet-type society is its political economy. Most civil-society theorists intentionally avoid this question precisely because it is so difficult, but avoidance does not overcome the barriers political–economic ignorance raises. For civil society to be constructed, some economic organization that allows a greater measure of formal rationality to return to the productive and distributive sphere is essential. But what kind of political–economic organization?

Most advocates of civil society's reconstruction recognize, even if they do not publicly acknowledge, capitalist economy's affinity with civil society. One Hungarian youth activist told me, for example, that although he himself is not a disciple of Friedman or Hayek, the struggle for civil society logically leads to the reconstruction of a political economy based on the premises of classical liberalism. Pluralism in the political and social sphere does indeed require a pluralism in the economic. The character of that economic pluralism is not obvious, however.

To the extent that Marxist and socialist accounts cannot incorporate civil society's advantages into their own reconstruction of a desirable alternative, that economic pluralism will be based on classical liberalism. The incorporation of civil society into socialist political economy does not depend only on Marxist willingness to rethink civil society's place, of course. Incorporation will depend far more on the result of the struggles of the age, as in the Polish economic reforms demonstrated in 1980–81. To the extent that workers were active in the self-management movement (which was variable to be sure), the democratic aspects of the reform were paramount. Engineers were on both sides of the question, viewing self-management as a means of increasing technical efficiency and ensuring democratization. But engineers were of that latter inclination only because of the conditions of their alliance with workers: there is no reason, in professional or national discourse, that they should be advocates of enterprise democratization. Their promotion of this truly self-managing transformation of the economy was itself a product of their alliance with workers. Self-management helped to secure what might otherwise be a tenuous link between classes. And with this ideological projection of their alliance, socialist political–economic foundations for the reconstitution of civil society were laid, even if not completed.

As this set of alternatives indicates, civil society can have very different consequences for the laboring classes. The emancipatory character of the civil society is shaped by the nature of the alliance promoting it. Civil societies constructed by class alliances between professionals, workers and peasants will be more universal than those which are a product of an alliance between professionals and the authorities. These alliances cannot be willed into existence, nor will they be determined structurally. For the conditions of alliance to be utilized, alliances must be made by intelligent and broadly informed actors.

Civil society is on the agenda for social transformation in Eastern Europe. The most important ingredient for establishing the character of that transformation is the class alliances which move it along. Marxism privileges workers in its theory, as both agents of transformation and their condition as indications of emancipation. Given that workers' contribution to the construction of civil society is central to the latter's emancipatory quality, Marxists must rethink civil society's place in their own socialist vision if only to remain relevant to the struggles and wishes of the age in Eastern Europe. The incorporation of civil society in Marxist theory will, at the theoretical level, increase the possibilities for giving a socialist face to civil society.

The principal theoretical problem facing Western Marxism in its incorporation of civil society is Marxism's continuing identification of utopia with classlessness. The only emancipatory alternative for Marxism is one in which classes themselves disappear. This need not mean some bland homogeneity, Marxists argue; it merely means that difference and pluralism will not be derived from relations of production. But what agent will ensure this form of classlessness? The typical answer has been the state, which means its domination, or elimination, of civil society.

The meaning of classlessness must therefore be reconsidered in the Eastern European struggle for civil society. Its most utopian dimensions have included an end to the division of labor, as Bahro suggested. But this basis for classlessness lends itself to ultimately vanguardist solutions, which are incommensurate with civil society's resurrection. Self-management, on the other hand, poses another means of creating classlessness. This does not eliminate a division of labor, but it provides an organizational solution to the possibilities of class exploitation by democratizing relations in production. This solves the dilemma of classlessness only within the enterprise, however, and offers no ready solution for the macroeconomic picture. Indeed, it does not tell us how the state relates at all to the economy.

Some Marxists continue to argue that a real self-management can be developed only under a strong central plan (Samary, 1988). By contrast, those like Horvat (1982) maintain that for self-management to be consequential, the plan must be reduced in significance and enterprises connected through a variety of other mechanisms, including those of the market. As the debate over the feasibility and desirability of socialist planning rages in Marxist journals (Mandel, 1986, 1988; Nove, 1987), its connection to civil society remains unexplained. Those who continue to argue against the market consider it self-evident that civil society is irrelevant to the emancipatory project; those who argue for socialist market relations find civil society a likely byproduct of this kind of reform. Also, those post-Marxist theorists of civil society who have addressed political economy at all typically find arguments along Horvat's line most convincing (Heller, 1988). Logically speaking, Horvat's macroeconomic vision of self-management seems to be more compatible with the recreation of civil society, because it emphasizes procedural rationality more than it does substantive rationality.

Self-management is not the only political–economic alternative advanced by post-Marxists as a foundation for civil society. Szelényi finds in the emergence of a petty-bourgeois class reason to believe an emancipatory alternative is immanent in Eastern Europe. Indeed, economic pluralism, not self-management, might be the most proximate economic foundation for the establishment of civil society.

This volume is not intended to argue how Western Marxism must be reconstructed in order to be more relevant to Eastern Europe. I hope merely to raise the most appropriate questions. One of the most important questions for critical sociology is to refigure socialism's relationship to civil society. The question most suitable for Marxists in this larger issue, and one of the most urgent problems facing real social transformation, concerns political economy. What political–economic reforms will most likely generate civil society with a socialist face? Until those debating socialist planning and markets place civil society at the center of their debates, these questions will not be answered, and Marxism will remain less relevant to the struggles of Eastern Europe.

I believe this volume is also relevant, however, to demonstrating that the projects for social transformation undertaken in Eastern Europe are shaped by the character of the class alliance underlying it. This will not come as a surprise to Marxists, of course. But it is not a major theme in the discourse of independent-society theorists, for there the struggle has been based on one culture against another.

Cultural identities and conflicts in civil society

In a system where the authorities simultaneously aim to control all spheres of social life and justify their intervention with claims to substantive rationality, autonomous collective identities are hard to make. Of course, any dialectic of domination and resistance generates its own antagonistic identities, but domination or exploitation by themselves do not automatically mean that identification with others similarly oppressed emerges. The residual utility of that recently much-criticized dualism, class in itself and class for itself, makes this explicit.

The organizational hegemony and substantive rationality characterizing power relations in Soviet-type society mean that autonomous collective identities are hard to form. Because the authorities sponsor organizations which cut across lines of domination and resistance, and because they repress those organizations which try to act in ways that reflect opposition to domination rather than its amelioration, expressions of collective organized resistance are difficult to mount. To the uncautious observer, these societies might then appear much as the ideology describes – relatively unified and non-antagonistic. Of course, no sociologist would make that mistake today, given the instabilities reform presents. No sociologist should even make that mistake after the demonstration of how Solidarity could form so quickly in 1980. And one would think that the experience of Czechoslovakia in 1968 would have led to a healthy skepticism about the integration of these systems. But what consequence do these changes in Soviet-type society have for the epistemology of its critical sociology?

Critical sociology has generally focused on the public sphere in economy or politics. Feminist theory rightly has challenged other critical sociologies for ignoring the power and exploitation that go on in those "private" worlds apparently based on consensus not coercion. These private spheres of oppression are difficult to penetrate, however, because very often the exploited themselves are not able or willing to acknowledge the oppression enmeshed in the tradition that binds them. Consequently, feminist theory has been obliged to take far more seriously the cultural and symbolic dimensions of domination. The study of domination and resistance in Soviet-type society also requires a cultural emphasis, but not because of the power of the "dominant" tradition.

It is, after all, difficult to establish what cultural framework is "dominant" in Soviet-type societies. There is a range of cultural "tool kits" (Swidler, 1986) within Marxism–Leninism, from Stalinism to the reformism we are witnessing presently, that actors might use to pursue their strategic interests. There is also a wider range of potential identities beyond Marxism–Leninism (with one's nation, with technology or as a military superpower) which might inform the authorities' activity. But these alternative identities are constrained to a considerable degree by the vassalage system. Unless these identities are reinforced by some kind of fiefdom, they will remain unexpressed within vassaldom. It is difficult to project on the basis of behavior within one context the likely practice of a vassal once an alternative range of action is permitted. Cultural dominance cannot therefore be "read off" the patterns of domination in the coercive power of the ruling group, in economic planning or in the party's organizational hegemony.

If one is interested in theorizing the alternativity of Soviet-type society, one must therefore attempt to discover the knowledgability of actors in their assumption of vassalage roles; in general terms, one must uncover the hermeneutic link between the intent of vassals' action and their intention in that action (Hayes, 1985; Kennedy, 1987a). All too often, theorists of independent society assume that the intent and intention of vassal action are identical; that, for instance, their intent to carry out their superior's recommendation reflects the intention to realize that goal rather than to demonstrate one's loyalty. If the theory of power relations advanced in chapter 6 makes sense, the limited exclusivity of vassal power resources makes it virtually impossible to identify in a vassal's routine practice much personal motivation other than survival. It therefore calls into question the relevance of any previous identity to vassal action in "critical situations" where there are radical disruptions of everyday routine. It also suggests that the power relations of vassalage, not the ideology of Marxism–Leninism, explains the motivation of vassals in everyday life.

Nevertheless, many independent-society theorists explain the antagonism between authorities and society in terms of an essential cultural antagonism between Marxism–Leninism and national culture. They construct neat dichotomies between cultures, but have difficulty fitting these cultural antagonisms with the social groups constituted by the power relations of the Soviet-type system. Which social group embodies Marxist–Leninist culture and which national culture?

There are different kinds of identification in each of these two culturally based groups. Some assume that "society" identifies unambiguously with the national culture. In order to translate the pure cultural antagonism into sociological categories, the authorities must become unambiguous representatives of Marxism–Leninism. Clearly this latter translation is dubious, given that the authorities' identity is not constructed by some "free" attachment to a cultural belief system, but based, rather, on a system of power relations which makes virtually irrelevant the private beliefs of its executors and absolutely central their public pronouncements. But does "society" identify so purely with a national culture either? Clearly this is also a contentious identification, for each national culture has a range of possible symbols, myths and identities around which it can form. It also has significant differences across regions and classes. Aspects of national culture are more and less apparent, too, across time. Where, for instance, does anti-Semitism fit in Polish culture? The effectiveness of this racism in mobilizing opposition to students, intellectuals and some party members in 1968 suggests an important streak in Polish "tradition." But it was precisely because of this offensive that in 1980–81 Solidarity struggled quite successfully against the resurrection of anti-Semitism (Warszawski, 1989).

Cultural studies in Eastern Europe are of limited value to critical sociology to the degree that they fail to explain the practical foundations of cultural identities and antagonisms. Often, cultural theorists attribute to Marxism–Leninism and to national culture essentialist qualities that seem to be moored more in ideas, beliefs or memory than in social practices. Idealist currents are poor foundations upon which to build a critical sociology, especially when the power relations constituting systems are themselves quite unstable. This is most apparent in the portrait independent-society theorists paint of the authorities.

If the identification with Marxism–Leninism, or a particular form of it, is mostly pragmatic from the vassal's point of view, shifts in power relations that grant to the vassal greater autonomy would lead that vassal to act in ways entirely inconsistent with an idealist determinism. Indeed, Polish managers may have maintained a facade of loyalty in the 1970s, but in 1980–81 they were able to shed quite readily their old presentation of self to adopt a new one more consistent with another frame of power relations.

Vassals acquire even greater capacity to act in new, independent ways when there is a shift in power relations at both the bottom and at the top: *perestroika* from Moscow and organization of popular fronts and independent movements in the Baltic republics have led to the creation of new party authorities that could not be predicted from past ideological affirmations. Social practices and power relations are not only useful in identifying the variability of the authorities' "culture," but also to identifying various differences and potentials in national culture.

The image we have of 1980–81 Solidarity is one of a united movement for labor, democracy and independence. This is legitimate, but only if we keep in mind that this "total" movement was *constructed*, and did not emerge *ex nihilo* out of some worker-centered, democratic and nationalist Polish culture. The primary identity for most members of the movement was one of self-organization and the rights of an independent trade union. This was very important for skilled workers in large factories, and an especially strong part of the movement's identity in Silesia. Professionals also saw the value of an independent trade union, but identified its value less for its defensive potential at the workplace and more for the institutional transformations it could foster. This professional role can be seen in the pressures for democratization, but especially in the programs for self-management and for health care's transformation.

If we were to leave the cultural realm with this conclusion, however, we might be guilty of the same essentialist mistake some culturalists commit. Working-class culture/interests and professional culture/interests might translate directly into their variable emphasis on

Solidarity's trade-union and transformative aspects; but a pragmatic (Rochberg-Halton, 1986) or practice–oriented account of culture (Ortner, 1984) would emphasize that the strategic alliance between professionals and workers also transforms the culture of each and consequently the character of the Solidarity movement they build together. Physicians' culture is a particularly good example. Polish physicians, as physicians in most parts of the world, participate in an elite occupational culture. Most of them consider their work to be of a fundamentally different kind than that of their co-workers. Their "culture" should lead them to advocate their own occupational association. While the *Izba Lekarska* was an important goal of the Solidarity movement, it was subordinated to the solidary organization of all health-sector workers. Physicians did not generally organize into their own group to press for demands that benefitted themselves disproportionately. Even within the movement, physicians supported a wage reform that benefitted them little and those more poorly paid a great deal. This practice of 1980–81 has even left an important cultural legacy with organizational consequences: before Solidarity, physicians, being largely apolitical and professional in their occupational culture, participated in official organizations; after Solidarity, their occupational culture has become far more political. Few physicians belonged to officially sponsored organizations after martial law, and a significant group of overtly political physicians kept alive the activist culture generated in 1980–81.

Classes and social groups therefore transformed, through their strategic action, each other's cultures. The organization of Solidarity also created new cultural identities. Polish culture has a legacy of cautious "organic work" and revolutionary romanticism, but Solidarity created new forms of these identities in the genuinely transformative programs of pragmatists and the cautious romanticism of the "true Poles." Both "tendencies" in Polish culture were reproduced in Solidarity, but were simultaneously transformed as each sought the means for maximizing their own radicalism within a general commitment to self-limitation.

Solidarity's organization also created new antagonistic cultures, between the "rank and file" and the leaderships of Solidarity. The leaderships of Solidarity were more "transformed" than the rank and file, as the former became simultaneously more "political" and more aware of the difficulties of negotiation with the authorities. The rank and file over 1980–81 reproduced their cultural legacy from the 1970s by becoming increasingly impatient with the failure of the Solidarity leadership to realize appropriate negotiations and by becoming more dissatisfied with their work and consumption. These different "cultures" within Solidarity were created as a consequence of the new practices allowed by the shift in power relations. But we cannot attribute to these groups differentiated by position within the movement some "essentialist" cultural difference. One of the most powerful implications of Touraine *et al.*'s (1983) work is that self-limitation in movements develops as a consequence of the analytical discussion of the possibilities for transformation. Rank-and-file workers become as "pragmatic" as their leadership when the former discuss in the same analytical fashion the very problems which led the latter to compromise and caution.

Cultural theorists of an independent society increase their relevance to critical sociology to the degree that they can establish how various symbols, beliefs and identities are rooted in the social practices and power relations of different milieus within Soviet-type society. Theorists of civil society tend to recognize this, even if they acknowledge it more in their practice than they do in their theory.

Civil-society theorists are tied closely to cultural theorists, inasmuch as the advocates of civil society find in certain cultural or historical traditions reasons why democratic civil society ought to be reborn in their own world. On the surface, these theorists appear to rely on some essentialist cultural identity, as they argue Central European history provides them with a legacy which mandates the resurrection of civil society in this imposed Eastern political economy. Although this is their apparent reasoning, they use the inevitability of history in such a way as to maximize the potential for cultural identities to be transformed into the necessary transformative vision. Instead of an evolutionist telos, the theorists of civil society rely on historical continuity for the inevitability of certain kinds of change, but, like orthodox evolutionary Marxism, Central European civil-society theorists see their own role as merely clarifying the logic of history.

Quite unlike socialism, however, this vision of civil society is not universally applicable to the world, much less to all the other Soviet-type societies. Only regions with certain historical legacies are able to generate this emancipatory alternative. The rest of the world is left to their own cultural legacies to find alternatives. It does not matter, for these theorists, what those legacies are so long as the Central Europeans can rejoin Europe. With this historicism and localism, these theorists of civil society abandon the critical sociological agenda.

Critical sociology has traditionally been defined by its commitment to uncover a praxis that would overturn existing forms of domination and help construct an emancipatory form of social organization. Although utopia has not always been so understood, in critical sociology utopia has always meant universality, where not only the citizens but also the slaves would be emancipated. It has also been understood as a form of social organization that exists nowhere, but serves as an uncompromised normative standard for critique of all existing forms of social organization. Many theorists of civil society abandon both of these commitments when they imply that its procedural universalism is relevant only to certain regions of this world and when they argue that they only seek that which Western Europe already enjoys.

These implications are probably quite useful for domestic praxis in Eastern Central Europe. To point to something which exists elsewhere is a much more powerful way of indicating the arbitrariness of extant injustice than is having to promise an alternative that exists nowhere. To argue, too, that civil society has a regional inevitability to it strengthens the commitment of its proponents, as they recognize history to be on their side. But to what extent should critical sociology be domestic? On the grounds of both scholarship and praxis, this is its greatest deficit.

In terms of scholarship, this leads to a kind of intellectual chauvinism that finds struggles in other parts of the world hopelessly naive or disingenuous. This means, of course, that one cannot penetrate beneath the level of ideological self-identification to find what in the struggles of others might clarify the meanings and potentials of one's own scholarship. This need for translation across experiences is obviously important for praxis too, if we believe that praxis is more than the negation of the oppression we suffer, involving also the positive construction of that which we seek (Lukes, 1985). Finally, to the extent praxis can avoid identification with any existing system, it can minimize the possibility that it will be manipulated for the ends of those already repressing struggles for emancipation in other parts of the world.

One of the most powerful reasons for avoiding localism is that a methodologically comparative and philosophically universal critical sociology can help to uncover those systematic silences which even emancipatory movements reproduce as they struggle. This is especially apparent with the feminist question in the Solidarity movement.

Gender and emancipation in Soviet-type society

Gender consciousness is noticeably low in Soviet-type societies. This, of course, is not the case during revolutionary struggles, when women typically challenge the patriarchal cultures which oppress them (Hart, 1989). But, as formerly revolutionary authorities consolidate their positions and move economic development and organizational hegemony to the center of their agendas, the prospects for feminist theory and practice decline (Salaff and Merkele, 1970). Although there are evolutionary trends toward greater equality in decision-making within families (Juviler, 1980), the possibilities for a more radical challenge to patriarchy within Soviet-type societies become limited.

One reason for this is that women ostensibly have been "liberated" from the private sphere and brought into the public sphere by the logic of economic development communist parties have fostered. Women's rates of employment and levels of education have closed in on men's rates, even while women remain in gendered occupational ghettoes (Jancar, 1978). It is not the "satisfaction" of public life that undermines the possibilities for gender consciousness, but rather that women have little time for the feminist organization that raising consciousness requires. Women continue to bear the greatest responsibility in the household economy (Nuss, 1984). This responsibility is even more onerous, given the lack of consumer amenities, labor-saving devices and services in the production-oriented Soviet-type economy. Thus gender consciousness is suppressed by time itself.

Time is, of course, not the only barrier to gender consciousness. Ideologically, women are at a greater disadvantage in Eastern Europe, given the cultural alternatives organizing struggle. Generally, both the Marxist-Leninist ideology of the authorities and the ideologies and cultures associated with traditional social patterns emphasize the identity of woman as defined by others, not woman as someone with autonomy to define herself. Traditional cultures are reinforced by the difficulties associated with household maintenance; the travails of shopping, cooking and other housework make kinship ties and roles even more important in everyday survival.

Finally, women do not have the organizational means by which to establish gender consciousness, even if they had the time and commitment to do so. Self-organization is itself, as we have argued throughout this volume, antagonistic to the structuring principles of Soviet-type society. Even self-organization within the party around feminist agendas has proved ineffective, as it apparently undermines the unity the party authorities require to maintain the illusion of their substantive rationality.

If barriers to self-organization are one of the principal reasons for limited gender consciousness, we should see in those periods where self-organization abounds, as in Poland in 1980–81, the emergence of a new feminism. Although there was more discussion of Western feminism (Persky and Flam, 1982:149–51), there was very limited popular movement around this vision. One of the most fertile grounds for such a movement might have been in Solidarity's health section, where women were numerically dominant and held leading positions. But feminism was not explicit.

My initial exploration of these matters suggests three main reasons. As Solidarity was developing its strength, the economic crisis was intensifying, making the reproduction of household economy all the more difficult. Because traditional gender roles were not challenged in this period, women were obliged to suppress any disruptive conscious-ness (which no doubt includes gender consciousness) in order to main-tain homes under even more difficult conditions. This applied not only to female laborers but also to female nurses and physicians. Solidarity also identified to a large degree with traditional Catholicism. The Church promoted its understanding of women as first and foremost wife and mother. This identity was strengthened all the more by the charisma of Danuta Wałęsa, Lech's wife, who appeared in public mainly as a supporter of her husband and a mother to their large family. Finally, the intensity of the struggle itself forced Solidarity to suppress even those conflicts its activists acknowledged. Conflicts of interest between regions, classes and strategies were minimized by the solidar-ristic ideology characterizing the movement. If these overt conflicts could be minimized, it is obvious that such a potent difference in a patriarchal system as that between men and women would be sup-pressed. This does not mean, however, that gender consciousness is not on the agenda of social transformation in Soviet-type society.

As civil society is recreated and institutionalized, the possibility for different and conflicting interests to be articulated within society will increase. In this sense, civil society is the precondition for the emer-gence of feminism. But civil society is not often associated with feminism, as it has always been constructed as the domain of a male citizen unencumbered by household duties (Fraser, 1987; Pateman, 1988). Although civil society has been understood traditionally as that sphere of social relations neither private (i.e. family) nor within the state, it need not remain so. Civil society is but a procedural form of social organization which allows new identities to form and sub-sequently to transform institutions in order to allow those new identities full participation and rights in social life. A strong feminist movement in civil society would probably mean that the "obvious-ness" of the distinction between public and private would fade, and new boundaries and connections be established.

Much as a strong working-class element in the construction of civil society in Eastern Europe would mean some kind of socialist political economy, a feminist social movement in the constitution of civil society would mean, too, new borders and transitions between the private and the public. The possibilities for a feminist face for Eastern European civil society seem quite remote, even more remote than for a socialist civil society, however.

One of the most important issues in critical sociology should therefore be to discover what might allow gender consciousness to emerge simultaneously with the recreation of civil society in the Soviet-type system. The economic, cultural and organizational odds are against it, but making explicit the barriers to gender consciousness is the first step towards raising that consciousness. In general, the discursive penetration of domination is a necessary first step before organized efforts to overturn it can be successful.

Critical sociology is easily contained within these three separate themes of class, nationality and gender. The most useful critical sociology would be one that facilitates the interaction of these different agendas. In this concluding section, I argue that socialist–feminist pragmatism not only offers the most fruitful vehicle for realizing a synthesis of these forms of critical inquiry, but also is quite useful for providing a foundation for the critical sociology of the Soviet-type societies we are likely to see in the 1990s.

Socialist–feminist pragmatism and the future of Soviet-type society

Pragmatism has been identified in lay discourse as a narrow, instrumentalist approach which prizes *Realpolitik* above any kind of ideologically defined or ideally motivated worldview. Given the changes facing Eastern Europe in the present, it is not surprising that most leaders and most commentators share the down-to-earth assumptions this pragmatism suggests. For instance, Timothy Garton Ash (September 29, 1988), one of the most astute Western journalists observing Eastern Europe, notes that socialism as an ideology is dead in Eastern Europe. The opposition is everything but socialist, and even the public authorities do not maintain a public facade committing themselves to socialism. But while public resistance to unlimited private enterprise is declining, according to recent public-opinion surveys (p.58), the majority of society still fears capitalism. For Ash, this is a "sad fact."

Why is this a sad fact? Certainly it cannot be because capitalism in general, and capitalist transition in Eastern Europe, is benign. But apparently this capitalism is, for Ash, the best of all possible worlds. In the lay sense of the word, Ash is pragmatic. His accounts are rooted in a normative framework that prizes the realism of rulers and assumes that the fears of ordinary people must be transcended by elites. Ash's tone suggests that it is passé and naive to vest any hope in socialism, and every hope in capitalism. Most philosophically informed pragmatists would reject such a posture, however.

The most vulgar pragmatism is one where the values informing practice are shaped more by the correlation of forces in the world than by the ideals which should inspire it. Pragmatism is about consequences, but not only those consequences defined by elites or the systems in which they predominate. Utopias were an integral part of John Dewey's pragmatism, at least. Without them, there can be no ideal that moves one against the injustices pragmatism was designed to overcome (Rochberg-Halton, 1986:3–40).

Pragmatism shares the same "final justifying ends" or "end in view" of Marxism, that of the "liberation of mankind" [sic] (Dewey, 1938[1973]). Without this normative vision, pragmatism ceases to be a theory of practice oriented toward the approximation of truth, and becomes the path of least resistance. Given that pragmatism has such a weak theory of structure, this loss of vision generates a theory which finds the possibilities shaped by the powerful and privileged not only the easiest to follow, but also the best of all possible worlds. When that happens, socialism dies. But when pragmatism remains constituted as a philosophy of lived experience informed by overarching ideals, structures, including ideological structures, are but organized habits and meaning derived from intelligible conduct rooted in a community (Rochberg-Halton, 1986). Socialism need not die if it remains tied to the alternative vision which once animated it. But socialism will die if it is not tied to a pragmatic method.

The debate between John Dewey and Leon Trotsky clarified the methodological difference essential to making socialism relevant to Eastern Europe again. Although they agreed in their "ends in view," the means to those final ends differed fundamentally. Dewey could not find any justification for Trotsky's claim that class struggle is the single means to realize this emancipatory alternative. Dewey acknowledged that it *could be*, but this means must be confirmed through the "inductive examination of the means–consequences in their interdependence" (Dewey, 1938[1973]:71). In effect, therefore, pragmatism argues that the means to realize emancipation cannot be deduced from theoretical laws, even those formed on the basis of past experience. Socialism, in so far as it is the systemic form to realize individual self-actualization, must be subject to revision too. This might involve, then, a reformulation of the place of civil society, the planned economy and even property relations in the definition of socialism. This flexibility is essential to understanding, and influencing, the future of Soviet-type society.

Even for those who do not find socialism an appealing framework to salvage in Soviet-type society, pragmatism could be quite useful to critical sociological analysis, given its commitment to evaluating theory on the basis of its outcomes. The party's substantive rationality has survived precisely by cloaking itself in a "dialectical" reality that makes irrelevant outcomes of a supposedly universal actor's programs. Pragmatism's dialectics do not allow such manipulation. Pragmatism's advocacy of procedural democracy also recognizes the utopia for which Eastern European emancipatory movements already strive. Its identification of communicative communities helps us understand the actors that strive for this democracy. Its notion of role-taking might even be useful to the emancipatory movements themselves, as it provides a means by which groups with long-standing enmities might begin to realize a greater sympathetic understanding of the antagonistic other.

This pragmatism thus might prove useful to emancipatory theory and practice within Soviet-type society, but it provides no answer by itself as to how these struggles might be incorporated in a general critical sociology. Indeed, it might help reproduce the problem. In order to avoid that, pragmatism must strengthen its historically weak utopian dimension or develop a stronger structural theory. Preferably, it might do both, not only in order to improve ties among critical sociologists across the globe, but also to understand better the likely outcomes of certain developments within a Soviet-type system.

Given that "truths" and values are always context-bound in pragmatism, the only way that struggles in Eastern Europe could inform struggles in the capitalist world system is through their explicitly common efforts. Given the bipolar world in which we have lived for most of the post-World War II era, the only contacts these movements have is as ideological nemeses. Emigrés from Communist Party-led societies are often the most committed to the policies and programs of those who dominate in the capitalist world system. The structure of this world system, where authorities in one sphere have identified with, or are identified as, the ally of anti-systemic movements in the other, works against their "pragmatic" unification. Instead, movements in the "other" world are treated as "manipulated" by one's own oppressors.

The structure of the Soviet world system also works against the construction of a common struggle on pragmatic grounds. In the USSR, "socialism" remains the aim of emancipation, but the leading force in that movement is professionals and authorities! In Poland, workers are the leading force, but they do not consider the socialism the Soviet authorities proclaim to be part of their agenda. The different structures of domination and praxis in these various Soviet-type societies, and between capitalist and Soviet-type systems, will not produce a common agenda that could link their efforts. One escape from this structural division is the construction of a utopia that is of no world, but relevant to all.

Habermas's utopia of the uncoerced and undistorted communication community is one such construction relevant to both capitalism and the range of Soviet-type societies. His "ideal society" is one where "people resolve contested issues consensually by observing procedural norms of democratic discourse, resulting in communicatively rational, voluntaristic social integration" (Antonio, 1989:734). The main problem with this, Antonio (1989:735) claims, is that because this utopia, this normative foundation, is so universalistic, "it has little substantive to say about any single context". Antonio is right, but whether the implication of this is to abandon "quasi-foundationalism" for a "pragmatic realism" is another question.

Habermas's project is not so useful for explaining the formation of social movements, given the theory's overly rationalistic and evolutionist aspects. It is, on the other hand, extremely useful for interpreting these struggles and helping to influence their wishes because it provides a conceptual vehicle for critics from different systems to recognize a universal community of interests that in the past was socialism's province. Until socialism is reconstructed so that civil society is a necessary part of its vision, socialism cannot provide a conceptual foundation upon which to build that universal interest, at least if we wish to include those who struggle in Eastern Europe in our community. The Habermasian communicative emphasis is in fact designed to reincorporate that civil society to socialism's utopia.

There is a more practical reason for Eastern European critical sociology to be more inclined toward this kind of socialist pragmatism. A too pragmatic approach to transformation in this period of East-West negotiation will lead, quite likely, to transformations directed by Western capital and by states on both sides of the old systemic divide. Because these actors have the resources to establish what is and is not feasible, pragmatists are likely to find collaboration with these actors necessary, and cooptation likely. Thus, not only should pragmatism be grounded in Habermasian utopia, but also in working-class identification.

Pragmatism was formed in politics, specifically in American progressivism. This reformist current failed in American politics precisely because it held an overoptimistic view of society's elites and a naive view of how communication could override material interests (Shalin, 1988). A self-conscious working class or *socialist* pragmatism, one that bases its experiential evaluation of truth on a power base that is rooted in the working class, will have at least one power resource as a barrier to its cooptation by more powerful actors. Indeed, where the working class is already so organized, as in Poland, this kind of socialist pragmatism will likely be inevitable as a strategy for the opposition, and as a means to interpret their achievements and possibilities.

As I write, Poland is struggling to realize political and economic reform. Solidarity has been legalized and has won in elections nearly all the seats available to it in both upper and lower houses of parliament. General Wojciech Jaruzelski has barely been elected president, and his intended prime minister, General Czesław Kiszczak, failed to survive a revolt of Peasant Party representatives. The editor of *Tygodnik Solidarność*, Tadeusz Mazowiecki, has been appointed premier. Some economic reforms have been implemented. The prices of basic goods have skyrocketed and wildcat strikes are occurring throughout the country.

By dint of Solidarity's organization in the working class, its leaders should pursue their own pragmatism in a socialist style, even if without socialist language. They strive to retain their alliance with workers through the means traditionally studied by pragmatist theory, through symbolic and discursive action. Solidarity's union leaders cannot appear too conversant with the political authorities, for fear of alienating their base. At the same time, they cannot act in an obstructionist or solely oppositional fashion, for to do so would merely guarantee the failure of the institutional transformations so badly needed for Poland's survival. Unrealistic price supports, central planning and an economy based on exclusively political rather than economic criteria have to be ended. But the alternative is extremely unclear. The alternative will have to be sought, much as Solidarity sought in 1980–81, in their own pragmatic analysis of opportunities and impossibilities, not in any ready plan. That might be why it is better to call this perspective one of socialist pragmatism, rather than pragmatic socialism. The latter implies certain definite characteristics of socialism as system; the former implies only that the means toward emancipation will be based on the struggle by those who are simultaneously most limited and most able to realize a better society in this system, and on the basis of this lived experience, should formulate the most effective means for emancipation.

Although the structure of Polish power relations suggests a *socialist* pragmatism, given working-class self-organization and empowerment, the structure of power relations in Hungary and the Soviet Union do not. Where workers are not self-organized, they are obliged to work in institutions formulated for them with resources delegated to them by others. In both Hungary and the USSR today, the highly educated are setting these conditions, and these conditions are likely to lead to a system that fits better into the capitalist world system. This is the outcome of vulgar pragmatism. Where this leads socialist pragmatism to next remains to be seen.

Although it is difficult to anticipate the outcome of the impending transformations of Soviet-type society, one dimension of its power relations remains certain. Gender will continue to structure social relations profoundly, and without significant strategic intervention by social movements, patriarchy will not abate. Indeed, it is quite possible that with the restoration of "traditional" cultures, gender relations will become more sexist.

A pragmatism that takes as its point of departure only the generalized other within Soviet-type society will not be based on feminist foundations, even if it might be grounded in socialism. In these societies, the generalized other remains overwhelmingly masculine. For pragmatism to realize its emancipatory aims, therefore, it need not only ground its theory in workers' organization, but also women's empowerment. Given the affinities feminist theory has with pragmatically informed theories, this synthesis may not prove so difficult on an intellectual level (Lengermann and Niebrugge-Brantley, 1988). But because feminist theory has not emerged strongly within either academic or public discourse, the social conditions for its link to Eastern European pragmatism are weaker. As intellectual ties between Eastern and Western critical publics grow, and as civil society is constituted in Eastern Europe, the possibilities for a socialist–feminist pragmatism, as a theory *of* Soviet-type society and a theory *in* Soviet-type society, become more real.

Soviet-type societies are in transition. As in every transitional period, the directions for change are uncertain. Some outcomes seem more likely than others. Return to the old Stalinist system seems very unlikely, while some kind of new, harsh capitalism or military dictatorship remain distinct possibilities. Despite the moves toward greater political democracy, an emancipatory alternative, one that combines economic rationality with greater freedom and equality, seems even less likely than any of the above. It becomes even less likely when that emancipatory vision is abandoned by vulgar pragmatists inside or outside of Soviet-type society. But Solidarity in 1980–81 reminded us that the realm of the possible is expanded by the innovations of practical social theorists in social movements. Critical sociology can live up to its name to the extent that it can take Solidarity's praxis as a lesson for the future, and contribute to an emancipatory alternative that is Solidarity's legacy.

Notes

Introduction

1 I use the term *Soviet-type society* to refer to those societies whose political–economic structure is modeled on the Stalinist–Brezhnevite Soviet Union. These are industrial societies with state ownership of the major means of production and an economy directed to some degree by a plan formulated under the leadership of a hegemonic Marxist–Leninist party. If the transformations undertaken in Gorbachev's USSR and other Soviet-type societies prove lasting and consequential, this term will require a new prefix to refer to the former Communist Party-led societies.

2 T. Anthony Jones (1984) identifies three general paradigms in Soviet studies: the political, political–economic and modernization. I discuss here only the first two because the last, modernization, tends to work with a more "collective" notion of power. Following Parsons (1967) and Lenski and Lenski (1987), power is conceived more as the generalized capacity to realize collective goals. Ironically, this view is quite similar to Lenin's vision of Soviet power paving the way to socialism (Lukes, 1978:638).

1 The historical genealogy of Solidarity

1 See Szporluk (1988b) for an insightful analysis of this relationship, as anticipated in the writings of Karl Marx and Friederich Liszt.

2 The Polish Socialist Party and the Polish People's or Peasant's Party–Liberation (*Polskie Stronnictwo Ludowe Wyzwolenia* or PSL–*Wyzwolenie*) were most influential. In national elections to the Polish Sejm and senate in November 1922, the KPRP received 132,000 votes, while the Polish Socialist Party received 907,000 votes. Two communist supporters (in the *Związek Proletariatu Miast i Wsi* or the Union of the Urban and Rural Proletariat) were elected to parliament, and through them the party gained some institutional influence. The entire left, however, received only 25 percent of the votes in this election; the center won 24 percent and right-wing parties 29 percent. National minority parties won 22 per cent. This conveys the extremity of political polarization in Poland at this time (Tomicki, 1983:262).

375

3 The execution of Polish communists and liquidation of their party is one of the "blank spots" the Polish–Soviet commission on history is supposed to fill in. Khruschev admitted this crime in 1956, and purged party members were reinstated. But the commission might bring new light on this. For instance, the co-chair of the commission, historian of the seventeenth century Professor Jarema Maciszewski, told Norman Davies (1988) that they have learned communists were executed and the party liquidated *before* the public announcement that these events would take place in the future.

4 During the 1950s and 1960s, Polish censorship policy forbade mention of the 15,000 Polish officers interned by Soviets in 1939 and the more than 4,000 corpses found buried in a mass grave in the Katyn Forest near Smolensk in 1943. In the 1970s, Polish censorship softened, and allowed reference to the event so long as it followed the line laid down in the *Great Soviet Encyclopedia* (see Curry, 1984:340–42). The Soviets had admitted the imprisonment of these well-educated officers between 1939 and 1941, but claimed that when the Soviets were forced out by invading German troops, the officers were left alive and the Nazis executed them in the autumn or winter of 1941. That seems doubtful, since the Poles were found buried in summer uniforms, suggesting their execution by Soviets in the spring of 1940 (Davies, 1984:452). In 1988–89, the offical Polish press has begun to reconsider the story and challenge the old Soviet version, demonstrating the significance of *glasnost'* for Poland.

5 The Western allies effectively ceded Poland to the Soviet sphere of influence. The current debate is over the amount of choice the allies had. Draper (1986) argues that unless the allies wanted to engage the Soviets militarily, there was no alternative. The Soviet Army had occupied most of Poland already. Kołakowski (1986), on the other hand, charges that Yalta's division of the world into these spheres of influence legitimated the Soviet takeover, and thus the allies should not have made the agreement even if force had decided the matter.

6 Political domination of a society can be said to be legitimate when that domination is acceptable to the population at large, and when obedience to those in power is considered obligatory or exemplary (Weber, 1978:31–38, 214–16). For a political order to be legitimate, however, it is not necessary that all members of a population view it as such. It suffices that one part of the population views that domination as valid and other parts fail to conceive of an alternative that is superior and feasible.

7 Raina (1977:146–48) does not think these events were provoked by any part of the authorities, Moczar included. In Raina's opinion the student demonstrations were autonomously generated. Staniszkis (1984a:281, 297) and Checiński (1982:225–36) see the March events as deliberate provocations, with the former believing that they were instigated by those seeking revenge for their being scapegoated at the 1956 October plenum. Whether these conflicts were or were not provocations, it is true that these disturbances were used by factions and individuals in their struggles for power in the party. Party members learned the lesson in 1956 that it is

possible to exploit social and economic difficulties in order to use social discontent in power struggles within the party elite itself. Where party control is so incomplete, as in Poland, political power is gained in the course of labelling games, portraying oneself as the hero of the rank and file seeking to eliminate the causes of problems, be they Stalinists, Zionists, or the corrupt.

8 This move to introduce a price hike less than a fortnight before Christmas has been explained as the stupidity of the authorities. It seems more reasonable to believe that it might have been a provocation by one faction. Knowing that there would be a strong reaction by the population, they might have planned to exploit the situation to gain power within the Politburo (Staniszkis, 1984a:281).

9 Roman Laba (forthcoming) has written an excellent social history of the conflicts on the coast in this period.

10 Szczypiórski (1982:80) wrote this about Gomułka: "He had the provincial habits of a poor artisan. He wore badly cut suits, smoked cheap cigarettes, ate as sparsely as a monk. He got angry at the sight of luxuries, and as luxuries he considered everything that transcended the most modest existence and the satisfaction of elementary needs. He demanded modesty from party members." Of course this is not to say that the entire leadership in Gomułka's day was as ascetic as him: "in Lansk, when they learned of his [Gomułka's] imminent arrival, an alarm would go off, and the delicacies, carpets, and some of the servants would vanish. Later, when the provincial politicos complained about the excesses at Lansk, Gomułka would cry, 'It isn't true, I was there! They serve you curdled milk with potatoes and kasha'" (Brandys, 1983:105). Gierek was something else entirely, and set the example for his lieutenants in his own conspicuous consumption. In the early 1980s, Warsaw cabarets featured satires of the abuses of the Gierek era. One of the favorites is the weekly trips made by Mrs Gierek to Paris in her husband's private jet to have her hair done at a special salon. As Niebuhr (1957) observed about second generations of religious sectarians who fail to follow the path of their forebears' self-denial, later generations of communists also seem to have less personal zeal to follow the asceticism of their elder comrades.

11 On the basis of the Warsaw Pact invasion of Czechoslovakia, Brown (1979:152) identifies these pillars as the leading role of the Communist Party, high centralization within that party, and political censorship of the means of communication.

2 The nature and causes of Solidarity

1 They included Tadeusz Mazowiecki, editor of the Catholic periodical Więź later to become the Solidarity's government's prime minister in 1989; economists Waldemar Kuczyński and Tadeusz Kowalik, later to serve as Wałęsa's economic advisors; Bronisław Geremek, a medieval historian; Andrzej Wielowiejski, a Catholic intellectual; and Jadwiga Staniszkis, a sociologist who was part of the March 1968 generation.

2 Macrocausal analysis compares historical cases with similar outcomes but different contexts in order to establish significant and causal antecedents. This style of comparative work is exemplified by Skocpol (1979), and as a method is systematized by Skocpol and Somers (1980).

3 Wright (1984:6–18), for instance, writes that Marxists consider several levels of analysis: the mode of production, the social formation and the conjuncture. The conjuncture is the least abstract and considers the relation between class and non-class relations in the context of concrete institutions and contingent historical factors. This is Woodall's interest. The social formation raises questions of how alliances between classes and class fractions becomes possible. The mode of production, however, is even more abstract and not directly accessible in empirical inquiry. It can be understood only in terms of the manifestations of its pure types. But because these pure types are not apparent, it does not mean that they are any less "real" (hence the appellation, "realist").

4 See Błasiak (1987) for one preliminary example.

5 These include Grażyna Gęsicka, Tadeusz Chabiera, Anna Kruczkowska, Ireneusz Krzemiński, Pawel Kuczyński, Anna Matuchniak, Małgorzata Melchior, Krzysztof Nowak, Włodzimierz Pańków, and Dorota Ręczek.

6 Sociological interventionism is a method of study for social movements, in which researchers enter social movements in order to help them clarify the vision invoked in their critique of domination, thereby facilitating their independent action and capacity for self-regulation. Researchers generally bring focus groups of activists together, and provide or act as an interlocuter in order to raise that group's vision (Touraine, 1978, 1984). Cohen (1982:215–16) has called this a kind of "sociological Leninism."

7 Michael Burawoy (1985) develops this term to distinguish between class relations engendered on the shopfloor and those which are derived from the mode of production itself, which are called relations *of* production. Thus, even if there is a unified class of employees that might unite against the state, within production there are still asymmetric relations that structure those who command against those who are commanded.

8 Crighton (1985:124, 125) is wrong on a couple of points: (1) professionals "specialized" only to the degree that they focused on issues related to their occupational concerns; many professionals were leaders of the trade union itself. Thus professionals *were not* specialized into their own SMOs, unless self-management can be considered a professional preoccupation; and (2) professionals *could join* Solidarity; physicians were indeed members of the union and among the most professionally self-conscious.

9 This suggests another reason why the Czechoslovak case of "competitive pluralism" differed from Poland's "consolidated pluralism" (Paul and Simon, 1982): when reform is initiated from above, and the authorities take initiative and not consolidate in defense, there are more possibilities for gaining access to political power.

3 The Solidarity movement as emancipatory praxis

1 The relationship between Solidarity and socialism is discussed in many places. Some of the best places to begin are Arato (1981), Ash (1983:226–31) and Persky and Flam (1982:127–28).

2 Pańków did not originate this list of stages; several of the participants in the research groups in Touraine's study also found similar stages. In general, there is widespread consensus in Poland that this evolutionary model fits Solidarity. There is less agreement on how to establish the alternative possibilities each stage represented.

3 Roman Laba (forthcoming) provides an especially interesting discussion of this decision, in which Warsaw intellectuals advocated centralization, and the Gdańsk presidium, Wałęsa included, favored the maintenance of a regionally decentralized movement. Laba explains the final centralized outcome as a consequence of the Gdańsk presidium being outmaneuvered. This may be true, but the structural pressures on the union to move toward national organization, suggested in the reasoning of the KOR intellectuals, was considerable.

4 In a meeting of hardline party activists in Katowice, Anton Zabiński suggested ways in which the independent movement might be weakened. One of those strategies was that the party should provoke leaders into taking action on controversial activities (Ascherson, 1982:211). Although the Naroźniak affair preceded this meeting, it is reasonable to believe that the Katowice meeting was not the first time this strategy was imagined.

5 The largest shift in opinion between 1980 and 1981 occurs with a decline in the USSR alone to socialist states in general. This presumably occurred because Czechoslovakia and East Germany were as severe, if not more severe, in their denunciations of Solidarity. The various German answers derive from the memories of World War II.

6 See Raina (1985:106–68) for a text of the Bill to Reform Higher Education.

7 The term "self-management" means the factory workforce's greater influence over factory decisions; "independence" means management's greater autonomy in deciding what and how much to produce; and "self-financing" means the closer link between workers' incomes and enterprise performance.

4 Solidarity, modernization and class

1 Even if we cannot define Marxism's boundaries, can we define the "core" of its research program, in the sense Lakatos uses these terms? Are there some core assumptions to Marxism that can enable us to discover what is more and less consistent with the Marxist tradition? Michael Burawoy (1988) suggests that three propositions from Marx's preface to *The Grundrisse* (Marx, 1859 [1970]) were central to Leon Trotsky's Marxism:

    1. At a certain stage of their development, the material productive forces of society come in conflict with the existing relations of production ... From forms of development of the productive forces these relations turn into their fetters.

2. Then begins an epoch of social revolution . . . In considering such transformations a distinction should always be made between the material transformation of the economic conditions of production, which can be determined with the precision of natural science, and the legal, political, religious, aesthetic or philosophic – in short, ideological forms in which men become conscious of this conflict and fight it out . . .

3. No social order ever perishes before all the productive forces for which there is room in it have developed; and new higher relations of production never appear before the material conditions of their existence have matured in the womb of the old society itself. (Burawoy, 1988:25)

Although these propositions may have been central to Trotsky's work, they were not shared universally by other Marxists and certainly are not commonly held today.

2 See the exchange between Kołakowski (1977) and Marković (1977) for an example of a dispute over Marxism's relationship to Stalinism. Besançon (1977 [1981]) and Lewin (1968) provide alternative views of Leninism's relationship to Stalinism.

3 For example, Kelly (1985) claims Sweezy (1980) embraces a set of Stalinist assumptions in his critique of Soviet-type society.

4 It is important to note that throughout his exile and the ever-increasing degeneration of the "workers' state," Trotsky never returned to his earlier critique of the Leninist Party. Before 1905, he criticized Leninist centralism for its wish to remain small; he charged it with "substitutionism," substituting the party leadership at the core of the socialist movement for the workers themselves; finally, he argued, inner-party democracy itself would be endangered. He even charged that this conception could lead to a dictatorship *over* the proletariat. He did not substantially alter his views until shortly before the October Revolution (Knei-Paz, 1978:175–233).

5 Mandel (1982:58) explains how the bureaucracy retains its working-class roots in terms of the following: its mode of appropriating privilege, its recruitment from the working class, its rejection of private ownership of the means of production, its inability to develop an original ideology and its continued reliance on a perverted "Marxism," and its links to the international working class. The bureaucracy nevertheless dominates the proletariat because a monopoly of political power is "the only way to defend its huge material privileges." But to show how great is the need to define domination in class terms, Mandel (1982:58) calls the bureaucracy a "petty bourgeois layer of the working class" by virtue of its cultural practices and international class alliances.

6 Mandel's subsequent critiques of Soviet-type societies have embraced these democratic elements, in which he calls for the right of self-expression for the working class, and not just members of the party. Mandel (1982:63) thus supported Polish Solidarity as the expression of legitimate working-class struggles.

7 For central planning to be so responsive, however, "classlessness" must be

accompanied by democracy, according to Mandel (1982:59). This is not the democracy of "bourgeois individualism," but democracy as "objective needs for a harmonious balanced functioning of Soviet economy and society, of any society in transition between capitalism and socialism." Democracy is the necessary addition in a planned society for a market which balances an economy's inputs and outputs. "The only way to assure efficient social planning is precisely through socialist democracy, universal and democratically centralized workers' control, full publicity and large public debate about what's happening everywhere in economic and social life." This vision of democracy is indeed inconsistent with bourgeois democracy, but it also illustrates how democracy is subordinated to the creation of classlessness. It also directs little attention to "difference," other than that between classes or that between economy and society.

8 This emphasis on development of the means of production under control of the ruling group is a common position among Eastern European and Soviet critics. See Fehér, Heller and Markus (1983:243); Szelényi (1982:318); Voslensky (1984:124).

9 Rational redistributive systems occur in planned economies in which most of the surplus is redistributed through the state budget, and, especially in earlier stages, devote a major portion of the surplus to the development of heavy industry.

10 That prospect is what leads Marc Rakovski to believe that experts and lower- and middle-level managers will prefer to work within the system rather than risk creating a society in which they would have to confront an autonomously organized working class (Rakovski, 1978:28). Hence, in contrast to Czechoslovakia in 1968, "it is unlikely that future crises in Soviet-type society will spring from the ruling class. There is nothing in our view of the consolidated post-Stalinist society which would lead us to expect that any eventual changes in the relative positions of the various ruling class groups will raise the question of power again. If there is a new division in the ruling class at all, it will be the consequence of crisis rather than its cause" (Rakovski, 1978:37). And so it was in Poland. Workers' protest enabled the breakup of the rulers into representatives of the world of work and representatives of the old order, not the other way around (Rychard, 1984). Gorbachev's *perestroika* might be the replay of the Prague Spring so unexpected. But we shall turn to this in the final chapter.

11 In remarks at the 1989 conference of the American Sociological Association, Szelényi finds Hungary to have become the very system he thought unlikely just a few years earlier. The intelligentsia has realized a ruling position in Hungary, as its culture of critical discourse (Gouldner, 1979) has become the language of rule, and its members have overwhelmed the state apparatus.

12 Bahro's emancipatory project is very far from the emphasis on equality in the consumption of privilege given by Trotsky or even Szelényi. Although Bahro is rather egalitarian in his program (p. 397), he considers the distribution of material privilege to be rather of secondary importance (p. 181). Bahro believes that once the "means of subsistence" are secured,

the "focal point of conflict of interests in society must move successively further from the distribution of compensation for labor towards the distribution of labor itself" (p. 211).

13 The experience of the Prague Spring informs Bahro's analysis. When given the opportunity, members of Novotny's Stalinist apparatus jumped at the chance to reform the society. Although Bahro does not mention it, similar events took place in Poland when Gomułka came to power. Members of the censorship office itself marched to demand the abolition of their own jobs. More generally, "the closer any sphere of society is to the politbureau, i.e. the closer it stands either intellectually or functionally to the power of disposal over the mechanisms of regulation of information, *without actually being admitted to this realm*, the more the rule of the apparatus finds there its dangerous enemies" (p. 325).

5 Solidarity, culture and civil society

1 By using the terminology of the political right in the USA, they can buttress their image as one of the most deserving opponents of communism.

2 Hungarian theorist Mihály Vajda (1988) exemplifies this resistance to systemic or "structural" analysis. He argues that structural analysis is simultaneously obvious and deceptive. Of course, there are similar organizational frameworks among Soviet-type systems, but this consistent framework interacts with fundamentally divergent "societies" to produce radically different experiences in these various places. The origins of these divergent experiences are found in various historical traditions, which above all separate "Eastern Europe" from "Eastern Central Europe". We shall return to this cultural emphasis later in the chapter.

3 One might include in this list Marcin Król and some around the journal *Res Publica*, Stanisław Stomma and the Dziękania club, Mirosław Dzielski and the Kraków Industrial Association, Aleksander Hall and some formerly associated with Young Poland and Antoni Macierewicz with those from the publication *Głos* (Frentzel-Zagórska and Zagórski, 1988; Walicki, 1988).

4 The utopia of their "democracy" then becomes the classical liberal right to dissent (*à la* Friedman) rather than the right to have equal say in governance (*à la* Rousseau), since it is the social question, i.e. social equality, itself which influences the possibility of equal participation in governance (Wolfe, 1977).

5 Given the pace of change, many sociologists have turned their attention to historically limited periods. Much of what I explain below refers to the 1970s before the formation of Solidarity. Inasmuch as explaining the initial formation of Solidarity is my principal substantive concern in this volume, I limit my account to this period. The cultural realm has, of course, changed dramatically with the initial success of Solidarity, the imposition of martial law and finally the reforms of the last few years.

6 Simmel (1908[1971]) suggests that a common trait of nobility culture is an emphasis on the personal elaboration of that which is internally specific,

hence an emphasis on subjective individuality even if in a context of aristocratic standardization.

7 Ash (1986:46–47) writes that Polish intellectuals, especially those not from Galicia, are less likely to promote the idea of Central Europe, because their cultural orientations extend more to the east, to Wilno and Lwów, than they do to Mitteleuropa.

8 Middle Europe and Central Europe have slightly different entymologies: the former was based on the German term and implied German hegemony; the latter was developed by Czechoslovak Thomas Masaryk in opposition to the Germans (Szporluk, 1982).

9 Vajda (1988), for instance, paints Russian rule as antagonistic to the general European tradition of the "flowering of individual and social autonomy" (p. 348). He acknowledges that, historically, Russia has been part of Europe as a whole, but its religious and political centralization blocked the rise of various autonomies (p. 347). The Soviet state apparatus today has the capacity to completely prevent any emergence of autonomy within its own society (p. 334). Its suppression of the "hereditary" (p. 341) need of Eastern Central Europeans to realize autonomy convinces him that "Russia is *not* Europe: it is not the socially, culturally and economically backward part of Europe" (p. 333); it has rejected all the values which distinguish European civilization (p. 334). This portrait of Eastern European/Eastern Central European difference is, for those tied to both worlds, politically dangerous. It suppresses the tension within the Russian intelligentsia, between its praise for things "truly European" and its pride in the Russian soul. What is worse, it alienates the Russian intelligentsia from the struggles to their west (Friedberg, 1988).

10 "Post-Marxism," as with most terms that enjoy a prefix, usually rests more on what it is not than what it is. Jean Cohen (1982:194), one of the members of this group, explains her relationship to Marxism and class theory by describing her new critical stratification theory as one that abandons the "overly ambitious" aspects and "dogmatic assumptions" of class analysis while nevertheless incorporating its insights.

11 Few post-Marxists include Lenin or Trotsky in their tradition. Indeed, some argue that Lenin is responsible for the conceptual transformation which led to the derailment of emancipatory politics in the USSR and Eastern Europe. Polan (1984:176) writes, for instance, that Lenin's post-revolutionary theory impoverished the Marxist alternative by denying that individuals could have political interests that were not based on class.

12 In a summer 1989 conversation, Ivan Szelényi told me that he considers his choice of terms one decade ago unfortunate. Civil society is a convenient way to avoid questions of political economy. He now believes that the question of "socialist civil society" is not central, but that the role of bourgeois property forms in the emancipatory agenda is.

13 In Eastern Central European discourse, this term is also called "independent society" and "parallel polis." The discussion by Czechoslovak intellectuals organized by Skilling (1988) illustrates the different nuances of meaning these various terms convey.

14 Heller (1988) argues that generalizing ownership through self-management (i.e. the positive abolition of private property) rather than its negative abolition by denying ownership to anyone and installing it within the state, is essential to the growth and survival of formal democracy. This article is one good illustration of the potential compatibilities between the classlessness of the self-management revision of Marxism and the post-Marxist concern for pluralism and civil society.

15 This distinction of the social and the political is one of the major objections post-Marxists have to Arendt's scheme. As Richard Bernstein (1984) notes, it is notoriously difficult to determine *a priori* what is and is not appropriate to political discussion. Arendt held that matters deserving political discussion are historically determined, but if they are so determined, and if the political discussion is not to be artificially circumscribed, Arendt's social question can become subject to political debate and resolution if that is how politics evolve. For the majority of the post-World War II period, the very idea of the welfare state is based on the consensus that the social question should be politically addressed.

16 Arato finds in the experience of 1980–81 Solidarity evidence that points 3, 4 and 5 are feasible, while point 7 is impossible.

17 Polish Socialist Party activist Zbigniew Szczypiński told me in a 1988 interview that this group is closer to the right-wing Young Poland (*Młoda Polska*) or Confederation for an Independent Poland (*Konfederacja Polski Niepodległej*) than to those whose political–economic programs should be similar: the Polish United Worker's Party. This reinforces the very common point of those with interests in Eastern Europe that the political labels of left and right make no sense in the context of Soviet-type society (Fehér and Heller, 1987).

18 Staniszkis bases her analysis on the insights of the Western property-rights school, although Fehér, Heller and Markus (1983) reach similar conclusions on the Soviet-type society's structure without invoking that perspective. Staniszkis considers property relations in Soviet-type society as incomplete because there are no concrete social groups that have the socially recognized right to use scarce resources in complete accord with their wishes. The absence of the right to the hereditary transfer of property ownership is one such example of incomplete property rights. Because property rights are incomplete, no social group actually enjoys the full benefits or suffers the full costs of decisions over the employment of scarce resources. This means, then, that property rights are non-exclusive.

19 See also Fehér, Heller and Markus (1983:180–82) for Heller's discussion of the paternalistic state.

6 A theory of power relations in Soviet-type society

1 In the Soviet Union, there are approximately 750,000 such positions (Voslensky, 1984:95). In Poland, the number increased in the 1980s. In the 1970s, it was estimated that over 100,000 posts were controlled directly by the party in this fashion (Smolar, 1983); in 1986, Marek Henzler (1986)

estimated that there were over 250,000 positions which required some kind of political approval by some level of the party. In Poland, as in the other Soviet-type societies, directors of enterprises, banks, cooperatives, hospitals and state farms are all subject to party approval (MacShane, 1981:163–69). Different levels of the party control different *nomenklatura* lists: the Central Committee of the national Communist Party will control a more important list of positions than will the provincial central committee, and likewise it will control a more important list than will the regional committee. This form of control affects between 1 and 4 percent of all jobs in the centrally planned economies of Soviet-type societies.

In recent years, changes have been introduced in *nomenklatura* as the authorities have initiated drives toward self-government. In Poland, a 1986 party document has changed the criteria of acceptance for some positions from demanding acceptance to that of "mutual agreement" (*uzgodzień*). For a discussion of this, see Kennedy and Białecki (1989). For the relevant discussion in China, see John Burns (1987).

2 Korpi (1985) distinguishes many more dimensions of power resources: (1) the context, or number of actors affected; (2) the scope, or range of activities affected; (3) the type, or whether resources reward or punish; (4) the scarcity, or availability of resources; (5) the centrality, or the necessity of those resources in daily life; (6) the concentration potential, or the degree to which a resource can be concentrated to a few actors; (7) the storage potential, or the possibility for a resource's preservation; and (8) liquidity, or the readiness for a power resource's use. Korpi's understanding of power is different from mine, and therefore leads him to emphasize different dimensions. He delimits power to be "power resources as the attributes (capacities or means) of actors (individuals or collective) which enable them to reward or to punish other actors" (Korpi, 1985:33). It seems here that the distinction between power and privilege is collapsed, since the use of power resources to enhance one's own privilege is excluded from consideration. Because I am not only interested in powers affecting others, but also expanding one's own opportunities for action including the pursuit of further privilege, I take a slightly different tack from Korpi. When I speak of the scope of resources under control, I include under that heading both Korpi's context and scope dimensions, but add to that the possibility for accumulating privilege. The notion of exclusivity bears some resemblance to Korpi's concentration potential, but also differs. While Korpi's concept seems to emphasize the dispersion among actors of control over a resource, exclusivity instead emphasizes the degree of discretion its holders have in its application.

3 Although there have been other legal political parties in postwar Poland, they are not competitive and rather cooperate under the leadership of a hegemonic party, the PZPR. For the classic statement on this in Polish sociology, see Jerzy Wiatr (1967[1978]).

4 Although nearly all macro-level power emanates from the upper reaches, the Politburo if you like, even that group cannot be completely arbitrary in its decisions. The upper reaches of the party are perhaps the most

autonomous power in the system (the *most* autonomous, of course, being the CPSU politburo), but even they are to some degree dependent on other levels within the party–state to implement their decisions. In Poland, many economic reforms have been successfully resisted by the central planning organs. The difficulty of controlling the secret police during the existence of Solidarity also shows this limited control. Individual members of the apparatus can be fired for insubordination, but an entire section cannot be eliminated (Białecki, 1985). A few members of the secret police can be held accountable for the murder of the pro-*Solidarność* priest, Jerzy Popiełuszko, but the entire apparatus cannot be brought to trial. Despite the infighting that goes on within the upper reaches of the party, the highest organs (in whatever mixture between army, secret police and party faction) have the greatest degree of autonomy in the society, and most power and privilege in the society is dependent on them. They have the greatest scope and exclusivity in the use of power, especially over individuals, but even their power over groups is quite limited. I elaborate upon this problem when I consider vassals and the system of *nomenklatura* in the subsequent section.

5 When asked in a recent interview who directly planned the introduction of martial law in 1981, Kiszczak (1986) replied that plans originated in "an inner circle" including Jaruzelski, himself and the vice-minister of national defense, Florian Siwicki. Kiszczak was also asked by Jaruzelski to run for Poland's president in the spring of 1989, when Jaruzelski thought that he could not win the post in the parliamentary election. Kiszczak also lost his bid to become prime minister in August.

6 I do not use the term "vassal" in this context because I think the vassal in Soviet-type society is identical to the feudal vassal. Historical analogies are never so precise. I nonetheless believe that the term merits use in the socialist context, given the similarities between socialist and feudal vassals, as I argue later in this note. I believe it is also useful to employ this term rather than the more neutral term "client" for its emotive power.

Clientalism implies a normal state of affairs and not something that demands transcendence. One of the principal barriers to emancipatory transformation in Soviet-type society is this vassalage behaviour, however. I use "vassalage" as a term, therefore, to imply that it is a barrier to transformation, and that those whose positions demand some kind of vassalage can contribute to social transformation by minimizing the vassalizing aspects of their behavior. By making the historical analogy, the potential for alternative behavior becomes more real.

In Max Weber's (1978:1006–1110) discussion of patrimonialism and feudalism, feudalism is considered a marginal case of patrimonialism (p. 1070) and is distinguished from the latter by the contractual relationship between ruler and vassal (p. 1072). Socialist vassals have the following characteristics in common with both feudal vassals or patrimonial officials: (1) their membership in a hierarchically graded stratum stands above the mass of society; (2) their positions of influence are granted in exchange for obligations of personal fealty to their superiors; (3) their privilege is contingent to a large degree on the continued power and support of their superiors and is hereditary only to the degree that their descendants "merit" their positions (p. 1074); and (4) the lord or ruling group is powerful before an individual, but powerless in the face of the entire group (pp. 1012, 1079).

The more important point is not whether these socialist officials are better described as vassals or retainers, but that they are better characterized as vassals or retainers than as bureaucrats. They do not have formally defined responsibilities which are preserved in practice. The exercise of power is discretionary and not based on the execution of impersonal tasks. They do not qualify for their positions by virtue of their professional competence. Their promotion and dismissal are imbued with a high degree of arbitrariness and discretion and thus in this sense are more similar to patrimonial officials than feudal vassals given the relative absence of "subjective rights." They occupy a position very similar to that of the patrimonial official Weber (1978:1030) describes, whose position "derives from his purely personal submission to the ruler, and his position vis-a-vis the subjects is merely the external aspect of this relation." Thus, to find my analysis of Soviet-type society support for Weber's warning against impending bureaucratic domination in all kinds of societies fails to note that what I describe is not bureaucracy.

I ultimately use the term "vassal" rather than "retainer" or "patrimonial official" because of the quasi-contractual relationship that exists between the superior and vassal in actual socialism. The support of vassals is one of the main power resources of those seeking to advance in the official hierarchy. At the same time, vassalage to the right superior is the means by which one improves one's status in official power relations (Willerton, 1979, 1987). Thus, as among feudal vassals, socialist vassalage need not be a demeaning status but a means by which advancement is made possible. Only under conditions where the status of the notable is illegitimate, as in Poland, is the vassal a demeaning status. As Soviet-type societies generate the possibilities for the creation of a socialist civil society, this vassalage will become increasingly illegitimate too.

Another similarity to the feudal condition is the possibility for conflict between vassals and superiors and among vassals themselves. Because of the uncertainty of the hierarchy, in Soviet-type society the vassals of vassals, or "subvassals," have contradictory loyalties, to both the ruling group and their immediate superiors, a condition which can generate conflicts of interest.

7 Andrew Walder (1985) also argues that industrial authority in communist China is best understood as constructed through clientalist networks. Although I developed my ideas on vassalage in Poland before reading Walder's work, there are considerable similarities in our analyses. Most importantly, we both emphasize the importance of informal ties alongside the more formal bureaucratic ones. His notion of "clientalistic bureaucracy" is an elegant way of conveying this combination. But we differ in the degree of significance we attach to the "twosidedness" of power relations. Walder emphasizes the dependence of workers on their patrons. While

that is also true for workers in Poland, Polish notables are dependent on their vassals, and Polish cadres are especially dependent on their workers. One reason for this difference in emphasis across enterprises might be a consequence of the relative power of individual workers in these systems. In China, there remains an oversupply of workers for industry; in Poland, skilled workers are still in great demand.

7 Professionals, power and prestige

1 The single "independent" (non-Solidarity) candidate elected to Poland's Senate, Henryk Stokłosa, is a successful private entrepreneur who used his wealth liberally to help assure his electoral victory.
2 In 1974, sociology students from Warsaw University under the direction of K. Słomczyński surveyed Warsaw residents who were old enough to have lived in the inter-war period and have been personally familiar with the status of the intelligentsia. The students asked these people to rank on a scale of 1 to 5 various occupations present in both the inter-war period and the contemporary scene (see table 7.3) (source: Bogdan Mach, personal communication).

8 Engineers in Solidarity

1 Who are the engineers? Need one work in a job that requires engineering skills to be identified as an engineer? Does one have to have a higher education in technical studies? Must this degree be from a day school at the polytechnic, or do we consider engineers to be those who have acquired their education at night school? Does self-identification as an engineer suffice? Different statistical sources and different studies rely on different definitions. In this chapter, I adopt the most inclusive definition of "engineer," where an engineer must have one of the following character-istics: (1) a masters (*magister*) degree in polytechnical education from day or night school; (2) employment in a job designated for someone with that background; or (3) self-identification as a professional engineer. In certain cases, however, it will be important to distinguish among these different "kinds" of engineers, and I do so when it becomes essential to the account.
2 Including two Solidarity activists, a Party activist, two members of the self-management group and a factory council member. Of this group, two were engineers and the rest unidentified by occupation.

9 Physicians in Solidarity

1 Although there is a considerable amount of Polish sociological research on engineers, research on physicians as anything other than deliverers of health care is quite limited. As such, this chapter relies very heavily on consultations I made. My consultants were selected via a snowball sam-pling method, with paths beginning at several different points. Most of my consultants are from Warsaw given that this was my own home for most of the eleven months I spent in Poland. I met some of these consultants only

once, while others I consulted several times over the course of the four years I researched these questions. Because of the sensitive nature of some of my questions, some of my respondents preferred that their names and the times of these informal consultations remain unspecified. Others were quite ready to offer their names, but in the interests of caution and consistency, I refer to them only by their number on the following list. Due also to the potential compromise that association with me might entail, I would not record these interviews on a tape recorder. I reconstructed conversations later to assure some level of privacy and security for my consultants.

2 I rely primarily on Cecylia Łabanowska's (1978) excellent doctoral dissertation for presenting the history of the Polish medical profession. Physicians' quotations from periodicals in this section are, unless otherwise noted, translated from her citations.

3 In the name of socialist ideals and worker–peasant unity, physicians associated with the Peasant Party protested this discrimination, but to no avail. The individual farmer who owned his own land was a relic of Poland's past, not considered to be part of the socialist social structure (Firkowska-Mankiewicz et al., forthcoming).

4 DiP began in 1973 as an informal discussion group among fifty former Życie Warszawy journalists who lost their jobs when a new, less independent journalist became editor-in-chief. On November 14, 1978, DiP expanded its scope when it held a public forum on welfare policy at the PAN Institute of History on the Warsaw Old Town Square. They planned another forum on the problem of "law and order", but were prevented from doing so by the authorities (Świdlicki 1982:137–50). Faced with this repression, the service unit organizing DiP decided to conduct further activities using surveys. In January 1979, the service unit sent out a six-question survey to intellectuals, the responses to which formed the basis for the "Report on the state of the republic." Another report, "Which way out?," was based on another survey conducted in December 1979 (DiP, 1981). After the Gdańsk agreement, a second plenary session was held with twenty-four participants. Five working groups were set up: law and order; agricultural affairs; public health; educational reform; and cultural affairs.

5 This reconstruction is based on interviews with three of the original ten members of the commission.

6 There are four principal sources for this section: (1) the data collected by Marek Latoszek in the summer and fall of 1980; (2) the insightful analysis of those data by Danuta Duch (1981); (3) analysis of original documents found in the microfilm collection called "Solidarity 1980–81"; and (4) my own consultations.

Physician consultants

	Type of work	Place of work	Region	Gender	1980–81 Activist*
1.	Medical researcher	institute	Lublin	male	yes
2.	Medical researcher	institute	Warsaw	male	yes
3.	Internist	medical academy	Warsaw	male	no
4.	Dentist	clinic	Warsaw	female	no
5.	Internist	factory	Warsaw	male	yes
6.	Anesthesiologist	hospital	Warsaw	female	no
7.	Surgeon	hospital	Warsaw	male	no
8.	Anesthesiologist	hospital	Warsaw	female	no
9.	Anesthesiologist	hospital	Warsaw	female	no
10.	Anesthesiologist	hospital	Warsaw	female	no
11.	Internist	clinic	Gdańsk	male	yes
12.	Internist	clinic	Gdańsk	female	yes
13.	Surgeon	hospital	Łódź	male	no
14.	Surgeon	hospital	Warsaw	male	no
15.	Radiologist	hospital	Warsaw	female	yes
16.	Anesthesiologist	hospital	Warsaw	female	yes
17.	Medical researcher	institute	Warsaw	female	yes
18.	Hematologist	hospital/clinic	Warsaw	female	yes
19.	Administrator	association	Warsaw	male	no
20.	Internist	hospital	Warsaw	female	no
21.	Orthopedist	hospital	Warsaw	male	no
22.	Medical researcher	institute	Warsaw	male	yes
23.	Internist	hospital	Warsaw	female	yes
24.	Orthopedist	clinic	Gdańsk	male	yes
25.	Pediatrician	hospital	Warsaw	female	yes
26.	Surgeon	hospital	Warsaw	male	yes
27.	Psychiatrist	institute	Warsaw	female	yes
28.	Radiologist	hospital	Warsaw	female	yes

*Activist defined as someone who was a member of some organizing body within Solidarity or in other medical-affiliated bodies. Of these 16 activists, 2 were student activists in the medical academy, and 2 were not members of Solidarity but were members of DiP.

References

Cited primary documents associated with Solidarity and contemporary articles from popular publications

The following list of references includes only those items which are directly cited in the text. The list is divided into primary and secondary sources. I have included in the list of primary sources those documents which are better understood as part of Poland's public sphere, and not part of the more specialized social scientific literature. These documents are generally not readily available to the non-Polish sociological community, although some, including the Solidarity-sponsored periodicals *Tygodnik Solidarność* and *Wiadomość Dnia*, are available on microfilm collections in some libraries. The following three groups of materials were also sponsored by Solidarity. These were not published in any regular periodicals, but rather on a smaller scale either in leaflets or bulletins. I have distinguished these items by whether they referred to the health sector or not, and for the former, from what region they came. *Przegląd Techniczny* and *Polityka* were published by the authorities and are available in some collections. *Zeszyty Niezależnej Myśli Lekarskiej* was an underground journal and comes from my own collection. Other primary periodicals which do not have multiple citations are listed under "other."

Those materials included in the list of secondary references include, most obviously, English-language materials, but they also include many Polish materials that also are not readily available in non-Polish collections. They are, however, potentially more accessible than those listed in the primary section as these contributions are made by academics who are prepared to collaborate internationally. Indeed, a major source of information for this study has been the research, often unpublished or at least not widely circulated, conducted by Polish social scientists.

Tygodnik Solidarność

Bulczak, Zbigniew, "Bank Leków," 15 (7/19/1981):16.
Grędziak, Anna, "Bank Leków 'Solidarność,'" 22 (8/28/1981):15.
Jakubowicz, Szymon, "Autentyczność: Warunkiem Zaufania i Poparcia," 2(4/10/1981):6–7.

Klimaszewski, Stanisław, "Zostanę inzynierem, będzie mi gorzej," 23 (8/21/1981):13.

Kopecki, Kazimierz, "Kiedy Wyjdziemy z Energetycznej Nędzy," 4 (4/24/1981).

Kozinski, J., St. Kielczewski, T. Listwan and St. Witkowski, "Konkurs na Dyrektora," 18 (7/31/1981):1, 6.

Kozlowski, Paweł, "Dyrektorzy," 26 (9/25/1981):9.

Kuczyński, Waldemar, "Upadek Absolutyzmu Fabrycznego," 4 (4/24/1981):4.

Kuratowska, Zofia, "Gorzej niz Źle," 33 (11/13/1981):7.

"Nieczynny Szpital," 16 (7/17/1981):16.

Pajdak, Marian, "Mądrzy po Szkodzie," 14 (8/3/1981):7, 9.

Rosner, Jan and Piotr Krasucki, "Trudne Dzis, Trudniejsze Jutro," 6 (5/8/1981):4.

Słabisz, Bozena, Letter to the editor, 7 (5/15/1981):16.

Wywrich, Mateusz, "Świębodzicki Czworokat," 27 (10/2/1981):14.

Wiadomość Dnia

"Czym Jest Solidarność i Dlaczego do Niej Wstępujemy?" 226 (11/11/1981):2.

"Jak Edward Gierek Został Inżynierem?" 50 (3/3/1981):2.

"Lekarze pracują 12 godziń," 71 (3/27/1981).

"Lokale dla Służby Zdrowia," 86 (4/17/1981).

"Z Prac OBSu," 113 (6/1/1981).

Coastal Region Medical Sector Materials

Gmaj, Piotr, "Stary Związek w Nowej Szacie," *Biuletyn Informacyjny NSZZ Służba Zdrowia "Pomost"*, Gdańsk, 2 (9/21/1980):4.

"Oświadczenia Komitet Strajkowy Studentów Pomorskiej Akademii Medycnej," (11/10/1980).

"Odpowiedni na Notatki Prasowe," Gdańsk (11/11/1980).

"Obywateli i Studenci Pam-u Informują," Pomorska Akademia Medycyna, 3 (11/13/1980).

"Studenci PAM-u Informują," Pomorska Akademia Medycyna, 5 (11/14/1980).

"Telefonogram z Gdańska," *Instytut Biochemii Pomorskiej Akademii Medycynej* (11/7/1980):9.

Mazowsze Region Medical Sector Materials

Moskwa, Jerzy, Anna Tymowska and Bogusława Dębicka, "Oświadczenia Sekcji Pracowników Służby Zdrowia Mazowsze," *Komitet Organizacyjny Branżowej Sekcji Pracowników Służby Zdrowia NSZZ Solidarność region Mazowsze* n.d., p. 9.

Pieńkowska, Alina, "Doświadczenia Komisji Porozumiewawczej Służby Zdrowia," in *NTO: Informator Wewnętrzny dla Kół Nauki, Techniki i Oświaty, NSZZ Solidarność Region Mazowsze* 7 (11/16/1980):8.

"Solidarność a Interesy Zawodowe i Branżowe," in *NTO: Informator Wewnętrzny dla Kół Nauki, Techniki i Oświaty, NSZZ Solidarność Region Mazowsze* 4 (10/26/1980):11.

Other Regional Materials of Solidarity

"Apel Lekarzy Polskich," *Solidarność Biuletyn Związkowy WSKPZL Świdnik* 25 (4/25–26/1981).

Choina, Bogusław, "Probelmy Miasta i Regionu," *Informator NSZZ Solidarność Politechniki Ślaskiej Gliwice* 26/81 (5/25/1981).

Jacek, Bronisław, "Jaka Ma Być Nowa Reforma Studiów?" *Informacyje NSZZ Solidarność przy Politechnice Wrocławskiej* (5/29/1981):4.

"Sięć," *Zeszyty Glosu PANu*, Kraków NSZZ Solidarność, 2 (August 1981).

"Wybory," *Gliwice Informator NSZZ Solidarność Śląsku* 34/81 (8/16/1981):2–4.

"Założenia Programowe OZ NSZZ Solidarność w PW," *Pismo OZ NSZZ Solidarność w Politechnice Warszawskiej* 4 (1981):9–11.

Przegląd Techniczny

"Samorządni, samodzielni i . . .," 26(1981):24–25.

"Dyskusje i Decyzje," 26(1981):38.

Wieczorkowska, Anna and Malgorzata Woźniak, "Za Kwidzyn pod Klucz," 27–28(1981):9–12.

Ochremiak, Witold, "Federacja i Nowy Statut," 29–30(1981):10–11.

Karwicka-Rychlewicz, Krystyna and Henryk Nakielski, "Kraj Mlekiem Płynący," 29–30(1981):20–24.

"W Nową Kadencją," 31–32(1981):9–10.

Kłoc, Kazimierz, "Nie Straszmy Sie Samorządem," 33–34(1981):10–13.

"Apel o Niezalezną Organizację Techniczną," 35(1981):8. See also *Tygodnik Solidarność* 20(8/14/1981).

"Do Inżynierów i Techników Polskich," 35(1981):16–17.

Mejro, Czesław, "Licencja na Produkcje Czadu," 35(1981):19–20.

Stankiewicz, Tomasz,. "Miejsce w systemie," 35(1981):16–18.

Polityka

Baczyński, Jerzy, "Zmaganie z Materia," 47(1983):3.

Biernacki, Janusz, "Czego chcecie poza pieniędzmi?" an interview by Andrzej Mozolowski (11/29/1980).

Kiszczak, Czesław, "Bedę Rozmawiał z Każdym," (7/14/1986).

Kulerski, Marek, "Liczy się tylko Solidarność," an interview by Andrzej Mozolowski (11/29/1980).

"Wielka Pięćsetka" (7/7/1984).

Zeszyty Niezależnej Myśli Lekarskiej

Dwugłos o spółdzielniach lekarskich: Znana, Maria, "Jakie powinny byc?" and Ryszard Płoński, "Na progu bankructwa," 6 (December 1985).

Biendota, Roman, "Leki-Odpowiedzialność Rzadu," 9 (December 1986).
Badanie Społecznego Komitetu Nauki i Społecznej Komisji Zdrowia, "Leki – Próby Analizy," 9 (December 1986).
Kuratowska, Zofia, "Służba Zdrowia: Kto Winien?" 11 (April 1987) (reprinted in *Kultura* [Paris] March, 1987:83–97).

Other

Brzeski, Jan, "Inżynier na Taryfie," *Odrodzenie* (4/24/1984).
Kania, Stanisław, "Zadania w Sprawie Dalszego Rozwoju i Doskonalenia Ochrony Zdrowia Społeczeństwa," *Nowe Drogi* 7(374)(7/1980):7–27.
Karas, Stanisław, "Kwalifakacje a Awans," *Życie Warszawy* (6/16/1981).
Kruszyński, Z., "Właściwy Człowiek na Własciwym Miejscu," *Życie Gospodarce* 47 (1958).
Kubicki, Wojciech, "Kto Wykształci Inżynierów Ruchu?" *Życie Warszawy* (11/14/1983).
Misiak, Marek, "Uchylanie Kurtyny," *Życie Gospodarcze* (7/15/1984).
Osa-Ostrowski, Sławomir, "Urodaj Inżynierów," *Expres Wieczorny* (1/23–24/1984).
Pięć Lat Po Porozumienia: Raport Stan Kraju. NSZZ Solidarność, 1985.
Polska Ludowa a Kosciół Katolicki. Warszawa: Książka i Wiedza, 1949.
Protokol Porozumienia zawartego między Komisją Rządową a delegacją Służby Zdrowia, NSZZ Solidarność. Wydawnictwo Związkowe Mazowsze, 1981.
Skalski, Ernst, "Praca i Płaca," *Tygodnik Powszechny* 24 (1986).

Statistical references cited

Rocznik Statystyczny
  1970 Warsaw: Główny Urząd Statystyczny.
  1981 Warsaw: Główny Urząd Statystyczny.
  1982 Warsaw: Główny Urząd Statystyczny.
  1983 Warsaw: Główny Urząd Statystyczny.
  1987 Warsaw: Główny Urząd Statystyczny.
Rocznik Statystyczny Ochronia Zdrowia
  1981 Warsaw: Główny Urząd Statystyczny.
Rocznik Statystyczny Szkolnictwa
  1981 Warsaw: Główny Urząd Statystyczny.
Spis Kadrowy
  1977 Warsaw: Główny Urząd Statystyczny.

Secondary sources and other general works

Adamski, Władysław 1982. "Przyzależność Związkowa i Miejsce w Strukturze a Interesy Grupowe," in Adamski *et al.* (eds.), 183–96.
Adamski, Władysław, L. Beskid, I. Białecki, K. Jasiewicz, L. Kolarska, A. Mokrzyszewski, A. Rychard, J. Sikorska, E. Skotnicka-Illasiewicz, A. Titkow and E. Wnuk-Lipiński 1982. *Polacy 81: Postrzeganie Kryzysu i Konfliktu.* Warsaw: PAN IFiS.

Anderson, Perry 1983. "Trotsky's Interpretation of Stalinism," *New Left Review* 139:49–58.

Antonio, Robert J. 1989. "The Normative Foundations of Emancipatory Theory: Evolutionary vs. Pragmatic Perspectives," *American Journal of Sociology* 94:721–48.

Apel, Karl-Otto 1980. *Towards a Transformation of Philosophy*. London: Routledge and Kegan Paul.

Arato, Andrew 1981. "Civil Society Against the State," *Telos* 47:23–47.

1982b. "Critical Sociology and Authoritarian State Socialism," in John B. Thompson and David Held (eds.) *Habermas: Critical Debates*, 196–218. Cambridge, Mass.: MIT Press.

Arendt, Hannah 1963 [1979]. *On Revolution*. New York: Penguin.

Ascherson, Neil 1982. *The Polish August*. New York: Viking Press.

Ash, Timothy Garton 1983. *The Polish Revolution: Solidarity*. New York: Scribner's.

1986. "Does Central Europe Exist?" *The New York Review of Books* October 9:45–52.

1988. "The Empire in Decay," September 29: pp. 53–60; "The Opposition," October 10:3–6; "Reform or Revolution," October 27:47–56. *The New York Review of Books*.

Aslund, Anders 1984. "The Functioning of Private Enterprise in Poland," *Soviet Studies* 36:427–44.

Avinieri, Shlomo 1968. *The Social and Political Thought of Karl Marx*. Cambridge: Cambridge University Press.

Babiuch, Jolanta 1988. "Analiza Funkcjonowania Pojęcia Inteligencji," unpublished doctoral dissertation, University of Warsaw.

Bahro, Rudolph 1978. *The Alternative in Eastern Europe*. London: New Left Books.

Bakuniak, Grzegorz and Krzysztof Nowak 1987. "The Creation of Collective Identity in a Social Movement: The Case of *Solidarność* in Poland," *Theory and Society* 16:401–29.

Barańczak, Stanisław 1986–87. "The Polish Intellectual," *Salmagundi* 70–71:217–28.

Bauman, Zygmunt 1972. "Officialdom and Class: Bases of Inequality in Socialist Society," in Frank Parkin (ed.) *The Social Analysis of Class Structure*, 129–48. London: Tavistock.

1976. *Socialism: The Active Utopia*. London: Allen and Unwin.

1980. *Memories of Class*. London: Routledge and Kegan Paul.

1981. "On the Maturation of Socialism," *Telos* 47:48–54.

1987. "Intellectuals in East-Central Europe: Continuity and Change," *Eastern European Politics and Societies* 1:162–86.

Beilharz, Peter 1979. "Trotsky's Marxism – Permanent Involution?" *Telos* 39:137–52.

Bell, Daniel 1973. *The Coming of Post Industrial Society: A Venture in Social Forecasting*. New York: Basic Books.

Bellis, Paul 1979. *Marxism and the USSR: The Theory of Proletarian Dictatorship and the Marxist Analysis of Soviet Society*. Atlantic Highlands, N.J.: Humanities Press.

Benhabib, Seyla 1986. *Critique, Norm and Utopia*. New York: Columbia University Press.

Bettelheim, Charles 1976. *Class Struggles in the USSR: First Period: 1917–1923*. New York: Monthly Review.

Bernstein, Richard 1984. "Rethinking the Social and the Political," paper presented at Philosophy and Social Science conference, Dubrovnik, Yugoslavia.

Besançon, Alain 1977 [1981]. *The Rise of the Gulag: Intellectual Origins of Leninism*, New York: Continuum.

Białecki, Ireneusz 1982. "Solidarity: The Roots of the Movement," *Sysyphus* 3:115–26.

    1985. "Authority and Privileges: The Logic of Distribution in a Centrally Planned Economy," unpublished manuscript.

    1986. "Wykształcenie i Ruchliwość Zawodowa," in I. Białecki, H. Domański, B. Mach, M. Pohoski and W. Zaborowski (eds.) *Przemiany Ruchliwości Społecznej w Polsce*, 51–110. Warsaw: Polish Academy of Sciences.

    1987. "What the Poles Thought in 1981," in J. Koralewicz, I. Białecki and M. Watson (eds.) *Crisis and Transition: Polish Society in the 1980s*. London: Berg.

Błasiak, Wojciech 1987. "Centra i Peryferie Masowego Ruchu Pracowniczego w Polsce 1980–81," in Ewa Lewicka-Banaszak, Piotr Marciniak and Wojciech Modzelewski (eds.) *Studia Nad Ruchami Społecznymi*, 135–76. University of Warsaw Institute of Sociology.

Blau, Peter 1964. *Exchange and Power in Social Life*. New York: Wiley.

    1977. *Inequality and Heterogeneity*. New York: Free Press.

Bobbio, Norberto 1988. "Gramsci and the Concept of Civil Society," in John Keane (ed.) *Civil Society and the State*, 73–100. London: Verso.

Bova, Russell 1987. "On Perestroika: The Role of Workers' Participation," *Problems of Communism* 36:4:76–86.

Brandys, Kazimierz 1983. *A Warsaw Diary: 1978–1981*. New York: Random House.

Bridge, Susan 1975. "Why Czechoslovakia? And Why 1968?" *Studies in Comparative Communism* 8:413–25.

Brown, Archie 1979. "Eastern Europe: 1968, 1978, 1998," *Daedelus* 108(1):151–74.

    1987. "A Reformer in the Kremlin," *The Nation* June 13:792–95.

Brown, Archie and Jack Gray (eds.) 1979. *Political Culture and Political Change in Communist States*. New York: Holmes and Meier.

Brumberg, Abraham 1983. *Poland: Genesis of a Revolution*. New York: Random House.

Bruszt, Laszlo 1988. "Without Us but for Us? Political Orientation in Hungary in the Period of Late Paternalism," *Social Research* 55:43–76.

Brzezinski, Zbigniew 1967. *The Soviet Bloc: Unity and Conflict*. New York: Praeger.

    1989. "Communism: Terminal Crisis," lecture at The University of Michigan, March 10.

Burawoy, Michael 1985. *The Politics of Production*. London: New Left Books.

1988. "Two Methods in Search of Science: Skocpol vs. Trotsky," unpublished manuscript.

1989. "Should We Give Up on Socialism?" *Socialist Review* 89(1):57–66.

Burks, R. V. 1970. "Technology and Political Change in Eastern Europe," in Chalmers Johnson (ed.) *Change in Communist Systems*, 265–312. Stanford: Stanford University Press.

Burns, John 1987. "China's Nomenklatura System," *Problems of Communism* 36(5):36–52.

Casanova, Jose 1988. "The De-privatization of Catholicism: State and Church Relations in Poland," paper given at the Conference on Religion and Marxism in East Central Europe, The University of Michigan, October 13.

Chałasiński, Józef 1946. *Społeczna Genealogia Inteligencji Polskiej*. Warsaw: Spółdzielnia Wydawnicza.

Checiński, Michael 1982. *Poland: Communism, Nationalism, Anti-Semitism*. New York: Karz-Cohl.

Cohen, Jean 1982. *Class and Civil Society: The Limits of Marxian Critical Theory*. Amherst: University of Massachusetts.

Collins, Randall 1979. *The Credential Society*. New York: Academic Press.

Commission of the Central Committee of the CPSU(B) 1939. *History of the Communist Party of the Soviet Union (Bolsheviks)*. New York: International Publishers.

Connor, Walter D. 1979. *Socialism, Politics and Equality*. New York: Columbia University.

1980. "Dissent in Eastern Europe: A New Coalition?" *Problems of Communism* 29:1–17.

Corrigan, Philip, Harvie Ramsay and Derek Sayer 1978. *Socialist Construction and Marxist Theory: Bolshevism and its Critique*. New York: Monthly Review.

Cottam, Kazimiera Janina 1978. *Boleslaw Limanowski (1835–1935): A Study in Socialism and Nationalism*. New York: Columbia University Press.

Crighton, Elizabeth 1985. "Resource Mobilization and Solidarity: Comparing Social Movements across Regimes," in Bronisław Misztal (ed.) *Poland after Solidarity*, 113–32. New Brunswick: Transaction.

Curry, Jane 1983. "Polish Dissent and Establishment Criticism: The New Evolutionism," in Jane Curry (ed.) *Dissent in Eastern Europe*, 153–72. New York: Praeger.

(ed.) 1984. *The Black Book of Polish Censorship*. New York: Vintage.

1989. "The Rise and Fall of Polish Intellectuals," paper presented at a conference, "Poland and Instability," Pennsylvania State University.

Dahrendorf, Ralf 1959. *Class and Class Conflict in Industrial Society*. Stanford: Stanford University Press.

Davies, Norman 1984. *God's Playground: A History of Poland in Two Volumes*. New York: Columbia University Press.

1988. "Polish–Soviet Relations, Past and Present," lecture at The University of Michigan, November 15.

Denitch, Bogdan 1977. *The Legitimation of a Revolution*. New Haven: Yale University Press.

Deutscher, Isaac 1984. "The Tragedy of the Polish Communist Party," in I. Deutscher, *Marxism, Wars, and Revolutions*, 91–127. London: Verso.

Dewey, John 1938 [1973]. "Means and Ends," in Leon Trotsky, John Dewey and George Novack, *Their Morals and Ours*. New York: Pathfinder Press.

de Weydenthal, Jan B. 1978. *The Communists of Poland: An Historical Outline*. Stanford: Hoover.

DiP 1981. *Poland Today: The State of the Republic*. White Plains: Sharpe.

    1983. "Health and Health Protection of the Polish Population," *International Journal of Health Services* 13(3):487–513.

Djilas, Milovan 1957. *The New Class*. New York: Praeger.

    1969. *The Unperfect Society*. New York: Harcourt Brace Jovanovich.

Doktór, Kazimierz 1982. "Industrial Conflicts and the Ultrastability of the System," *Sysyphus* 3:69–80.

Draper, Theodore 1986. "NeoConservative History," *New York Review of Books* January 16.

Drążkiewicz, Jerzy and Andrzej Rychard 1981. "Strajki w Regioni Warszawskim w Lecie 1980," unpublished manuscript.

Drewnowski, Jan (ed.) 1982. *Crisis in the East European Economy*. London: Croom Helm.

Duch, Danuta 1981. "Kryzys i Konflikty w Służbie Zdrowia," unpublished manuscript.

Duran-Arenas, Luis and Michael D. Kennedy forthcoming. "The Constitution of Physicians' Power: A Theoretical Framework for Comparative Analysis," *Social Science and Medicine*.

Dziecielska-Machnikowska, Stefania 1966. *Farmaceuci w Polskiej Rzeczypospolitej Ludowej*. Wrocław: Ossolineum, PAN.

Dziewanowski, M. K. 1976. *The Communist Party of Poland*. Cambridge, Mass.: Harvard University.

Eisenstadt, S. N. 1968. "Prestige, Participation, and Strata Formation," in John A. Jackson (ed.) *Social Stratification*, 62–103. Cambridge: Cambridge University Press.

Farrell, John P. 1981. *"Growth, Reform, and Inflation: Problems and Policies,"* in Maurice D. Simon and Roger E. Kanet (eds.) *Background to Crisis: Policy and Politics in Gierek's Poland*, 299–328. Boulder, Colo.: Westview.

Fehér, Ferenc 1988. "Eastern Europe's Long Revolution Against Yalta," *Eastern European Politics and Societies* 2(1):1–35.

Fehér, Ferenc and Agnes Heller 1983. *Hungary 1956 Revisited*. London: Allen and Unwin.

    1987. "Eastern Left – Western Left: Part I: Reflections on a Problematic Relationship," *Socialist Review* 89:25–48; and "Part II: After 1968," *Socialist Review* 90:33–48.

Fehér, Ferenc, Agnes Heller and György Markus 1983. *Dictatorship over Needs*. New York: St Martin's Press.

Firkowska – Mankiewicz, Anna, Marek Czarkowski, Danuta Duch and Anna Titkow forthcoming. "Ideology in Politics – Health," *Sisyphus* 6:

Fiszman, Joseph 1972. *Revolution and Tradition in People's Poland*. Princeton: Princeton University Press.

Foucault, Michel 1977 [1984]. "Truth and Power," in Paul Rainbow (ed.) *The Foucault Reader* New York: Pantheon.

Fraser, Nancy 1987. "What's Critical about Critical Theory?" in Sylvia Benhabib and Drucilla Cornell (eds.) *Feminism as Critique*, 31–55. Minneapolis: University of Minnesota Press.

Frentzel-Zagórska, and Krzysztof Zagórski 1988. "The Intelligentsia in Poland and East Central Europe," paper presented at the Annual Meeting of the American Sociological Association.

Friedberg, Maurice 1988. "Culture and Ideology: East Europe and the Soviet Neighbor," paper given at the conference on Religion and Marxism in Eastern Central Europe, University of Michigan, October 14.

Friedman, Milton 1962. *Capitalism and Freedom*. Chicago: University of Chicago Press.

Gans, Herbert 1972. "Positive Functions of Poverty," *American Journal of Sociology* 78:275–89.

Gella, Aleksander 1971. "The Life and the Death of the Old Polish Intelligentsia," *Slavic Review* 30:1–27.

Giddens, Anthony 1973. *The Class Structure of the Advanced Societies*. New York: Harper and Row.

1979. *Central Problems in Social Theory*. Berkeley: University of California Press.

1981. *A Contemporary Critique of Historical Materialism*. Berkeley: University of California.

1984. *The Constitution of Society*. Berkeley: University of California Press.

1987. *The Nation State and Violence*. Berkeley: University of California Press.

Gouldner, Alvin 1970. *The Coming Crisis of Western Sociology*. New York: Basic Books.

1979. *The Future of Intellectuals and the Rise of the New Class*. New York: Seabury.

1980. *The Two Marxisms: Contradictions and Anomalies in the Development of Theory*. New York: Seabury.

Green, Peter 1977. "The Third Round in Poland," *New Left Review* 101/102.

Gross, Jan 1988. *Revolution from Abroad*. Princeton: Princeton University Press.

Grzelak, Andrzej 1965. "Problemy Adaptacji Młodych Inżynierow," in Maria Hirszowicz (ed.), *Problemy Kadry Przemysłowej*. Warsaw: Wydawnictwo Związkowe CRZZ.

Habermas, Jürgen 1971. *Knowledge and Interests*. Boston: Beacon.

Halamska, Maria 1988. "Peasant Movements in Poland, 1980–81: State Socialist Economy and the Mobilization of Individual Farmers," *Research in Social Movements, Conflicts and Change* 10:147–60.

Hankiss, Elemer 1988. "The Second Society: Is there an Alternative Social Model Emerging in Contemporary Hungary?" *Social Research* 55:13–42.

Hann, C. M. 1985. *A Village without Solidarity*. New Haven: Yale University Press.

Harrington, Michael 1989. "Markets and Plans," *Dissent* Winter: 56–70.

Hart, Janet 1989. "Empowerment and Political Opportunity: Greek Women in Resistance, 1941–1964," unpublished dissertation, Cornell University.

Havel, Václav 1988. "Anti-Political Politics," in John Keane (ed.) *Civil Society and the State* 381–98. London: Verso.

Hayek, Friederich 1944. *The Road to Serfdom*. Chicago: The University of Chicago Press.

Hayes, Adrian C. 1985. "Causal and Interpretative Sociology," *Sociological Theory* 3:1–10.

Heller, Agnes 1988. "On Formal Democracy" in John Keane (ed.) *Civil Society and the State* 129–46. London: Verso.

Henzler, Marek 1986. "Najlepsi czy loyalni," *Polityka* 23 (June 7):6.

Hewitt, Ed 1988. *Reforming the Soviet Economy: Equality vs. Efficiency*. Washington, D.C.: Brookings.

Hirszel, Krzysztof 1983. *Robotnicy i Inżynierowie: Postawy wobec Pracy i Wybranych Wartości Społecznych*. Warsaw: Ksiazka i Wiedza.

Hirszowicz, Maria 1980. *The Bureaucratic Leviathan*. New York: New York University.

Holzer, Jerzy 1984. *Solidarność, 1980–81: Geneza i Historia*. Paris: Instytut Literacki.

Hornowski, Jozef 1981. "Historia Izb Lekarskich w Polsce," *Medycyna, Dydaktyka, Wychowanie* 13:198–206,220.

Horvat, Branko 1982. *The Political Economy of Socialism*. White Plains, N.Y.: M.E. Sharpe.

Horvat, Branko, Mihailo Marković and Rudi Supek (eds.) 1975. *Self Governing Socialism*. White Plains, N.Y.: IASP.

Hoser, Jan 1970. *Zawód i Praca Inżyniera*, Wrocław, Warsaw, Kraków: Ossolineum.

Hraba, Joseph 1985. "Consumer Shortages in Poland: Looking Beyond the Queue into a World of Making Do," *The Sociological Quarterly* 26(3):387–404.

Hryniewicz, Janusz 1983. "Własność i Dysponowanie Środkami Produkcji w Polsce," unpublished manuscript.

Indulski, Janusz and Grażyna Rzepka-Koniarek 1982. "Funkcjowanie Prywatnej Praktyki Lekarskiej w Polsce w Opinii Społecznej", unpublished manuscript. Institute of Industrial Medicine in Łódź.

Jaakkola, Magdalena and Wacław Małkarczyk 1980. "Social Networks" in Erik Allardt and Włodzimierz Wesołowski (eds.) *Social Structure and Change: Finland and Poland, Comparative Perspective*. Warsaw: PWN.

Jancar, Barbara 1978. *Women under Communism*. Baltimore: Johns Hopkins Press.

1985. "Women in the Opposition in Poland and Czechoslovakia in the 1970s" in Sharon L. Wolchik and Alfred G. Meyer (eds). *Women, State and Party in Eastern Europe*. Durham, N.C.: Duke University Press.

Jasiewicz, Krzysztof 1982. "Polityczny Wymiar Kryzysu," in W. Adamski *et al.*, 127–58.

1988. "Political Conflict in Poland: Sociological Interpretations," lecture at The University of Michigan, April 14.

Jaśkiewicz, Włodzimierz 1977. *Uczelnia, Przemysł, Inżynier*. Warsaw: Panstwowe Wydawnictwo Naukowe.

Johnson, Terence J. 1972. *Professions and Power*. London: MacMillan.

Jones, T. Anthony 1976. "Modernization Theory and Socialist Development," in Mark Field (ed.) *Social Consequences of Modernization in the USSR* 19–49. Baltimore: Johns Hopkins Press.

1981. "Work, Workers and Modernization in the USSR," in Richard Simpson and Ida Harper Simpson (eds.) *Research in the Sociology of Work* 249–83. New York: JAI Press.

1984. "Models of Socialist Development," in Gerhard E. Lenski (ed.), *Current Issues and Research in Macrosociology*, 86–99. Amsterdam: E.J. Brill.

Jones, T. Anthony, David Bealmear and Michael D. Kennedy 1984. "Public Opinion and Political Disruption," in Jack Bielasiak and Maurice D. Simon (eds.), *Polish Politics: Edge of the Abyss*, 138–68 New York: Praeger.

Jowitt, Kenneth 1987. "Moscow Centre," *Eastern European Politics and Societies* 1:296–348.

Judt, Tony R. 1988. "The Dilemmas of Dissidence: The Politics of the Opposition in East Central Europe," *Eastern European Politics and Societies* 2(2):185–241.

Juviler, Peter H. 1980. "The Soviet Family in Post-Stalin Perspective," in S. Cohen, A. Rabinowitch and R. Sharlet (eds.), *The Soviet Union Since Stalin*, 227–51. Bloomington: Indiana University Press.

Kahk, Juhan 1988. "Perestroika and the Situation in the Baltic states," lecture at The University of Michigan, October 26.

Karpiński, Jakub 1982. *Countdown*. New York: Karz-Cohl.

Kaser, Michael 1976. *Health Care in the Soviet Union and Eastern Europe*, Boulder, Colo: Westview.

Kautsky, Karl 1919[1964]. *The Dictatorship of the Proletariat*. Ann Arbor: The University of Michigan Press.

Keane, John 1988. "Introduction," and "Despotism and Democracy," in John Keane (ed.) *Civil Society and the State*, 1–72. London: Verso.

Kelly, Kevin D. 1985. "Capitalism, Socialism, Barbarism: Marxist Conceptions of the Soviet Union," *Review of Radical Political Economics* 17(4):51–71.

Kemp-Welch, A. (ed. and trans.) 1983. *The Birth of Solidarity: The Gdańsk Negotiations*. New York: St Martins.

Kennedy, Michael D. 1982. "Towards an Explanation of Political Instability in Industrial Socialism," paper presented at the annual meeting of the American Sociological Association.

1987a. "Hermeneutics, Structuralism and the Sociology of Social Transformation in Soviet-type Society," *Current Perspectives in Social Theory* 8:47–76.

1987b. "Polish Engineers in the Solidarity Movement," *Social Forces* 65:641–69.

Kennedy, Michael D. and Ireneusz Białecki 1989. "Power and the Logic of Distribution in Poland," *Eastern European Politics and Societies* 3(2):299–327.

Kennedy, Michael D. and Konrad Sadkowski 1990. "Constraints on Professional Power in Soviet-type Society: Insights from the Solidarity Era in Poland," in T.A. Jones (ed.) *Professions and the State: The Organization of Professional Work in the Soviet Union and Eastern Europe*. Philadelphia: Temple University Press.

Kirschner, Henryk 1988. "Postac Marcina Kacprzaka na tle Rozwoju Medycyny Spolecznej w Polsce," *Archiwum Historii i Filozofii Medycycny* 51:1.

Klegon, Douglas 1978. "The Sociology of Professions: An Emerging Perspective," *Sociology of Work and Occupations* 5:259–83.

Knei-Paz, Baruch 1978. *The Social and Political Thought of Leon Trotsky*. Oxford: Oxford University Press.

Kołakowski, Leszek 1977. "Marxist Roots of Stalinism," in Robert Tucker (ed.) *Stalinism* 283–97. New York: Norton.

  1983. "The Intelligentsia," in A. Brumberg (ed.) *Poland: Genesis of a Revolution*, 54–67. New York: Random House.

  1986. "Yalta and the Fate of Poland," *New York Review of Books* August 14:43.

Kolankiewicz, George 1973. "The Working Class," and "The Technical Intelligentsia," in David Lane and George Kolankiewicz (eds.) *Social Groups in Political Society*, 88–151 and 180–232. New York: Columbia University.

  1979. "Translator's Introduction," to W. Wesolowski, *Classes, Strata, and Power*, ix–xx. London: Routledge and Kegan Paul.

Kolarska, Lena and Andrzej Rychard 1982a. "Ład Ekonomiczny i Ład Polityczny," in Adamski *et al.* (eds.) 197–268.

  1982b. "Visions of Social Order," *Sysyphus* III:206–51.

Kolosi, Tamas 1984. "Status and Stratification," in Rudolph Andorka and Tamas Kolosi (eds.) *Stratification and Inequality*, 51–103. Budapest: Institute for Social Sciences.

Konrád, György 1984. *Antipolitics*. New York: Harcourt, Brace, Jovanovich.

Konrád, György and Ivan Szelényi 1979. *The Intellectuals on the Road to Class Power*. New York: Harcourt Brace Jovanovich.

Koralewicz(-Zębik), Jadwiga 1984a. "Current Perceptions of Inequality in Poland in 1960–80," *British Journal of Sociology* 18(2):225–38.

  1984b. "Lęk a Stratyfikacja Społeczna," unpublished manuscript.

  1987a. "Changes in Polish Social Consciousness during the 1970s and 1980s: Opportunism and Identity," in Koralewicz, Bialecki and Watson (eds.), 3–25.

  1987b. *Autorytaryzm, Lęk. Konformizm*. Warsaw: Ossolineum.

  1987c. *Społeczenstwo Polskie Przed Kryzysem*. Warsaw: PWN.

Koralewicz-Zębik, Jadwiga, Ireneusz Białecki and Margaret Watson (eds.) 1987. *Crisis and Transition: Polish Society in the 1980s*. Oxford: Berg.

Korboński, Andrzej 1965. *The Politics of Socialist Agriculture in Poland 1945–60*. New York: Columbia University Press.

Kornhauser, William 1959. *The Politics of Mass Society*. Glencoe: The Free Press.

Korpi, Walter 1985. "Power Resources Approach vs. Action and Conflict: On Causal and Intentional Explanations in the Study of Power," *Sociological Theory* 3(2):31–45.

Kostecki, Marian and Krzysztof Mreła 1984. "Collective Solidarity in Poland's Powered Society," *The Insurgent Sociologist*. 12(1–2):131–42.

Kowalewski, Zdzisław 1962. *Chemicy w Polskiej Rzeczypospolitej Ludowej*. Wrocław, Warsaw, Kraków: Zakład Narodowy im Ossolińskich Wydawnictwo Polskiej Akademii Nauk.

Kowalewski, Zbigniew 1982. "Solidarity on the Eve" in Persky and Flam (eds.) 230–42.

Kowalik, Tadeusz 1983. "Experts and the Working Group," in Kemp-Welch (ed. and trans.), 143–67.

Kozek, Wiesława 1986. "Zwiększona Odpowiedzialność Kierowników w Świetle Badań," in Witold Morawski (ed.) *Gospodarka i Społeczenstwo*, 99–128. Warsaw: University of Warsaw Institute of Sociology.

Krystufek, Zdenek 1982. *The Soviet Regime in Czechoslovakia*. New York: Columbia University.

Krzemiński, Ireneusz 1983. "Jak Powstał i Działał Niezależny Samorządny Związek Zawodowy Pracowników Nauki, Techniki, i Oświaty," in Ireneusz Krzemiński, Grzegorz Bakuniak, Henryk Banaszak and Anna Kruczkowska, *Polacy-Jesień 80*, 328–434. Warsaw: University of Warsaw Institute of Sociology.

Kuczyński, Paweł 1983. "Dwa Modele Swiadomości Politycznej Robotników: Analiza Ruchu Społecznego w Okresie 1980–81," in Witold Morawski (ed.) *Demokracja i Gospodarka*, 461–90. Warsaw: University of Warsaw Institute of Sociology.

Kundera, Milan 1982. Interviewed by Alain Finkielkraut in *Cross Currents* 1:15–29.

Kurczewski, Jacek 1982. "The Old System and the Revolution," *Sysyphus* 3:21–32.

Kurczewski, Jacek and Jan Solarz 1972. *Zawód Lekarza w Opinii Publicznej*. Warsaw: Ośrodek Badania Opinii Publicznej i Studiów Programowych. Komitet do Spraw Radia i Telewizji.

Kuroń, Jacek 1973. "Spór o Wydarzenie Marcowe," *Zeszyty Historyczne* 24. Reprinted in Jacek Kuroń, *Polityka i Odpowiedzialność*. London: Aneks, 1983.

  1981. "Not to Lure the Wolves Out of the Woods: An Interview with Jacek Kuron," *Telos* 47:93–97.

Kuroń, Jacek and Karol Modzelewski 1966. "An Open Letter to the Party," *New Politics* 5:5–47.

Laba, Roman forthcoming. *The Roots of Solidarity*. Princeton: Princeton University Press.

  1986. "Working Class Roots of Solidarity," *Problems of Communism* July–August:47–67.

Łabanowska, Cecylia 1978. "Przemiany Wzoru Osobowego Lekarza," Ph.D. dissertation, University of Warsaw.

Lane, David 1984. "The Structure of Soviet Socialism: Recent Western Theoretical Approaches," *Insurgent Sociologist* 12:101–12.

Larson, Magali Sarfatti 1977. *The Rise of Professionalism*. Berkeley: University of California Press.

Latoszek, Marek 1987. *Więzi i Przejawy Integracji w Grupach i Zbiorowościach Społeczenstwa Gdańskiego pod Koniec Lat Siedemdziesiątych*. Gdańsk: University of Gdańsk Press.

Layton, Edwin T., Jr. 1971. *The Revolt of the Engineers*. Cleveland: Case Western Reserve University Press.

Lengermann, Patricia Madoo and Jill Niebrugge-Brantley 1988. "Contemporary Feminist Theory," in George Ritzer (ed.) *Sociological Theory*, 400–43. New York: Knopf.

Lenin, V. I. 1918 [1975]. "The Proletarian Revolution and the Renegade Kautsky," in Robert Tucker (ed.) *The Lenin Anthology*, 461–76. New York: Norton.

Lenski, Gerhard E. 1966. *Power and Privilege*. New York: McGraw Hill (reprinted 1984, Chapel Hill: University of North Carolina Press).

1978. "Marxist Experiments in Destratification: An Appraisal," *Social Forces* 57:364–83.

Levine, Andrew, Elliot Sober and Erik Olin Wright 1987. "Marxism and Methodological Individualism," *New Left Review* 162:67–84.

Lewin, Moshe 1968. *Lenin's Last Struggle*. New York: Random House.

1988. *The Gorbachev Phenomenon*. Berkeley: University of California Press.

Lewis, Paul G. 1982. "Obstacles to the Establishment of Political Legitimacy in Communist Poland," *British Journal of Political Science* 12:125–47.

Lichtheim, George 1961. *Marxism: An Historical and Critical Study*. New York: Praeger.

Lipski, Jan Jozef 1985. *KOR: Workers' Defense Committee in Poland*. Berkeley: University of California Press.

Lowit, Thomas 1979. "Le Parti polymorphe en Europe de l'est," *Revue française de science politique* 29:812–46.

Lukas, Richard 1985. *Forgotten Holocaust: The Poles under German Occupation, 1939–44*. Lexington: University of Kentucky Press.

Lukes, Steven 1978. "Power and Authority," in Tom Bottomore and Robert Nisbet (eds.) *A History of Sociological Analysis*, 633–76. New York: Basic Books.

1985. *Marxism and Morality*. Oxford: Oxford University Press.

Lutyński, J. 1982. "Conditions of Success in Negotiations as Illustrated by the Students' Strike in Łódź," *Sysyphus* 3:135–48.

Luxemburg, Rosa 1899 [1977]. *The Industrial Development of Poland*. New York: Campaigner Industries.

1918 [1961]. *The Russian Revolution and Leninism or Marxism*. Ann Arbor: University of Michigan.

MacDonald, Oliver 1983. "The Polish Vortex: Solidarity and Socialism," *New Left Review* 139:5–48.

Mach, Bogdan 1987. "Zróżnicowanie Autoidentyfikacji Społecznych," in Edmund Wnuk-Lipiński (ed.) *Nierówności i Upośledzenia w Świadomości Społecznej*, 153–206. Warsaw: Polish Academy of Sciences Press.

Maciejewski, Jarosław and Zofia Trojanowiczowa (eds.) 1981. *Poznanski Czerwiec 1956*. Poznań: Wydawnictwo Poznanskie.

Mackiewicz, Maciej and Henryk Skrzypek 1981. "O Lokalny Samorząd Zdrowotny," unpublished manuscript.

MacShane, Denis 1981. *Solidarity: Poland's Independent Trade Union*. London: Spokesman.

Mallet, Serge 1974. *Bureaucracy and Technocracy in the Socialist Countries*. Nottingham: Spokesman.

Manchin, Robert and Ivan Szelényi 1985. "Eastern Europe in the 'Crisis of Transition': The Polish and Hungarian Cases," in Bronisław Misztal (ed.) *Poland after Solidarity*, 87–102. New Brunswick: Transaction.

Mandel, Ernest 1978. "On the Nature of the Soviet State," *New Left Review* 108:23–46.

1981. "The Laws of Motion of the Soviet Economy," *Review of Radical Political Economics* 13:35–40.

1982. "The Class Nature of the Soviet Union," *Review of Radical Political Economics* 14:55–67.

1986. "In Defense of Socialist Planning," *New Left Review* 159:5–38.

1988. "The Myth of Market Socialism," *New Left Review* 169:108–20.

Marcuse, Herbert 1958. *Soviet Marxism*. New York: Columbia University.

Markiewicz, Stanisław 1981. *Państwo i Kosciół w Polsce Ludowej*. Warsaw: Ludowa Spółdzielnia Wydawnicza.

Markovic, Mihailo 1977. "Stalinism and Marxism," in Robert Tucker (ed.) *Stalinism*, 299–319. New York: Norton.

Markovic, Mihailo and Robert Cohen 1975. *Yugoslavia: The Rise and Fall of Socialist Humanism, A History of the Praxis Group*. Nottingham: Spokesman.

Markus, Maria 1985. "Constitution and Functioning of Civil Society in Poland," in B. Misztal (ed.) *Poland after Solidarity*, 57–66. New Brunswick: Transaction.

1987. "Women, Success and Civil Society," in S. Benhabib and D. Cornell (eds.) *Feminism as Critique*, 96–109. University of Minnesota Press.

Marody, Mira 1987. "Social Stability and the Concept of Collective Sense," in J. Koralewicz, I. Białecki and M. Watson (eds.) *Crisis and Transition: Polish Society in the 1980s*, 130–58. Oxford: Berg.

1988. "Antinomies of Collective Subconsciousness," *Social Research* 55(1–2):97–110.

Marx, Karl 1852 [1977]. "The Eighteenth Brumaire of Louis Bonaparte," in Robert Tucker (ed.) *The Marx–Engels Reader*, 594–617. New York: Norton.

1959 [1970]. *A Contribution to the Critique of Political Economy*. New York: International Publishers.

Matejko, Aleksander 1982. "The Structural Roots of Polish Opposition," *Polish Review* 27:112–40.

Mattick, Paul 1978. *Anti-Bolshevik Communism*. White Plains, N.Y.: M. E. Sharpe.

Merton, Robert 1967. *Social Theory and Social Structure*. New York: Basic Books.

Michnik, Adam 1976 [1985]. "The New Evolutionism," in *Letters from Prison and Other Essays*, 135–48. Berkeley: University of California Press.

1977a. "The New Evolutionism," in *Letters from Prison and Other Essays*, 135–48. Berkeley: University of California Press.

1977b. *Kosciół, Lewica, Dialog*. Paris: Kultura.

1981. "What We Want to Do and What We Can Do," *Telos* 47:66–77.

1985. *Letters from Prison and Other Essays*. Berkeley: University of California Press.

Mihalyi, Peter 1988. "Common Patterns and Particularities in East European Business Cycles," *Soviet Studies* 40:444–59.

Mills, C. Wright 1951. *White Collar*. London: Oxford University Press.

1956. *The Power Elite*. London: Oxford University Press.

1958. *The Causes of World War III*. New York: Simon and Schuster.

1964. "Mass Media and Public Opinion," in Irving Louis Horowitz (ed.) *Power, Politics, and People*, 577–98. London: Oxford University Press.

Misztal, Barbara and Bronisław Misztal 1986–87. "Uncontrolled Processes in the Socialist City: A Polish Case Study," *Politics and Society* 15:145–56.

Moczulski, Leszek 1979. *Rewolucja bez Rewolucji*. Warsaw: Wydawnictwo Polskie.

1987. "The Possibilities for Polish Revolution without Revolution," lecture at the University of Michigan.

Mokrzyszewski, A. 1982. "Społeczna Ocena Władzy i 'Solidarnosci'" in Adamski *et al.* (eds.), 109–26.

Morawski, Witold 1987. "Self Management and Economic Reform," in J. Koralewicz, I. Białecki and M. Watson (eds.) *Crisis and Transition: Polish Society in the 1980s*, 80–110. Oxford: Berg.

Morris, Aldon 1984. *The Origins of the Civil Rights Movement*. New York: Free Press.

Najduchowska, Halina 1974. "Dyrektorzy Przedsiębiostw Przemysłowych," in Jolanta Kulpińska (ed.) *Socjologia Przemysł*, 248–74. Warsaw: PWE.

New Left Review 1972. "Polish Workers and Party Leaders – A Confrontation," 73:35–53.

Niebuhr, H. Richard 1957. *The Social Sources of Denominationalism*. New York: Meridian.

Noble, David 1977. *America by Design*. Cambridge, Mass.: MIT Press.

Norgaard, Ole and Steven L. Sampson 1984. "Poland's Crisis and East European Socialism," *Theory and Society* 13:773–801.

Norr, Henry 1985. "Solidarity and self-management, May–July 1981," *Poland Watch* 7:97–122.

Nove, Alex 1987. "Markets and Socialism," *New Left Review* 161:98–104.

1983. *The Economics of Feasible Socialism*. London: Allen and Unwin.

Nowak, Krzysztof 1988. "Covert Repressiveness and the Stability of the Political System: Poland at the End of the Seventies," *Social Research* 55:179–208.

Nowak, Stefan 1981. "Values and Attitudes of the Polish People," *Scientific American* 245(1):45–53.

Nuss, Shirley 1984. "Family Maintenance Activities: Husbands' Participation in Centrally Planned and Market Oriented Countries," *Insurgent Sociologist* 12:13–24.

Nuti, Domenico Mario 1981. "The Polish Crisis: Economic Factors and Constraints," in Ralph Miliband and John Saville (eds.) *Socialist Register*, 104–43. London: Merlin. Reprinted and expanded in Jan Drewnowski (ed.) *Crisis in the East European Economy*, 18–64. London: Croom Helm.

Opara, Stefan 1982. "Polish Tradition and Ideology," *Dialectics and Humanism* 2:95–101.

Orchowski, Adam 1980. "Przebieg Strajku Okupacynego w Stoczni Gdańskiej im. Lenina w dniach 14–31 Sierpnia 1980 roku," *Punkt Gdańskich Środowisk Twórczych* 12 (December):9–44.

Ortner, Sherry B. 1984. "Theory in Anthropology since the Sixties," *Comparative Studies in Society and History* 126–66.

Pakulski, Jan 1986. "Leaders of the Solidarity Movement: a Sociological Portrait," *Sociology* 20:64–81.

Pańków, Włodzimierz 1987. "The Solidarity Movement, Management and the Political System in Poland," in J. Koralewicz, I. Białecki and M. Watson (eds.) *Crisis and Transition: Polish Society in the 1980s*, 111–29. Oxford: Berg.

Park, Henry 1987. "Secondary Literature on the Question of the Restoration of Capitalism in the Soviet Union," *Research in Political Economy* 10:27–58.

Parkin, Frank 1971. *Class Inequality and Political Order*. London: Paladin.

Parry, Albert 1966. *The New Class Divided*. New York: Macmillan.

Parsons, Talcott 1939. "Professions and Social Structure," *Social Forces* 17:457–67.

 1967. "On the Concept of Political Power," in Talcott Parsons (ed.), *Sociological Theory and Modern Society*, 297–354. New York: Free Press.

Pateman, Carol 1988. "The Fraternal Social Contract," in John Keane (ed.) *Civil Society and the State*, 101–28. London: Verso.

Paul, David W. and Maurice D. Simon 1981. "Poland Today and Czechoslovakia 1968," *Problems of Communism* September–October:25–39.

Pearson, Raymond 1983. *National Minorities in Eastern Europe 1848–1945*. London: MacMillan.

Pełczyński, Z. A. 1988. "Solidarity and 'The Rebirth of Civil Society,'" in John Keane (ed.) *Civil Society and the State*, 361–80. London: Verso.

Persky, Stan 1982. *At the Lenin Shipyard*. Vancouver: New Star Books.

Persky, Stan and Henry Flam 1982. *The Solidarity Sourcebook*. Vancouver: New Star Books.

Peter, Laszlo 1988. "Church–State Relations in Nineteenth Century Hungary and Civil Society: A Historical Perspective," paper presented at the conference on Religion and Marxism in East Central Europe, The University of Michigan, October 14.

Petrovic, Gajo 1983. "Praxis," in Tom Bottomore (ed.) *A Dictionary of Marxist Thought*, 384–89. Cambridge, Mass.: Harvard University Press.

Pohoski, Michał 1984. Presentation at the Polish Academy of Sciences.

 1986. "Social Inequality and Mobility," in K. Slomczynski and T. Krauze (eds.) *Social Stratification in Poland*, 30–51. Armonk: M. E. Sharpe.

Pohoski, Michał, K. Słomczyński and W. Wesołowski 1975. "Occupational Prestige in Poland, 1958–1975," *Polish Sociological Bulletin* 4:63–77.

Polan, A. J. 1984. *Lenin and the End of Politics*. Berkeley: University of California Press.

Pravda, Alex 1982. "Poland 1980: From 'Premature Consumerism' to Labour Solidarity," *Soviet Studies* 34:167–99.

Raina, Peter 1977. *Political Opposition in Poland, 1954–77*. London: Painters and Poets Press.

 1985. *Poland 1981: Towards Social Renewal*. London: George Allen and Unwin.

Rakovski, Marc 1978. *Towards an East European Marxism*. London: Allison and Busby.

Reszke, Irena 1984. *Prestiż Społeczny a Płeć*. Wrocław: Ossolineum.

Rev, Istvan 1984. "Local Autonomy or Centralism: When was the Original Sin Committed?" *International Journal of Urban and Regional Research* 8(1):38–63.

Reynolds, Jaime 1978. "Communists, Socialists and Workers, Poland 1944–48," *Soviet Studies* 30:516–30.

Rigby, T. H. 1964. "Traditional, Market, and Organizational Societies and the USSR," *World Politics* 16:539–57.

Rochberg-Halton, Eugene 1986. *Meaning and Modernity: Social Theory in the Pragmatic Attitude.* Chicago: University of Chicago Press.

Rona-Tas, Akos 1990. "The Second Economy in Hungary: the Social Origins of the End of State Socialism," unpublished dissertation, University of Michigan.

Roth, Julius 1974. "Professionalism: The Sociologist's Decoy," *Sociology of Work and Occupations* 1:6–23.

Rupnik, Jacques 1979. "Dissent in Poland 1968–78: The End of Revisionism and the Rebirth of Civil Society," in Rudolph Tokes (ed.) *Opposition in Eastern Europe*, 60–112. Baltimore and London: Johns Hopkins University.

  1988. "Totalitarianism Revisited," in John Keane (ed.) *Civil Society and the State*, 263–90. London: Verso.

Russell-Hodgson, Chris 1982. "Health Policy and Health Service Reform in the 1970s," in Jean Woodall (ed.) *Policy and Politics in Contemporary Poland*, 171–94. New York: St Martin's.

Rychard, Andrzej 1981. "Social Needs and the Management System: The Case of Poland," *Polish Sociological Bulletin* 2:15–25.

  1984. "Ład Społeczny w Gospodarce: Pomiędzy Odrzuceniem a Przyzwoleniem," forthcoming in *Polish Sociological Bulletin*.

  1987a. "The Legitimation and Stability of the Social Order in Poland," in J. Koralewicz, I. Białecki and M. Watson (eds.) *Crisis and Transition: Polish Society in the 1980s.* Oxford: Berg.

  1987b. "Health Care in the Region of Łódź in 1967–69 as compared with Eleven Selected Regions in Other Countries," *Sysyphus* 4:175–200.

Sabel, Charles and David Stark 1982. "Planning, Politics and Shopfloor Power: Hidden Forms of Bargaining in Soviet Imposed State Socialist Societies," *Politics and Society* 11:439–75.

Salaff, J. and J. Merkele 1970. "Women and Revolution: The Lesson of the Soviet Union and China," *Berkeley Journal of Sociology* 15:166–91.

Samary, Catherine 1988. *Plan, Market and Democracy: The Experience of the So-Called Socialist Countries*, Notebooks for Study and Research, 7/8. Amsterdam: International Institute for Research and Education.

Scanlon, James 1988. "Reform and Civil Society in the USSR," *Problems of Communism* 37(2):41–47.

Sciulli, David 1986. "Voluntaristic Action as a Distinct Concept: Theoretical Foundations of Societal Constitutionalism," *American Sociological Review* 51:743–66.

Scott, James 1985. *Weapons of the Weak.* New Haven: Yale University Press.

Semprich, J. "Petraktacje," *Służba Zdrowia* 43.

Shalin, Dmitri 1988. "G. H. Mead, Socialism and the Progressive Agenda," *American Journal of Sociology* 93(4):913–51.

Shanin, Teodor 1988. "The Question of Socialism in Gorbachev's Political Universe," lecture at the University of Michigan, September 21.

Shils, E. 1968. "Deference," in J. A. Jackson (ed.) *Social Stratification*, 104–32. Cambridge: Cambridge University Press.

Siemińska, Renata 1985. Comments at the International Sociological Association Session on the Polish Crisis.

Šik, Ota 1976. *The Third Way: Marxist Leninist Theory and Modern Industrial Society*. White Plains: International Arts and Sciences Press.

Sikorska, Joanna 1979. *Społeczno-ekonomiczne Zróżnicowanie Wzorów Konsumpcji w Pracowniczych Gospodarstwach Domowych*. Wrocław: Ossolineum.

1987. "Wpływ Regresu Warunków Konsumpcji na Społeczne Zróżnicowania jej Wzorów," in Lidia Beskid (ed.) *Warunki i Sposób Życia Społeczenstwa Polskiego w Sytuacji Regresu*. Warsaw: PAN IFiS.

Silver, Geoffrey and Gregory Tarpinian 1981. "Marxism and Socialism: A Response to Paul Sweezy and Ernest Mandel," *Review of Radical Political Economics* 13:11–22.

Simmel, Georg 1907 [1978]. *The Philosophy of Money*. London: Routledge and Kegan Paul.

1908 [1971]. "The Nobility," in *On Individuality and Social Forms*. Chicago: University of Chicago.

Singer, Daniel 1981. *The Road to Gdańsk*. New York: Monthly Review Press.

1984. "Comment," *Insurgent Sociologist* 12:165–68.

Sirianni, Carmen 1983. *Workers Control and Socialist Democracy: The Soviet Experience*. London: New Left Books.

Skilling, H. Gordon 1988. "Parallel Polis or an Independent Society in Central and Eastern Europe: An Inquiry," *Social Research* 55:211–47.

Skocpol, Theda 1979. *States and Social Revolutions*. Cambridge: Cambridge University Press.

Skocpol, Theda and Margaret Somers 1980. "The Uses of Comparative History in Macrosocial Inquiry," *Comparative Studies in Society and History* 22:174–97.

Smolar, Aleksander 1983. "The Rich and the Powerful," in Abraham Brumberg (ed.) *Poland: Genesis of a Revolution*, 42–53. New York: Random House.

Sokołowska, Magdalena 1974. "Social Science and Health Policy in Eastern Europe: Poland as a Case Study," *International Journal of Health Services* 4(3):441–51.

1982. "Health as an Issue in the Workers' Campaign," *Sysyphus* 3:91–106.

Sokołowska, Magdalena and Bożena Moskalewicz 1986. "Health Sector Structures: The Case of Poland," *Social Science and Medicine* 24(9):763–76.

Staniszkis, Jadwiga 1979. "On Some Contradictions of Socialist Society: The Case of Poland," *Soviet Studies* 31:167–87.

1984a. *Poland's Self Limiting Revolution*. Princeton: Princeton University Press.

1984b. "Reflections on Property Rights, Rationality, and Social Structure," presentation at the Polish Academy of Sciences.

1987. "The Political Articulation of Property Rights: Some Reflections on the

Inert Structure" in J. Koralewicz, I. Białecki and M. Watson (eds.) *Crisis and Transition: Polish Society in the 1980s*, 53–79. Oxford: Berg.

Stark, David 1986. "Rethinking Internal Labor Markets: New Insights from a Comparative Perspective," *American Sociological Review* 51:492–504.

Starr, Paul 1982. *The Social Transformation of American Medicine*. Cambridge Mass.: Harvard University Press.

Starski, Stanisław 1982. *Class Struggle in Classless Poland*. Boston: South End Press.

Strasser, Hermann 1976. *The Normative Structure of Sociology: Conservative and Emancipatory Themes in Social Thought*. London: Routledge and Kegan Paul.

Sweezy, Paul 1980. *Post-Revolutionary Society*. New York: Monthly Review Press.

Swidler, Ann 1986. "Culture in Action: Symbols and Strategies," *American Sociological Review* 51:273–86.

Świdlicki, Andrej 1982. "'Experience and the Future' and the Polish Crisis," *Telos* 53:137–49.

Święcicka, M. 1980. "Samoocena Pozycji Społecznej Inteligencji," in A. Borucki (ed.) *Polska Inteligencja Współczesna* 77–96. Warsaw: Polska Akademia Nauk IFiS.

Szczepański, Jan 1962. "The Polish Intelligentsia: Past and Present," *World Politics* 14: 406–20.

1980. "Perspectives on Development of Social Macrostructure in Poland," in Jan Danecki and Jerzy Krycki (eds.) *Towards Poland 2000: Problems of Social Development*, 47–70. Wrocław: Zakład Narodowy Imienia Ossolinskich Wydawnictwo Polskiej Akademii Nauk.

Szczypiórski, Andrzej 1982. *The Polish Ordeal: The View From Within*. London: Croom Helm.

Szelényi, Ivan 1978. "Social Inequalities in State Socialist Redistributive Economies," *International Journal of Comparative Sociology* 19:64–82.

1979. "Socialist Opposition in Eastern Europe: Dilemmas and Prospects," in Rudolph Tokes (ed.) *Opposition in Eastern Europe*, 187–208. Baltimore: Johns Hopkins University Press.

1982. "The Intelligentsia in the Class Structure of State-Socialist Societies," in M. Burawoy and T. Skocpol (eds.) *Marxist Inquiries*, 287–326. Chicago: University of Chicago Press.

1986–87. "The Prospects and Limits of the East European New Class Project," *Politics and Society* 15:103–44.

1989. "Intellectuals, Knowledge and Power," presentation at the annual meeting of the American Sociological Association.

Szkolny, Michael 1981. "Revolution in Poland," *Monthly Review* 33(2):1–21.

Szporluk, Roman 1982. "Defining Central Europe: Power, Politics and Culture," *Cross Currents* 1:30–38.

1988a. "Imperial Legacy in Soviet Nationality Problems," unpublished manuscript.

1988b. *Communism and Nationalism*. Oxford: Oxford University Press.

Szücs, Jenö, "Three Historical Regions of Europe," in John Keane (ed.), *Civil Society and the State*, 291–332. London: Verso.

Szymanski, Albert 1979. *Is the Red Flag Still Flying? The Political Economy of the USSR Today.* London: Zed.

1984. "Class Struggle in Socialist Poland," *Insurgent Sociologist* 12:115–30.

Taras, Ray 1984. *Ideology in a Socialist State: Poland 1956–83.* Cambridge: Cambridge University Press.

Tarkowski, Jackek 1983. "Patronage in a Centralized Socialist System: The Case of Poland," *International Political Science Review* 4:495–518.

Tarpinian, Gregory and Geoffrey Silver 1982. "Class Analysis and the Transition to Socialism: A Rejoinder to Ernest Mandel," *Review of Radical Political Economics* 14:68–75.

Taylor, J. 1952. *The Economic Development of Poland: 1919–1950.* Ithaca: Cornell University Press.

Tellenbeck, Sten 1978. "The Logic of Development in Socialist Poland," *Social Forces* 57:436–56.

Titma, Mikk 1989. "Recent Developments in Soviet Sociology," a presentation at the annual meeting of the American Sociological Association.

Tomicki, Jan 1983. *Polska Partia Socjalistyczna 1892–1948.* Warsaw: Książk i Wiedza.

Torańska, Teresa 1987. *Them: Stalin's Polish Puppets.* New York: Harper and Row.

Touraine, Alain 1978[1981] *The Voice and the Eye: An Analysis of Social Movements.* Cambridge: Cambridge University Press.

1984[1988]. *The Return of the Actor.* Minneapolis: University of Minnesota Press.

Touraine, Alain, with F. Dubet, M. Wieviorka and J. Strzelecki 1983. *Solidarity: The Analysis of a Social Movement, Poland 1980–81.* Cambridge: Cambridge University Press.

Treiman, Donald J. 1977. *Occupational Prestige in Comparative Perspective.* New York: Academic Press.

Trotsky, Leon 1920[1961]. *Terrorism and Communism.* Ann Arbor: University of Michigan Press.

1927[1965]. *The New Course.* Ann Arbor: University of Michigan.

1937[1972]. *The Revolution Betrayed.* New York: Pathfinder.

Trotsky, Leon, John Dewey and George Nowack 1973. *Their Morals and Ours.* New York: Pathfinder.

Tymowski, Andrzej 1982. "What Use of Freedom? The Dilemmas of the Polish People," *Sysyphus* 3:127–34.

Tymowski, Janusz 1980. *Organizacja Szkolnictwa Wyższego w Polsce.* Warsaw: Panstwowe Wydawnictwo Naukowe.

1982a. *Problemy Kadr Wysoko Kwalifikowanych.* Wrocław: Ossolineum.

1982b. "Sytuacja Inżynierów," unpublished manuscript.

1983. *Sytuacja Finansowa Pracowników Technicznych w Polsce.* Warsaw: NOT.

1984. "Ludzie Czekają na Cud," interview in *Kierunki*, March 11.

Vajda, Mihály 1981. *The State and Socialism.* London: Allison and Busby.

1988. "East Central European Perspectives," in John Keane (ed.) *Civil Society and the State*, 333–60. London: Verso

Veblen, Thorstein 1965. *The Engineers and the Price System.* New York: Viking.

Voslensky, Michael 1984. *Nomenklatura*. New York. Doubleday.

Walaszek, Zdzisława 1977. "Recent Developments in Polish Sociology," *Annual Review of Sociology* 3:331–62.

Walder, Andrew 1985. *Communist Neo-Traditionalism*. Berkeley: University of California Press.

Walicki, Andrzej 1983. *Polska, Rosja, Marksizm*. Warsaw: Książka i Wiedza.

    1984. "Myśli o Sytuacjach Politycznej i Moralno-psychologicznej w Polsce," *Aneks* 35:82–104.

    1988. "Liberalism in Poland" *Critical Review* 2:8–38.

Wałęsa, Lech 1987. *A Way of Hope: An Autobiography*. New York: Henry Holt.

Warszawski, David 1989. "Poland: The Impact of March '68," *New Politics* 2(2):49–54.

Wasilewski, Jacek 1981. *Kariery Społeczno-Zawodowe Dyrektorów*. Wrocław: Ossolineum.

Weber, Max 1978, *Economy and Society*. Berkeley, University of California Press.

Webster, Thomas G. 1982. "Health Policy Issues and the Predicament in Poland," *New England Journal of Medicine* February 4 308–12.

Wejnert, Barbara 1988. "The Student Movement in Poland, 1980–81," *Research in Social Movements* 10:173–81.

Wesołowski, Włodzimierz 1966a [1979]. *Classes, Strata and Power*. London: Routledge and Kegan Paul.

    1966b. "Changes in the Class Structure in Poland," in Jan Szczepański (ed.) *Empirical Sociology in Poland*, 7–36. Warsaw: Polish Scientific Publishers.

    1978. *Teoria, Badania, Praktyka*. Warsaw: Ksiazka i Wiedza.

Wesołowski, Włodzimierz and Bogdan Mach 1986. "Unfulfilled Systemic Functions of Social Mobility," *International Sociology* 1:19–36 and 173–88.

Whalley, Peter and Stephen Crawford 1984. "Locating Technical Workers in the Class Structure," *Politics and Society* 13:39–52.

White Stephen 1974. "Contradiction and Change in State Socialism," *Soviet Studies* 26:41–55.

Wiatr, Jerzy 1967[1978]. "The Hegemonic Party System in Poland," in *Essays in Political Sociology*, 186–99. Wrocław: Ossolineum.

Wilensky, Harold 1964. "The Professionalization of Everyone?" *American Journal of Sociology* 70:137–58.

Willerton, John P. 1979 "Clientalism in the Soviet Union," *Studies in Comparative Communism* 12:177–211.

    1987. "Patronage Networks and Coalition Building in the Soviet Union," *Soviet Studies* 39:175–204

Wnuk-Lipiński, Edmund 1982. "Dimorphism of Values and Social Schizophrenia: A Tentative Description," *Sysyphus* 3:81–90.

    1987. "Social Dimorphism and its Implications," in J. Koralewicz, I. Białecki and M. Watson (eds.) *Crisis and Transition: Polish Society in the 1980s*, 159–76. Oxford: Berg.

Wojtisiak, Grażyna 1980. "Kontakty Towarzyskie Inteligencji," in A. Borucki (ed.) *Polska Inteligencja Współeczesna*, 133–50. Warsaw: Polska Akademia Nauk IFiS.

Wolfe, Alan 1977. *The Limits of Legitimacy*. New York: Free Press.

Wood, Ellen Meiksins 1986. *The Retreat From Class: A New 'True' Socialism*. London: Verso.

Woodall, Jean 1981. "New Social Factors in the Unrest in Poland," *Government and Opposition* 16:37–57.

1982. *The Socialist Corporation and Technocratic Power*, Cambridge: Cambridge University Press.

Wright, Erik Olin 1984. *Classes*. London: Verso.

Wyszyński, Stefan Cardinal 1983. *A Freedom Within*. New York: Harcourt Brace Jovanovich.

Yakowicz, Joseph Vincent 1979. *Poland's Postwar Recovery*. Hicksville, N.Y.: Exposition–University Press.

Zaborowski, Wojciech 1983. *Obrazy Struktury Klasowej w Świadomości Mieszkań-ców Warszawy*. Warsaw: PAN IFiS.

Żarnowski, Janusz 1964. *Struktura Społeczna Inteligencji w Polsce w latach 1918–1939*. Warsaw: Panstwowe Wydawnictwo Naukowe.

1973. *Społeczenstwo Drugiej Rzeczypospolitej*. Warsaw: Panstwowe Wydaw-nictwo Naukowe.

Zaslavskaja, Tat'yana 1988. "Perestroika and Sociology," *Social Research* 55(1–2):267–77.

Zielinski, Janusz G. 1973. *Economic Reforms in Polish Industry*. London: Oxford University Press.

Żukowski, Tomasz 1987. "Między Kooptacją a Rewolucją," in Ewa Lewicka-Banaszak, Piotr Maraniak and Wojciech Modzelewski (eds.) *Studia Nad Ruchami Społecznymi*, 177–204. Warsaw: University of Warsaw Institute of Sociology.

Zussman, Robert 1984. "The Middle Levels: Engineers and the Working Middle Class," *Politics and Society* 13:217–37.

Index

414

Soviet and East European Studies

Soviet and East European Studies

Soviet and East European Studies